Inside the Japanese System

Inside the Japanese System

Readings on Contemporary Society and Political Economy

EDITED BY

Daniel I. Okimoto and Thomas P. Rohlen

STANFORD UNIVERSITY PRESS

STANFORD, CALIFORNIA

Stanford University Press
Stanford, California

© 1988 by the Board of Trustees of the
Leland Stanford Junior University

Printed in the United States of America

CIP data appear at the end of the book

To M A R I U S   J A N S E N ,

Y A S U S U K E   M U R A K A M I ,   *and*

R O N A L D   D O R E ,

whose scholarship and values have

served as an inspiration

Preface

A M O N G the world's great industrial states, Japan is the newest, most dynamic, and most distinctive. It is so different from the United States and other Western nations that various labels have had to be coined to capture its uniqueness, such as "Japan, Inc." and "Confucian capitalism." The need to know and understand Japan is very great today, but the growing attention the country is receiving has not yielded a clear picture. Take Japan's economic power: some people describe the system as a planned economy; others view it as market-driven. Some attribute Japan's phenomenal economic growth to the government, especially to the effectiveness of its industrial policy; some credit Japanese culture and education for creating an orderly, dedicated, and very competent population; some focus on Japanese management; and still others argue that the underlying causes lie in such private-sector economic factors as the high rate of capital formation. The fascination is that so many explanations are plausible. The answers are undoubtedly complex, but it is certain they will portray a national system that we have much to learn from, one to which we in the West will find our destiny more and more closely tied as we approach the twenty-first century.

As Japan grows more important, as both ally and competitor, the questions and interpretations multiply. We are told that competition in Japan's private sector is often so intense that it borders on the "excessive"; but if that is true, why is there a persistent belief that competition is actually quite controlled? Many foreign observers extol the virtues of Japanese management, including its unsurpassed capacity to forsake short-term profit for the long-term expansion of market share, but other observers call attention to its shortcomings, and particularly to its inability to foster basic technological innovation. The Japanese say their economy is open to foreign imports; many foreign exporters deny that it is. We are told Japan is the land of disciplined, loyal workers, but families are changing and the values of the young appear to be in flux.

What are we to make of these contradictory images? More than anything else, they reflect the complexity of Japan's industrial system and the difficulties of grasping those complexities. In such areas as government-business interactions, finance, industrial relations, and intercorporate relationships, Japan presents a striking contrast to patterns with which Westerners are familiar. No wonder misperceptions abound.

This book is designed to highlight this complexity and to help clarify Japan's distinctive qualities, as well as the nation's similarities with other industrial societies, by offering the reader a selection of the most insightful and informative interpretations available.

For six years, from 1977 to 1982, we were involved in a series of executive seminars focused on Japan at the Aspen Institute for Humanistic Studies, for the express purpose of educating leaders from business, government, the media, and universities about how that nation in fact works. The readings selected for this volume are essays that proved most stimulating and productive to our seminars. They have been chosen to provide a broad and incisive introduction to the structure and inner workings of Japan's system. The seminars taught us that juxtaposing different interpretations was very fruitful, and we tried to keep that spirit in our choice of readings. The selections cover many levels, from workers and managers, through company organization, to the nexus of ties between companies and their subcontractors, subsidiaries, banks, shareholders, and business "group" affiliations. The book's scope also encompasses the controversial but important subjects of industrial policy, government-business relations, financial markets, sociocultural factors, and the political context within which the whole system functions. A concrete illustration of the overall system in operation can be found in the case study concerning the near-bankruptcy and subsequent turnaround of Mazda Motors, especially as its recovery contrasts with that of Chrysler.

We were also guided by some basic questions. What are the central features of Japan's industrial system? What are the core institutions and practices that have to be understood in order to know how it functions? What distinctive characteristics set Japan apart from other industrial systems, notably that of the United States, with which the reader may be more familiar? Is the Japanese system changing, and if so, how? As these questions indicate, this anthology is not a primer on how to do business in Japan, nor is it a polemic for a particular approach to Japan. Rather, it has been conceived as a broad conceptual guide to Japan's overall modern system, how it is structured and how its institutions function.

The book is organized to accommodate different approaches to the readings. One can proceed sequentially, from start to finish, following what we think is a logical progression. Or depending on one's interests, one can go directly to a particular section, read it for its own value, and then proceed to sample more widely. Whatever the approach, we hope that by the time the book is put down, the reader will have gained a much clearer picture of the Japanese industrial system in all its richness, internal logic, and contradictions, both apparent and real.

The selections we present are relatively short, being in most cases extracts or abridgements of longer works. We have not indicated elisions, but we note where each selection can be found in its entirety so that interested readers will be able to explore the subject more fully. We have lightly edited all selections in this anthology to ensure consistency in style, punctuation, and capitalization, and in the handling of numbers, proper names, and foreign words and phrases. In some cases explanatory or digressive elements (such as parenthetical comments, lengthy notes, and tables) have been silently dropped to give the excerpt a sharper focus. The sequence within some texts has been slightly altered for the sake of clarity. With regard to the treatment of Japanese names, the names of those scholars working primarily in Japan are given surname first; in the source notes the names appear as they do in the original publication.

We would like to acknowledge the institutions and individuals without whose help the publication of this book would not have been possible. For financial support, research assistance, and secretarial help, we wish to thank the Northeast Asia–United States Forum on International Policy, Stanford University, and especially Nancy Okimoto, Stacey Green Tanaka, Josephine Harris, John Rogers, Kyle Koehler, and Sam Rasmussen. Our thanks go to all the participants at the Aspen seminars, especially Robert S. Ingersoll, Mikio Kato, Hugh Patrick, Henry Rosovsky, and Tadashi Yamamoto; also to Gail Potter and Marty Krasney, both formerly of the Aspen Institute. We feel fortunate to have worked with Stanford University Press. A special debt of gratitude is owed Betsey Scheiner for her fast, efficient, and marvelously competent editing.

D.I.O.
T.P.R.

Contents

Part I: Culture and Society

A S T H E F I R S T non-Western nation to reach an advanced state of modernization, Japan illustrates the myriad ways in which traditional patterns of meaning persist and are made vital in the present. The vexing question is assessing the degree of influence these patterns, developed over a long, rich, and quite distinct history, have in shaping contemporary economic behavior. There is little to be gained by either asserting cultural determinism (i.e., making culture the sole or dominant explanation) or ignoring the influence of culture altogether. Yet just what distinguishes Japanese culture is the first question to ask, a question the following readings answer in rather different ways.

In most societies and certainly in Japan, the family or household is the cradle of culture, both because it exemplifies the basic patterns to be found in social relations in general and because it is where feelings, thought patterns, and behavior are learned by each new generation. Many of the selections that follow highlight qualities of family life and childrearing practices that contrast with behavior in the West. The astute reader will note some significant differences in emphasis among the readings and is likely to discover paradox and seeming contradiction (given the Western model) (1) between dependence needs and the self-discipline evidenced in education and work; (2) between the emphasis on group membership and the workings of large-scale institutions; (3) between hierarchy and intimacy; (4) between emotionality and the necessities of rational calculation; and (5) between consensual and hierarchical processes in decision-making. The nature of competition also emerges as problematic in a society that values harmony and cooperation. Together the selections on the family establish a general portrait of relationships and values that, when contrasted to those in the contemporary West, highlights many of the vast patterns undergirding modern institutions. It is very helpful to keep in mind the fact that companies, unions, government agencies, political parties, and financial institutions, and the interactions between them, have evolved over the past hundred years through the interaction of Western models, Japanese cultural influences, and historical pressures. The mix is invariably complex and is still in flux.

Several selections offer insights into Japan's general sociological character. The school system shapes both population and many of its social and cultural characteristics. Japan is a nation preeminently dependent on the skills and diligence of its people. Education is thus crucial to the national destiny. From Inagami's article on the Japanese work ethic we learn about the income distribution pattern and its relation to worker morale and participation. The issues of equality and participation constitute important themes taken up by other readings throughout the book.

Finally, although Japanese tradition owes much to Buddhism and to Shinto, the role of Confucianism is the most immediate and apparent historical influence shaping the social ethics of the past century. Japanese thought has been greatly altered by Western culture, and in both public ideology and intellectual conversation there has been, until recently, a paucity of explicit traditionalism. But at the level of daily social morality, within the ideologies of many organizations, and in the implicit patterns of political decision making, a significant Confucian influence can be discerned. Around this ethic—which stands in marked contrast to the individualism and liberalism that are the analogous legacies in the West—can be gathered much of the most salient cultural explanations for Japan's modern distinctiveness. The last author in Part I even credits much of Japan's economic miracle to the behind-the-scenes influence of Confucianism. Here is the extreme cultural explanation, one readers can judge and weigh for themselves as the more concrete workings of the Japanese system are discussed in subsequent sections of the book.

1. The Family as an Ethical System

Watsuji Tetsurō

In 1928, the Japanese philosopher and cultural historian Watsuji Tetsurō returned from a year's travel in Europe, puzzled by the extreme contrasts he had seen between European culture and that of Japan. He began to study the role of climate in the formation of ethical thought and social institutions. The result was a comprehensive work entitled *Climate and Culture*, published in 1935, in which he concluded that Japan's unusually high humidity brought about the creation of institutions unique to that country. In this selection, Watsuji examines the concept of *ie* (household or, in the translation used here, house), a concept that continues to be used by social scientists in explaining how Japanese society works.

The term "house" (*ie*) signifies the family as a whole. The latter is represented by the head of the house, but it is the family as a whole that gives the head of the house his authority. It is not the case that the house is brought into existence at the whim of its head. The house is given a substantial and distinctive character by the fact that its unity is understood in historical terms. The family of the present shoulders the burden of this historical house and undertakes a liability for its unity from the past down into the future. Therefore, the good name of the house can make a victim even of the household head. The household member is not merely parent or child, husband or wife. He is also a descendant of his ancestors and an ancestor to those who are to come. The house evinces most starkly the fact that the family as a whole takes precedence over its individual members.

The house in this sense stands out prominently as part of the Japanese way of life; the family system appears as an elegant and beautiful custom. But where does the special character of this family system lie? Will Japan's distinctive way of life disappear as the family system falls into disuse?

In the family system, the relationship between husband and wife, parent and child, elder and younger brother or sister is, above all, that of gentle affection, aiming at a completely frank union. The artless ancients, when speaking of quarrels between husband and wife or of jealousy, displayed this sense of warm and unreserved family affection. The fine poem of the Manyō poet Yamanoue no Okura (ca. 660–733):

> Silver or gold or jade,
> None is as precious as my child.

From Tetsurō Watsuji, *Climate and Culture*, tr. Geoffrey Bownas (Tokyo: Hokuseido Press, 1961), pp. 141–49. Copyright © 1935, 1987, by Watsuji Masako. Originally published in Japanese by Iwanami Shoten, Publishers, Tokyo, 1935. By permission of the publisher.

expresses well the heart of the Japanese. Okura's family affection is revealed even more directly by his poem "On Going Home from a Party":

> My sobbing child and his mother
> Now wait for me to go home.

Such gentle affection can even be seen in the warriors of the Kamakura period (1185–1333) who brought about a great social revolution; Kumagai Renshōbō, for example, had a reversal of heart that sprang from his affection for his child. Again, in the Nō chants of the Ashikaga period, love between parent and child displays a deep and fundamental power. It goes almost without saying that the writers of the Tokugawa period used affection between parent and child when they wished to draw tears. Through every age, Japanese have striven to eradicate selfishness within the family and to realize fully the fusion of self and other. But even though this affection is calm, it is full of passion. The calmness of affection is not a mere fusion of emotions sunk in the depths of gloom. It is achieved only at the cost of purging and purifying powerful emotions. In spite of its outward calm, the force that is directed toward unreserved unity within the family is essentially very intense. The sacrifice of the self does not stop short at the needs of convenience but is carried through to its extreme limits. Whenever it meets with an obstacle, this quiet affection turns into ardent passion, forceful enough even to overwhelm the individual for the sake of the whole family. Then the family relationship takes the form of a heroic and martial attitude, unsparing even of life itself. Notions of vendetta carried on for the sake of parents in, for example, the *Tales of the Soga* indicate just how much such sentiments stir the hearts of the Japanese. A man is ready to sacrifice his life for his parents or for the good name of his house, and, for the individual concerned, this sacrifice is felt to possess the greatest significance in life. Such a person was the heroic samurai, who was prepared to lay down all for the good name of his house. The house as a whole is always of greater importance than the individual, so the latter throws away his life with the utmost selflessness. The most striking feature of Japanese history is this readiness to stake one's life for the sake of a parent or a child, or to cast away one's life for the house. The calm of family affection contains within it the sacrifice of self-centeredness. Thus, valor for the good of the family is not grounded in selfishness and precludes a dogged clinging to life.

The house represents the realization, through the family, of a distinctive Japanese relationship—the fusion of calm passion with martial selflessness. This relationship further becomes the basis of the development of the house itself, for this calm affection does not permit man to be viewed either artificially or abstractly. As a result, it is inappropriate to the development of a larger community of men built on consciousness of the individual. The concept of house in Japan takes on a unique and important significance as, if you like, the community of all communities. This is the real essence of the Japanese way of life, and the Japanese system, built on this foundation, has roots that lie deeper than any ideology.

Exactly the same phenomenon is revealed in architecture. The house as a structure of human relations is reflected in the layout of the house as a building. Above all, the physical house exhibits an internal fusion that admits of no discrimination.

No room is set off from another by lock and key; in other words, there is no distinction between the individual rooms. Even if there is a partitioning by shoji (sliding doors) or *fusuma* (screens), this is a division within the unity of mutual trust and not the sign of a desire for separation. The close and undiscriminating unity of the house does permit partitioning by shoji or fusuma, but the very fact of the need for partition is an indication of the passion it contains. Partitions indicate the existence of antagonisms within the house, yet their removal is in itself a show of a completely unbarriered and selfless openness.

The house is, however, quite unmistakably distinguished from what is outside. Even if there are no locks on the doors of the rooms, there is always one on the door that leads to the outside. Beyond this there may also be a fence, a wall, and, in extreme cases, a protective thicket or a moat. When a Japanese returns home from the outside, he removes his *geta* or shoes. By this very act he draws an explicit distinction between inside and outside.

The house continues unchanged in Japan—and continues not just as a formal entity but as a determinant of the Japanese way of life. The degree to which the character of the latter is unique becomes clearer with a comparison to the European way of life. A house in Europe is partitioned off into individual and independent rooms that are separated by thick walls and stout doors. These doors can all be secured by intricate locks so that only key-holders may come and go freely. In principle, this is a construction stressing individuality and separation.

Even the awakening of the Japanese people at the time of the foreign wars of the Meiji period is not a theoretical topic in and for itself but, rather, can be interpreted in terms of traditional family unity. The Japanese, it was said, are one great family that regards the imperial house as the home of its deity. The people as a whole are nothing but one great and unified house, all stemming from an identical ancestor. Thus, the entire state is "the house within the household," and the fence that surrounds the latter is broadened conceptually to become the boundaries of the state. Within the borders of the state as a whole, there should be the same unreserved and inseparable union that is achieved within the house. The virtue that is called filial piety from the standpoint of the house becomes loyalty from the standpoint of the state. Filial piety and loyalty are essentially identical virtues, which define the individual in accord with the interests of the whole.

The claims of loyalty and filial piety include a fair degree of patent irrationalities, whether regarded theoretically or historically. The family is the alpha of all human communities, as a unit of personal, physical, community life; the state is the omega of all human communities, as a unit of spiritual community life. The family is the smallest, the state the largest unit of union. The nature of the connections within each is different. To regard family and state as similar human structures is a mistake. Furthermore, the filial piety that was stressed so heavily in the Tokugawa period (1600–1868) does not by any means exhaust the prescriptions laid on the individual by virtue of his membership in the house as a whole.

Even so, there is much historical sense in the assertion of an identity between loyalty and filial piety rising from an understanding of the nation as a whole in terms of the analogy of the house. This kind of interpretation, which attempts to interpret the state in terms of a distinctive Japanese way of life, is common in Japan. And the simple fact that this is possible hints that, while the distinctiveness of the Japanese is best exemplified in the way of life of the house, a similar distinctiveness is reflected in the way of life of the nation as a whole.

2. The Family as an Economic Unit

Thomas C. Smith

A continuous flow of talented people from the countryside to the cities has provided much of the dynamism for Japan's modernization. Yet the values of these people were influenced by the values of the villages from which they came. The economic historian Thomas C. Smith argues in *The Agrarian Origins of Modern Japan*, published in 1959, that it was the importance of the family unit in the organization of farming villages which led to the continuation of conservatism in rural areas.

During the Tokugawa period (1600–1868), peasant society took on an unprecedented mobility; agriculture became competitive, productivity increased, commercial and industrial activity in the countryside flourished; there were even profound shifts of political power in many villages. Some elements of society, however, remained relatively unchanged, even well into the twentieth century. The most important were the small size of the farming units, family organization of production, and the unsparing use of hand labor. Whatever the reasons for these extraordinary continuities—and they are hotly debated—they had the effect of perpetuating the peasant family as an economic unit, thus allowing little change in its social character. The family's welfare continued to be of transcendent value, its authority immense. Solidarity and obedience were taught to the young as conditions of survival, and these traditional values carried over to behavior outside the family.

Another repository of tradition was the village. In many countries industry broke up the peasant village and dispersed its population, or greatly weakened its solidarity by creating deep class divisions. Neither development occurred in Japan, at least not on a comparable scale. Family farming remained the almost invariable rule, preserving the pattern of compact settlements and blocking the growth of large capitalist farms. Landownership did tend to concentrate, but large owners turned their land over to families of tenants or part-tenants rather than work it themselves. Despite increasing differences of income and the growth of non-agricultural employment, therefore, the village remained predominantly a community of small peasants faced with similar problems of small-scale cultivation and marketing. Sentimental and organizational ties from an earlier period persisted with special force, and the authority of the village over its members remained exceedingly strong.

From Thomas C. Smith, *The Agrarian Origins of Modern Japan* (Stanford, Calif.: Stanford University Press, 1959), pp. 208–10. By permission of the publisher.

Rice culture also contributed to the cohesiveness of the village. Rice was cultivated wherever soil, climate, and terrain permitted, which is to say on at least part of most holdings. Because rice must be made to stand in water much of the growing season to get maximum yields, there was need in nearly every village for an extensive system of ditches, dams, dikes, ponds, tunnels, and water gates. Since these could be constructed and maintained only by community effort, their use was subject to community control. A rice farmer never owned or controlled all of the essential means of production himself, and he could not individually make all the critical decisions of farming. He might wish, for instance, to turn an unirrigated field into a paddy, but he would not be allowed to do so if this would impair the water supply of others. And, if this was the case, he would refrain from insisting on his wish because he had been taught he must and because village opinion would be ranged solidly against him if he did not. The habit of obedience to community opinion where water was concerned likewise carried over to other community affairs (including the preservation of tradition), since any serious breach of solidarity directly threatened the communal foundations of farming.

Family farming and the emphasis on rice as a crop tended to preserve tradition among the peasantry in another way. These two factors kept farming less commercial than one might think in a country with as large an urban market as Japan. Most peasant families supplied all or nearly all of their own food, and food took a relatively large share of individual output. Hence, about one-third of the total agricultural income of the average peasant family in 1935 was received in kind, which is to say without marketing. Thus, the Japanese peasant's involvement in the market was far from complete; commercial values did not penetrate a very large area of economic relations, which remained embedded in custom-bound social groups.

Thus, although modernization generated in towns and cities new attitudes destructive of tradition, and greatly affected some important aspects of agriculture, the countryside remained a vast and populous hinterland of conservatism. Nor did the demographic ratio between town and country alter with the growth of industry as rapidly as in some countries. Owing to the intensive nature of farming, the agricultural population was almost perfectly stable from 1868 to 1940. As a result, persons employed in agriculture in Japan in 1930 accounted for 50.3 percent of the total labor force—as compared with 18.8 percent in the United States in 1940, 16.3 percent in Germany in 1933, and 6.2 percent in England in 1938! Here, then, was one of the most important reasons the state was able to sustain tradition even in the face of breathless change.

3. Hierarchy in Japanese Society

Nakane Chie

Nakane Chie's book *Japanese Society*, published in 1970, analyzes those elements of traditional Japanese social organization that have survived the pressures of modernization and Western influence. In the selection presented here, she discusses the characteristics of group formation, focusing primarily on the Japanese company as "the expression of group consciousness." A social anthropologist, Nakane was the first woman to become a professor at Tokyo University.

In any society, individuals are gathered into social groups or social strata on the bases of attributes and frame. The way in which these underlying factors are commonly weighted bears a close reciprocal relationship to the values that develop in the social consciousness of the people in the society. For example, the group consciousness of the Japanese depends considerably on the immediate social context, or frame, whereas in India it lies in attribute (most symbolically expressed in caste, which is fundamentally a social group based on the ideology of occupation and kinship).

The ready tendency of the Japanese to stress situational position in a particular frame, rather than universal attribute, can be seen in the following example: When a Japanese "faces the outside" (confronts another person) and affixes some position to himself socially, he is inclined to give precedence to institution over kind of occupation. Rather than saying, "I am a typesetter" or "I am a file clerk," he is likely to say, "I am from B Publishing Group" or "I belong to S Company." Much depends on the context, of course, but where a choice exists, he will use this latter form.

In group identification, a frame such as a "company" or "association" is of primary importance; the attribute of the individual is secondary. The same tendency is found among intellectuals: among university graduates, what matters most, and functions the strongest socially, is not whether a man holds or does not hold a Ph.D. but, rather, from which university he graduated. Thus, the criterion by which the Japanese classify individuals socially tends to be one of institutional affiliation rather than universal attribute. Such group consciousness and orientation fosters the strength of an institution, and the institutional unit (such as school or company) is in fact the basis of Japanese social organization.

The term *kaisha* (company) symbolizes the expression of group consciousness. Kaisha does not mean that individuals are bound by contractual relationships into a corporate enterprise, while still thinking of themselves as separate entities; rather, kaisha is "my" or "our" company, the community to which one belongs primarily and which is all-important in one's life. Thus, in most cases, the com-

From Chie Nakane, *Japanese Society* (Berkeley: University of California Press, 1970), pp. 2–99.
© 1970 The Regents of the University of California. By permission of the publisher.

pany provides the whole social existence of a person and has authority over all aspects of his life; he is deeply emotionally involved in the association. The sort of reasoning involved here, that Company A belongs not to its shareholders but rather to "us," is carried to such a point that even modern legal arrangements must compromise in the face of this strong native orientation. I would not wish to deny that in other societies an employee may have a kind of emotional attachment to the company or his employer; what distinguishes this relation in Japan is the exceedingly high degree of the emotional involvement. It is openly and frequently expressed in speech and behavior in public as well as in private, and such expressions always receive social and moral appreciation and approbation.

The resulting system of lifetime employment has advantages for both employer and employee. For the employer, it serves to retain the services of skilled workers against times of labor shortage. For the employee, it gives security against surplus labor conditions; whatever the market circumstances, there is little likelihood of the employee finding better employment if he leaves his job. The system has, in fact, been encouraged by contradictory situations—a shortage and a surplus of labor. Here is demonstrated a radical divergence between Japan and America in management employment policy: a Japanese employer buys potential labor for the future, and an American employer buys labor immediately required. According to Japanese reasoning, any deficiencies in the current labor force will be compensated by the development of maximum power in the labor force of the future; the employer buys his labor material and shapes it until it fits his production need. In America, management buys ready-made labor.

The characteristics of Japanese enterprise as a social group are, first, that the group is itself familylike and, second, that it pervades even the private lives of its employees, for each family joins extensively in the enterprise. These characteristics have been encouraged consistently by managers and administrators since the Meiji period. And the truth is that this encouragement has always succeeded and reaped rewards.

A cohesive sense of group unity, as demonstrated in the operational mechanisms of household and enterprise, is essential as the foundation of the individual's total emotional participation in the group; it helps to build a closed world and results in strong group independence or isolation. This inevitably breeds household customs and company traditions. These in turn are emphasized in mottoes that bolster the sense of unity and group solidarity and strengthen the group even more.

Consciousness of "them" and "us" is strengthened and aggravated to the point that extreme contrasts in human relations can develop in the same society, and anyone outside "our" people ceases to be considered human. Ridiculous situations occur, such as that of the man who will shove a stranger out of the way to take an empty seat but will then, no matter how tired he is, give up the seat to someone he knows, particularly if that someone is a superior in his company.

These characteristics of group formation reveal that Japanese group affiliations and human relations are exclusively one-to-one: a single loyalty stands uppermost and firm. There are many cases of membership in more than one group, of course, but in these cases there is always one group that is clearly preferred while the others are considered secondary.

In the foregoing discussion it has been shown that a group where membership is based on the situational position of individuals within a common frame tends to become a closed world. Inside it, a sense of unity is promoted by means of the members' total emotional participation, which further strengthens group solidarity. In general, such groups share a common structure, an internal organization by which the members are tied vertically into a delicately graded order.

A functional group always consists of heterogeneous elements, and their vertical relation becomes the actuating principle in creating cohesion among group members. Because of the overwhelming ascendancy of vertical orientation, even a set of individuals sharing identical qualifications tends to create differences within it. As this is reinforced, an amazingly delicate and intricate system of ranking takes shape.

There are numerous examples of this ranking process. Among lathe operators with the same qualifications, differences of rank exist which are based on relative age, year of entry into the company, or length of continuous service; among professors at the same college, rank can be assessed by the formal date of appointment; among commissioned officers in the former Japanese army, the differences between ranks were very great, and it is said that, even among second lieutenants, distinct ranking was made on the basis of order of appointment.

Ranking-consciousness is not limited merely to official groups but is found also among writers and actors—that is, groups that are supposed to be engaged in work based on individual ability and should not therefore be bound by any institutional system. A well-known novelist, on being given one of the annual literary prizes, said, "It is indeed a great honor for me. I am rather embarrassed to receive the award when some of my *sempai* [predecessors or elders] have not yet received it."

A Japanese finds his world clearly divided into three categories: *sempai* (seniors), *kōhai* (juniors), and *dōryō*. *Dōryō*, meaning "one's colleagues," refers only to those with the same rank, not to all who do the same type of work in the same office or on the same shop floor; even among dōryō, differences in age and year of entry or of graduation from school or college contribute to a sense of sempai and kōhai. These three categories would be subsumed under the single term "colleagues" in other societies.

Once established, vertical ranking functions as the charter of the social order, so that whatever the change in an individual's status, popularity, or fame, there is a deeply ingrained reluctance to ignore or change the established order. In this kind of society, ranking becomes far more important than any differences in the nature of the work. Even among people with the same training, qualifications, or status, differences based on rank are always perceptible. Because the individuals concerned are deeply aware of their existence, these distinctions tend to overshadow and obscure even differences of occupation, status, or class.

In Japan, once rank is established on the basis of seniority, it is applied to all circumstances and to a great extent controls social life and individual activity. Seniority and merit are the principal criteria for the establishment of a social order, and every society employs these criteria, although the weight given to each may differ according to social circumstances. In the West, merit is given considerable importance, while in Japan the balance goes the other way. In other words, in Japan in contrast to other societies, the provisions for the recognition of merit are weak, and the social order is institutionalized largely by means of seniority.

In everyday affairs a man who is not aware of relative ranking is not able to speak or even to sit or to eat. When speaking, he is always expected to be ready with differentiated, delicate degrees of honorific expressions appropriate to the rank order between himself and the person he is addressing. The expressions and the manner appropriate to a superior are never to be used to an inferior. Even among colleagues, it is only possible to dispense with honorifics when both parties are very intimate friends. The English language is inadequate to supply appropriate equivalents in such contexts, but behavior and language are intimately interwoven in Japan.

The ranking order that produces delicate differentiations between members of a group develops firm personal links between superior and subordinate. Such relationships form the core of the system of a group organization. A group structure based on a vertical line of this strength is demonstrably different from one based on a horizontal line.

Most Japanese, whatever their status or occupation, are involved in *oyabun-kobun* (boss-subordinate) relationships. The oyabun-kobun relationship comes into being through one's occupational training and activities and carries social and personal implications, appearing symbolically at the critical moments in a man's life. The oyabun often plays the role of the father, and it is by no means exceptional for him to play an even more important role.

It is said that the greatest battle weakness of the former Japanese army was the disruption that ensued when a platoon leader was killed. A platoon that had lost its organizational pivot because of the death of its lieutenant easily degenerated into a disorganized mob, committing gross errors of judgment. In the British and American armies there is no such disruption; a substitute platoon leader quickly steps out from the ranks, and control of the platoon continues undisturbed until there is only one soldier left.

Herein, then, lies the supreme importance of the role of the leader: he is both the holder of legitimate status and the outstanding personality, able to synthesize the members and suppress antagonisms among them. Even though a leader's absence from his men is only temporary, it may give rise to increased antagonisms among them. Legitimacy is based on seniority (not necessarily of age but of years of service in the group); the most senior man is also very probably the man who is highest in rank after and most closely linked with the leader, since the group hierarchy is formed according to the order of entry into the group. If there is more than one man in such a position, the most senior in age would become the first candidate for succession to the leadership.

Whatever their size, Japanese groups share common structural characteristics. Regardless of the size of the whole group, the functionally effective core is fairly small, usually of one or two dozen members. This is a size that enables each member to have direct contact with all the others, which can be organized on two or three levels, including the leader on the top level. Thus, members on the lowest level do not stand too far (i.e., through too many levels) from the leader. The ideal type of effective group is organized on two levels, with all members linked directly to the leader. When a group becomes larger, with an increased number of levels, the effectiveness of the entire system tends to decrease, and a functional core develops at each level.

These factors contribute to inefficiency of organization, in the matter of poor communication from the lower sectors to the top and between sections. However, such inefficiency is perhaps more than balanced by the extreme efficiency of communication from the top to the lowest level. Indeed, the swiftness by which the members of a group can be mobilized from the top in Japan is not paralleled in any other society. The secret of such swift action and the source of the high level of group energy seems to lie in the nature of the core of group organization, based on the relationship between two immediately linked men. The golden rule is that the junior man should invariably carry out any order from his immediate superior, for this immediate link between the two men is the source of the existence of the junior man in the organization. Hesitation or refusal constitutes a violation of the system, even if the execution of the order takes a man outside his assigned role, for what is important is the working of the vertical system, rather than the nature of the work or the formal assignment of roles. The prompt acceptance of an order by a junior predisposes his senior in his favor, and the accumulation of such give-and-take contributes to the mobilization of the entire group.

However, at the same time this highly involved relationship between the two men entails the phenomenon of "the creation of groups within a group" (*tochu to o tsukuru* in Japanese)—the sectionalism from which Japanese organizations regularly suffer. This precludes horizontal relations. It is difficult for a horizontal link or balanced cooperation between sections to function in Japan. The equal balance of powers between peers or collaboration between two equally competing groups is almost nonexistent in Japanese society, for when there is more than one faction within a group one will dominate. The existence of equally competing powers is a most unstable situation in Japan; stability always resides in imbalance between powers where one dominates the others.

A de facto coalition of equally strong factions is unlikely in Japan, for one of the factions is always invested with disproportionate weight. On this basis the leader mediates between opposing factions in order to arrive at group consensus, and will appeal to the weaker faction to concede its point "for the sake of my face"—that is, for his standing and reputation; and if the leader's face is saved, so is that of the opponent. Given such group structure and the use of emotional appeals, the majority opinion readily emerges. Thus, though the issue itself may never be subjected to logical examination, the group can reach agreement to act on a generally accepted decision. General agreement prompts readiness to act, and if a recalcitrant minority adamantly resists concession, radical action might finally be taken by which this minority could be made outcasts from the group.

From the above discussion two negative characteristics of group structure can be deduced: first, that the group is always under the risk of internal fission, and second, that it has the crucial external weakness of not permitting cooperation between groups. On the positive side, when the group is functioning at its best, great power and efficiency can come from concentrating and mobilizing its members' energies, since the ties binding individuals are emotional and stable. It follows, however, that efficiency is open to impairment through ambitions that upset the balance of power.

It is demonstrable that the informal hierarchy and the factions that develop among a group's members overlap and supersede an institution's formal administrative organization. In firmly established institutions, such as long-founded companies and governmental organizations, the instability and disintegration of informal groups are well compensated for by the institutional frame itself. Even when the informal hierarchy is deformed or destroyed, individual members still remain within the frame. Even while its efficiency is lowered, the group can preserve itself by means of the formal administrative organization. The institutional frame fulfills the important function of keeping the members together, whatever factions are found within it. Since members are classified primarily by the institution, whatever internal rivalries they may feel, they realize that they are all in one boat racing with other boats. It goes without saying that the degree of effectiveness of an institutional frame (the coherence of its members) is heightened when the institution itself possesses wide prestige and an important role in the society.

The overall picture of society resulting from such interpersonal (and intergroup) relations is not that of horizontal stratification by class or caste but of vertical stratification by institution or group of institutions. The construction of social groups based on vertical organization stresses their unitary aspects and brings about numerous vertical schisms within the society. Even if social classes like those in Europe can be detected in Japan, and even if something vaguely resembling the classes that are illustrated in the textbooks of Western sociology can also be found in Japan, the point is that in actual society this stratification is unlikely to function. It does not really reflect the social structure. In Japanese society, it is really not a matter of workers struggling against capitalists or managers but of Company A ranged against Company B. The protagonists do not stand in vertical relationship to each other but instead rub elbows from parallel positions. The organization of unions in Japan, their ideals, and the peculiarities to be seen in the union movement cannot be understood without this kind of analysis. The antagonism and wrangling between management and labor in Japan is unquestionably a "household" problem, and though their basic divergence is the same as it is the world over, the reason it cannot develop in Japan into a problem intimately and powerfully affecting society as a whole lies in the group structure and the nature of Japanese society.

Competition takes place between parallel groups of the same kind, and the prize in the race is the rating. A common Japanese reaction may well take the form, "Their rating is higher than ours, so . . ." Among governmental organizations, the ranking is known in an informal way, though in a manner sufficiently overt for those closely concerned. The Finance Ministry stands out at the top, and the Education Ministry, for example, is placed considerably lower. Generally, earlier entrants (those having a longer history) have the higher ratings, but the fact that rating can be changed through the acquisition of additional political and economic power and influence is a primary factor in whipping up the race.

The ranking order among institutions is likewise of immediate concern to individuals, in that individual status and prestige go according to this ranking as well as according to the individual's rank within each institution. Even typists and drivers take pride in belonging to a company with a high ranking, for they are able to feel superior to typists and drivers employed by lesser-ranked companies, even though they receive the same pay. The Japanese are not so much concerned with social background as with institutional affiliation. Since the hierarchy of each field is so clearly perceived and widely known, and since the hierarchy within individual institutions also extends beyond the institution, taken together they offer a fairly distinct picture into which an individual can be fitted.

The building of a hierarchy based on the ranking order of institutions is further complicated by the tendency for a set of institutions to be organized in the manner of the inverted v, in just the same way as individuals form a group. It is usual, for example, for a large business firm or industrial plant to attach to itself a considerable number of affiliated and subordinate companies, many of which are called its "child companies." The nature and degree of the relationships between parent company and child company vary considerably. A child company may be created by separating a part of the original company, or by investing a part of the capital of the latter; or an independent smaller company may establish a parent and child relationship with a large one. Personnel and finance may be transferred from the one to the other. However, some child companies have a considerable degree of independence from the parent company and an autonomy not found in the case of, for example, an American subsidiary company. Indeed, there are examples of a child company which develops and becomes so successful that it reaches a status comparable to that of its parent company. On the other hand, a child company may be closely tied to the parent company, forming one distinct hierarchical organization with it and the other companies affiliated at various levels. Such a case is usually centered on a large company, say, with more than 10,000 employees—at the lowest level there may be a very small enterprise consisting of the members of a single family.

Clusters of this kind, which exist in all business sectors in Japan, are at their most pronounced in such fields as automobile production and the building industry. Toyota Motor Corporation, one of the largest automobile enterprises in Japan, is a convenient and telling illustration. Centered on Toyota Motor Corporation are twelve companies known as the Toyota Group. These companies are closely linked with Toyota Motor Corporation through activities or business such as sales, exports, production of parts, and supply of materials.

An examination of the interinstitutional relations in any such group reveals the operation of the same structural mechanism as exists in the single institution—immobility, both within and between groups. For this reason, a group, on whatever level, is organized vertically and keeps its solidarity and exclusiveness. For the same reason, any element built into the body of the group is virtually unexchangeable. Thus, the one-to-one, single-bond affiliation, solidly fixed, contributes to the maintenance of order in the overall structure of society. It is not a simple matter of "loyalty," for the structure of the group is significant. A society having this type of social organization does not spontaneously put its resources into a pool from which every group can take supplies whenever they are needed. In this system of organization, therefore, a group tends to develop self-sufficiency so that it can function by itself. Otherwise, it would not survive.

4. Childrearing and Personality Formation

William A. Caudill and Carmi Schooler

In the early 1960's, the American anthropologist William A. Caudill began a long-term comparative study of Japanese and American childrearing practices. Part of his research consisted of observing 40 Japanese and 30 American three- to four-month-old infants and their mothers. After Caudill's death in 1973, his associate at the National Institute of Mental Health, Carmi Schooler, published an "interim report" on the study, using Caudill's words as much as possible. In the report, Caudill and Schooler conclude that differences in childrearing methods do indeed play an important role in personality formation and in the transmission of culture from one generation to the next.

A comparison of the data on infant behavior in Japanese and American cultures shows a basic similarity in the biologically rooted behavior of the infants in the total time spent for the intake of food (sucking on breast or bottle and eating of semisolid food) and in sleep, and also shows a basic similarity in the behavior of the mothers in the two countries in the time they spend feeding, diapering, and dressing their infants. Beyond these similarities, however, there are distinct cultural differences. American infants show greater amounts of gross bodily activity, play (with toys, hands, and other objects), and happy vocalization; in contrast, Japanese infants seem passive, having only a greater amount of unhappy vocalization. American mothers do more looking at, positioning the body of, and chatting to their infants; Japanese mothers do more carrying, rocking, and lulling of their infants.

The general findings indicate that the mothers in the two cultures engage in different styles of caretaking: the American mother seems to encourage her baby to be active and vocally responsive, while the Japanese mother acts in ways which she believes will soothe and quiet her baby. Infants in both cultures seem to have become habituated by three to four months of age to respond appropriately to these different styles of caretaking. The responses of the infants are strikingly in line with the general expectations for behavior in the two cultures: in America, the individual should be physically and verbally assertive; and in Japan, he should be physically and verbally restrained.

It is noteworthy that the greater happy vocalization of the American infant is significantly correlated with the mother's looking at and chatting to her baby. In contrast, the Japanese infant's lesser amount of happy vocalization does not show any clear pattern of relationship with his mother's behavior. This patterning of correlations suggests that vocal communication between infant and mother in the two cultures serves different purposes. But such correlational findings do not an-

From William A. Caudill and Carmi Schooler, "Child Behavior and Child Rearing in Japan and the United States: An Interim Report," *Journal of Nervous and Mental Disease*, vol. 157, no. 5 (Nov. 1973), pp. 323–38. Copyright © 1973 by Williams & Wilkins. By permission of the publisher.

swer the question of how the flow of vocal communication actually proceeds in daily life in each culture. This problem is more fully explored by making use of the sequential property of the data. This was accomplished by examining all of the instances in which an infant is awake and alone to discover, within the limits of the block of forty observations covered by each record sheet, what happens when he begins a string of unhappy, happy, or mixed vocalizations. This method enables us to see how quickly the mother responds to each of these kinds of vocalizations, or alternatively, what happens when the mother does not respond and the infant must himself resolve the matter. The usual response for the infant when he "handles" the situation himself is to go to sleep. When this happens, there are no differences in the amount of time it takes the Japanese or the American infant to go to sleep; this argues for the essential biological similarity of infants in the two cultures. There are, however, great cultural differences in the responses of Japanese and American mothers to these various situations, and these differences go a long way toward answering the question of why the American infant produces a greater amount of happy vocalization while the Japanese infant produces a greater amount of unhappy vocalization.

First, the sequential analysis indicates that the pace of the American mother is livelier. She is in and out of the room more and thus provides more naturally occurring opportunities to speak to her baby and for him to respond vocally as she comes to care for him. Second, the American mother in general responds more quickly to her baby's vocalizations, regardless of whether they are happy or unhappy; and third, and even more importantly, the American mother differentiates more sharply between kinds of vocalizations by responding more quickly to his unhappy sounds than she does to his happy sounds. In this latter regard, the American mother appears to be teaching her infant to make a more discriminating use of his voice. Fourth, the American mother has more vocal interaction with her baby, especially by chatting to him at the same time he is happily vocal. All of these findings are part of the American mother's style of caretaking, which serves to increase her infant's happy vocalizations and, more broadly, to emphasize the importance of vocal communication.

In contrast, the pace of the Japanese mother is more leisurely and, although she does not spend more total time in the care of her baby, her periods of caretaking are fewer and longer in duration. She is more involved than is the American mother in the process of her baby's going to sleep and waking up. Part of the Japanese mother's style of caretaking is to carry, rock, and lull her baby to sleep, with the result that when the sleeping baby is put down, he tends to awaken and cry, and the process begins again. Here, obviously, is one reason for the greater amount of unhappy vocalizations on the part of the Japanese babies in our sample. In checking on her sleeping baby, the Japanese mother is more likely to go beyond just glancing in at him to other caretaking acts which bring her into physical contact with the baby, and these often result in the baby waking and crying for a brief period. Thus, while the American mother tends merely to glance into the room where the baby is sleeping, the Japanese mother goes beyond this to adjusting the baby's covers, wiping the sweat off the baby's forehead, and so on. These additional actions have the effect of interfering with the baby's normal rhythm of sleep. As a result of this greater intervention by the Japanese mother, the Japanese baby is in and out of sleep more frequently and is, consequently, more unhappily vocal during these transitions. The Japanese mother is also slower in general in her response to her infant's vocalizations; when she does respond, she does not discriminate between his unhappy and happy sounds by responding more quickly to one than to the other. Finally, the Japanese mother has less vocal interaction of any type with her baby during caretaking. This is especially evident in those situations where mothers of both cultures chat to happily vocalizing babies. These aspects of the Japanese mother's style of caretaking help to explain why the Japanese infant has a greater amount of unhappy vocalization; they also point to a lesser reliance on and refinement of vocal communication between mother and infant while, at the same time, emphasizing the importance and communicative value of physical contact.

Looking at the cultural contexts of these cross-national differences in the behavior of mothers and infants, it would appear that in America the mother views her baby, at least potentially, as a separate and autonomous being who should learn to do and think for himself. For her, the baby is from birth a distinct personality with his own needs and desires that she learns to recognize and care for. She helps him to learn how to express these needs and desires through her emphasis on vocal communication so that he can "tell" her what he wants and she can respond appropriately. Obviously here, in psychological terms, we have the beginnings of a greater separation of mother and infant, and the development of sharper ego boundaries. The American mother deemphasizes the importance of physical contact such as carrying and rocking, and encourages her infant through the use of her voice to explore, and learn to deal with, his environment by himself. The American mother does more encouraging of her baby to reach out for toys, and to be more physically active (indeed, one of our mothers was encouraging her baby, at three to four months of age, to use a spoon by himself). Just as the American thinks of her infant as a separate individual, so also does she think of herself as a separate person with her own needs and desires, which include time apart from her baby to pursue her own interests, and to be a wife to her husband as well as a mother to her baby. For this reason, the pace of caretaking is quicker, and when she is caretaking, her involvement with the baby is livelier and more intense. Partly this is true because she wishes to stimulate the baby to activity and response when he is awake so that when it is time for him to go to sleep, he will remain asleep and give her a chance to do other things—both during the day and at night. In Japan, in contrast to America, the mother views her baby much more as an extension of herself, and psychologically the boundaries between them are blurred. Because of the great emphasis in Japan on the close attachment between mother and child, the mother is likely to feel that she knows what is best and that there is no particular need for him to tell her verbally what he wants because, after all, they are virtually one. Given this orientation, the Japanese mother places less importance on vocal communication and more on physical contact; also, for her there is no need for hurry as the expectation is that she will devote herself to her child without any great concern for a time away from him, or even for a separate time to be with her husband. This expectation extends throughout the night because of the Japanese custom of parents and children sleeping together in the same room.

From these results of the infant study it seems likely that a considerable amount of culturally patterned behavior has already come into being by three to four months of age, including the forerunners of what will become attitudes toward one's body and its management. In America, even the infant is encouraged in some ways to care for his own needs, whereas in Japan the infant has learned that his needs will be taken care of by others if he complains hard enough.

5. Children and Their Mothers

The following selection compares the findings of two studies of 2,236 American and 1,658 Japanese children aged seven to eleven. The results suggest that personality and cultural differences created by differences in infant childrearing methods continue as children grow older. The article appeared in 1978 in *Focus Japan*, a Japanese magazine which publishes English translations of articles that have appeared in Japanese newspapers and journals.

Compared with their counterparts in the United States, Japanese grade school children have more lenient mothers and are slower in developing self-awareness, concludes a report by the Japan Youth Research Institution (JYRI). The institution, a private research organization founded in 1976, recently conducted an interview survey of grade school children and their mothers concerning child discipline, the mother-child relationship, and children's psychological development. The JYRI utilized the method employed in a similar study undertaken in the United States by the Foundation for Child Development (FCD) and then compared the two findings.

According to the report, Japanese children are given more freedom in choosing daily activities than American youngsters. Asked if they were allowed to choose their own "TV viewing time," "TV programs," "playmates," and "bedtime," the majority of Japanese children answered "yes" to all but "bedtime." More than half the American children, on the other hand, replied that they were restricted in the choice of all but playmates. However, 68 percent of the Japanese children said that their mothers frequently told them to "study harder," and more Japanese than American mothers expressed dissatisfaction with their children's grades. This probably reflects the rigorous educational system in Japan, in which a child's future is largely determined by whether he or she passes the entrance examination for a "good" high school or college.

American mothers, the survey revealed, tend to discipline as well as reward their children more than Japanese mothers. A high percentage of both Japanese and American children said that their mothers praised them when they behaved well or did something good. But twice as many American children indicated that

From "Growing Up with Mom," *Focus Japan*, June 1978, pp. 9–10. By permission of the Japan External Trade Organization, JETRO.

their mothers also rewarded them with money or goodies. On the other hand, American children are more often subjected to punishment when they misbehave. In addition to scolding and spanking, American youngsters said that they were "shut up in their room" (63 percent vs. 11 percent for Japanese children), "not allowed to play with friends" (55 percent vs. 20 percent), or "not allowed to watch TV" (47 percent vs. 27 percent). Japanese children tend to be reprimanded more with verbal threats and disparaging remarks ("I don't like children like you," "People will laugh at you," etc.).

Questioned whether their mothers treated them "more like a grown-up or a baby," 65 percent of the American children answered "more like a grown-up," compared to only 10 percent of the Japanese children. Though the differing nuances of "grown-up" and "baby" in the two languages may be a factor behind the wide disparity in the two sets of responses, Japanese mothers' reluctance to recognize their young children's independence was confirmed by other questions. The JYRI's question "When will you consider your children independent?" brought answers of when he or she "finishes school and starts working," "gets married," or "attains the voting age of twenty." In addition, a large majority of Japanese mothers pointed to "obedience" as their child's best personality trait.

Perhaps the biggest difference revealed by the two surveys is that Japanese children are less self-aware and less self-confident than American children. Questioned about the aspect of themselves that they are most proud of, one-third of the Japanese children answered that they didn't know, and 11 percent said "none." Those offering specific qualities cited "nice and kind," "athletic ability," "cheerful," "peppy and active," etc. On the other hand, American children gave a variety of answers, such as "athletic ability," "good student," "being myself," "easy to get along with," "popular," and so on. "Don't know" and "none" accounted for only 8 and 2 percent, respectively. Similarly, a question asking what aspect of themselves they wanted to change most drew "don't know" responses from a quarter of the Japanese children polled, as opposed to a mere 7 percent of their American counterparts. Answers of "none" accounted for 17 percent of Japanese and 23 percent of American children's responses. Aspects of themselves that they did want to change showed an interesting contrast: the top five answers from Japanese children indicated that they wished to become "more patient," "a better student," "less shy," "more intelligent," and "better-looking." American children, on the other hand, wanted to change their "hair," "height," or "weight," or to become "more attractive" or "older."

"Whom are you most afraid of?" brought very different answers from the two groups of children. Among Japanese children, mother came first, followed by father, schoolteachers, brother or sister, and other children. Among American youngsters the order was father, children in the neighborhood, older children in the neighborhood, brother or sister, and the devil. Japanese children's primary fear of mother seems to reflect the recent tendency to leave child upbringing and discipline entirely to the mother, with the father remaining indifferent. The survey also confirms the general observation that children fight more physically in the United States than in Japan. Although Japanese children do seem to quarrel just as often as American youngsters, far fewer of them have experienced getting hit, knocked off their bicycle, etc., or having toys or money taken by other children.

6. Dependency in Human Relationships

Doi Takeo

The psychiatrist Doi Takeo is famous for his theory that *amae* (dependency) underlies all human interaction in Japan and that it is the institutionalization of this concept which distinguishes Japan from other societies. This selection is drawn from an article entitled "*Amae*: A Key Concept for Understanding Japanese Personality," published in English in 1962; a book entitled *The Anatomy of Dependence*, which appeared in Japanese in 1971 as *Amae no kōzō*; and an article entitled "The Japanese Patterns of Communication and the Concept of Amae," published in English in 1973.

The Concept of Amae

I am particularly interested in the problem of personality and culture in modern Japan for two reasons. First, even though I was born and raised in Japan and had my basic medical training there, I have had further training in psychiatry and psychoanalysis in the United States, thus exposing myself for some time to a culture different from that of Japan. Second, I have had many opportunities to treat both Japanese and non-Japanese (mostly American) patients with psychotherapy. These experiences have led me to inquire into the differences between Japanese and non-Japanese patients and also into the question of what is basic in Japanese character structure.

The essence of what I am going to talk about is contained in one common Japanese word, *amae*, the noun form of *amaeru*, an intransitive verb that means "to depend and presume upon another's benevolence." This word has the same root as *amai*, an adjective that means "sweet." Amaeru has a distinct feeling of sweetness and is generally used to describe a child's attitude or behavior toward his parents, particularly his mother. It can also be used to describe the relationship between two adults, such as the relationship between a husband and a wife or a master and a subordinate. I believe that there is no single word in English equivalent to amaeru, though this does not mean that the psychology of amae is totally alien to the people of English-speaking countries.

The state of amae basically refers to what a small child feels toward his mother. It is therefore not surprising that the desire to amaeru still influences one's adult years and that it becomes manifest in the therapeutic situation. Here we have a perfect example of transference in the psychoanalytic sense. But then is it not strange that amaeru is a unique Japanese word? Indeed, the Japanese find it hard

From Takeo Doi, "*Amae*: A Key Concept for Understanding Japanese Personality," in R. J. Smith and R. K. Beardsley, eds., *Japanese Culture: Its Development and Characteristics* (Chicago: Aldine, 1962), p. 132; *The Anatomy of Dependence* (Tokyo and New York: Kodansha International, 1973), pp. 15, 84–87, and 94–95; and "The Japanese Patterns of Communication and the Concept of Amae," *Quarterly Journal of Speech*, vol. 59, no. 2 (1973), pp. 180–83. By permission of the publishers.

to believe that there is no word for amaeru in European languages; a colleague once told me he could not believe that the equivalent for such a seemingly universal phenomenon as amae did not exist in English or German, since, as he put it, "Even puppies do it, you know."

There is a social sanction in Japanese society for expressing the wish to amaeru. Parental dependency is encouraged, whereas the opposite tendency prevails in Western societies. We can speak of parental dependency as being institutionalized in Japanese society. For instance, in marriage a husband does amaeru toward his wife, and vice versa. It is strongly present in all formal relationships, including those between teacher and student and between doctor and patient.

The desire to amaeru is entirely contingent upon the actions of others for its gratification. One cannot receive gratification by a verbal message, as sometimes can be done in the case of "I love you." In fact, Japanese seldom say "I amaeru." Still, the gratification of amaeru stands as a norm in Japanese society. Perhaps it is better to define it as the principle of mutuality that must be present to guarantee smooth transactions. All interpersonal communications in Japanese society have an emotional undertone of amae. It is not surprising, then, that Japanese tend to have many short breaks in their conversation. During those breaks they try to feel out one another and assess the situation, because what is most important for them is to reassure themselves on every occasion of a mutuality based upon *amae*. One could say that for the Japanese, verbal communication is something that accompanies nonverbal communication and not the other way round. In other words, they are very sensitive to the atmosphere that pervades human relationships. To explain this point further, let me introduce you to some very interesting comparative research by William Caudill and Helen Weinstein. Caudill and Weinstein selected as samples 40 Japanese and 30 American three- to four-month-old infants and studied the interactions of those infants and their mothers. The conclusions the authors drew from this study are astounding. To quote: "The American baby appears to be more physically active and happily vocal, and more involved in the exploration of his body and his environment than is the Japanese baby, who, in contrast, seems more subdued in all these respects." Moreover, these patterns of behavior learned so early by the infants are likely to lead to different expectations for adult behavior in the two cultures.

I remind you that the conclusions were based on relations in three- to four-month-old babies. At that early age there are already cultural differences. One can easily see from this that Americans are conditioned from the very beginning of life to associate human contact more with verbal communication and Japanese more with nonverbal and passive communication.

Japanese Ambiguity

In this connection, I'd like to tell you my first reaction to Americans when I went to the United States in 1950. I was greatly surprised, almost perturbed, by the fact that Americans loved to talk incessantly, even during meals. As a matter of fact, they sounded almost hypermanic to me. This impression was undoubtedly partly due to the language barrier that I was painfully aware of, and partly due to the difference in customs between the United States and Japan. (When we were growing up, we used to be chided if we talked during a meal. One was supposed to eat without saying much.) But I thought there was more to it. I couldn't help feeling that Americans hate silence, whereas Japanese can sit very comfortably without talking to one another. To tell you the truth, even though I no longer feel the pinch of the language barrier, it is still a strain for me to keep pace with Americans during a social evening. But I can't hide behind a curtain of silence as I do when I am acting professionally. I am often thankful that I am a psychiatrist because of the privilege of keeping silent.

One more example will prove the point. I know a Japanese simultaneous translator who often interprets at key international conferences in both Tokyo and Kyoto. He told me that it was simply amazing how little Japanese participants communicate with Americans. I remind you that they don't have to speak English because they can count on the ample services of simultaneous translators. Still, according to my informant, they don't talk much but sit looking stiff and stony-faced. Don't think that they are awed by the dignified-looking Americans, though this might have some influence.

Japanese just don't talk much—even at a conference for Japanese only. But they are congenial to one another. They usually spend a long time fishing for clues as to where each stands on the question at issue, so that they can somehow reach the unanimous agreement which is so important for them. Unanimous agreement has a very important social function for the Japanese. It is a token that the mutuality of all the members has been preserved. In other words, it is a token satisfaction of amae. The Japanese hate to contradict or to be contradicted—that is, to have to say "no" in a conversation. They simply don't want to have divided opinions, and if such an outcome appears to be inevitable, they will get so heated emotionally that it becomes almost impossible to continue any reasoned discussion. I think this explains why disagreements become violent in the Diet [parliament] and other groups in Japan. The greater the power of cohesiveness, the more violent the effect of a break. It is like splitting the atom.

The well-known Japanese fondness for hesitation or for ambiguities of expression can also be explained along the same lines. Japanese hesitate to speak or to say something ambiguous when they fear what they have in mind might be disagreeable to others (that is, when they have to say "no"). I think this has been deeply ingrained in the Japanese people from time immemorial.

The Japanese fondness for unanimous agreement which I mentioned above may also contribute to ambiguity. Curious as it may seem, for the Japanese, the form of unanimous agreement is not strictly binding if all agree to respect it—which I am afraid is an ambiguous statement. But what I mean is this: since unanimous agreement is a token that the mutuality of all the members has been preserved, an individual member may harbor his own thoughts and beliefs, so long as he does not openly challenge the agreement.

This involves the very Japanese double standard of *tatemae* (principle or rule) and *honne* (one's true intention). Tatemae is any rule of conduct which Japanese accept by unanimous agreement, and you would be wrong if you think that Japanese do not take it seriously. They do. It is like a certificate that secures them membership in a coveted group. Nevertheless, it is a formal front—rather than a principle in the English sense—behind which one may safely and continuously entertain one's honne. The discrepancy between the two—tatemae and honne—is borne, and not at all vaguely, in good conscience. For the Japanese themselves, there's nothing ambiguous about the double standard of tatemae and honne. As a matter of fact, this is a measure of maturity in the Japanese sense: that people have the knowledge and existence of such a double standard and adjust their lives accordingly.

Amae and Freedom

The Japanese word *jiyū*, usually used to translate the English word freedom and other Western words of similar meaning, is of Chinese origin but seems to have been used in Japan from an early date. What is interesting for us here is that the meaning in which it was traditionally used—as suggested by the combination *jiyū-kimama* (fancy-free)—seems to have a close connection with the desire for amae. "Freedom" in Japan has traditionally meant the freedom to amaeru, to behave as one pleases without considering others. Never was it freedom from amae. Willfulness, of course, is not considered to be a good thing and, judging from examples found in old Chinese and Japanese documents, the word jiyū often has overtones that are to a certain degree critical. In this it is the exact opposite of freedom and liberty (for which jiyū served as the translation following the Meiji Restoration), which in the West signify respect for the human being and contain no trace of criticism. For this reason, the word jiyū has come in recent years to partake of both its good, Western sense and its bad, Japanese sense, with an extreme ambiguity as the result.

First, something should be said concerning the idea of freedom in the West. Historically speaking, it seems to have begun with the distinction between freeman and slave in ancient Greece. Freedom meant an absence of the enforced obedience to another implied in the state of slavery. It is precisely because of this that in the West, freedom became tied up with such ideas as the rights and dignity of man and came to be seen as something good and desirable. As a logical extension, the Western-style idea of freedom also served as a basis for asserting the precedence of the individual over the group, in which respect it again affords a marked contrast with the Japanese idea of jiyū. If, as I have done above, we interpret jiyū as the right to do what one pleases (*wagamama*), we could certainly apply it to the desire of individuals to avoid, for example, interference by the group. Here, though, it is because the group will not fall in with the individual's wishes that the desire for freedom arises, and the individual himself remains fundamentally unable to transcend the group. In other words, the Japanese-style idea of jiyū cannot serve as the basis for asserting the superiority of the individual over the group. There is nothing surprising in this when one considers that originally Japanese-style jiyū had its origins in amae and that amae requires the presence of others: it might make the individual dependent on the group, but it would never allow him to be independent of it in the true sense. Contrary to this, in the West, with its emphasis on the freedom of the individual, people have always looked down on the type of emotional dependency that corresponds to amae.

All kinds of arguments could probably be adduced to show that the Western concept of freedom depends on a rejection of amae, but I would like here to quote the following passage attributed to the Renaissance scholar Juan Luis Vives (1492–1540): "Passive love, that is, the tendency to be the recipient of love, produces gratitude; and gratitude is always mixed with shame. Shame would naturally interfere with the sense of gratitude." When I came across this quotation in Gregory Zilboorg's history of psychology, I was immediately reminded of the Japanese *sumanai* (unpardonable), a word that is used as an apology for a burden imposed on another person. People in the West, however, as the Vives quotation suggests, seem to feel that thanks carry with them feelings of shame, which in turn hinder feelings of gratitude. In an attempt to wipe out the sense of shame, the Westerner has striven for long years not to feel excessive gratitude, which is the result of passive love. There is no doubt, of course, that this has fortified the individual's sense of freedom.

Thus, the spirit of amae and freedom of the individual seem to be contradictory. If this is true, then contact with Western-style freedom following the Meiji Restoration must have been a considerable shock for the Japanese. Most of them were fated to suffer emotionally because they were not able to attain the freedom they desired. Ironically, the Western-style freedom they thought they were seeking was probably, in fact, a Japanese-style freedom. The trouble stems from confusion concerning the meaning of jiyū; it has even been suggested that jiyū is a mistranslation, but in any case, since Meiji times the Japanese have been obsessed by a conflict concerning freedom, something clearly illustrated in modern Japanese literature.

I wish to pose the following question: Is the freedom of the individual, that magnificent article of faith for the modern Western world, really to be believed in, or is it merely an illusion cherished by one section of the population of the West? Western man in the early twentieth century, even after the experience of World War I, still harbored a great pride in the idea of freedom that was his spiritual legacy. That fine historian and sociologist Ernst Troeltsch, for example, wrote as follows: "The idea of Personality, which, in the form of Freedom, determines everything in the morality of conscience, and, in the form of Object, everything in the ethic of values—this idea is, after all, a Western belief, unknown in our sense to the Far East, and preeminently and peculiarly the destiny of us Europeans." It is true that even today men in the West still act on the assumption that the individual is free, so that there is considerable difference between their behavior and that of the Japanese who lack their faith. But there are signs that that faith has recently begun to degenerate into an empty shell.

In short, modern Western man is gradually becoming troubled by the suspicion that freedom may have been only an empty slogan. The incisive analyses of Marx, who insisted that capitalism inevitably alienated the human being; the writings of Nietzsche, who proclaimed that Christianity was the morality of slaves; and the psychoanalysis of Freud, who emphasized the control of the spiritual life by the unconscious, all helped to open the eyes of modern Western man on this point. As a result, his faith in freedom has been cruelly broken. Admittedly, there are thinkers like Sartre, who cling to human freedom as the only absolute in a society whose superstructure is in the process of collapse. Yet where does this type of freedom lead? Ultimately, it can only mean, if not the simple gratification of individual desires, solidarity with others through participation—in which case, the Western idea of freedom becomes ultimately something not so different from the Japanese.

7. Education in Japanese Society

Thomas P. Rohlen

Thomas P. Rohlen is an anthropologist at Stanford who writes about Japanese business and education. In this article, he discusses the factors that have brought about Japan's extraordinary record of educational accomplishment, focusing particularly on the role of university entrance examinations. Rohlen argues that the qualities of diligence and organization that characterize Japanese education also characterize Japanese society as a whole, and that in both domains they lead to similar strengths and weaknesses.

Contemporary Japan is about as developed and organized a society as one can find today. It is a society of employers and employees, where educational credentials and educated skills are central to employment, promotion, and general social status. Japan is a meritocracy shaped by educational competition. And this is fitting, for Japan is a nation which, lacking natural resources, must live by its wits. The skills and cooperation of its citizenry must combine into highly efficient organizations, ones that are adept at learning borrowed and new technology. It is not a society with a privileged traditional class, nor is it one divided between a small, educated elite and the masses. Rather, the modern sectors require the skilled participation of the great majority of Japanese.

It is not surprising, therefore, to discover that in terms of both quality and inclusiveness, Japanese education is outstanding. On international tests of achievement in science and math, Japanese students outperform all others. Her newspaper readership level is the world's highest. A considerably larger proportion of Japanese (90 percent) than Americans (73 percent) or Europeans (in most countries below 50 percent) finish the twelfth grade, and a greater proportion of males complete university B.A. degrees in Japan than in other countries. Japanese children attend school about 50 more days each year, which means that by high school graduation they have been in school the equivalent of three to four more years than their American counterparts. If we add to this the fact that requirements in all basic subjects are heavier in Japan, and that elementary education in art and music is universal and quite advanced, we have a most impressive portrait of national achievement. It would not be an exaggeration to say that in many respects the average high school graduate in Japan is equal or superior to the average American college graduate in the sciences, math, geography, history, music, art, and foreign language skills. The West has hardly noted these accomplishments, and the Japanese themselves have rightly been concerned with the costs incurred in achieving such success, but the fact remains: Japanese education, like the nation's overall industrial system, has been made into an extraordinarily efficient engine for economic advancement. Today, Japan sets the world standards in mass education.

Some points of comparison between the Japanese and American education systems (1984) are summarized here.

Total education expenditures (percentage of gross national product):
Japan   10%   United States   7%

Four-year-olds attending school:
Japan   63%   United States   32%

Students graduating from twelfth grade:
Japan   90%   United States   73%

Average daily hours of homework during high school:
Japan   2.0   United States   .5

Daily absentee rate:
Japan   under 2%   United States   9%

Years required of high school mathematics:
Japan   3   United States   1

Years required of foreign language (grades 7–12):
Japan   6   United States   0

Matriculation rate to higher education:
Japan   36% (universities 27%)   United States   52%

Engineering majors in undergraduate population:
Japan   20%   United States   5%

Women in university population:
Japan   21%   United States   44%

One explanation for the Japanese level of achievement is the firm hand of the national Education Ministry in setting standards and curriculum, but equally important is the motivation of students to succeed on university entrance exams. Pick up any one of Japan's national news magazines in early spring, and you are certain to find the lead story to be the country's university entrance examinations. Momentarily each year these ordeals surpass political scandals, international economic problems, and gossip about entertainers as the matter most interesting and important to the reading public. The magazines' cover photographs depict the character of the annual drama. The scene is the campus of an important but unidentified university where families, friends, and interested observers have gathered to read the results posted on a large bulletin board. The moment of victory is captured by the cameraman in a picture that centers on an elated candidate leaping in the air or joyfully embracing a friend, while in the background unsuccessful aspirants struggle to maintain their composure. The presence of newsmen, television cameras, and a host of media commentators and social critics all attest to the centrality of entrance examinations to Japanese society. Schooling is geared to it, jobs are based on it, and families are preoccupied with it. Exam results by university are published in the nation's weekly magazines (the equivalents of *Time* and *Newsweek*), and high schools are ranked according to their records of success.

Accession rates for Japanese high school and university education increased rapidly over the quarter century from the Occupation period to the mid-1970's. In 1950, only 43 percent of all fifteen-year-olds were going on to high school (compulsory education ends with ninth grade), whereas by 1975 the figure had risen to 93 percent. Drop-outs from high school are but 2–3 percent. In 1955, only 8 percent of college-age Japanese enrolled in higher education; today nearly 40 percent are going on to universities or junior colleges. The university population has swollen from about half a million in 1950 to over two million. Universities are clearly overcrowded, and the quality of education has suffered. In sum, the demand for education in Japan is extraordinary. It surges past what the public system is able to provide, and it sponsors a competitive environment beyond the imagination of Americans.

The ratio of candidates to openings in the freshman class of almost any university starts at 3:1 and rises to an average of 5:1. Many private universities attract eight or nine candidates per opening, and competition for entrance to departments that lead to a degree in medicine regularly reaches a ratio of 20:1. The national total of applicants, furthermore, annually exceeds the number of university openings by approximately 200,000.

Many who fail to enter the school of their choice decide to try again. They join a particular category of students who have graduated from high school but have not yet entered college. The main occupation of this group is cramming for the next annual round of entrance examinations. (As with the ancient Chinese examination system, there is no limit on how many times one may try and no age limit.) Known as *rōnin* because they are akin to the wandering, disenfranchised warrior-heroes made familiar by samurai movies, these students are very largely male and in most cases academically talented. Attracted to the best universities, they prefer to persevere even for several years rather than resign themselves to a lesser university. Their lonely pursuit of fame and glory is often romanticized, but, in fact, it is a dreary, expensive existence. The annual rōnin population is estimated at 140,000 young people, and approximately one in every five male high school graduates is fated to make this particular detour in the system.

Consider the situation at the most prestigious university, Tokyo University. Annually, there are over 12,000 applicants for 3,075 places in the freshman class of Japan's oldest and greatest public institution of higher learning. Of the successful applicants, about 55 percent have taken the exam once, 35 percent twice, and 10 percent at least three times. A few finally enter on their sixth or seventh attempt! What kinds of examinations are involved, not just for Tokyo University, but across the nation? Comprising almost entirely multiple choice and short-answer questions, the exams are designed to test (1) comprehension of mathematical and scientific principles (high school math goes beyond trigonometry; physics, chemistry, biology, and earth sciences are required), and (2) memorization of enormous bodies of factual material pertaining to social studies (including economics and geography, and European, Japanese, Chinese, and United States history), and the English language (six years are required). Every question has but one correct answer. Interpretive skills are not tested, but skills in natural science problem solving are important, and the degree of detailed knowledge required is astounding. For example, the level of factual knowledge necessary to pass the history sections of the exams for the better universities would tax American graduate students specializing in history. In sum, the exams are the kind for which the capacity to grind away at preparation year after year makes a difference. Intelligence is important, but self-discipline and willpower are equally essential. Only the exam results count toward admission. High school grades, extracurricular activities, teachers' recommendations, and special talents play virtually no role, except in a small percentage of cases where universities are experimenting with American-style practices.

Nothing better illustrates the pressure to begin preparations early than the popularity of cram schools, or *juku*, which today enroll one in three middle school students and one in four upper elementary school students across the nation. In Tokyo and other large cities, fully two-thirds of all seventh, eighth, and ninth graders are either attending cram schools or being tutored at home.

Juku are privately run after-school academies designed to supplement public education. There are juku for slow students, juku for average students, and juku for bright students. The public system has no gifted programs, eschews tracking within schools, and forbids individually paced learning. The typical pattern for juku is a couple of hours a few days a week, but more aggressive and fast-paced cram schools hold classes more regularly, even on weekends and during vacations. Juku are like tactical weapons in an escalating educational arms race. Juku management is now a booming growth industry, complete with franchising and educational conglomerates. Private entrepreneurship and parental anxiety have combined with entrance exam pressures to create an unprecedented phenomenon, which some critics feel threatens to make Japanese childhood a tightly scheduled existence in which children are shuttled from home to school to juku to home, with no time for friends or play.

Is the effort required to enter Tokyo University and the other elite schools worth it? Clearly, the extraordinary thirst for educational success is based on the knowledge that companies offer jobs on the basis of university name, not university grades. In fact most students, upon gaining entry to a university, take a one- or two-year holiday from serious study as a reward for the killing effort to pass the examinations. Just how dominant the top schools have been in supplying the country's managerial elite can be seen from a few notable statistics. Tokyo University, which accounts for less than 3 percent of university graduates, alone produces nearly a quarter of the presidents of Japan's leading companies. The picture of elite dominance is even more pronounced in the upper level of the national bureaucracy, where Tokyo graduates have occupied the majority of jobs and nearly all the top positions since before the turn of the century. Much the same picture emerges from the nation's elected representatives. In the lower house of the national Diet, one in four are Tokyo graduates. The ruling Liberal Democratic party and the Communist Party both appear particularly well stocked with Tokyo graduates; better than 30 percent of their members are Tokyo alumni. The point is clear: success on entrance exams is associated with career success, and ultimately with power and status. Even if it takes a few extra years as rōnin to finally enter a top school, the career opportunities and ultimate rewards make the sacrifices worth the effort.

The powerful engine of exam preparation is fueled by this rather tight calibration between academic and career success. Those wishing to reform Japanese education realize they must first ease the tight relationship to employment. Others privately fear, however, that without future employment as the driving motive of entrance exam competition, students, parents, and schools would slacken their effort and the present high standards in basic subjects would begin to fall.

We turn next to the question of social mobility. Just how open is the education system to the upward mobility of talent? Compulsory education was a crucial ingredient in breaking down many nearly absolute social categories when it was first established in Japan in the 1870's and 1880's. Samurai, peasant, and merchant children were led to attend the same public schools. By the turn of the century, some students of all social origins were entering Tokyo University and subsequently moving into leadership roles within the larger society. Public education also introduced coeducation in primary schools. Before World War II, women were advancing to separate girls' high schools in significant numbers, and a small percentage were gaining the equivalent of a university education. The American Occupation's reforms extended the process considerably by opening up high school and university opportunities to much greater numbers and by extending coeducation throughout the public education system.

Since 1945, democratic mass education has been coupled to an elite public university system and a newer mass private university system. Secondary education articulates the mix. The intensity of the "examination hell" is largely the result of this hybridization.

Since the war, the public system has been free of all tracking until high school. During the first nine years, in fact, special efforts are made to mix abilities in each classroom. At the point of high school entrance, however, the separation of students by ability begins in earnest. High school entrance examinations are crucial to the overall ranking of high schools. The question of where the ablest students go, where the least able go, and all the fine shadings in between has been thoroughly worked out in every prefecture and city. The public and private high schools, the vocational and academic ones—they all have a commonly known position on a single totem pole. In a number of areas, one or a few private schools have risen to the top as a result of the greater latitude they enjoy in collecting the best students and gearing up singlemindedly for success on the entrance exams; yet in some areas public schools are very strong. Nearly half of all successful applicants to Tokyo University now come from elite private and "laboratory schools" associated with universities.

The ranking of high schools and universities provides two sensitive yardsticks by which to measure the influence of family background factors on educational outcomes. The pattern revealed reflects income levels and a trend toward a greater rather than a lessening role for this factor in educational outcomes. Entrants to the elite national universities in the early 1960's came from a broad cross section of the population, with little relationship between income and success. Private uni-

Table 7.1.   *Family Background and High School Attendance in Kobe, 1975*

Background category	Private academic (elite)	Prefectural academic (2d rank)	City academic (high 3d rank)	City vocational	City nighttime vocational
Ave. no. of siblings in family	2.1	2.3	2.4	2.8	2.9
Pct. of working mothers	15%	22%	21%	30%	34%
Pct. lacking one or both parents	1%	.07%	2%	13%	15%
Pct. of university-educated fathers (including *senmon gakkō*)	69%	—	33%	6%	2%
Pct. with own room for study	99%	86%	77%	71%	58%
Pct. ever attending tutoring or cram school	91%	78%	68%	57%	39%
Pct. attending tutoring or cram school in elem. school	74%	43%	37%	40%	24%

SOURCE: Statistics compiled by Kobe school officials.

versities (more expensive and easier to enter), on the other hand, were filled primarily by students from families in the upper half of the income scale. By the mid-1970's a significant shift was perceptible, with fewer and fewer students from poor families entering the elite universities. In 1974, for example, 25 percent of the places in national universities went to candidates from the lowest 40 percent of the population in terms of family income, whereas fifteen years earlier, 30 percent had come from that sector. The reasons have to do, I think, with the rising significance of privately purchased advantages in the preparation process, namely, juku and elite private schools.

In 1975, I investigated five Kobe high schools chosen as representative of five distinct points in that city's hierarchy of secondary schools (Table 7.1). The results indicate a number of very strong associations between school rank (and therefore academic achievement as measured by entrance exams) and a host of family background factors. Family qualities may be influential from an early point in the child's schooling, but only with high school entrance examinations does the overt sorting take place. So that the reader can better appreciate the difference in outcome represented by each of the five schools, let me add that the private elite school studied sends more than 100 of its 250 graduates to Tokyo University each year, whereas the second- and third-rank public academic high schools (each considered quite good locally) send but a handful of their students to any national university. Very few vocational school students go on to higher education at all. Drop-out rates for the night school are about 25 percent.

The school system at the high school level does not just reflect differences in family background; by its very organization it undoubtedly extends and elaborates these differences through the creation of distinct, stratified school subcultures. Delinquency rates, for example, correlate closely with the academic rank of high schools. Entrance exams serve a function somewhat analogous to that of residential segregation in the United States. Japanese cities remain residentially heterogeneous; one reason is the competitive entrance exam system that supersedes residential location (and thus housing expenditures) as the key to access to better public schooling.

Also notable is inequality between the sexes. Slightly more women than men now enter institutions of higher learning, but this is explained largely by the rapid growth of junior colleges, where enrollments are 90 percent female. The number of university places also grew rapidly in the 1970's, and the percentage of women enrolled in four-year universities increased from 16.2 percent in 1965 to 23.1 percent in 1984. Yet the fact remains that four of every ten females in higher education are attending a junior college, whereas nine of every ten males in higher education are in four-year universities. Furthermore, the percentage of women in Japan's top universities has remained very small. Only about 6 percent of those accepted by Tokyo University are women. These differences, it must be emphasized, do not stem from overt discrimination in the examination or admission process. The simple fact is that many fewer women apply. In 1975, only 17 percent of the women graduating from high school applied to universities, whereas 52 percent of the male graduates applied. The underlying reasons have to do primarily with cultural attitudes about gender in the Japanese family.

The distinguishing features of Japanese education—a very high average level of accomplishment based on diligence and organization, an orderly singlemindedness, and an exceptional educational fever centering on exams—also seems to characterize Japanese society as a whole. These qualities characterize the vast, hard-working middle class that works in Japan's highly efficient and demanding modern industries and offices. As we might expect, both education and society share some of the same deficiencies. By our standards of individualism, Japan seems so busy and well organized—so like an anthill—that idiosyncratic potentials do not receive much recognition. Both society and education suffer from very rapid growth and from an obsessive preoccupation with success as measured by economic output standards. These very efficiencies have masked problems of unattended spiritual values and national identity. Finally, prosperity easily undermines character strength, and Japan, of all nations, cannot afford to allow economic success to spoil the young. Exam pressures keep things challenging and rigorous, but very narrowly focused. In the last decades of the twentieth century, a prosperous, successful Japan must also discover its own ways of maintaining the will to hard work, the high standards, the fascination with learning, and the discipline that have been its hallmarks, while encouraging innovative diversity and discouraging inequalities of income and gender. The twenty-first century will challenge Japan in new ways, and a nation that relies so heavily on its human resources must be particularly adaptive in the area of education.

8. The Japanese Will to Work

Inagami Takeshi

In this essay, Inagami Takeshi analyzes the Japanese work ethic and how it affects Japanese working conditions. Inagami teaches sociology and labor-management relations at Hōsei University. The article first appeared in 1981 in *The Wheel Extended*, a quarterly magazine published by Toyota Motor Corporation, in which various aspects of economy, industry, and society are discussed.

The motive power behind the advancement of an industrialized society is determined largely by the will of its labor force to work. In Japan, there is no sign of a decline in the work ethic, despite the emergence of an affluent society during the 1960's. The extended economic recession, in the aftermath of the oil crisis, witnessed a widespread implementation of employment adjustment measures—primarily in the large manufacturing enterprises—but these measures did not result in any deterioration of labor-management relations. One reason for this was greater worker participation, achieved mainly through an expanded role for the nation's joint labor-management conference system. Following a peak period in 1974, the number of labor disputes has undergone a sharp decline. In contrast, worker participation in small-group activities and the use of worker suggestion systems have been on the rise since the time of the oil crisis.

In this report, we shall examine the underlying factors that produce this strong will to work, which has played a vital role in Japan's economic development.

Work Ethic Indicators

There is no agreement among labor experts concerning the exact indicators that ought to be used to gauge the will to work. Nevertheless, the following indicators and accompanying figures point to a strong will to work on the part of the Japanese labor force.

First of all, we observe a high rate of work attendance (a low rate of absenteeism). In twelve cases studied by Koshiro Kazutoshi, one of Japan's foremost authorities on labor economics, the average rate of absenteeism was an extremely low 0.53 percent. In other words, the average attendance rate was 99.47 percent. (The absences in question were recorded on attendance sheets, together with an explanation such as illness or accident.) Even counting absences due to annual paid leaves and special paid leaves for births, marriages, and deaths in the family, the average attendance rate was 92.8 percent.

Second, we can see that Japanese workers are intensely interested in their work. In a study comparing the same age groups in 1971 and 1977, the percentage of

From Takeshi Inagami, "The Japanese Will to Work," *The Wheel Extended*, vol. 10, no. 3 (Jan.–March 1981), pp. 21–29. By permission of the publisher and the author.

young Japanese who replied that they "live for their work" shows a noticeable decline, but even those workers who were more oriented toward leisure activities in their twenties gradually tended to shift toward "living for work" when they reached their thirties. This change of heart toward what makes life worth living is due more to growing older than to any generation gap.

Third, concerning work preferences, there is a strong desire for work that enables workers to make use of their abilities and improve their knowledge and skills. According to a Labor Ministry study conducted in July 1977, those workers who expressed such a desire constituted 82.7 percent of the workers covered in the survey, including 91.7 percent and 92.6 percent of male workers aged twenty to twenty-four and twenty-four to twenty-nine. The desire of young workers to improve their knowledge and skills is quite strong, despite their professed intention to live for leisure activities.

Fourth, vigorous implementation of small-group activities and suggestion systems may be cited. A study by the Japan Human Relations Association indicates that use of suggestion systems has spread at an ever-increasing rate since the oil crisis, with the number of suggestions submitted growing in geometric progression. The Association's latest survey, conducted in 1980, shows that the number of suggestions submitted at 400 business enterprises during 1979 totaled an impressive 13.5 million, or an average of 7.19 suggestions per worker. According to a Labor Ministry study conducted in July 1977, as many as 74.1 percent of all business enterprises employ suggestion systems. Increasing participation in small-group activities and suggestion systems represents not only the traditional tendency of Japanese workers to involve themselves, in word as well as in deed, in the concerns of their companies and coworkers, but also a trend toward turning blue-collar work into "gray-collar" work. This trend has been stimulated by the gradually increasing involvement of engineers in work-related blue-collar activities.

Explaining the Will to Work

Many factors underlie the intense will to work exhibited by Japanese workers. Professor Koshiro, who has perhaps done the most exhaustive research on this subject thus far, has suggested that six are most important:

1. *Capital intensity*, i.e., the pressure of capital costs incurred by importing technology, which has demanded ever higher rates of production, encouraging formulation of measures to reinforce the workers' will to work.

2. *Distinctive cultural characteristics*, e.g., such typically Japanese modes of behavior as group-oriented mores and giving priority to common interests over individual interests.

3. *Stiffening competition among business enterprises*, which reinforces the self-preservation mentality of employees who subscribe to the "company as family" philosophy.

4. *The company union factor.*

5. *The internal labor market factor*, i.e., the high stage of development of the labor market in Japan as compared to the nations of the West, which means that the long-term interests of employees and corporations tend to overlap.

6. *The scarcity of employment opportunities*, which means that the will to work is strengthened as a result of fierce, open competition in which everyone has an equal chance.

Of these six points, Professor Koshiro maintains that the last is the most influential.

The author of this paper sees four factors as the most important.

The first is lifetime employment, which is becoming more widespread than ever before. In 1978, the Economic Planning Agency's Economic Welfare Bureau conducted a study of "standard workers"—workers who join a company immediately after school graduation and remain with the same company permanently—calculated for different industries and various sized enterprises, from figures supplied by the Labor Ministry. The percentage of "standard workers" for all industries, which stood at 29.7 percent in 1954, reached 49.6 percent in 1974 and 54.0 percent in 1978. These figures signify that lifetime employment is more firmly rooted in Japanese corporate practice than ever before.

Most Japanese executives come up in the company from the ranks of regular employees through systems of internal promotion. According to a survey conducted by the Japan Committee for Economic Development in 1977, which polled the boards of directors at various firms (2,398 full-time directors at 134 companies), the proportion of those executives who were promoted from the company ranks was as high as 91 percent.

Since the number of employees spending their entire occupational lives within the same company is increasing, and since the companies themselves are engaged in fierce competition with one another, it is understandable that the employee's sense of belonging to the company (which must be differentiated from a sense of indiscriminate loyalty) has become ever stronger. Given the lifetime employment system, it is indispensable for workers—regardless of their degree of loyalty to the firm—to have a desire to protect and improve their own working conditions. Only then will the company's competitive market strength be increased and its share of the pie made larger.

The second crucial factor is job consciousness. One salient characteristic of the large majority of Japanese workers is that they do not regard their jobs simply as a means of earning an income. Instead, they attach a great deal of importance to the intrinsic compensation derived from the work itself—for example, from opportunities to use aptitudes and abilities. Belonging to a company can be interpreted more clearly as a sense of belonging to the whole company as a place of employment rather than to any specific job. While the expectation of some intrinsic compensation derived from work remains strong, "work" does not connote a specific job but encompasses a rather wide range of diverse occupations. This characteristic clearly reflects a situation where (1) labor unions are organized into enterprise-based units in which all employees of individual companies are members, regardless of their occupations or job classifications; (2) especially in the case of white-collar work, corporate organizations typically promote generalized personnel training programs in an effort to avoid specialization of personnel in specific jobs; and (3) there is, as a result, ample flexibility in assignment of personnel to suit the company's particular needs.

The human relations formed within the occupational and corporate framework extend to the realm of private life, outside the company. There are, however, reports that note signs of decline in social intercourse based on corporate and occupational relationships. One white paper published in 1980 by the Economic Planning Agency points out that employees show an inclination to separate their leisure activities from their company life. Nevertheless, the company role in human relationships remains deep-rooted and strong, especially in comparison to workers in other countries.

The third important factor is resource distribution and mobility, within both the national community and the corporations. (Resources in this context include human resources in addition to wealth—i.e., income and assets, influence and information.)

A comparison of income distribution in different nations is available in the Organization for Economic Cooperation and Development (OECD) report "Income Distribution in OECD Countries / Public Sector Budget Balances." As stated in this report, Japan, along with Australia and some others, belongs to the group of countries with the least inequity of income distribution. According to an Economic Planning Agency study of social mobility, intergenerational mobility in Japan is also at a high level when compared to other nations. These findings suggest that (1) resource distribution and mobility meet the expectations and aspirations of a large segment of those people who hold the view, "If we work hard, our lives will improve accordingly"; (2) efforts to distribute resources fairly have fostered healthy, free competition; and (3) these efforts have promoted an open society, inhibiting formation of a rigid class system.

Much the same can be said of resource distribution and mobility on the corporate level. In other words, the seniority rule, a pivotal element of the rules of resource distribution, has functioned in tandem with the widespread practice of lifetime employment to ensure stable employment and wages commensurate with lifetime needs, with promotions determined by employee age and duration of continuous service. The wage differentials between white-collar and blue-collar workers in Japan and differentials that reflect academic background are relatively low compared to other nations. However, the egalitarian seniority rule does not restrict competition among employees. The element of competition is definitely taken into account, especially in deciding on promotions. Excellence in job-related knowledge and skills, and being trusted by co-workers, are criteria far more important for promotion than age or duration of continuous service. This promotion system, in combination with the lifetime employment system, has worked to prevent any schism due to an "us-and-them" attitude.

The last factor is work mores. A comparison of the workplace structure and position and roles of foremen in Japan with those in the United States or Great Britain shows features peculiar to Japan.

In the case of Japan, job descriptions are less precise and not so narrowly defined. Moreover, the practice of overlapping on-the-job duties of superior and subordinate levels is more widespread in Japan. This difference is extremely important for the following reasons:

1. In the United States and Europe, on-the-job duties assigned to individual workers are clearly defined, and workers are not held responsible for, or given authority over, anything beyond those specific tasks. The practice of not becoming

involved in other people's work is thus firmly entrenched. But not so in Japan, where collective involvement is rather common. As a result, human relations within the Japanese work organization assume great importance.

2. On-the-job training activities are stimulated by the overlapping of tasks.

3. This broader view of individual tasks, together with extensive, far-reaching internal promotion opportunities, frequent rotation, and increasing versatility in skills, contributes to wider competence and work enrichment, enhancing the overall quality of work life itself.

It is interesting to note that in Japan a foreman's role is rather diffuse. His duties include listening to subordinates' complaints concerning work life, participating in their weddings, funerals, and other family affairs, and even such emotionally taxing involvements as listening to subordinates' intimate personal problems—all of which require him to maintain close communication with his subordinates.

The foreman is also obliged to hold a position akin to leader of a work team and to represent his section of the organization. In the latter capacity, he is responsible for communicating his team's consensus to his superiors—whatever the issue. This is quite distinct from being a leader entrusted with management control of a work section. If pressure that may be harmful to the aims or advancement of work in his section is brought to bear by superiors, or by other departments within the organization, the foreman may often have to reject the pressure and demand a reconsideration of the matter. In other words, he must not only be an expert on all work matters but is also expected, by his subordinates, to function in a number of other capacities. The leadership and authority that a foreman is allowed to exercise thus depends largely on how well he can handle his overall role. A foreman may hold a position of leadership in the enterprise union as well, but only if he can be a leader to his subordinates in that context.

The fact that small-group activities and suggestion systems are being extensively implemented indicates that the mode of execution of work is, in practice, left largely up to the autonomously regulated creativity, ingenuity, and spontaneity of groups of workers. This factor should not be overlooked, nor should the fact that a foreman also plays the role of a spokesman representing the interests of his particular section. And the small-group activities, suggestion systems, and foreman activities are but a few of the channels for worker communications with executives.

9. Confucianism as a Basis for Capitalism

Morishima Michio

Morishima Michio suggests here that the nature of Asian capitalism is fundamentally different from that of the West because it developed out of a specifically Japanese historical experience, based on Confucianism, rather than out of the historical experiences shared by

From Michio Morishima, "The Power of Confucian Capitalism," *The Observer* (London), June 1978. Reproduced courtesy of *The Observer*, London.

most European countries. Morishima, who was trained at Kyoto and Oxford, is an economist affiliated with the London School of Economics and Political Science. He has written about Leon Walras and Karl Marx, as well as on the subject of econometric models. The present essay first appeared in 1978.

The economic disputes between Japan and the West are not merely problems of yen, cars, television sets, or tariff barriers. They are symptoms of basic social-philosophical conflicts. The West can no longer afford to ignore the Japanese outlook, particularly because Asian countries that follow Japan economically—such as Korea, Taiwan, Singapore, and Hong Kong—all have similar social philosophies.

The modern countries of Europe evolved in very different ways from Japan. Modern European political organizations were the product of clashes and compromises between feudal lords and the middle class; feudalism was abolished in Japan in 1868 not because the Japanese bourgeoisie demanded it, but because it appeared that under feudalism the country would never become a great power and match the strength of the European powers. Compulsory education was instituted in Japan as early as 1872, not because the government recognized the significance of education for its own sake, but because of the belief that the general level of education had to be raised to establish a great nation. Thus, to build a modern state, Japan adopted many Western systems despite the absence of conditions similar to those from which these systems had emerged in Europe.

Capitalism began in Japan in a unique way. When Japan began to build a modern state after the Meiji Restoration of 1868, there was no powerful bourgeoisie, so she introduced state capitalism and established factories with money raised by taxation or by issuing paper currency. The government soon fell into financial distress and had to sell most of its factories at low prices to retired government officials, or to private firms in which they were executives. These individuals suddenly became big capitalists. This is in contrast to the emergence of Western capitalists, who had to establish themselves by their own efforts, often in opposition to the state.

The very spirit of Japanese capitalism is different from that of Europe. Max Weber stressed that European capitalism was related to the Protestant ethic of asceticism. In the early years of Western capitalism, neither the accumulation of capital (which Marx called "primitive accumulation") nor the propensity to invest (which Marx described in the famous line, "Accumulate, accumulate; that is Moses and the Prophets") would have been possible had Protestants not prevailed among capitalists. It would also have been impossible for Western capitalists to exploit workers had the latter not been sober and industrious and regarded work as a life purpose.

In Japan the two main religions, Buddhism and Shintoism, have had almost no influence on secular or economic conduct. This is one consequence of the educational policy of the Tokugawa government before the Meiji period, which for more than two centuries supported and encouraged Confucianism. In Japan today, Confucianism influences the everyday conduct of Buddhists and Shintoists and even Christians.

Confucianism, which the Japanese view as an ethic rather than a religion, holds the following virtues as most important: loyalty to the state or the emperor, filial piety, faith in friendship, and respect for elders. It is primarily concerned with the individual's relationship to various communities. Confucianism discourages individualism. It is intellectual and rational in character, rejecting the mysticism and incantation common to other religions. The ability of the Japanese to assimilate Western technology and science with astonishing rapidity after the Meiji Restoration was due, at least in part, to their education under Confucianism; Western rationalist thinking was not entirely foreign.

In Confucian political thought, those who play the most important roles in society are the bureaucrats. Under that philosophy, the feudal age of the Tokugawa was an era of bureaucratic rule in which a samurai was a civil as well as a military officer. The Meiji government was an advanced modern bureaucracy from the outset.

An important element in the development of the modern Japanese economy was the country's almost total involvement in war from 1931 to 1945. When World War II ended, most men under forty had no working background except as soldiers. With no managerial experience, they operated firms the way they had commanded platoons. The workers, who as soldiers had existed precariously between life and death, found monotonous factory work by no means unbearable. Loyalty to firms took the place of wartime loyalty to the state. In this way, the collectivist character of Confucian capitalism was strengthened.

One may console oneself with the belief that Japan will become Westernized because of her economic achievements. But no one really knows what course an economically mature Confucian capitalist country will take.

Part II: The Economy

O V E R   T H E   postwar period, Japan has achieved the fastest sustained rate of economic growth among the major industrial countries of the world. Its economy has grown from being 5 percent of the size of America's economy in 1950 to roughly 50 percent by 1987, making it the second largest economy in the world. As a percentage of world GNP, Japan's share has more than tripled since 1960, expanding from 3 to 10 percent.

Japan's pace-setting rate of growth is reflected in the rapidly changing structure of employment. In 1950, the primary sector (especially agriculture) employed nearly 50 percent of the workforce, the secondary sector (manufacturing) accounted for 21 percent, and the tertiary (the services) 29 percent. Less than a generation later (1985), employment in the primary sector had dropped to only 8.8 percent, the secondary sector had risen to 34 percent, and the tertiary sector had jumped to 57 percent.

How is this dynamic and fascinating economy organized? What, if anything, makes it different? The readings in this section provide insights into some of its distinctive features. In contrast to America's open and decentralized financial markets, for example, Japan's financial system—until the 1980's—had been closed and tightly regulated. Tight financial regulations can be traced back to the period of wartime mobilization, when extensive controls were imposed; they were later carried over (more or less intact) to the early postwar period. This insulated, heavily regulated system, as one of the readings points out, functioned to absorb an extraordinary level of household savings, which Japanese banks then allocated to meet the investment needs of industry. By allowing the Japanese government to allocate credit, in effect the system gave government the means to preside over the reconstruction of the country's war-devastated economy.

As the funnel through which household savings were redirected to private corporations, banking institutions played a key role in the rapid growth of the Japanese economy. Because Japanese companies relied heavily on bank loans to meet their need for capital, and because Japanese banks could buy stock in companies to which they made loans, the relationship between banks and businesses became very close and interdependent—in contrast to the situation in the United States, where the two dealt with each other extensively but at arm's length. This interdependence, which one article in this section refers to as Japan's "banking-industrial complex," has served the interests of both sides, giving private industry huge amounts of capital and providing banks with multiple outlets for profitable lending and investment. It has also served as an effective mechanism, one of many in Japan's political economy, for risk reduction during downturns in business cycles.

Structural interpenetration, long-term commitments and relationships, mutual trust, and flexible accommodation pervade the Japanese economy at all levels, including industrial groups (*keiretsu*), patterns of intercorporate stockholding, and subcontracting networks. The readings in this section deal with each of these distinctive institutions. Like the "banking-industrial complex," these organizations function to reduce risks and uncertainties, make smooth adjustments to fluctuations in business cycles, solidify long-term relationships, coordinate complex sequences of business activities, and facilitate flows of vital information. Such economic organizations help to give Japan's market economy its remarkable combination of stability, flexibility, and dynamism.

If, for analytical purposes, the Japanese economy is broken down into two basic elements—market (referring especially to the reliance on the system of price signals) and organization (extra-market institutions)—Japan's distinctiveness can be immediately understood to reside in the pervasiveness and importance of such extra-market organizations as subcontracting networks, intercorporate stockholding arrangements, and industrial groups. Such organizations affect management practices, influence corporate strategies, and provide a structure within which market competition takes place.

The importance of such organizations should not be misconstrued to mean that Japan is not a market economy or that the market mechanism is somehow enfeebled. Nothing could be further from the truth. Market competition between firms is arguably stronger in Japan than anywhere else. Producer groups compete fiercely for market share, striving to reduce production costs and raise product quality, slashing prices to the barest margins, marketing aggressively, and offering the best possible follow-up service. The Japanese economy is productive and dynamic precisely because Japanese firms have learned to survive in the crucible of market testing.

Instead of stifling market competition, extra-market organizations in Japan provide an orderly structure within which the interplay between private companies takes place. It is surprising that organizational structures like industrial groups and subcontracting networks do not interfere with, or retard, market competition. Readers of this book might want to ask themselves why the maze of organizational structures has not led, as one might expect, to a variety of undesirable consequences—institutional rigidities, costly inefficiencies, disincentives to compete, high transaction costs, and an inability to adapt to ever-changing business conditions. Risk-reducing structures in the United States and Western Europe, after all, have often had the effect of diminishing the discipline of the marketplace. How is it that organizational structures have not weakened competition in Japan? How is it that the existence of such organizations has tempered the pursuit of profit but not dampened the spirit of market capitalism?

By pondering the organizational characteristics of the Japanese economy, readers can deepen their understanding of what makes Japan different. Discerning readers interested in this topic should be able to identify many of the critical elements that constitute what some people have called "Confucian capitalism"—or at least a variant form of capitalism when compared to those that have evolved in the West—as they progress through these readings and those on the government-business relationship.

10. Organization for Economic Reconstruction

Sakakibara Eisuke and Noguchi Yukio

How was Japan able to achieve its remarkable postwar economic growth? Economists Sakakibara Eisuke and Noguchi Yukio argue that until recently Japan possessed a unique economic structure, one that combined the efficiency of wartime financial institutions with the energy released by a new egalitarian ideology. The article, which originally appeared in *Chuō Kōron* magazine, suggests that political changes have begun to produce a new, more stable, economic system.

The Economic System at War's End

Financial controls constituted the core of the economic system for all-out war, as is made clear by the Bank of Japan Law. Patterned after the Reichsbank Law of Nazi Germany, the law was promulgated in 1942 as a consummation of the wartime institutions for the control of financial activities, and today it remains in existence as a fundamental part of the Japanese financial system, thirty-odd years after the end of the war. True, the bank's goal of contributing to "appropriate application of the state's total economic power" changed from the execution of war to the achievement of economic growth in the postwar period, but the system itself, geared as it was to all-out war, remained intact in spite of Japan's defeat.

A similar observation may be made about commercial banks. In the early years of the Shōwa era, commercial banks numbered over 1,000, but gradually they were reorganized owing to the persisting financial panic and the regimentation of the Japanese economy for purposes of waging war, until only 61 commercial banks remained when the war came to an end. To date, no significant change has taken place in their number, nor in the composition of the banking industry. It is indeed surprising that the banking industry alone retained the wartime structure, in the midst of the all-transforming economic growth of the postwar years.

Playing a central role in the wartime financial regime were "special banks" like the Industrial Bank of Japan. Some of them, like the Bank of Taiwan and the Bank of Korea, were shut down after the war, while others, like the Nippon Kangyō Bank and the Hokkaidō Takushoku Bank were reorganized as ordinary commercial banks. But established in their place were the Long-Term Credit Bank of Japan, the Japan Development Bank, and the Japan Export-Import Bank. These newly created special banks controlled the bulk of fund flows until the mid-1950's

From Eisuke Sakakibara and Yukio Noguchi, "Dissecting the Finance Ministry–Bank of Japan Dynasty," *Japan Echo*, vol. 4, no. 4 (1977), pp. 88–124. By permission of the publisher.

in much the same way as did the old special banks during the war. The role of the Industrial Bank of Japan was to serve as the mainstay vehicle to finance Japan's wartime industry. In the postwar "total-war" economy, this role was amplified rather than diminished.

Another major instrument of economic control was the Foreign Exchange and Foreign Trade Control Law, which served as the bulwark of Japan's closed monetary system. Promulgated in 1949, the law completed Japan's efforts, which started with the Capital Flight Prevention Law of 1932, to build a system of controls over external monetary transactions. The substance of the Foreign Exchange and Foreign Trade Control Law remained unchanged until 1980.

Postwar Occupation reforms thus did not bring a complete liquidation of the old economic order. What the Occupation forces achieved was a reorientation. If they had any impact on the wartime Japanese economic system, that impact concerned internal arrangements within the system and not the existence of the system itself.

There was a time in the pre-Occupation policy debate within the United States government when the "old China hands" in the State Department, represented by such men as Owen Lattimore, and in the Treasury Department, under the command of Henry Morgenthau, called for a fundamental remodeling of Japan's economic system. But by the time the Allies won the war and General Douglas MacArthur arrived in Japan as the supreme commander, a pro-Japan group rallying around former Ambassador Joseph Grew prevailed over the hard-liners, and a relatively moderate occupation policy, in comparison with the one for Germany, was formulated. In line with the Morgenthau Plan, drastic reforms were imposed on Germany—the country was divided into separate occupation zones by the victor nations; the central government was reorganized to hand over greater autonomy to local communities; and the economy, too, was extensively reorganized. By contrast, the moderate occupation policies applied in Japan were the most important reason why the substance of the wartime economic system survived the defeat.

Bureaucracy Preserved

Another factor contributing to the continuation of the wartime economic structure is that SCAP (the Supreme Commander for the Allied Powers) chose indirect rule through the Japanese administrative machinery instead of direct military rule as in the case of Germany.

The wartime bureaucratic organization in the economic field was allowed to survive without significant change. While the armed forces and the Internal Affairs Ministry were dismantled, the Finance Ministry and other economic agencies of the government succeeded in maintaining roughly the same organization as before the war, in spite of such changes introduced by the Occupation authorities as a revision of the Civil Service Law and reforms in the recruiting and control of civil servants under the newly created National Personnel Authority. This point may be shown by comparing the present Finance Ministry with what existed in 1937. The only differences are the addition of two bureaus (the Securities Bureau and the Customs and Tariff Bureau) and the renaming of two departments (the former Repairs and Assets Bureau is now a number of "national property" sections within the Financial Bureau; the former Exchange Bureau is now the International Finance Bureau). One of the more severe steps taken by the Occupation authorities was the purge of some 210,000 Japanese from public life, but most of the people affected were military personnel. Only 2,000 civil servants were purged, of which the Internal Affairs Ministry accounted for the bulk and the Finance Ministry for only nine.

If the reorientation of Japan overseen by the Occupation forces had any impact on the economic system, it was restricted to the system's internal composition. In January 1948, when developments on the Chinese mainland brought Cold War politics to Asia, United States Secretary of the Army Kenneth Royal emphasized the importance of accelerated efforts to put Japan on its feet economically. A recommendation was made shortly afterward by Under Secretary of the Army William Draper in favor of redirection of the Occupation policy, following his visit to Japan with a mission led by Perch Johnston, chairman of the Chemical Bank.

The Draper report led to a succession of economic policy changes, such as reduction of Japanese war reparations and relaxation of the Law Against Excessive Concentration of Economic Power. The United States policy changes opened the way for indirect control of the economy through the balancing of the budget and financial regulations. Suspension of an earlier plan for breaking up Japan's five largest banks, which was made possible by the relaxation of the Law Against Excessive Concentration, proved to be an event of decisive importance to the subsequent evolution of the Japanese economy. Saved from the application of this law and what otherwise would have been stringent reforms directed against it, Japan's financial system was retained in much the same form as before the war, with the Bank of Japan at its apex.

The newly charted policies of the Occupation were later established more firmly with programs recommended by two advisers to SCAP, Joseph Dodge and Carl Shoup. The fiscal and monetary reforms introduced at their recommendation called for, basically, (1) a balanced budget based on classical economic theory, (2) strengthened tax assessment, and (3) establishment of a single foreign exchange rate for the yen. However, even greater importance should be attached to the fact that these reforms led to strengthened financial controls on the wartime pattern of limiting credit expansion and price increases, and that they also brought into being a prototype of the system of national financial isolation of subsequent years through the imposition of extensive restrictions on foreign exchange transactions. The immediate objective of the "Dodge line" was to bring inflation under control. By adopting the policy pattern of tight financial control and a balanced budget, however, it had the effect of completing the fundamental institutions for the postwar Japanese economy.

Egalitarian Ideology

Although the economic system and especially the financial establishment were preserved without major changes, the defeat in the war brought a major transformation in Japanese social perception. This means that while continuity was retained in the economic system, Japanese society faced a major discontinuity in publicly upheld values. A revolution in the governing ideology of society was promoted through an overhaul of the Civil Code, the breakup of the armed forces, the democratization of the police organization, and the reform of the civil service, besides the enactment of a new Constitution. This revolution also pushed its way into ordinary life by the liberalization of the mass communication media and the remaking of the educational system.

The Occupation destroyed the prewar fiction of the nation as a large patriarchal household headed by the emperor. It also remade the traditional family system in Japan through the abolition of the old Constitution and a thoroughgoing revision of the Civil Code. Occupation reforms did not, however, touch the quasi-family system existing in a modernized form in business organizations and government bureaucracy. This quasi-family system was instead reinforced in subsequent years through the unionization of seniority wage and lifetime employment systems. Business corporations, particularly larger ones, as the surviving and reinforced machinery of control, became the engine of economic reconstruction and growth in the following years.

Mechanisms of High Growth

Bipolar Structure

Our basic view of the postwar economic growth is that it was made a reality by human energy released by the newly introduced ideology of egalitarianism, as well as by financial controls. We also hold that the effusive, buoyant growth of the economy, in turn, helped to sustain dynamically this bipolar structure.

Viewed from the standpoint of macroeconomics, one requirement for economic growth is the availability of high savings and an industrious, high-quality labor force. In postwar Japan, savings and labor power were supplied voluntarily under the egalitarian ideology, in the absence of the ideological compulsion present under the wartime emperor system. But this factor alone is not enough to achieve high growth. The second requisite condition is the availability of established social institutions capable of absorbing and activating the savings and labor resources thus generated. This role was performed, without question, by large corporations. Further, indirect economic controls channeled the flow of funds and gave direction to growth. High growth was thus an elaborate system organically made up of a trio of elements—(1) an egalitarian ideology, (2) large corporations, and (3) quasi-wartime financial controls. Lacking any of these, high economic growth could not have materialized.

Labor Motivation

The force of competition set loose by egalitarian ideology enhanced worker morale, stimulated competition among companies, and provided the most powerful motivation supportive of high economic growth. Large corporations were on the receiving end of the supply of a workforce imbued with such motivation. The seniority wage lifetime employment system had begun to be adopted by large Japanese corporations in the course of the industrial modernization following World War I. It was firmly established in the mid-1930's and further developed into a central social institution in Japan after World War II. The *ie* (household) concept survived as the organizing principle of business in spite of its rejection in the revolutionary switch in orthodoxies at the end of World War II. This may be because the other major concept of social organization in Japan—that of the *mura* (village)—is an effective organizing principle of small farming communities but could not be applied realistically to the large corporations of modern industrial society.

Effect of High Savings

The high savings ratio in postwar Japan has conventionally been explained by an uneven distribution of income, the low ratio of liquid assets to income, and the inadequacy of social security. Explanations of this type seem to overemphasize the relative poverty of Japanese households as a cause of high savings. We think that the increased leveling of income standards resulting from the postwar reforms and various factors associated with the prevalence of an egalitarian ideology played no small part in raising the Japanese savings ratio. The need to prepare for future expenditures for children's education and the purchase of housing also had a major influence on family saving behavior.

High savings cannot be translated into high growth unless they are linked to a high rate of investment. It was large companies that turned the high savings generated by egalitarian changes in social life into investment. In this respect, the companies played as important a role here as they did in absorbing the supply of labor resulting from the collapse of the ie structure in households and rural villages.

In the years immediately after the war, economic recovery from the war's devastation was sought under the priority production system, which called for the concentrated allocation of resources to certain key industrial sectors. Demand related to the Korean War then provided the initial push for high economic growth. The subsequent years saw the continued process of self-sustaining, self-accelerating growth (high growth—expectations of high profits—high investment demand—high growth).

Financial Controls

Controlled Economic Growth

High growth presupposes the existence of an abundant and industrious labor force and high savings. It is also a process in which savings are continuously converted into additional production capacity, each investment calling forth a new investment. But in Japan, extensive regulation applied through the money market controlled the flow of capital, strongly influencing the industrial structure and the pattern of economic growth. Financial control was implemented through the Bank of Japan and other financial institutions, particularly large banks, with support from the bureaucracy in the economic field. The banks and the economic bureaucracy functioned as a general staff behind the battlefield in this total war called high economic growth.

The controls were designed to bring into being a national monetary system closed to the rest of the world, shutting out international flows of capital. They were also used to allocate credit through a policy of artificially low rates of interest for industries of strategic importance to the domestic economy as well as export industries. It is hard to say whether high growth could have been achieved in the absence of such controls. We think, however, that at least this much may be said.

First, without the isolated national system of financial policy, it would have been impossible to keep the Japanese rate of interest at a low level far removed from the prevailing international level for long. If liberalization had been carried out at an early date, Japan would probably have suffered from flight of capital, as has been the case with some developing countries; domestic savings thereby would have been prevented from going into domestic capital formation.

Suppose, next, that the domestic financial flow had been left to the workings of the free market. Given the absolute shortage of capital and the sheer abundance of labor in the postwar Japanese economy, the money market would have functioned in such a way as to direct most of the available investment funds to labor-intensive industries instead of heavy industries. Capital would also have been invested in unproductive assets, such as real estate and jewelry, in a financial climate not conducive to stepped-up accumulation of production capacity.

These considerations lead us to the conclusion that the allocation of funds to priority capital-intensive industries was made possible only by the existence of preferential financial controls. The controls may thus be credited with having played a key role in the development of the heavy industries that provided the sinews of Japan's postwar high economic growth. In this sense, the preservation of the wartime financial controls, together with the failure of the Occupation authorities to reform the financial sector extensively, proved to be of decisive importance in determining the pattern of Japan's economic expansion.

Institutional Underpinnings of Financial Controls

The institutional basis for controlling the Japanese economy with financial tools consisted of (1) the Temporary Money Rates Adjustment Law, which maintained a policy of artificially low interest rates; (2) the Foreign Exchange and Foreign Trade Control Law, which shielded Japan against international monetary flows; (3) the Banking Law, which established powerful surveillance machinery and leadership power over financial institutions; (4) strategic financing organizations (the Reconstruction Finance Corporation in the early postwar years, followed by the Industrial Bank of Japan in later years and including the Japan Development Bank, the Japan Export-Import Bank, and other government-affiliated financial institutions); and (5) the doctrine of the balanced budget.

Let us turn now to how financial controls were implemented under these institutions. Under the Temporary Money Rates Adjustment Law, the government set a controlled price (controlled rate of interest) at a level lower than the point of equilibrium between demand and supply, thereby causing an excess of demand over supply. A variety of other requirements had to be met, however, before such controls became fully effective. Let us review them one by one.

Bank of Japan's Growth Financing

In general, new issues of bank notes result from such developments as fiscal deficits, increases in foreign currency holdings (balance of payments surpluses), and increased lending by the central bank. Federal budget deficits were the primary cause in the United States after the war, while increased foreign exchange reserves were most important in the case of West Germany. In contrast, new issues of bank notes in Japan resulted primarily from increased lending by the central bank during the years of high growth. This was because the Japanese government adhered to the policy of a balanced budget, even after the Dodge reforms, and enjoyed a surplus in the fiscal sector. (The government started floating bonds in the mid-1960's, but borrowing activity was extremely limited in scale until the 1970's.) In Japan, growth currency was supplied through the Bank of Japan—commercial bank channels to industry, which was the deficit sector of the economy. Before and during the war, the government made use of the Temporary Funds Adjustment Law to channel long-term investment funds to defense industries on a priority basis. In the postwar period, growth currency was supplied to the economy through the Bank of Japan, holding down the banks' loan rates to an artificially low level under the Temporary Money Rates Adjustment Law. This enabled the government to allocate funds arbitrarily to priority industries.

Direct Financing Underdeveloped

Even if currency were available through the Bank of Japan, the government could not control the economy through monetary instruments if companies had ready sources of financing other than commercial banks to meet their demand for funds. But in Japan, direct financing by companies or financing from non-bank sources remained underdeveloped.

The ratio of direct financing to indirect financing through banks (funds supplied to industry on a rate-of-change basis), which was roughly 9:1 in 1931, changed steadily in favor of indirect financing in the subsequent years until it reached 7:3 in 1935. The two forms of financing reached parity, or 5:5, in 1940, and radically reversed to 1:9 in 1945. For the first thirty years after the war, the reversed ratio showed no major change, posting 1.25:8.75 in 1975. In the last one-year period, funds raised through sales of securities managed to reach about one-third of the total funds supplied to industry.

A number of factors contributed to preventing the continuation of direct financing in Japan. First, the direct financing of the prewar period was mostly in the form of share ownership by the holding companies of the *zaibatsu* (giant financial combines) and credit supply between non-bank firms themselves. The postwar economic reforms, including the disbandment of the zaibatsu and a wider distribution of stock ownership, shattered the zaibatsu-centered financing structure, virtually eliminating the possibility of a revival of the direct financing system that had existed in the Taishō era and the early Shōwa era.

Second, the prewar practice of direct coordination of new bond issues, originally coordinated by the defunct Temporary Funds Adjustment Law, has continued to date. In place of the Bond Issue Planning Council created in 1930, two organizations, the Bond Issue Council and the Bond Issue Liaison Committee, were set up in 1949 to continue the quantitative coordination of newly planned bond flotations.

By far the single most decisive factor thwarting direct financing is the fact that the government refrained for years from floating state bonds, in faithful observance of the balanced budget doctrine introduced by the Dodge reforms. Since the government's bonds, which otherwise would have held the central place on the market for public and corporate bonds and debentures, were absent, markets for absorbing and distributing bonds and debentures failed to develop adequately. No market was even created to handle government bonds, which began to be issued in significant quantities in 1965. Instead, a syndicate formed mainly by city banks accepts government bonds, and about 90 percent of the outstanding state bonds were held by financial institutions.

The vacuum created by the restrained borrowing policy of the government was filled by debentures issued by the special banks. Those private funds that otherwise would have flowed broadly to the fiscal sector were channeled by the long-term credit banks to large private corporations. On this score, the Industrial Bank of Japan, resuscitated as a long-term financing bank, played an extremely large role in the high economic growth of the postwar period.

Financial Hierarchy Preserved

The policy of low interest rates induced fund flows to city banks and large companies and helped form a hierarchical order in Japan's banking industry. If there had been no such interest policy, smaller banks, operating from a regional base— local banks, mutual savings and loan banks, and credit associations—would have lent their funds profitably to their own regular customers, most of which were small businesses. Instead, they were banned from raising the rate beyond a specified point and also faced stiff regulations if they attempted to improve the real rate through various means at their disposal. Therefore, it was infeasible for them to extend loans to small businesses and individual clients of less than top credit-worthiness. Since they have few regular customers among larger companies, they inevitably suffer a redundancy of funds; the surplus funds are applied to city banks via the interbank markets, such as the call loan market. This is what is known as the problem of maldistribution of funds in Japan's banking industry. In other words, the government's low interest policy made it possible to channel the flow of funds into city banks and large corporations.

This has led to the formation of a well-ordered hierarchy in the financial world. Located at the top are long-term credit and city banks, followed by local banks, mutual banks, credit banks, and credit associations on successively lower levels of the hierarchical structure. The Industrial Bank of Japan and other long-term credit banks, with their entrenched status in the monopolistic flotation of financial bonds, supplies the absorbed funds to key industries on a priority basis. City banks, especially those having their origin in the prewar zaibatsu, also have close links with key industries. They absorb funds from local and mutual banks and credit associations via the call market and other channels and supply them to key industries.

The Finance Ministry's Banking Bureau has been instrumental in maintaining the hierarchical order of the banking industry because of its licensing power over the establishment of new banks and new branches of existing banks. Since the war, the Finance Ministry has issued not one permit in response to an application to establish a new bank. Nor has it allowed any existing bank to fold. By its regulatory administration of the banking industry, which has been likened to the escort of a convoy of ships by a warship, the Finance Ministry has successfully preserved the Japanese financial hierarchy. Smaller financial institutions obtain some compensation for cooperating with the low interest policy manifestly working to the benefit of the bigger city banks—the Finance Ministry guarantees their existence by preventing the entry of newcomers in the banking business. The artificially maintained low interest rates have given rise to intense competition among the existing banks, regulated through the licensing of new bank branches. Competition taking place under control of this kind is not competition in the real sense of the word. Where price is a nonvariable constant, competition is bound to become a struggle for a larger share of the business. No rational standard exists for competition of this kind; rivalry must take a covert form.

System Closed to the World

The main participants in building the financial machinery of postwar Japan were large corporations of mainstream industries, serving as the engines of high economic growth; financial institutions through which fund flows were directed; and the Finance Ministry, which acted as the guardian of the hierarchy. Plainly absent were two other major participants that would be present in the system under normal circumstances: the overseas financial sector and the suppliers of savings.

The domestic financial structure was completely separated from the external financial sector through the "noninternationalization of finance" provisions under the Foreign Exchange and Foreign Trade Control Law. The controls on yen conversion isolated domestic finance totally from international finance. They made outward flight of Japanese capital impossible and created extreme difficulties for Japanese companies trying to raise capital in overseas money markets. This made the task of controlling the economy easier. We must not forget that Japan could maintain a domestic rate of interest far removed from the international rate determined in New York and London and allocate domestic funds arbitrarily only because of the existence of the isolated national monetary regime. Not a few Japanese have been angered at the frequent charges raised in recent trade disputes with the United States and Western Europe that Japan follows an isolationist policy, but as far as the system of foreign exchange controls centering on the restrictions on yen conversion is concerned, foreign complaints about Japanese isolationism seem to be justified.

The savings sector was shut out from the financial structure. To borrow from the vocabulary of left-oriented intellectuals, the Japanese people were denied opportunities for earning a high return on their modest savings because of a "capitalist system of monopolistic financing closed to the people." Without a doubt, the Japanese system of financial controls was a closed system not admitting suppliers of savings. But there were other means by which the fruits of high growth were fed back outside the framework of that system.

We must reckon first with the fact that high economic growth resulted in an extremely rapid increase in the wage level not limited to workers of large corporations alone, but including those of smaller and self-owned businesses, as demand for labor outstripped supply. The fact that consumer prices rose in the high growth period in spite of a high degree of stability shown by wholesale prices is indicative of the narrowing wage differentials in different sectors of the economy, which changed relative prices. In addition, income compensation was offered to backward sectors of the economy through public finance. High economic growth caused a steady rise in tax revenues, part of which was preferentially distributed to backward industries, such as agriculture, and underdeveloped regions.

Partial Adjustments Offered by Public Finance and Politics

In the process of high economic growth, public finance played a supporting role—a powerful supporting role, in fact. It did not, however, match the central place occupied by banks. Public finance was prevented from dominating the high-growth mechanism partly for the institutional reason that the budget was subject to the direct control of the Diet. But more fundamentally, unlike the monetary-financial sector, the fiscal sector was not sheltered against public exposure by impenetrable technicalities.

Qualitative Importance of Public Finance

What exact function did public finance play in high growth? Its most important function was, by limiting its own scale to a minimum, to pass on the savings in the private household sector to large corporations.

But there were two reasons why the quantitatively small government managed to wield a major qualitative influence on the economy. First, only very small outlays were made for defense, giving the government more freedom of action in fiscal policy. In fiscal 1975, defense expenditure as a percentage of gross national product was 0.9 percent in Japan, far lower than the 5.9 percent for the United States and 2.7 percent for West Germany. Second, expenditures for social security, mostly comprising payments under insurance and pension schemes, did not yet entail a major burden on Japan's public finance. Until the beginning of the 1970's, the combined sum of social security outlays and pension payments for retired civil servants remained stable at only about 20 percent of the general account budget. The success in controlling the size of defense and social security expenditures meant that the government was left with considerable freedom of action in fiscal policy despite the limited quantitative scale of fiscal expenditures. Comparison of the budget components in different countries is not entirely accurate because of differences in national fiscal systems, but the simple sum of defense outlays plus social security expenditures was 30 percent of Japan's budget in 1976, compared with 74 percent for the United States and 62 percent for West Germany.

Another role played by public finance was to provide piecemeal assistance to those sectors left behind in the high growth process. The following mainly concerns general account outlays, since special measures for tax relief and the treasury loans and investments program do not lend themselves to simple characterization.

Compensating for Uneven Growth

In adjustment distortions created by high economic growth, the fiscal sector (1) offered assistance to mitigate economic differentials between different regions through the transfer of income from developed areas to less developed areas, and (2) extended income compensation to low-productivity sectors, such as agriculture and small business.

Most typical of the assistance to reduce regional imbalances is the system for transfer of the central government's tax revenues to local governments. The system calls for transferring a fixed proportion of the revenues from individual and corporate income taxes and the liquor tax to local governments according to their financial status. The proportion of tax transfer, 20 percent in fiscal 1955, was raised through successive revisions until it is now 32 percent.

The government also plays a role in correcting income disparities by adjusting the distribution of public works projects. Public works are not, of course, planned primarily for this purpose. However, their distribution is under the strong control of the central government in the case of at least three categories of projects—those in which the central government invests directly, those financed in part by subsidies from the central government, and those financed indirectly by the treasury loans and investments program.

Tax transfer to local governments and public works investments accounted for less than 30 percent of the total outlays in the general accounts of the mid-1950's. The proportion began to rise in the first half of the 1960's, when high economic growth was under way, and reached close to 40 percent in the 1970's. The government offers many other varieties of subsidies, including assistance to defray half the salaries of public school teachers. These subsidy programs, too, are believed to have had an effect in adjusting disparities to income levels of different regions.

Most representative of income compensation by fiscal management to low-productivity sectors is the rice pricing policy under the food control system. Although expenditures related to rice price support occupy a relatively modest portion of the total budget expenditures, this percentage began to increase rapidly when, in spite of a decrease in the farm population, the lag in income improvement in the agricultural sector became prominent with the start of high economic growth from the mid-1950's onward. Fiscal aid is also extended to the agricultural sector through public works projects (land improvements in particular) and priority treasury loans and investment projects (lending is done mostly by the Agriculture, Forestry, and Fishery Finance Corporation). In addition, tax assessment on farm income is far less comprehensive than that on some other forms of income. The liberal leeway allowed farmers in tax collection may be regarded as yet another form of fiscal subsidy to the agricultural sector.

It is clear that rice price support under the food control system is meant not for improvement of farm productivity, but as a retroactive supplement to farm income. It does not represent a general expansion of social security, but a sectoral measure addressed to a specific industry. These features are exactly what characterize the corrective function played by the fiscal sector to alleviate the inequities caused by high economic growth. Similar sectoral and income compensation measures are taken for the benefit of smaller businesses under the general account and treasury loans and investments program, and in the form of deficit-covering subsidies to the national health insurance plan and fiscal grants to support the financial rehabilitation of the Japanese National Railways.

Conservative Politics and Public Finance

Of the fiscal adjustment measures, the tax transfer to local governments leaves little room for arbitrary decisions by the central government, since it is done automatically under fixed procedures. Since, however, other fiscal aids are determined for individual cases, they are open to discretionary decision making, whether they concern the regional distribution of public works projects or subsidies to agriculture and small businesses. These are prone to use as instruments of politics. In fact, fiscal expenditures of the latter type have been exploited by the conservative government as one of the principal supports which keep it in power.

It is well known that the conservative party has electoral strongholds in the Japanese economy's underdeveloped sectors, notably in rural areas and small-business industries. Conservative politicians have not played the same role as the business establishment in the postwar high economic growth. Instead, their role has been one of coordinating on behalf of the less-favored sectors. Their function has been to repair some of the broken parts of economic society, which could not be repaired through the workings of the high-growth machinery. By doing this service, the conservative politicians indirectly helped protect the security of the financial establishment.

11. The Banking-Industrial Complex

M. Therese Flaherty and Itami Hiroyuki

M. Therese Flaherty and Itami Hiroyuki argue that industry in Japan is governed by a system of relationships between companies and city banks. The system controls the actions of existing companies and, in a nation where the development of venture capital businesses is discouraged, also directs the growth of new enterprises. The selection is drawn from Daniel I. Okimoto et al., *Competitive Edge: The Semiconductor Industry in the United States and Japan.*

In Japan, the relationships among the city banks and the two-way relations between firms and their lead banks amount to a virtual "banking-industrial complex" analogous to the United States's "military-industrial complex." The dealings between the banks and the firms in this complex are not arm's-length transactions. The high level of bank borrowing by the Japanese semiconductor manufacturers means that information flows with the loans at all levels of the organizations. The transactions are "quasi-internal." In terms of modern organizational economics, the banking-industrial complex is a governance system shaping the actions of companies and banks. The Japanese banks are willing to lend and the Japanese firms are willing to borrow so much money, not because of Japan, Inc., and government loan guarantees, but because they have consistent, long-term, mutual interests, large amounts of bank-controlled capital, and the power and information to protect them. Japanese firms borrow from the bank at the loss of some independence, with more information disclosures and the two-way demands of a long-term relationship. Sometimes this means that firms borrow even when they have no real investment needs.

From M. Therese Flaherty and Hiroyuki Itami, "Finance," in Daniel I. Okimoto et al., *Competitive Edge: The Semiconductor Industry in the United States and Japan* (Stanford, Calif.: Stanford University Press, 1984), pp. 151–53. By permission of the publisher.

Close long-term relations between banks and large firms in Japan probably increase the effectiveness of the Japanese financial system's support of the semiconductor industry. The banks, for example, make loans available to large and profitable firms even when credit is tight. Just as long as the city banks believe that the highly leveraged semiconductor firms will profit from international competition in the long run, the banks will continue to make financing available to them. Just as important, the banks will make loans available to these firms even during tight money conditions when they cut back their credit to other firms.

We should note that this system of two-way relationships in Japan did not prevent serious competition among the city banks during the 1970's and early 1980's. During the late 1970's, many large companies carried large debts but were not at risk operationally, and Japanese bond and stock markets began to be more accessible to borrowing companies and investors. The city banks competed vigorously for business, and several large companies changed their lead banks. During the same period, many large Japanese companies were developing international operations with significant overseas investments. The foreign exchange laws were beginning to be liberalized. The control of interest rates and capital availability by the Finance Ministry was beginning to weaken. Thus the dominance of the city banks, and the prevalence of highly leveraged large firms in Japan, might not survive the long-term trend of freer access to markets. This has definitely been a slow change, which only began during the late 1970's.

In the 1970's and 1980's, not only has Japan had virtually no venture capital market such as exists in the United States, but furthermore the Japanese banking-industrial complex has made it almost impossible for venturesome entrepreneurs to obtain seed money in the form of bank loans. Not surprisingly, there are very few, if any, venture businesses in Japan even in the high technology area.

The main reason is that the Japanese equity market has not developed enough to enable successful venture businesses (and their capitalists) to sell their stocks to realize capital gains. Whereas in the United States some 298 firms went public in NASDAQ in 1980, in that same year there were only 14 new public equity offerings in the Japanese over-the-counter market. In another market for public offerings, the American Stock Exchange (AMEX) and the second section of the Tokyo Stock Exchange, the difference in 1980 was less dramatic but still very substantial: 65 new entrants in the United States and 12 in Japan. This difference was not a temporary anomaly. From 1976 through 1980, the total numbers of new public offerings were 600 in NASDAQ and 33 in Japan.

Japanese requirements for going public, set by both the government and the securities industry, are far more stringent than United States market standards. Among other requirements, the firm has to be larger than a certain level, and it has to submit dividend and profitability records for many years.

A second reason for the lack of venture capital in Japan is again related to the limited supply of capital for risks not intermediated by the city banks. There is no special tax incentive for the affluent to provide venture money like the tax shelters allowed in the United States tax code. Moreover, capital gains are treated as a part of regular income, and regular income tax rates apply for both corporations and individuals, whereas in the United States, the maximum rate is reduced, in effect, to 28 percent. For a small amount of public trading (trading in the stock exchange) of securities, a capital gain is not taxable in Japan for personal income tax. But this actually favors large established firms.

Third, the nature of the labor market limits the supply of entrepreneurs who demand venture capital. Low labor mobility in Japan—at least among top-flight engineers—means that an entrepreneur has a very small chance of returning to any established or well-regarded firm if he fails in a spinoff attempt. This high cost of failure naturally has the effect of discouraging venture attempts.

Finally, a cultural factor may work against a labor supply of entrepreneurs in Japan. Belonging to an established organization seems to be valued more highly in Japan, whereas independence seems to be more highly valued in the United States.

12. Japanese Bond and Stock Markets

Edward J. Lincoln

As foreign participation in Japanese financial markets and Japanese participation in foreign markets increase, it is important to understand how differences in regulations and operating methods affect investment. This report, which was published by the United States–Japan Trade Council in 1980, traces the development of postwar Japanese financial markets. It argues that early growth was hindered by restrictive government policies and that their gradual relaxation is leading to a greater flexibility.

With Japan the second-largest market economy in the world, it is important to understand how and why its financial markets work as they do. Even though Japan is not likely to become a major international financial center in the near future, foreign participation is increasing and is expected to continue to do so, as is Japanese participation abroad.

This report focuses on the bond and stock markets in Japan. To some extent the bond market remains underdeveloped because of restrictive government policies that are discussed in this report. The direction of change, however, is toward greater flexibility. Stocks in Japan are viewed somewhat differently from the way they are viewed in the United States, but the stock market is an active and well-developed one.

Role of Stocks and Bonds in Personal Savings

The major difference between personal savings in Japan and in the United States is that in Japan a much lower proportion goes into corporate equities (Table 12.1). Why have Japanese investors placed such a small share of their savings in corporate equities? Since interest rates on bank deposits have been controlled by

From Edward J. Lincoln, "Financial Markets in Japan," *United States–Japan Trade Council Report*, no. 47, Dec. 19, 1980.

Table 12.1.   *Composition of Personal Assets, 1978*
(In percentages)

Personal assets	United States	Japan
Cash and demand deposits	6.5%	13.6%
Time and savings accounts	32.7	55.1
Bonds	9.6	8.1
Central government	4.1	2.3
Public corporation	1.0	1.0
Local government	2.6	0.2
Corporate and foreign	1.9	4.6
Corporate equity	23.5	10.0
Mutual funds	1.3	1.8
Life insurance	15.7	12.6
Other[a]	8.1	0.6

SOURCES: Bank of Japan, *Economic Statistics Annual*, 1979; and Department of Commerce, *Statistical Abstract of the United States*, 1979.

NOTE: United States data are for December 31, 1978, Japanese data for the end of fiscal year 1978 (March 31, 1979).

[a]Includes, for the United States, pension fund reserves, security credit, mortgages, corporate paper, money market funds, and miscellaneous; for Japan, mainly company savings plans.

the government at levels generally considered to be below market-clearing rates, it would be reasonable to expect savers to put a greater proportion of their funds into other financial assets. The stock market is a true market, with no opportunity for the government to control rates of return. The rate of return on bonds is controlled in the new issue market, but not in the secondary market. The preference for bank deposits therefore seems to be due to a greater aversion to risk than prevails in the United States. While stocks provide a higher return than bank deposits, they carry a capital risk since the price of the shares may decline.

The Role of Stocks and Bonds in Corporate Finance

Equity and bonds represent two ways in which corporations can raise funds to finance their corporate creation and expansion. During the high growth era (1958–69), Japanese companies were characterized by much heavier reliance on bank loans as a source of funds than is the case in the United States (Table 12.2). However, this does not mean that Japanese corporations relied less than their American counterparts on bond and equity issues. The big difference between Japan and the United States was a much lower dependence on internal funds (retained earnings and depreciation), leading to a correspondingly higher dependence on banks. Conditions in Japan have changed considerably since then. With slower growth in the economy, retained earnings and depreciation provided a much larger share of corporate funds in fiscal year 1978 than during the 1950's and 1960's. Except for a very low reliance on bonds, the source of funds appears to be much closer to patterns in the United States. While neither bonds nor equity are a dominant source of new corporate funds in either country, they remain important financial instruments and a substantial part of the portfolios of investors.

Table 12.2.   Sources of Corporate Funds, Japan and United States
(In percentages)

	Japan		United States	
Source of funds	1958–69 (average)	1978	1958–69 (average)	1978
Equity	6.4%	2.6%	2.0%	0.8%
Depreciation	23.5	37.4	47.2	35.6
Retained earnings	4.5	24.7	23.2	19.2
Bank borrowings	33.4	18.7	9.1	20.5
Bonds	5.5	1.8	10.3	8.6
Other[a]	26.7	14.7	8.2	15.3

SOURCES: The 1958–69 averages are from Ryoichi Mikitani, "Monetary Policy in Japan," in Karel Holbik, ed., *Monetary Policy in Twelve Industrial Countries* (Boston: Federal Reserve Bank of Boston, 1973); 1978 data for Japan are from Bank of Japan, *Economic Statistics Annual*; and 1978 U.S. data are from Board of Governors of the Federal Reserve System, *Flow of Funds Accounts, 1949–1978*.

[a]Includes trade credit received. This is a very ambiguous source of funds since it is largely supplied from other firms within the corporate sector; it is a shifting of funds, not a net inflow from other sectors.

The Stock Market

Japan has eight stock exchanges, located in Tokyo, Osaka, Nagoya, Kyoto, Hiroshima, Fukuoka, Niigata, and Sapporo. The Tokyo market dominates, with 74 percent of all shares traded. Stocks on the exchanges are divided into two sections on the basis of various corporate size criteria, with approximately one thousand companies listed in the first section and another seven hundred in the second section.

At the top of the securities industry in Japan are the "big four"—Nomura, Daiwa, Yamaichi, and Nikkō. Securities firms in Japan act as underwriters and brokers and also buy for their own accounts. For the big four, purchases on their own accounts amount to about half of their total trading; the underwriting business has never become particularly important as a source of profits. Of the big four, Nomura is by far the largest, and it is acknowledged to be the largest securities company in the world. As Japanese investors have become more active in buying foreign securities, a number of the securities companies have established overseas offices. American brokerage houses have also begun moving into Japan over the past few years. They have entered the market to service both American customers buying or selling Japanese securities and Japanese dealing in foreign securities.

History

The stock exchanges, closed by Occupation command when the war ended, remained shut until passage of the Securities Transaction Law in 1948. One of the main features of this law, patterned on the United States's example, was the prohibition of commercial banks from underwriting securities (except for government securities).

From 1955 to 1960, the average daily volume of shares traded increased tenfold, and by more than twenty times in terms of sales value, as stock prices more than doubled. This heady atmosphere was dealt a severe blow during the economic slowdown of 1962, when the pace of gross national product growth dropped to only 2.4 percent and business investment fell by 2.5 percent. This slowdown apparently triggered a decline in stock prices, with the average price of a share falling from a high of 219 yen in July 1961 to a low of 86 yen in June 1965 (and the Tokyo Stock Exchange Price Index dropped from 344 to 192 over the same period). As prices fell, the volume of shares sold on the exchanges also dropped, from a high of 59 billion shares in 1963 to 42 billion in 1964, with volume showing no sustained rise until 1968. The drop in prices and business caused a crisis in the securities industry and resulted in the creation of two special corporations—the Japan Cooperative Security Company (established in January 1964) and the Japan Securities Holding Union. These companies were formed to buy shares and hold them to prevent prices from falling further. Together they bought some one billion dollars in securities. Despite their intervention, one firm, Yamaichi Securities, was in very poor financial condition and had to be given extensive aid by the Bank of Japan to prevent a collapse.

After this period of crisis, the stock markets recovered fully. Volume has fluctuated widely, but by 1979 it was more than double that of 1965. Sales volume increased more than eight times over the same period, while the Tokyo Stock Price Index increased five times. Stock prices in Japan, unlike stock prices in the United States, have more than kept up with inflation during this period, with the consumer price index increasing only 2.85 times over the same time span. By 1979, the sales volume on the Tokyo Exchange was 34.9 trillion yen, or $160 billion, not much less than the $200 billion in sales on the New York Stock Exchange.

Important Features

One of the main differences between Japan and the United States is in stock ownership patterns. A high proportion of Japanese stock is owned by corporations, and that proportion has been slowly rising (Table 12.3). Limits on the holdings by financial corporations, however, are set by the Antimonopoly Law. From 1953 to 1977, financial institutions were limited to 10 percent of the outstanding stock of any single corporation, but since 1977 the limit has been lowered to 5 percent.

A large part of the stock ownership by financial institutions and corporations represents more than portfolio management. Corporations belonging to a *kei-*

Table 12.3.   *Stock Ownership in Japan, 1965–1978*
(In percentages)

Owner	End of fiscal year			
	1965	1970	1975	1978[a]
Government	0.2%	0.3%	0.4%	0.2%
Financial institutions	26.8	30.9	31.2	38.8
Security companies	5.4	1.2	1.3	1.8
Corporations	21.0	24.7	30.3	26.2
Individuals	44.4	40.0	34.0	30.8
Foreigners[b]	2.1	3.2	2.8	2.1

SOURCE: Bank of Japan, *Economic Statistics Annual.*
[a]Includes only companies listed on the stock exchanges; previous years include unlisted companies as well.
[b]Includes both corporations and individuals.

retsu, or business grouping, engage in mutual stockholding with other members of the group as a means of creating tangible (but loose) ties within the group. This motive for stockholding means that those shares are not thereafter sold. As a result, individuals dominate trading on the stock exchanges even though they do not dominate share ownership. According to one report, individuals accounted for about two-thirds of the activity on the Tokyo Stock Exchange.

An important difference between stock transactions in Japan and the United States is the absence in Japan of what are known as unfriendly takeovers. Since a corporate takeover requires the agreement of the board of directors, the stock market is simply not the scene of contests for the control of corporations. In fact, stockholders are not expected to challenge the management at all; there are no proxy fights to unseat members of the board or to alter management policies. The professional troublemakers who own single shares and threaten to ask embarrassing questions at annual meetings unless paid off fall in the nuisance category and do not attempt to exert stockowner control of the corporation. In the United States, too, management has become increasingly divorced from ownership, but the separation is far more complete in Japan, reducing the stockholders to something like another creditor of the firm.

Foreign Participation

Foreign stock was not sold in Japan until the 1970's; purchases by Japanese individuals began in July 1971. At the end of 1973, Dow Chemical became the first foreign firm to be listed on the Tokyo Stock Exchange. However, foreigners were permitted to purchase stock in Japanese firms in the 1960's. According to Table 12.3, foreigners owned 2.1 percent of the outstanding stock of all Japanese companies listed on the Japanese stock exchanges of 1978. Of this, 2 percent was owned by corporations and .1 percent by individuals. Some of this ownership may represent holdings of subsidiaries or joint ventures incorporated in Japan, but many subsidiaries are not listed on the exchanges.

Foreign ownership of Japanese stock is subject to certain restrictions. Until the new Foreign Exchange Law went into effect at the beginning of December 1980, there were limits on the maximum percentage of outstanding shares that a single foreigner or foreigners as a category could hold. The limit was 10 percent for a single investor or 25 percent for total foreign ownership. Any level of ownership beyond those limits required approval by the board of directors. Under the new law, there are no general limits, but the Finance Ministry may establish them for designated companies. Eleven companies have been so designated as of this writing, with total foreign ownership frozen at present levels ranging from 25 to 50 percent: the Arabian Oil Company (with the limit set at 25 percent), Shōwa Oil (50 percent), Mitsubishi Oil (50 percent), Tōa Nenryō Kōgyō (50 percent), Kōa Oil (50 percent), General Sekiyu (40 percent), Fuji Electric (26 percent), Hitachi (30 percent), Tokyo Keiki (32 percent), Katakura Industries (25 percent), and Sankyō (25 percent). In all cases, the maximum amount of foreign participation was set close to the current foreign ownership levels.

Different attitudes about the role of the stockowners have led to some cases of international friction, illustrated by a recent case. A Hong Kong investor, Wang Tseng Hsiang, attempted to buy considerable amounts of two Japanese companies

(Ōji Paper and Katakura Industries) in 1977 through a securities investment company he ran. Although apparently within the legal limits (it was unclear if the 10 percent or the 25 percent level applied in the case of his firm), he discovered that Japanese securities companies were refusing to execute his purchase orders as his ownership became substantial. The explanation for such refusals remains unclear, with the Finance Ministry, the Tokyo Stock Exchange, and the companies all denying they put pressure on the brokerage houses. However, it is clear that Mr. Wang's activity could be viewed as undesirable in Japan on at least two grounds— ethnic prejudice against the Chinese and dismay over his intentions to use a strong minority ownership position to force management policy changes. As noted above, stockholders are not expected to raise their voices against management. As a result of the change in the law and the increasing number of foreign brokerage houses establishing branches in Tokyo, the possibility of action to prevent foreign purchases of Japanese corporate equities has been weakened. Even under the new law, however, a foreign investor buying more than 10 percent of a firm's shares must at least notify the Finance Ministry of its action.

Bond Market

The Japanese bond market has been hampered in the postwar period by the government's desire to control interest rates (and thereby hold down the cost of government debt). The regulation has eased somewhat, but it is not entirely gone.

A number of different types of bonds are sold in Japan, mostly in longer maturities. Bonds are issued by the central government, local governments, some government-owned corporations, long-term credit banks, and nonfinancial corporations. Central government bonds are mostly of a ten-year maturity, although two- and three-year bonds appeared beginning in 1978. There are short-term government securities, but very little of this is held outside government financial institutions. Local government bonds and government corporation bonds are all of a ten-year maturity. The government corporation bonds are issued mainly by the Japanese National Railways (to cover its large operating deficits) and the Nippon Telephone and Telegraph Company (NTT); one of the conditions for obtaining a telephone in Japan is to purchase an NTT bond. Long-term credit bank bonds are issued instead of collecting deposits and come in one- and five-year maturities. Industrial bonds are of longer-term maturities (seven to twelve years), and there is no commercial paper market.

History

Until 1965, the Japanese government was not able to engage in deficit financing. As a result, it had few outstanding long-term or short-term securities. Since 1965, government debt has mushroomed, largely in the form of long-term bonds, reaching a total amount of 67 trillion yen by the end of fiscal 1979 (March 31, 1980), or $292 billion at the average exchange rate for the fiscal year. This extraordinarily rapid rise in government debt brought it up to a level comparable with that of the United States (which had an economy twice as large and a government debt of $619 billion at the end of 1978). The Japanese bond market may remain underdeveloped in certain respects, but in terms of the size of government debt, this characterization is no longer apt.

Local government debt also rose rapidly after 1965, but by no means as fast as central government debt. It reached 15.4 trillion yen at the end of fiscal 1979 ($66.9 billion). This remains far less than half the United States state and local debt figure of $285 billion. Bank debentures, issued by long-term credit banks in Japan in lieu of collecting deposits, have also increased dramatically, reaching 24.3 trillion yen at the end of fiscal 1979 ($105.6 billion). There is nothing really comparable to these in the United States, except perhaps certificates of deposit (CD's), but even here there are many differences between the two. Nonfinancial corporate bonds are the one type of long-term bond that has not grown at the same high rates. In 1965, outstanding industrial bonds outnumbered central government securities by 2.5 to 1; in 1979, government securities outnumbered industrial bonds 6 to 1. As the amounts of outstanding bonds have increased, the volumes traded in the secondary market have risen as well. Total volume of over-the-counter bond sales in Tokyo came to 204.2 trillion yen ($932 billion) in 1979.

Important Features

The government of the bond market was hindered by the government's insistence on fixing the interest rates for new bond issues and essentially forcing commercial banks to buy the bonds and hold them for a minimum of one year, whether or not interest rates were attractive. Because the bonds were forced upon them, the banks have complained loudly if faced with capital losses when they sell the bonds after the one-year limit. Because of these complaints, the Bank of Japan and the government's Trust Fund Bureau (which administers the money from the secondary market) have begun to buy up bond issues in order to placate the banks. These buying actions are in no sense comparable to the open market operations of the United States Federal Reserve; the aim is to aid the banking industry—not control interest rates.

As a result of the system of issuing government bonds, commercial financial institutions hold 50 percent of government debt, the Bank of Japan 22 percent, the Trust Fund Bureau 20 percent, and the nonfinancial private sector only 8 percent. Combining the Bank of Japan holdings and the Trust Fund Bureau, fully 70 percent of the debt is held by government agencies. In the United States, the ratios are very different. Despite the need to hold government debt for open market operations, the Federal Reserve system holds only 18 percent of United States government debt, and commercial banks hold only 15.7 percent, while the nonfinancial sector (including nonfinancial corporations, individuals, and foreigners) holds 48.8 percent.

One feature of government bonds making them attractive is that they can be used in a form of short-term lending called the *gensaki* market, which began in the late 1960's. Under this system, bonds owned by the borrower are sold to the lender with a repurchase agreement, with the lending period varying from several weeks to about six months, and with interest rates determined by the market. Central and local government bonds, government-owned corporation bonds, and long-term credit bank bonds can all be used for these transactions. The outstanding amount of lending through the gensaki market was 4.7 trillion yen (about $22 billion) by June 1980.

The establishment of relatively low interest rates for new bond issues is generally given as the major reason that corporations have had limited access to the bond market, since (unlike the government) they cannot coerce commercial banks into acquiring them. However, it is unclear how the long-term credit banks have been able to expand their bond issues faster than nonfinancial corporations. A possible explanation is their shorter maturity and greater similarity to time deposits. As the size of new debt issue by the government has risen, it has been forced to alter the rates of interest on new issues more frequently and to keep them closer to the market-determined rates prevailing in the secondary market. This greater flexibility still falls short of making public offerings and accepting market interest rates, and it has not removed the complaints of commercial banks.

Corporate bond sales may have been hindered by other factors as well, most of which are now changing. Until recently, all corporate bonds had to be secured by collateral. Even now, the Finance Ministry has very strict standards for determining which firms can issue unsecured bonds, guidelines most firms cannot meet. Until 1971, the securities industry rating system for all bonds was based on the issuer's capitalization; that system has now been replaced by one that relies on profitability and assets. Convertible bonds have also been growing in popularity. In 1979, 22 percent of nonfinancial corporate bonds issued were convertible and amounted to 14 percent of all outstanding corporate bonds. Trading activity in convertible bonds has been intense, with a sales volume on the Tokyo Stock Exchange in 1979 more than two hundred times as large as that for regular corporate bonds, which suggests that they have become a speculative item.

Foreign Participation

Like the market for stock purchases, the international bond market began in the 1970's and was heavily regulated. Foreigners were first allowed to issue yen-denominated bonds (called samurai bonds) in Japan in 1970 and foreign-currency-denominated bonds in 1972. Initially, borrowers were limited to international institutions (the first was a 6-billion-yen bond floated by the Asian Development Bank in 1970); then, foreign governments were included (beginning with Australia in 1972). Each new issue required Finance Ministry approval. All new issues were halted in November 1973 in order to slow capital outflow. With a trade deficit resulting from the oil crisis, the Finance Ministry did not want capital outflows compounding the deficits, and it intervened directly by refusing to allow foreigners to issue bonds in Japan. Beginning in 1970, Japanese investors had been allowed to make another capital outflow in the form of portfolio investments overseas. This permission was extended to insurance companies and individuals in 1971, but as with the samurai bonds, activity was temporarily suspended in 1974.

As Japan's trade position recovered from the oil shock, new samurai bonds were issued in 1975, and by the end of 1978, a foreign debt of $6 billion was outstanding in Japan. Another step was taken in 1979, when Sears, Roebuck and Company became the first foreign corporation allowed to issue a bond in Japan. Also unusual was the fact that it was an unsecured bond, and, not surprisingly, this led to further pressure from Japanese companies to ease the rigid guidelines and allow them to issue unsecured bonds of their own.

An additional regulation on the samurai bonds is that, when issued, foreign purchase is limited to 25 percent of the issue. No control is imposed on the secondary market, and one estimate is that foreigners own about 40 percent of the outstanding bonds. Their relative attraction to foreign investors over Japanese bonds is unclear, but it may be due to greater foreign investor familiarity with the credit ratings of the issuers.

Japanese companies have been allowed to float foreign currency bonds (in dollars and West German marks) since the beginning of the 1960's, but the amounts raised were severely restricted, and the outstanding amount remained at the $500 million level until 1975. To slow capital inflow at a time when Japan was running a large current account surplus, flotation of these bonds was temporarily suspended in 1972 and 1973, but after the oil shock the policy was reversed and new issues were encouraged. By the end of 1979, the outstanding amount of foreign currency bonds was $6.5 billion.

Conclusion

Over the past year, foreign portfolio investment in Japan has accelerated. Oil-producing countries, in particular, have become much more active in investing in Japan, including purchases of both equity and bonds. As the oil-producing countries continue to seek outlets for their funds, and as foreigners become more familiar with Japanese financial markets, foreign participation is likely to increase. The new presence of United States securities firms in Japan attests to their concurrence in that conclusion.

During the postwar period, the Finance Ministry has moved very slowly to remove controls over domestic financial markets and international transactions. At times, the justifications offered for the delays reflected an attitude that the Japanese investors were children who had to be guided. At other times, international bond sales or purchases were shut off to fit the needs of domestic monetary policy. During the 1970's, however, the trend has been toward greater flexibility and freedom, and that trend is likely to continue. The new Foreign Exchange Law allows transactions unless prohibited, a reversal of philosophy from its predecessor. Although the new law means little in terms of actual conditions of access at the moment, it does represent another step in the continuing shift toward liberalization.

13. The Japan–United States Savings-Rate Gap

Nagato Kazuhiko

Japan's savings rate has been gradually declining since the oil crisis of 1973–74. Even so, the rate remains exceptionally high by international standards. In recent years Japanese families have been saving some 17–19 percent of their disposable income, compared with

From Kazuhiko Nagato, "The Japan–U.S. Savings-Rate Gap," in *Economic Views from Japan*, Part 5 (Tokyo: Keizai Koho Center, 1986), pp. 228–35. By permission of the publisher and the author.

an average figure of about 6 percent in the United States. Here Nagato Kazuhiko, a Japanese economist, examines the causes behind this large gap.

Taxes and Social Security

The first question to consider is the relationship between savings on the one hand and taxes and social security contributions on the other. Over the 1964–81 period the disposable income of the average Japanese family was 88 percent of gross income. The 12 percent of income that was not available for consumption went for taxes and social security premiums. In the United States taxes and social security take a larger bite out of paychecks. Over the same period the disposable income of American families was only 80 percent of their gross income.

Given this differential in disposable income, how large is the consequent differential in savings behavior, or the family's decision as to how much of the available flow of funds to set aside for later use? People planning household budgets have two basic alternatives when tax and social security payments go up: they can maintain their previous level of consumption and put less money into savings accounts, or they can continue to save at the same rate and cut back on consumption.

A variety of factors will influence their decision. Families may decide that they cannot reduce their saving because it is needed to meet their plans for consumption or investment in the future. Or the saving may be of an involuntary nature, which a family is unable to reduce even if it would like to. Depending on the systems in effect in a given country, families may arrive at different decisions on how much money to save. To illustrate this point, let us compare the total of money used for taxes and social security and money saved in Japan and the United States.

As shown in Table 13.1, in the 1964–81 period the share of gross income used for taxes and social security was 12 percent in Japan and 20 percent in the United States, while the percentage of gross income saved was 16 percent in Japan and 6 percent in the United States. Japanese families, in other words, enjoyed a tax and social security burden 8 percentage points lower than that borne by American families, and they maintained a savings rate 10 percentage points higher. Thus when tax and social security payments are added to money saved, we find a differential of only 2 percentage points between the two countries.

In more recent years, especially since the second half of the 1970's, social security in Japan has been catching up with that in the West. The pension system in particular has been expanded, and relatively generous benefits are now granted to many more people. At the same time, pension premiums and other social security contributions have also been rising.

How has household saving been affected by this rise in social security premiums and benefits? Until 1975 Japan's savings rate continued to rise despite a gradually growing burden of tax and social security payments. When the tax and social security burden began to increase rapidly, however, the savings rate started to decline. Since 1975 a trade-off relationship has been observed between savings and the tax and social security burden.

The conclusion to be drawn is that social security serves to some extent as a substitute for savings. Thus one of the causes of the savings-rate gap between Japan and the United States is apparently the differential in the level of social security payments in the two countries. We can further speculate that as Japan's social se-

Table 13.1.   Savings and Tax and Social Security Payments
as Share of Gross Income, 1964–1981 Average
(In percentages)

Payments and income	Japan (a)	United States (b)	Difference (a − b)
Taxes and social security payments (1)	12.1%	19.9%	−7.8%
Savings (2)	15.8	6.3	9.5
Taxes, social security payments, and savings (1 + 2)	27.9	26.2	1.7
Disposable income	87.9	80.1	7.8

SOURCE: OECD, National Accounts of OECD Countries, 1983.

curity system matures, the savings rate will continue to decline. Gradually the relationship between savings and payments for taxes and social security should move closer to the American pattern.

Saving for Acquisition of Housing

Although the savings rate of households can be defined as the percentage of disposable income that is not consumed, an alternative definition is provided by the ratio to disposable income of gross investment, that is, property investment plus additions to financial assets less additions to financial liabilities. The latter definition permits a breakdown of the savings rate into such components as housing investment, land investment, other fixed capital formation, and the net increase or decrease in financial assets and liabilities.

In this breakdown of savings components, the largest Japan-U.S. gap can be found in the category of housing investment. (In the discussion here, the purchase of land by the household sector and the capital consumption of nonfarm, noncorporate businesses are both excluded from consideration.) As Table 13.2 indicates, in the 1970–81 period the Japanese set aside 8 percent of their gross income for the purchase of housing, double the 4 percent allocated by Americans for the same purpose. About 40 percent of the 10-percentage-point spread between the Japanese and American savings rates, we may say, is a function of this difference in housing investment.

The cost of housing is the primary factor involved. The cost of a single-family house (with land) in the Tokyo area is equivalent to about six times the average Japanese family's annual income. United States housing costs have been on the rise, but even so an American family needs to pay only about three years' income to buy a house. Differences in the structure of housing demand help explain this large differential in housing starts. After World War II Japan faced a shortage of housing, and in urban areas this shortage became critical during the ensuing years of high growth. In addition to the influx of people into cities, the increased prevalence of nuclear families led to a sharp increase in the number of households. These factors worked in combination with the cramped and aged quality of much of the existing housing to produce a strong demand for new homes, the typical goal being to purchase land and build a house on it. And as the price of land in ur-

Table 13.2.   Housing Investment and Purchase of Consumer
Durables as Share of Gross Income, 1970–1981 Average
(In percentages)

Category	Japan (a)	United States (b)	Difference (a − b)
Housing investment (1)	7.9%	4.0%	3.9%
Increase in other assets (2)	7.9	2.3	5.6
Purchase of consumer durables (3)	4.0	9.7	− 5.7
Housing and durables (1 + 3)	11.9	13.7	− 1.8
Other savings and durables (2 + 3)	11.9	12.0	− 0.1

SOURCES: Bank of Japan, *Shikin Junkan Kanjo* (Flow of Fund Accounts), 1982; Federal Reserve Board, *Flow of Fund Accounts 1945–83*, 1984; Federal Reserve Board, *Balance Sheets for the U.S. Economy*, 1984.

ban areas shot up in response to this demand, people began to invest in housing and land as a hedge against inflation, further fueling the price spiral.

The resulting differential between Japan and the United States in the cost of housing has had an impact on financial assets going beyond the difference in the percentage of income allocated for housing. When money is borrowed to pay for a house, in both countries there is a similar upper limit on the monthly loan repayments that a family can afford. If this limit is assumed to be about 25 percent of income, a family in the United States can purchase a house even if all or almost all the money is borrowed.

The much higher cost of housing in Japan, however, virtually eliminates this possibility. In order to be able to afford housing loan repayments, the average family must save enough money to make a substantial down payment of about three times the family's annual income. Money set aside for housing, moreover, tends not to be employed for other purposes and can be seen as a type of "fixed savings." Thus the savings rate of the Japanese has been pushed up partly because of the need to save for the purchase of housing in the future.

Repayments of housing loans also work to keep the savings rate at a high level. This comes about because payments to reduce indebtedness are included as a component of savings. When a house is built using a loan, in other words, at first the value of the house is added to both the family's property assets and its financial liabilities in offsetting entries, and the family's savings rate is not affected. Each repayment of the loan is then included in the family's savings. Since these loans require many years to repay, all the people repaying them, a fairly large segment of the population in Japan, must sustain a high savings rate over a long period.

We may conclude from these observations that differences in the cost of housing work to drive the Japanese savings rate well above that in the United States. The factors involved include the higher cost of Japanese housing, and the repayment of the long-term liabilities incurred.

Purchase of Consumer Durables

Next let us look at the impact on savings of the purchase of consumer durables. Economists classify the act of purchasing a durable good as consumption, but from the family's viewpoint the purchase has the nature of an investment in that the useful life of the product can be expected to extend over many years. We can perhaps gain further insight into the Japan-U.S. savings-rate gap by viewing consumer durables as a sort of property investment.

Looking again at Table 13.2, we see that during the 1970–81 period Japanese households devoted 4 percent of their gross income to the purchase of consumer durables (value before depreciation). This percentage varied little from year to year.

One factor amplifying these differences is the consumer credit system. To the extent that consumer credit is provided, consumption rises and saving drops. The well-developed consumer credit arrangements in the United States have led to a heavy dependence on borrowing for consumption. Although the level of dependence fluctuates radically, over the last decade the average ratio of new borrowing to increased consumption was on the order of 25 percent.

At the end of 1981 total U.S. consumer credit outstanding was about five times the Japanese level, and U.S. borrowing per household was about three times the Japanese average. Behind such differences are a greater willingness on the part of American financial institutions to lend to individuals and less reluctance on the part of American consumers to rely on credit for consumption. Of total U.S. consumer credit outstanding, credit financing of auto sales accounts for 60 percent. Revolving credit schemes are another important element. On the average over the 1973–83 period, revolving credit accounted for more than 20 percent of net credit growth.

Inflation and Consumer Behavior

During times of rapid inflation, a key factor encouraging Americans to step up purchases of durable products has been the availability of revolving credit and second mortgage loans from finance companies. Inflationary expectations have also promoted the "Buy now, pay later" psychology of many consumers. Studies have shown that Japanese consumers are more cautious in the face of inflation. Unlike their American counterparts, who tend to move spending forward on the assumption that today's prices represent bargains compared with what the same items are likely to cost in the future, Japanese consumers are apt to hold off on purchases.

The reason for this cautious attitude toward the purchase of durables is the higher level of uncertainty about future income that an inflationary period gives rise to. Despite the advantage of purchasing durable goods before prices go up, Japanese consumers worry that their real income may rise little or even drop in the future, which would upset their credit repayment plans. With this rather pessimistic outlook, they scale down the income level they anticipate, hold current consumption in line with their reduced expectations, and devote more effort to building up savings for future consumption. Such features of the behavior of Japanese consumers are becoming less marked, however. Recent years have seen an expansion of consumer credit systems, and the younger generation is less reluctant to buy on credit. In this respect Japan is becoming more like the United States.

With these points in mind, let us look once more at Table 13.2. When property investment is defined as the total of housing investment and the purchase of consumer durables, we find that the two countries invest in property to a comparable extent. Expressed as a percentage of gross income, money used for housing and consumer durables (item 1 + item 3) in the period surveyed came to 12 percent in Japan and 14 percent in the United States. To be sure, Japanese households devoted a larger proportion of their income to housing, and American households spent more on durables. But when the two items are combined, people in both countries allocated a similar portion of their annual income flow to these property assets.

Savings other than for housing mainly represents net accumulation of financial assets (additions to financial assets less additions to financial liabilities). When the savings in this category are combined with money used for consumer durables (item 2 + item 3), again we find that a similar share of income is devoted to them by families in Japan (11 percent) and in the United States (12 percent).

A trade-off relationship can be observed between investment in financial assets and purchase of durables. A very high degree of substitutability is suggested in Table 13.2. While the Japanese devoted 5.6 percent more income to financial assets than did Americans in the 1970–81 period, Americans devoted 5.7 percent more income to durables than did the Japanese. These figures express the difference between Japan and the United States in people's preference for financial assets versus consumer durables.

Objectives of Saving

As a final topic of discussion, let us review the accumulation of financial assets in Japan and the United States. The differential between the two countries in the rate of net financial asset accumulation is primarily a result of differences in additions to assets, not in additions to liabilities. The main factors causing the gap seem to arise from the motivations for saving and the scale of financial stock.

The most basic reason for putting money aside in both countries is to prepare for accidental misfortune, such as illness or injury. This is known as the precautionary motive for saving. Since the money laid away may be needed unexpectedly, people prefer liquidity to high yield and therefore place the savings in a demand account or some similar financial instrument that can be quickly converted into cash.

The Japanese cite the need to have money for their children's education and marriage expenses as the second most important reason for saving. The money put aside for this purpose can be seen as fixed savings, as in the case of money saved for housing, since the funds cannot readily be diverted to other uses. The form the money is held in need not be as liquid as the savings accumulated for precautionary purposes, although a relatively liquid instrument is desirable. Most Japanese apparently select time deposits and other longer-term financial assets.

The third most important reason for saving mentioned by the Japanese is to provide for old age. In the United States this is given as the second most important reason, with children's education and marriage expenses in third place. The Japanese also place emphasis on saving for housing, which they give as the fourth most important reason, but in the United States this objective ranks only sixth, following such items as saving for travel.

The scale of financial stock desired by a family is a function of several factors. One psychological aspect is the degree of expectation or unease regarding the future. Generally the more cautious one's outlook, the more money one will try to accumulate in liquid assets. The presence or absence of institutional guarantees of money for old age and unforeseen expenses will also influence the desired scale of financial assets. Such guarantees as pensions and health insurance serve to some extent as substitutes for family savings. Another factor is the size of the financial assets the family has already accumulated. As the scale of existing assets moves up, generally the proportion designated for precautionary purposes declines as a percentage of the total.

When we compare the scale of financial assets in Japan and the United States with such considerations in mind, we find first that Americans possess a far higher level of financial assets than the Japanese. Whereas Americans hold financial assets equivalent to 27 months' income, the Japanese hold assets amounting to only nine months' income on the average. In the category of liquid assets as well, including time deposits and other fairly liquid instruments, the Japanese still place somewhat behind Americans despite a rapid accumulation of reserves in recent years. We may conclude from the observations that the motivation to build up savings in the form of financial assets is stronger in Japan than in the United States.

Demand deposits and other highly liquid assets account for about 15 percent of the net financial assets of the Japanese, as opposed to about 7 percent in the case of Americans. Somewhat less liquid assets like time deposits make up some 60 percent of the total in Japan, as opposed to about 25 percent in the United States. These ratios, coupled with the rapid buildup in such assets as time deposits in recent years, indicate that the high Japanese savings rate is being sustained in part by efforts to accumulate fixed savings, that is, savings earmarked for set objectives and held in fairly liquid instruments.

14. Industrial Groups

Rodney Clark

In this selection, which is taken from *The Japanese Company*, published in 1979, Rodney Clark describes the three major patterns into which postwar Japanese industrial groups are organized. Each pattern creates its own type of intra- and intergroup relations. Nevertheless, Clark asserts, there are a number of similarities among all three patterns which tend to distinguish them from the industrial groupings of other countries.

There are three main types of industrial groups. The first, most familiar to Westerners, is the descendant of the prewar *zaibatsu* (giant business combine). The second is the bank group, consisting of companies dependent for funds on a

From Rodney Clark, *The Japanese Company* (New Haven, Conn.: Yale University Press, 1979), pp. 73–87. Copyright © 1979 by Rodney Clark. By permission of the publisher.

major bank. The third type is the industrial family, comprising a major manufacturer and its related subsidiaries.

The prewar zaibatsu (the four biggest of which were Mitsui, Mitsubishi, Sumitomo, and Yasuda) were groups of companies partly owned and entirely controlled by a family holding company which stood at the center of the whole zaibatsu. Each zaibatsu contained a bank, a trust company, and an insurance company to provide funds and financial services, and a trading company to buy and sell goods on behalf of the member firms. These latter, operating in a number of different industries, were bound not only to the central holding company but to each other by interlocking shareholdings, directorships held in common, and preferential business arrangements. The zaibatsu were broken up by the Occupation authorities, and the family firms were abolished. But after the Allied troops left and Japan regained her independence, some of the companies of the prewar zaibatsu began to knit themselves together. They exchanged shares with other firms which bore the common zaibatsu name, deliberately relied on the group banks, trust banks, and insurance companies, and did business with each other through the trading companies. They also exchanged directors and set up clubs where the presidents of companies could meet. In this way there took place between 1952 and 1965 a revival of the prewar zaibatsu, and the word is commonly used for the collections of companies with the names of Mitsubishi, Mitsui, or Sumitomo, which were all once divisions of giant combines.

By comparison with their progenitors, however, the postwar zaibatsu are loose alliances, in which member companies cooperate only to a limited extent, and there is scarcely an attempt at central direction. (See, for example, Table 14.1.) Let us take the example of the Mitsubishi zaibatsu before and after the war. Before the war, each major company in the Mitsubishi combine had several directors who also sat on the boards of other Mitsubishi companies. Mitsubishi Heavy Industries and Mitsubishi Electric had had 11 and 12 such directors, respectively. Most of the interlocking directorships were held by the directors of the holding company: in 1937 the 17 holding company directors held among them 96 directorships in 19 major core companies. In 1976, however, no Mitsubishi company appeared to share directors with more than four other companies, most companies shared only one or two directors, and one important company, N.Y.K., seemed to have no interlocking directorships at all. The most common arrangement seemed to be that the presidents of two companies would sit as junior directors on each other's boards. The density of the connections was consistent with the interpretation that Mitsubishi companies were keeping abreast of each other's activities, but no more.

Instead of the prewar arrangement of shareholdings, in which the family holding company alone controlled a majority or near-majority of the shares of most of the companies of a zaibatsu, today, when holding companies are illegal, zaibatsu members do not hold more than a few percent of each other's shares. As Table 14.2 shows, even the total group holding in any one group member falls short of a majority of the capital.

It is also likely that the modern zaibatsu differ from the prewar versions in the extent to which member companies take in each other's business. Intragroup trade in the prewar zaibatsu was substantial, though firms did not buy from each other

Table 14.1.   The Sumitomo Group

CENTRAL SUMITOMO GROUP MEMBERS

Sumitomo Trust and Banking	Sumitomo Marine and Fire Insurance	Sumitomo Mutual Life Insurance
Sumitomo Realty and Development		Sumitomo Warehouse
	Sumitomo Chemical	
Sumitomo Bakelite		Sumitomo Aluminum Smelting
Sumitomo Heavy Industries	Sumitomo Bank	Nippon Electric (NEC)
		Sumitomo Construction
Sumitomo Electric Industries	Sumitomo Metal Industries	Sumitomo Light Metal Industries
Sumitomo Cement	Sumitomo Trading	Sumitomo Coal Mining
Sumitomo Forestry	Nippon Sheet Glass	Sumitomo Mining

MAJOR SUBSIDIARIES

Anritsu Electric	Seitetsu Kagaku
Daikin Kogyo	Shinto Paint
Inabata and Company	Sumitomo Precision Products
Nihon Spindle Manufacturing	Sumitomo Special Metals
Nippon Electric Industries	Sumitomo Rubber Industries
Nippon Pipe Manufacturing	Tohoku Metal Industries
Nippon Stainless Steel	Tokai Rubber Industries
Nisshin Electric	Tokyo Tungsten
Nitsuko	Toyo Communication Equipment

MAJOR AFFILIATED BUT INDEPENDENT COMPANIES

Asahi Chemical	Kinki Railway	Mazda Motors
Bridgestone Tire	Komatsu Ltd.	Sanyo Electric
Hankyu Railway	Kubota Ltd.	Takeda Chemical Industries
Idemitsu Kosan		

if they could get better terms from outsiders. Today zaibatsu companies will still deal with each other for preference. A shipper through Mitsubishi Corporation will perhaps pay less if he uses N.Y.K. ships and insures with Tokyo Marine. Yet even a casual observer of the Japanese industrial scene will notice occasions when group companies go outside the group for goods and services. Mitsubishi companies may employ trading companies from other zaibatsu. Buildings owned by Mitsubishi Real Estate do not necessarily have equipment made by Mitsubishi Electric.

Frequently the way people think and the principles upon which organizations are run become more clearly apparent when something goes wrong. In December 1974, an incident occurred which revealed a great deal about the cohesion of a present-day zaibatsu. An oil leak took place from the storage tanks of the Mizushima Refinery of Mitsubishi Oil. Oil poured into the Inland Sea, desecrating one of the most beautiful regions of Japan and destroying marine life in the area. It quickly became obvious that the costs of restitution and repair would be far too large for the company alone to bear—the eventual cost was about 50,000 million yen, or twice the net assets of Mitsubishi Oil as shown on the balance sheet at the

Table 14.2.   Cross-Shareholdings Among Selected Major Companies of the Mitsubishi Group, 1974
(In percentages)

Issuer	M. Bank	M. Trust Bank	Tokyo Marine	Meiji Life	M. Heavy Industries	M. Corporation	M. Electric	Asahi Glass	Kirin Beer	M. Chemical	N.Y.K.	Total of top 20 Mitsubishi companies
M. Bank		1.3%	4.7%	5.9%	3.3%	2.0%	1.4%	2.0%	0.8%	1.1%	1.1%	26.9%
M. Trust Bank	2.2%		1.7	7.7	3.1	3.7	1.7	2.2	1.0	0.8	1.4	32.3
Tokyo Marine	5.8	2.9		3.9	2.0	0.7	0.1	1.8	0.5	—	1.1	21.7
Meiji Life[a]	—	—	—		—	—	—	—	—	—	—	—
M. Heavy Industries	5.8	2.7	3.2	3.6		2.5	1.4	1.0	0.3	—	0.9	23.2
M. Corporation	7.9	4.1	7.8	4.8	5.9		2.0	1.6	0.5	—	2.7	42.2
M. Electric	3.4	1.0	1.6	4.5	2.6	1.7		0.2	0.1	—	0.0	16.3
Asahi Glass	7.7	4.1	6.1	4.3	1.6	1.7	0.3		1.0	—	0.3	29.3
Kirin Beer	3.0	1.5	0.7	3.7	0.7	0.9	0.2	1.0		—	0.2	12.7
M. Chemical	5.7	2.2	3.8	8.0	—	—	0.3	0.7	—		0.2	24.5
N.Y.K.	4.4	3.6	6.7	2.5	7.2	1.7	—	0.3	0.3	—		27.5

source: Okumura Hiroshi, *Hōjin Shihonshugi no Kōzō: Nihon no Kabushiki Shoyū* (The Structure of Corporate Capitalism: Share Ownership in Japan) (Tokyo: Hihon Hyoronsha, 1975), p. 175.
[a]A mutual life insurance company.

time. Now, Mitsubishi Oil, like most other Japanese oil companies, was partly owned by the foreign oil company which supplied it with oil: 48.7 percent of its shares were held by Getty Oil and only a few percent by other Mitsubishi companies. It was, in fact, Mitsubishi in name but not in nature. As the huge extent of the damage became known, the Mitsubishi Group was notably reluctant to come to the aid of what was described as an "outside lord" of the group—the reference being to those feudal lords in the Tokugawa period who were not of the Tokugawa family or its associates. In a newspaper article two months after the incident, the president of the Mitsubishi Bank is reported to have remarked that Mitsubishi Oil was Getty's company rather than Mitsubishi's; the president of Mitsubishi Mining and Cement rejected the idea that his firm should pay a higher price for oil from the Mitsubishi Oil Company to help the latter overcome its problems. Mr. Fujino, the representative of the association of presidents of the Mitsubishi Group, said, "If this were the time of the zaibatsu of the old days, then management would have been from a common kitty, and there would have been joint responsibility. But now, even though companies are members of the group, they are mutually independent companies and their shareholders are separate." And yet, as the leaders of the group admitted, Mitsubishi had its name both on the company and, by extension, the episode. Eventually, as the losses piled up at Mitsubishi Oil, and in the absence of any offers of help from Getty, the Mitsubishi Group did decide to rally round and arrange a substantial loan to reestablish the stricken company.

The second type of industrial group is that centered on a bank, in much the same way as the German Deutsche bank or Dresdner bank groups. Sanwa, to take the best-known example, is a major city bank. Its group consists of a dozen or so major companies, to which the bank lends money and in which it owns shares. Among these companies are Teijin, a large manufacturer of artificial fibers, and Takashimaya, one of the biggest department stores. A bank group such as Sanwa's is substantially less cohesive than a modern zaibatsu. The various companies that belong to it, though all indebted to the group bank, need not be particularly closely associated with each other. There is no sense of common history, no illustrious name to bring them together. It is not surprising, therefore, that the industrial companies in the Sanwa group do not feel the need to hold each other's shares.

There is also a tendency for large companies to become independent of any particular bank, and this, too, explains the comparative looseness of bank groups. The power of the banks in Japan has been and is very great. For most of Japan's modern history, capital has been in short supply, and the banks, which have traditionally acted as money-pumps—collecting funds from small depositors and pushing them into large industrial firms—have been able to influence industrial decision making. Even so, the preponderance of the banks has perhaps been overrated. The availability of other sources of finance has enabled a number of companies, like Makita Electric Works, Maruichi Steel Tube, or Brother Industries, to do without bank borrowing altogether, while some companies have very little debt. Matsushita Electric Industrial, Nippon Musical (the makers of Yamaha musical instruments), Shiseidō (the largest cosmetic company in Japan), and Taishō Pharmaceutical are all leading companies in their fields with little or no reliance on bank finance.

If banks as a whole are not as powerful as they are sometimes thought to be, the influence of any one bank, even over companies that belong to its group, is moderated by the intense competition that exists among banks. Japan is a grossly overbanked country. There are now more than 50 commercial banks with deposits in excess of 500,000 million yen, besides numbers of foreign banks, insurance companies, and governmental banks, all capable of large-scale lending. Add to these the myriad smaller banks, quasi-banks, and cooperatives, and it will be apparent that the treasurer of a big company can easily choose from whom to borrow. Now, as a company in a bank group gets bigger, two things happen. The group bank becomes less able and less willing, for reasons of financial prudence, to provide the growing company with most of its funds. At the same time, the company becomes attractive as a potential borrower to a number of outside banks. As the company borrows more from these outside banks, its relations with the group bank are attenuated.

Bank groups suffer, therefore, from an inherent defect, that the more successful their member companies are, the less likely they are to remain largely under the control of the central bank. Bank groups are also liable to be affected adversely by the government's recent policy of requiring banks to keep their loans to any one company below a certain proportion of the bank's capital. Since the capital of Japanese banks is small in relation to their loans, some banks will have to reduce their loans to favored customers and so risk losing influence over them. In the longer run, the coherence of bank groups is further threatened by the prospect that capital will no longer be in short supply, and that other sources of capital than the domestic banks—notably the stock exchange at home and banks and underwriters from abroad—will become relatively more important.

The last type of industrial group is formed around a large manufacturing company such as Hitachi, Nissan, or Toyota and consists of a constellation of subsidiaries, affiliates, and subcontractors. Table 14.3 shows details of some of the more important companies of the Matsushita Electric Industrial group.

Around the major company and each of the important affiliates and associates in a group like Matsushita there will be dozens, perhaps even hundreds, of smaller suppliers and sales companies, in which one or another of the Matsushita companies may have a shareholding. The group as a whole will present a clear example of both specialization and industrial gradation. Nearly every company will be engaged in a narrow range of activities, so that each will be dependent on the rest. At the same time, every company will have its place in a hierarchy, with the large, powerful, and stable leaders of the group at the top, and companies of decreasing size, stability, and efficiency arranged beneath them. The order will be maintained by subcontracting and the extension of credit.

Groups like this are formed by a combination of two processes. One is the conscription into the group of small companies which come to depend on large group members for their custom or their credit. The other is the hiving off of specialized divisions from the large companies at the center of the group. It is easy to see why Japanese firms establish subsidiaries. If the main firm is trying to diversify into a new business, then the creation of a subsidiary, a distinct and separate corporation in law, can have legal and administrative advantages. The establishment of a subsidiary may also be good for morale. It is easier to give loyalty to a separate small

Table 14.3. *Selected Companies Belonging to the Matsushita Group, 1976*

Company	Percentage of equity owned by MEI[a] in 1976	Annual sales (billion yen)	Business (pct. of sales)
LEADERS			
Matsushita Electric Industrial (MEI)	—	1,066	Radio equipment (46%), household electrical goods (36%)
Matsushita Electric Works	27.1%	266	Lighting and electrical installation (57%), materials (23%)
SUBSIDIARIES			
Matsushita Electric Trading	52.2	372	Export-import (100%)
Victor Company of Japan	51.1	110	Stereo, etc. (48%), TV (29%)
Matsushita Reiki	53.0	98	Refrigerators (68%), freezing equipment and air conditioners (17%)
Matsushita Communication	73.5	72	Communications equipment (21%), electronic equipment (21%), audiovisual equipment (27%), automobile equipment (31%)
Matsushita-Kotobuki	66.6	53	Electrical goods, especially heaters (75%)
Matsushita Seikō	52.5	45	Air conditioners and coolers (82%)
Kyushu Matsushita Electric	61.8	34	Radio equipment (55%), electrical engineering (25%)
ASSOCIATES			
National House[b]	33.3	35	Housing materials (69%), houses (15%), land (16%)
Fukuoka Paper	40.3	24	Corrugated board (83%)
Miyata Industries	45.0[c]	17	Bicycles (71%), fire extinguishers (21%)
Asahi National Lighting	22.1	10	Domestic lighting (87%)

SOURCE: Tōyō Keizai Shinposha, *Kaisha Shikihō* (Company Handbook), 1977 (1st quarter).
[a]MEI = Matsushita Electric Industrial; group companies have different year ends so that sales and shareholding figures are not strictly comparable.
[b]Matsushita Electric Works had as many shares as MEI in this company.
[c]Covers a 13-month period.

company, even if it is owned by another firm, than to the Fine Chemicals Division of a huge organization; it is more satisfactory to be a director of the former than assistant chief manager of the latter. These arguments apply in the West as much as in Japan, but in Japan there is the additional reason that people think it natural that a company should belong to one industry and desirable that it should have the homogeneous work force that specialization permits.

But why is a Japanese subsidiary given so much more latitude than a Western one, so that subsidiaries and parents form relatively loose industrial groups rather than centralized conglomerates? One important advantage is that the arrangement allows the parent company to be very flexible in its dealings with outside firms. Each ostensibly independent subsidiary or associate in a group can have a different set of relations with rival suppliers or trading partners, in a way that mere divisions of a large company cannot. The group as a whole can therefore distribute its patronage widely. The Matsushita companies, for example, rely on—or rather use, for the degree of dependence is low—a number of banks. Most call Sumitomo their main bank, but Reiki associates itself with Daiwa and Nippon Victor with the Industrial Bank of Japan. In this way, certain group companies can develop relations with the major rivals of Sumitomo, but without endangering the group's general commitment to that bank.

A second reason why parent companies give their subsidiaries, and particularly their successful subsidiaries, a considerable degree of freedom is in order to enable the subsidiaries to be listed on stock exchanges. Once a subsidiary is listed, the large number of its shares that are held by the parent company become much more freely negotiable. The parent company can sell some, and so reap the benefits of its diversification, but without necessarily relinquishing ultimate control over the subsidiary.

There is another reason why confederations consisting of parent and semi-independent subsidiary companies are so common in Japan. It is, however, a reason that applies less to the Matsushita group, which is outstandingly powerful and well-managed, than to certain others. This is that such confederations allow the managements of the large companies at their centers scope for smoothing over difficulties and concealing problems from the public.

What do the industrial groups of various types have in common? One feature shared by all is a sense of community. In the case of the new zaibatsu, the sense of community, the idea that certain companies with common origins ought still to be associated with each other, is the principal reason why there is a community at all. Even where the group hangs together for material reasons, the members of the group recognize that they are connected with each other and that the informed public is aware of the connection. A second feature of all the industrial groups is that they are hierarchically organized and that industrial gradation is evident in all of them. The new zaibatsu are led by vast firms like Mitsubishi Heavy Industries, financial institutions like Mitsubishi Bank, and trading companies; these exert their influence on lesser group members, and these in turn on numerous affiliates, subsidiaries, and subcontractors. In the bank groups, by definition, the bank leads the group. In the Matsushita-type federations, the large companies at the center provide not only business but also financial help for the smaller suppliers or sales agencies.

A third common feature is the degree to which member companies of groups are specialized. In the new zaibatsu and the industrial families, especially, each company will operate in its own field of business, partly so as not to compete and partly in order to do business with other group members. In the bank groups, it is true, the division of labor is less marked. In the Sanwa bank group, there are two major trading companies: Nisshō-Iwai and Nichimen. Even so, their strengths lie in different areas, the former in metal trading and engineering and the latter in textiles and foodstuffs.

The corollary of the idea that every company in an industrial grouping belongs to a particular industry is that belonging to the same industry is a common attribute of a number of rival companies from different industrial groupings. The managers of Japanese companies pay great attention to what is happening in the "other firms of the industry," and company enterprise unions take conditions in them as their main points of reference. There may well be institutional ties among the firms of an industry. Companies may belong to an industrial association and even engage in price-fixing or enter into a cartel under its auspices. The company unions may have corresponding institutional associations with their opposite numbers in rival companies; they may well belong to the same union federation. Thus, the managers and workers in a company like Mitsubishi Electric will keep an eye on what is going on in Toshiba, the equivalent company in the Mitsui group. Management will read about Toshiba's new extension to a factory in the specialist journals and perhaps hear gossip about it at the Japan Electrical Manufacturers' Association; the Mitsubishi Electric Union people will know through their union federation about the demands being made at Toshiba for extra overtime payments. The same division of labor, then, that provides a raison d'être for the industrial groupings in which companies find themselves, also gives scope for contacts and the exchange of information among companies of the various groups.

The fourth feature of industrial groups of all sorts is the way in which group members buy shares in each other as an expression of corporate relations. The constitutional and legal view of shareholders and shareholdings in Japan, as in the West, is that shareholders are the residual owners and ultimate controllers of a company through the board of directors whom they elect. It is a commonplace that, in Western industry, power has passed from the shareholder to the management of companies, but it is a commonplace with an element of confusion.

Commonly held large blocks of shares in individual companies can, from time to time, exert influence over their administration. This influence, however, is not exerted directly by the investing public, the beneficiaries of insurance and pension funds. Instead, it is exercised by professional managers. In one sense, the shareholders of individual companies have an element of control, but the important relations between shareholders and managers are really between different sets of managers. Power over industry as a whole has passed to a category of professional managers and away from the individual private investor, who either buys a few hundred shares directly or, more commonly, leaves his shares to be managed professionally.

In Japan, the rise of professional management teams and of institutional shareholders took place at the same time. After World War II, family holding companies were abolished so that managers became independent, but companies began to buy each other's shares. They did so, and still do so, for many reasons. One is to prevent foreign takeover bids, though the regulations hindering the inflow of foreign capital are so effective that there has never been a genuine need for mutual shareholding as a second line of defense. A more significant reason, perhaps, is that buying shares enables companies to provide for a rainy day. Shares once bought do not have to be revalued on the balance sheet, so that if they rise in real value over fifteen or twenty years, they come to constitute a "hidden asset." Such hidden assets can be pledged, and by mortgaging property with only a small book value, a company can secure a large loan. In harsh times they can be sold, and an apparently trivial disposal of book value assets will produce large revenues. Another reason for mutual shareholdings is that in Japan, unlike in Great Britain or the United States, shareholdings are widely publicized in, for example, company handbooks and popular magazines. Buying a company's shares is therefore a public affirmation of a relationship. Yet another reason is that by buying each other's shares companies can insulate each other from the stock exchange, which has still not shaken off its historical association with unhealthy speculation. In any event, the typical large Japanese company today will have ten or twenty important institutional shareholders, in which it in turn will hold shares. Unlike Western institutional shareholders, which invest largely for dividends and capital appreciation, Japanese industrial shareholders tend to be the company's business partners and associates; shareholding is the mere expression of their relationship, not the relationship itself. It is certainly an advantage of this arrangement that Japanese managements do not need to be afraid of the influence of shareholders interested only in short-term financial gains. But a major disadvantage is that company managements are—even more effectively than their Western counterparts—protected from having to deal with anyone outside a coterie of government officials and industrial and financial managers very like themselves.

A final point to be made about the three types of industrial groups is that the relations between companies within them frequently change. Bank groups are the most obviously susceptible to internal rearrangements, but in industrial families and zaibatsu, too, there are continual adjustments. Some companies find themselves doing more and more business outside the group, and so gradually weaken their constitutional and sentimental attachments to it. Other companies may fall into difficulties and have to be rescued by powerful group members. Such companies lose much of their independence and may become mere subordinates of the group leaders. Among the smaller companies attached to any group, there will be a great deal of movement, as new firms are recruited or old ones edge toward other groups or go bankrupt. It is this mutability of the relations between companies, the formation of and disengagement from alliances, and the gain and loss of independence that most conspicuously differentiates any of these groups from the centralized conglomerate.

15. A Statement Against Free Competition

Morozumi Yoshihiko

In the following selection, Ministry of International Trade and Industry (MITI) official Morozumi Yoshihiko outlines some of the reasons for Japan's support of a policy of "moderate concentration," or organized industrial cooperation. Morozumi made a number of such statements; this one dates from 1962.

The classic belief that the public welfare will be promoted by the invisible hand of free competition is held even today, but actually it is something else. Free competition provides neither the most suitable scale nor a guarantee of proper prices. Free competition means excessive equipment and low profits. In our country, the problem of excessive competition is being discussed. There are 64 Japanese trading companies in New York and 38 in Hong Kong. Fifty-three Japanese companies have entered into technical arrangements with RCA. Peabody and Company receives royalties from 17 Japanese companies on the Sanforizing process. Can one conclude from this that there is an "invisible hand" at work?

We must conclude that a policy of moderate concentration is a desirable thing, which will eliminate excessive competition and promote economies of scale. Increased concentration results in greater technical specialization and eliminates inefficient enterprises. By providing the conditions for workable competition, it will stabilize the rise in Japan's gross national product (GNP) and, especially, its exports. Free competition has a stifling effect on the economy. We must not allow it to be used in distributing the benefits of high growth—prices, wages, profits. If we have a problem in the suitable distribution of the economies of scale, we should correct it through public finance measures or the Fair Trade Commission. Our pressing, urgent business is the formation of a business system that will promote economic growth. [This statement was made in 1962, when growth of the GNP had averaged 15.6 percent per year for the previous three years.]

When the role of moderate concentration in the Japanese economy is being discussed, it is necessary to give consideration to developments in the division of labor, production specialization, equipment modernization, and operations of an efficient scale. There is an unstoppable trend taking place here. We cannot pause to theorize about the sort of influence that a policy of concentration will have. If our export strength is assured, the growth of our economy is assured.

From Eleanor M. Hadley, *Antitrust in Japan* (Princeton, N.J.: Princeton University Press, 1970), p. 397. Copyright © 1970 by Princeton University Press. By permission of the publisher.

16. The Closed Nature of Japanese Intercorporate Relations

Okumura Hiroshi

Japanese business is characterized by the strong cohesion of its corporate groups. In this article, which appeared in *Japan Echo* in 1982, Okumura Hiroshi suggests that these intercorporate relationships allow Japanese companies to assume a regulatory role that is played elsewhere by governments.

Transactions between Japanese companies are large in number, tend to be one-way in the vertical direction but reciprocal in the horizontal direction, and evolve into permanent ties. Such a situation has come about because strong cohesion in various forms prevails within the corporate groups. Intercorporate transactions first became numerous because companies had cohesive ties, and then these ties became even more cohesive through the high frequency of intercorporate dealing. The strengthening of cohesion is a natural result of the effort to stabilize the high volume of intercorporate transactions, although the question of whether this cohesion should be legally condoned is an entirely different matter.

Stockholdings, interlocking directorates, and group-controlled financing are among the tools by which cohesion is maintained. In particular, the holding of one company's stock by other companies plays a central role. Because rules governing the holding of stock are loose, banks and other corporate entities own more than 60 percent of the combined stock of the firms listed on Japan's stock exchanges. Whereas antitrust laws in the United States prohibit commercial banks from holding stock in other companies, Japan's Antimonopoly Law puts restraints on such possession of stock but does not outlaw it altogether. And whereas United States antitrust laws severely limit the types of stocks a corporation can acquire, the corresponding provisions in the Japanese Antimonopoly Law have been removed through amendments, throwing stock acquisition wide open.

In the United States, the takeover of one company by another is, as everybody knows, an everyday affair. Antitrust regulations are in force to limit this phenomenon, but they can be skirted by acquiring companies in different lines of business, as a result of which conglomerate-style diversification has become rampant. In Japan, by contrast, outright takeover in the American fashion is virtually unknown, and mergers are unusual even among large firms.

The main cause of this difference lies in the stock-securing maneuvers that Japanese companies execute. Each company extends to the companies it deals with a

From Hiroshi Okumura, "The Closed Nature of Japanese Intercorporate Relations," *Japan Echo*, vol. 9, no. 3 (1982), pp. 59–61. By permission of the publisher.

block of shares of a sufficient size to frustrate outside intervention. Because this form of intercorporate cohesion has progressed to an advanced degree, takeover bids are thwarted from the outset. The role of the merger in the American context is played in Japan by intercorporate links via stock possession.

Since the Japanese antimonopoly regulations now in force are based on American theories of industrial organization, they focus on market share. Antimonopoly guidelines are therefore strict with regard to mergers that could lead to a dominant market share but lax with regard to intercorporate cohesion through group formation. This renders antimonopoly surveillance ineffective. Only haphazard restraints have been placed on group-based control of distribution and unfair business practices, because little attention has been paid to intercorporate dealing.

Liberalization of Japanese trade took place from around 1955 through the first half of the 1960's; liberalization of capital transactions then got under way, lasting through the first half of the 1970's. In the beginning, business leaders, government representatives, and the mass media issued frantic warnings about both these programs: "Unrestricted imports will flood the Japanese market," they clamored. "Japanese companies will be gobbled up by foreign capital." Of course, nothing like that happened. Now the opposite refrain is being heard: "The excellence of Japanese companies has enabled them to weather trade and capital liberalization unharmed."

The crisis mongers undeniably assisted the response to trade decontrol by rousing workers to come to the aid of their companies, leading to improved productivity and product quality. But what of the warnings about capital decontrol? The government implemented a series of liberalization steps as scheduled, but foreign firms did not thereupon set out to absorb Japanese firms. Although the amended Securities and Exchange Law introduced a system of public stock offering, paving the way for American-style takeover bids, only one case of a takeover has occurred—the acquisition of the stock of an auto-component maker by Bendix Corporation of the United States. This was not, moreover, a true takeover in the American sense of the term.

As it turned out, while the government went about the liberalization of capital, Japanese companies were busily implementing their own plans for keeping foreign capital out by means of stock-securing maneuvers. These involved the placement of a large bloc of the stock issued by one company in the hands of other companies—typically its bank and leading partners. The companies thus entrusted with stock did not accept it merely because they were asked to. They became stockholders to enhance intercorporate cohesion and to bind the group together more firmly. The main reason almost no Japanese companies have been absorbed by foreign capital is that each corporate group met the capital liberalization program with its own stock-defense program.

It is to be cautioned that the intercorporate relations we have been considering here do not lead ipso facto to an absence of competition in the Japanese market. On the contrary, different firms in the same field of business compete fiercely to increase their market share and raise their ranking. But these firms have strong connections in other business fields. When it comes to deals between corporate buyers and sellers, competition through the market mechanism does not take place. Of course, if the terms of a deal are too unfavorable, a firm may indeed switch partners, but usually the mere threat to take business elsewhere leads to a resolution of the problem.

With these close links among companies as a foundation, corporate executives become joined in relations of mutual confidence, leading to the formation of a close-knit business community. Since the various segments of this community exchange confidences and derive support from each other, they become even more closed to the outside. The government as well, from its vantage point at the top, undertakes "administrative guidance" in conformity with the business community's logic. While, on the one hand, it decontrols capital transactions, on the other hand, the government assists the counteroffensive by encouraging stock-securing manipulation. And whenever it sniffs a takeover bid in the wind, it quickly comes to the rescue through administrative guidance. When Americans refer to "Japan, Inc.," this is what they are talking about.

The distinctive relations binding Japanese companies together are a cause of trade friction and also a barrier to the liberalization of capital. Of course, peculiar intercorporate relations are not confined to Japan; every country has its own brand of business ties. But since company-to-company transactions are relatively more numerous in Japan and cohesion in the business world is especially powerful and multifarious, the intercorporate ties of this country stand out more than the ties in the United States and elsewhere. With the growing intensity of trade disputes in the increasingly harsh external environment, an understanding of these relations will throw light on problems both at home and abroad.

17. Japan's Subcontractors: The Buck Stops Here

Japanese business appears to consist of large industrial firms, but much of the actual work of these firms is performed by small subcontractors. Parent companies can pass on problems arising from market and monetary fluctuations to their subsidiaries. This article, which appeared in *Focus Japan* in 1978, describes the advantages and disadvantages of such a system.

Behind Japan's great industrial firms stands a loyal legion of "independent" subcontractors without whose assistance Japanese big businesses would flounder and sink. Japanese automakers, for instance, have become the world's top auto exporters only with the support of thousands of subcontractors which supply them with parts. A single large automaker typically deals with as many as 170 primary subcontractors, which in turn consign parts manufacturing to 4,700 secondary

From "Japan's Subcontractors: The Buck Stops Here," *Focus Japan*, Sept. 1978, pp. 10–11. By permission of the Japan External Trade Organization, JETRO.

subcontractors. The secondary concerns enlist the help of 31,600 tertiary subcontractors even further removed from the parent automaker. Manufacturers in other industries also benefit from using subcontractors to share the burden of parts manufacture and assembly. Subcontractors are not cast in any fixed roles, and some are even trying to loosen the bonds with their parent company by developing new product lines. The majority, however, seem content to continue their symbiotic relationship with contractors, despite the fact that it is the subcontractors which are bearing the lion's share of the task of coping with the sharply appreciating yen.

Of the 814,000 manufacturing companies operating in Japan in 1975, 60.4 percent were subcontractors (firms doing work on consignment), according to the governmental Small and Medium Enterprise Agency. As of 1977, each of the manufacturing firms listed on any one of the nation's three stock exchanges used an average of 68 subcontractors, with the manufacturer's orders amounting to 17 percent of the value of the subcontractor's total shipments. The importance of subcontractors is especially great in industries where diverse parts, processing, and a high level of technology are required, such as in the general machinery, electrical machinery, motor vehicle, and precision machinery industries. In these four industries, leading manufacturers each deal with more than 90 subcontractors, with each manufacturer's orders amounting to at least 21 percent of the total shipment value.

For contractors, farming out parts manufacture to subcontractors has definite advantages. Large firms have experienced a great deal of difficulty in cutting labor costs, since many of their employees are hired under a lifetime employment system. The yen's sharp rise has therefore forced large firms to pass the burden for trimming costs onto their subcontractors, which have lower labor costs and can lay off workers when necessary. Subcontractors usually get the short end of the stick, since contractors not only cut back orders when economic conditions are unfavorable, but also deal with the appreciating yen by "asking" subcontractors to reduce the price of parts in order to keep dollar prices low. Subcontractors usually comply with these demands, since the parent firm's logic is mercilessly persuasive: if exports slow down, so do orders to subcontractors. A study conducted by the Tokyo Metropolitan Government in February 1978 revealed that of all the firms in Tokyo which used subcontractors, 45 percent had either negotiated price reductions or cut back their orders because of the yen spiral.

Despite the pressure, few subcontractors have gone under because of the yen's rising value. In fact, only 100 manufacturing firms in Japan have gone bankrupt for reasons directly related to the yen's steep rise in value. Subcontractors have been able to keep afloat, according to one official at the Tokyo Chamber of Commerce and Industry, "because, like the big firms at the top, they too can pass the buck—to their own subcontractors. Eventually the little guy at the bottom, often a housewife or a retired worker, is the one who 'gets the ax.'"

The Individual Bears the Brunt

Subcontracting firms vary widely in size. At the top of the scale are firms with a few hundred employees which deal with dozens of secondary subcontractors. At the other end are individuals working in their homes on a part-time basis. The average firm, however, is small, with more than 70 percent of subcontractors having 10 or fewer employees and only 10 percent employing more than 20 workers. One large subcontractor in Nagano Prefecture represents a typical pattern. This firm, which produces variable resistors for television and stereo manufacturers, employs about one hundred workers—80 percent of whom are housewives from nearby farming communities who work on a part-time basis. The firm also consigns manufacture of some products to six smaller subcontracting firms. In line with common practice, it also leases labor-saving assembly machines to these companies. The six firms, which together produce nearly half of the primary subcontractor's shipment value, each have from 10 to 30 employees and also consign manual jobs to another 50 housewives who work in their homes. These housewives are the first to lose their jobs when the demand for televisions and stereos drops. But since many work only to supplement the main household income, unemployment causes less serious consequences than when the main household income is cut off.

According to the Labor Ministry, the total number of households where at least one member was working on a subcontracting basis at home was 1.4 million in 1977 (about 4 percent of all Japanese households). Many household subcontractors are engaged in apparel (sewing, lacing, darting), textiles (weaving, knitting), mechanical assembly (assembling parts for electrical appliances, etc.), and sundry assembly work (dolls, toys, artificial flowers, and fireworks). Of these four main types of household subcontractors, 93 percent are women, who earn a mere 244 yen per hour, in contrast to the 1,239 yen of an average full-time employee in the manufacturing sector. Home-based subcontracting, however, does enable women with young children to contribute to the household income. Two to three million more individuals would take on part-time work at home if jobs were available, the Labor Ministry estimates.

Hard Times

The yen spiral and the resulting pressure on exporters to trim costs have made the going tough for many subcontractors, and some report harsh treatment by parent companies. Subcontractors in both hard chrome and cast iron manufacturing have complained to the Fair Trade Commission that contractors are forcing unreasonably low order prices by taking advantage of the fierce competition among subcontractors. In the textile industry, the situation deteriorated to the point that, earlier this year, the Fair Trade Commission of Japan had to order textile contractors to cease unfair price cutbacks and arbitrary refusals of products ordered. But those who have the roughest time making a go of subcontracting are home-based subcontractors. The number of home-based subcontractors dropped 4.4 percent last year from the previous year, the fourth annual decline. The number of complaints about delinquent payments has also risen sharply; during the period from March to September 1977, complaints received by the Labor Ministry tripled to more than 2,000 cases per month.

And these grievances are not unfounded. Though the Subcontracting Law requires complete payment within 60 days after delivery, the law also permits payment by bill. According to the Association of Tokyo Credit Associations, contracting companies in Tokyo in December of last year made 23 percent of their payments in notes cashable an average 120 days after the date of issue. However, some firms issued notes requiring delays of up to six months or even a year. In addition, the Fair Trade Commission and the government believe from the complaints they have received that subcontractors also suffer unjust product rejections, default on contract prices, and other heavy-handed treatment by parent firms. Subcontractors are urged to file complaints, but the majority remain silent, apparently out of fear of retaliation.

A recent survey by the Small and Medium Enterprise Agency revealed that a large number of subcontractors (32 percent) wish to lessen their dependence on a single parent firm by trying to develop new product lines. But an even larger percentage of those polled (45 percent) are completely satisfied with the present relationship with their parent company and seek no changes. Apparently, for this group the security of a steady flow of orders from a parent company makes up for slipping profitability. Access to the machinery and materials of the parent company is also a major drawing card for subcontractors. But even more important for most is the independence of running their own businesses. Of those who operate subcontracting firms, an estimated two-thirds were at one time employees in a similar line of work but say that they have changed positions because "running your own business gives you much more room for creativity." Though subcontractors are bearing the brunt of Japanese industry's attempt to cope with the rising yen, most have no intention of giving up their independent, dependent businesses.

18. Small Business in Japan

Robert C. Wood

Large manufacturing concerns occupy a position of prominence in Japan, but their share of Japanese manufacturing is less than 50 percent of value added. Robert C. Wood argues in this 1981 article, taken from the *Christian Science Monitor*, that government support of small businesses has virtually eliminated poverty in Japan and aided large businesses as well. Wood, a writer and business consultant, is the author of *Why the Japanese Grow Richer and We Don't*.

The United States has largely ignored Japan's way of aiding its lower classes, and Japan's results suggest that the United States has been making a mistake. But because Japan's approach is cheap and relies heavily on business—small business—it may appeal to the Reagan administration. Since at least the mid-1950's, the Japanese have emphasized helping small business to aid the poor and the lower middle class. And during that time they have virtually eradicated poverty. The

From Robert C. Wood, "Strength of Small Businesses in Japan Aids Lower Class," *Christian Science Monitor*, Jan. 7, 1981, p. 11. By permission of the author.

lower classes tend to depend on small business for jobs in every country. Because workers in large companies have power and their bosses tend to pay them better than do small companies, big companies generally automate more and pick and choose more among applicants. The gap between workers in big and small companies has been especially dramatic in Japan, where big companies are run largely for employees. Large Japanese companies almost exclusively hire new school graduates, leaving other workers little hope of entering.

Thus, about twenty-five years ago the Japanese decided that nothing they could do for their lower classes would help more than effective aid for small business. The more vigorous were the small businesses, the thinking went, the more they could pay their employees and the more money they could offer people who needed jobs. Today, all of Japan's political parties—including the Communists—portray themselves as small business's best friend. The Japanese system is designed to ensure that every small business wanting to borrow money gets a careful analysis from a loan officer. More than 1,000 private lenders are especially chartered to serve small business, and an array of government-operated finance agencies employs some of the nation's most talented bureaucrats. From 1955 to 1977, long-term lending to small business in Japan increased more than 200 percent.

The government also aids industrial associations that sponsor seminars, research, and reports for small business and funds 558 local research institutes that serve them. Though Japanese pollution and safety regulations have been strong enough to reduce emissions and accidents more than America's, Japan's environmental agency and Labor Ministry have been careful to administer them with sensitivity to small business. Special loan programs help small businesses pay for mandated changes.

Other programs discourage bigness in small business's traditional fields, though these may find it harder to administer programs that aid small companies directly. A man who wants to open a supermarket in an old Japanese neighborhood, for instance, not only must comply with zoning regulations and building codes, but also must negotiate directly with small neighborhood merchants angered by the threat of low prices. A college professor assigned to mediate may force him to reduce his store's size or hours. This obviously may hurt consumers, but it does protect jobs in small stores. Japanese small business also benefits from the practice of subcontracting, where smaller firms perform many nonmanufacturing functions in and around the factories of large companies. Unions at the big companies often encourage subcontracting to lower-wage companies because they know subcontracting increases profits, permitting increased wages. And subcontractors can be let go in recessions, increasing job security for workers at the big companies.

All this results in a vast small business labor market that provides decent jobs for nearly 80 percent of Japan's private labor force. Compared with the United States, where small manufacturing businesses benefit from few of the rules that protect small retailers and where the share of small business has declined sharply over the last generation, the share of small business in Japan has risen. All 3,000 manufacturers that Japanese statistics count as "large" have about the same share of Japan's manufacturing as the largest 200 manufacturers alone do in America—about 45 percent of value added.

The strength of small business means Japanese can find jobs fairly easily. The Reverend Iwao Masu, a Christian minister who works with derelicts in Yokohama, says he could readily find a job paying perhaps 200,000 yen a month for any healthy man who wanted one. Japan's unemployment rate rarely rises above 2 percent, and a study by the Organization for Economic Cooperation and Development found that the poorest 20 percent of Japanese received a share of the nation's income about 50 percent larger than the share received by the poorest 20 percent of Americans. Japan's experience suggests the United States can help its poor without spending more or making its economy less efficient. The poor's most important need is for jobs to get them out of poverty. Americans—like Japanese—probably produce better jobs when their industrial leaders and bureaucrats understand and remember the special problems of small business.

19. Japan's New Bankruptcies

Gary R. Saxonhouse

From 1968 to 1978, Japanese bankruptcies increased at an astonishing rate. Gary R. Saxonhouse argues in this article, which is drawn from a 1979 issue of the *Journal of Japanese Studies*, that bankruptcies occurring at the end of this period were not only more numerous than those occurring at the beginning; they were also different in both cause and effect. Saxonhouse teaches economics at the University of Michigan.

Even as the corporate net worth ratio was making an unprecedented improvement in 1977, Japanese bankruptcies were reaching a record high. This is not surprising, given the diverse performance of Japanese industries. Record profits in 1977 for some industries went hand in hand with more than 18,000 Japanese bankruptcies. In contrast, there were fewer than 800 bankruptcies in 1977 in the United States. The liabilities of Japanese corporate failures in 1977 were more than $16 billion. At a little more than $3 billion, the liabilities of American corporate failures in 1977 were less than 20 percent of this amount. Again in 1977, more than 18,000 Japanese bankruptcies occurred in a population of 1,400,000 corporations. The bankruptcy rate was a very high 1.31 percent. The American bankruptcy rate was one-quarter as large!

As the Japanese economy has weakened in past recessions, the number of bankruptcies has gone up substantially. Similarly, when financial conditions have ameliorated, the number of bankruptcies has declined. What is unusual about the present recession is that until spring 1978, even though the Japanese bank rate had been cut eight times after mid-1975 and financial opportunities for enterprises had improved, the number of bankruptcies went right on increasing. This is no doubt

From Gary R. Saxonhouse, "Industrial Restructuring in Japan," *Journal of Japanese Studies*, vol. 5, no. 2 (Summer 1979), pp. 289–320. Copyright © 1979 Society for Japanese Studies. By permission of the author and the publisher.

partly the result of the depth and length of the current recession. In part, it is also the result of structural changes being required of an economy where familiar rates of expansion have slowed dramatically.

The number of bankruptcies increased in all manufacturing industries between 1973 and 1977, especially in textiles, wood products, and shipbuilding. The scale of individual bankruptcies also increased. For example, in 1977, 28 Japanese firms, each with more than $50 million in liabilities, went bankrupt. This is a 400 percent increase in the number of firms of this size going bankrupt since 1974. In 1978, with the Eidai Plywood Group collapse, Japan experienced its second $1 billion bankruptcy.

With a new structural situation facing the Japanese economy, and with an increasing number of bankruptcies, the consequences of these bankruptcies have been changing. In 1968, only 37 percent of the companies going bankrupt actually stopped operations. In 1968, in contrast to 1977, many of the companies went bankrupt as a result of temporary critical conditions. In 1977, structural causes were a more prominent cause and, more often than not, no hope was held out for the ultimate recovery of the firm. Even for the minority of firms that did continue in business in 1977, more drastic steps were needed than in 1968. In 1968, temporary suspension of credit was the most prominent means of getting a bankrupt enterprise on its feet. In 1977, suspension of credit remained prominent, of course, but reducing the size of the enterprise, cutting the labor force, and selling off assets, which were measures of a structural character, came to assume equal prominence. Almost as interesting is the increasing use of enterprise ownership's private assets during reorganization.

The increasing incidence of bankrupt firms ceasing operations entirely or undergoing drastic restructuring has posed special problems for employees of these enterprises. Of the 49 percent of the bankrupt firms continuing operations, more than 80 percent reduced their labor force after bankruptcy. Indeed, almost half of those companies reduced their labor forces by more than 50 percent.

Workers laid off in this way and workers losing their jobs because their bankrupt firms had ceased operations entirely have had an increasingly difficult time securing new jobs within a reasonable period of time (less than six months). The number of bankrupt firms of which less than 50 percent of their employees could find new jobs has been steadily increasing. Given that at least one attractive portion of the Japanese labor market, i.e., employment at large companies, is in all likelihood closed to the employees of bankrupt companies, and given the precipitous drop in new employment during the past few years, such a result is hardly surprising.

Since there are a record-breaking number of bankruptcies in Japan, since the rate of bankruptcy in Japan is four to five times that of the United States, and since the average bankruptcy in Japan involves a firm with twice the liabilities of the average bankrupt firm in the United States, what is one to think of "Japan, Inc."? Clearly, whatever the substance of relations between government-business and bank groups is, it is not able to prevent all Japanese bankruptcies. There have been many famous bank and government rescues of ailing companies in Japan (Tōyō Kōgyō, Yamaichi Securities), just as there have been famous rescues in the United States (Lockheed and Chrysler). There have also been enormous corporate collapses in both countries (Kojin and Eidai in Japan, Penn Central in the United States). It is plain for all to see that the higher debt-to-equity ratio in Japan does, in fact, subject Japanese corporations to greater risks of bankruptcy. With about one-third the net worth ratio of American corporations, Japanese corporations suffer bankruptcy five times as frequently.

20. Goodwill and the Spirit of Market Capitalism

Ronald Dore

In this essay, British sociologist Ronald Dore examines the role of goodwill, or obligated relational contracting, in Japanese business. He suggests that contrary to the theories of many Western economists, goodwill contributes to rather than detracts from the smooth and profitable functioning of the market. Dore is the author of *Flexible Rigidities: Industrial Policy and Structural Adjustment in the Japanese Economy, 1970–1980*. This essay was originally delivered in 1983 as the Hobhouse Memorial Lecture.

Why have large factories given way to the coordinated production of specialized family units in segments of the Japanese textile industry? One reason is the predominance of "obligated relational contracting" in Japanese business. Consumer goods markets are highly competitive in Japan, but trade in intermediates (unfinished items), by contrast, is for the most part conducted within long-term trading relations in which goodwill give-and-take is expected to temper the pursuit of self-interest.

Cultural preferences explain the *unusual* predominance of these relations in Japan, but they are in fact more common in Western economies than textbooks usually recognize. The recent growth of relational contracting (in labor markets especially) is, indeed, at the root of the "rigidities" supposedly responsible for contemporary stagflation. (That is, by instituting job, wage, and cost of living guarantees, for example, we have made our labor markets less efficient.) Japan shows that to sweep away these rigidities and give markets back their pristine vigor is not the only prescription for a cure of stagflation. The Japanese economy more than adequately compensates for the loss of allocative efficiency by achieving high levels of other kinds of efficiency—in many respects thanks to, rather than in spite of, relational contracting. We would do well to be more concerned about those kinds of efficiency, too.

One of the economists' favorite Adam Smith quotations is the last passage in the *Wealth of Nations*, in which he sets out one of his basic premises. "It is not from the benevolence of the butcher, the brewer, and the baker that we expect our

From Ronald Dore, "Goodwill and the Spirit of Market Capitalism," *The British Journal of Sociology*, vol. 34, no. 4 (1983), pp. 459–81. Published by Routledge and Kegan Paul. By permission of the publisher.

dinner, but from their regard to their own interest. We address ourselves, not to their humanity, but to their self-love, and never talk to them of our necessities but of their advantages." I wish to question that sharp opposition between benevolence and self-interest. Perhaps, so that he should be alert for signs of possible bias, the reader should be warned that a prolonged soaking in the writings of Japanese eighteenth- and nineteenth-century Confucians at an early age has left me with a soft spot for the virtue of benevolence, even a tendency to bristle when anyone too much disparages it. At any rate, I wish to argue, apropos of benevolence, or goodwill, that there is rather more of it about than we sometimes allow, further that to recognize the fact might help in the impossible task of trying to run an efficient economy and a decent society.

My title refers to goodwill rather than benevolence because benevolence, in my Confucian book, though not I think in Adam Smith's, is something shown in relations between unequals, by superior to inferior, the reciprocal of which is usually called loyalty. Goodwill is more status-neutral, more an expression of Leonard Trelawney Hobhouse's "principle of mutuality." And it is that broader meaning which I intend. A formal definition of my subject might be: the sentiments of friendship and the sense of diffuse personal obligation that accrue between individuals engaged in recurring contractual economic exchange.

I have been caused to ponder the role of goodwill in economic life by the recent experience of studying the organization of the textile industry, or to be more precise, the weaving segment of it, in Great Britain and Japan. One place I visited in the course of that research was the small town of Nishiwaki in western Japan, whose industry is almost wholly devoted to the weaving of ginghams, chiefly for export to Hong Kong to be made up into garments for Americans to wear when square dancing in the Middle West. This is an area where hand-loom weaving goes back some centuries. Power looms came in in the late nineteenth century, and they brought with them the factory system as they did everywhere else. Twenty-five years ago, although many small weaving establishments had survived, the bulk of the output was accounted for by larger mills, many of which were part of vertically integrated enterprises with their own cotton-importing, spinning, and finishing establishments.

By 1980, however, the picture had changed. The larger mills had closed. The integrated firms had retreated to their original base in spinning. Small operations survived, however, in large numbers. The key family business was that of the merchant-converter, who contracted with the spinning company to turn its yarn into a certain type of cloth at a given contract price. The converter would send the yarn to another small family concern specializing in yarn dyeing; then it would go on to a specialist beamer, who would wind it onto the warp beams in the desired pattern and also put the warp through the sizing process. Then it would be delivered to the weaver, who might do his own weft preparation and the drawing in (putting the harness on the beams ready for the looms) or might use other family businesses—contract winders or drawers in—for the process. And so on, to the finishers who did the bleaching or texturizing or overprinting.

What is the reason for this fragmentation? What changes in Japanese society and the Japanese economy account for what, by most orthodox notions of the evolution of modern economies, would count as a regression—the replacement of a system of production coordination within a vertically integrated firm by a system of production coordination between a large number of fragmented small firms; the replacement, to use Oliver Williamson's terms, of coordination through hierarchy by coordination through the market?

The reason the dominant trend in the West seems to be away from coordination through the market toward coordination through the hierarchy of a vertically integrated firm lies, as Williamson never tires of telling us, in the transaction costs entailed, the costs arising from the imperfections of markets with small numbers of buyers and sellers, in which bargaining transactions are made difficult by what the jargon calls "impacted information." These features so enhance the bargaining power of each party that, when there are no significant economies of scale to be gained by their mutual independence, one party (usually the stronger one) buys out the other to put a stop to his "opportunism" (rapid response not only to price signals—which of course is always admirable—but also to information about vulnerable weaknesses of the other party). Here is another of those timeless generalizations about "capitalist economies" about which Japan gives pause. Transaction costs for large Japanese firms may well be lower than elsewhere. "Opportunism" may be a lesser danger in Japan because of the explicit encouragement and actual prevalence in the Japanese economy of what one might call moralized trading relationships of mutual goodwill.

The stability of the relationship is the key. Both sides recognize an obligation to try to maintain it. If a finisher re-equips his plant with a new and more efficient dyeing process that gives him a cost advantage and the opportunity of offering discounts on the going contract price, he does not immediately get all the business. He may win business from one or two converters if they have some *other* reason for being dissatisfied with their own finisher. But the more common consequence is that the other merchant-converters go to their finishers and say: "Look how X got his price down. We hope you can do the same because we really would have to reconsider our position if the price difference goes on for months. If you need bank financing to get the new type of vat, we can probably help by guaranteeing the loan."

It is a system, to use a distinction common in the Williamson school, of relational contracting rather than spot contracting—or to use Williamson's more recent phrase, "obligational contracting." It is more like a marriage than a one-night stand, as Robert Solow has said about the modern employment relation. The rules of chastity vary. As is commonly the case, for those at the lower end of the scale, monogamy is the rule. A weaver with a couple of dozen automatic looms in a back garden shed will usually weave for only one converter, so that there should be no dispute about prior rights to the fruits of his looms—no clash of loyalties.

As in nearly all systems of marriage, divorce also happens. That is why I said that a finisher with a cost advantage could attract other converters who happen to be dissatisfied with their finisher for other reasons. When I use the analogy of divorce, I mean traditional divorce in obligation-conscious societies, rather than the "Sorry, I like someone else better; let's be friends" divorce of modern California. That is to say, the break usually involves recriminations and some bitterness, because it usually has to be justified by accusing the partner of some failure of goodwill, some lack of benevolence—or, as the Japanese phrase is more often translated, "lack of sincerity." It is not enough that some external circumstances keep his prices high.

But how on earth, the economist will want to know, do the prices and ordered quantities get fixed? The answer seems to be that, once established, prices can be renegotiated at the initiative of either party on the grounds of cost changes affecting either party, or changes in the competitive conditions in the final market in which the branch cloth is sold. There are also fringe spot markets for cotton yarn and gray cloth, and the prices ruling in these markets and reported in the daily textile press provide guides. To further complicate the issue, there is some collective bargaining. The basic principles on which these price and quantity negotiations rest appear to be threefold. First, that the losses of the bad times and the gains of the good times should be shared. Second, that in recognition of the hierarchical nature of the relationship, a fair sharing of a fall in the market may well involve the weaker weaver suffering more than the converter—by having his profits squeezed harder. But, third, the stronger should not use his bargaining superiority in recession times and the competition between his weavers to drive them over, or even to, the edge of bankruptcy.

It is in the interpretation of these principles, of course, that ambiguity enters. Benevolence all too easily shades into exploitation when the divorce option, the option of breaking off the relationship, is more costlessly available to one party than to the other. There is even an officially sponsored Association for the Promotion of the Modernization of Trading Relations in the Textile Industry in Japan, which urges the use of written rather than verbal contracts in these relationships, and which is devoted to strengthening moral constraints on what it calls the abuse—but which our economic textbooks would presumably call the legitimate full use—of market power. As for the nature of such abuse, surveys conducted by the association show that suppliers with verbal contracts are more likely to have goods returned for quality deficiencies than those with proper written contracts. Weavers will wryly remark that returns become strangely more common when the price is falling (and a rejected lot contracted at a higher price can be replaced by a newly contracted cheaper lot).

That pattern is repeated in many other areas of the Japanese economy—between, for example, an automobile firm like Toyota and its subcontractors. Here, again, the obligations of the relationship are unequal; the subcontractor has to show more earnest goodwill, more "sincerity," to keep its orders than the parent company does to keep its supplies. But at the same time, the obligation is not entirely one-sided, and it does limit the extent to which the parent company can, for example, end its contracts with a subcontractor in a recession in order to bring the work into its own factory and keep its own work force employed.

These relations are not confined to the hierarchical case. Even between firms of relatively equal strength, the same forms of obligated relational contracting exist. Competition between Japanese firms is intense, but only in markets that are (a) consumer markets and (b) expanding. In consumer markets that are not expanding, cartelization sets in rather rapidly, but that is a different story which does not concern us here. What does concern us here are markets in producers' goods, in intermediates. And for many such commodities, markets can hardly be said to exist. Take steel, for instance, and one of its major uses, for automobiles. The seven car firms buy their steel through trading companies, each from two or three of the major steel companies, in proportions that vary little from year to year. Prices in this market are set by the annual contract between the champions, Toyota on the one side and New Japan Steel on the other.

It is the concentration of such relationships that is the dominant characteristic of the famous large enterprise groups, known to Japanese as *gurūpu* and to foreigners usually as *zaibatsu* or *keiretsu*.

But the main raison d'être of these groups is as networks of preferential, stable, obligated *bilateral* trading relationships, networks of relational contracting. They are not conglomerates because they have no central board or holding company. They are not cartels because they are all in diverse lines of business. Each group has a bank and a trading company, a steel firm, an automobile firm, a major chemical firm, a shipbuilding and plant engineering firm, and so on—and, except by awkward accident, not more than one of each (the "one set" principle, as the Japanese say). Hence, trade in producer goods within the group can be brisk. To extend earlier analogies, it is a bit like an extended family grouping, where business is kept as much as possible within the family, and a certain degree of give-and-take is expected to modify the adversarial pursuit of market advantage—a willingness, say, to pay more than the market price for a while to help one's trading partner out of deep trouble.

How does one explain the difference between Japan and other capitalist economies? Williamson has "theorized" these "obligational relationships" and explained the circumstances in which they will occur: when the extent to which the commodities traded are idiosyncratically specific (such that the economies of scale can be as easily appropriated by buyer or by seller), and the extent to which either party has invested in equipment or specialized knowledge for the trading relationship is not quite such that vertical integration makes sense, but almost so. He also asserts that in such relationships, quantity adjustments will be preferred to price adjustments, and price adjustments will be pegged to objective exogenous indicators (though he allows, in passing, for the not very "relevant" or "interesting" possibility that "ad hoc price relief" might be given as an act of kindness by one party to the other). Perhaps Williamson has evidence that that is the way it is in America, and the fact that his argument is couched in the terms of a timeless generalization merely reflects the tendency of American economists to write as if all the world were America. Or perhaps he does not have much evidence about America either, and just assumes that "Man" is a hard-nosed, short-run, profit maximizer, suspicious of everyone he deals with, and allows everything else to follow from that. At any rate, Williamson's account does not provide the tools for explaining the difference between the Japanese and the British or American economies.

Clearly, we have to look elsewhere for an explanation. Try as one might to avoid terms like "national character" in favor of the scientific pretensions of, say, "modal behavioral dispositions," it is clearly national differences in value preferences, or dispositions to action, with which we are concerned.

One possible explanation is that the Japanese are generally oriented toward the long-term future. At this moment, for example, the Industrial Structure Council of Japan's Ministry of International Trade and Industry is already composing what it calls a "vision" of the shape of the world economy in the mid-1990's. The economist is likely to seize on this explanation with relief, because it will allow him to ignore all dangerous thoughts about benevolence and accommodate the relational contracting phenomenon in the conventional microeconomics of risk aversion and low time discounts. Any sacrifice of short-run market advantage is just an insurance premium for more long-term gains. He would find some good evidence. Nakatani Isao has recently done an interesting calculation comparing 42 large firms inside one of the large kinship groupings like Mitsui and Mitsubishi that I have just described and a matched sample of 42 loners. The loners had higher average profit levels and higher growth rates in the 1970's. But they also had a considerably higher dispersal around the means. The group firms were much more homogeneous in growth and profit levels. What went on in the groups, he concluded, was an overall sacrifice of efficiency in the interests of risk-sharing and greater equality.

Relational contracts, in this interpretation, are just a way of trading off the short-term loss involved in sacrificing a price advantage for the insurance that, one day, you can call in the same type of help from your trading partner if you are in trouble yourself. It is a calculation that perhaps comes naturally to a population that, until recently, was predominantly living in tightly nucleated hamlet communities in a land ravished by earthquakes and typhoons. Traditionally, you pitched in to help your neighbor rebuild his house after a fire, even though it might be two or three generations before yours was burnt down and your grandson needed the help returned.

But you could be sure that the help would be returned. And this is where we come back to Adam Smith. The Japanese, despite what their political leaders say at summit conferences about the glories of free enterprise in the Free World, and despite the fact that a British publisher with a new book about Adam Smith can expect to sell half the edition in Japan, have never really caught up with Adam Smith. They have never actually managed to bring themselves to believe in the invisible hand. They have always insisted—and teach in their schools and in their "how to succeed" books of popular morality—that the butcher and the baker and the brewer need to be benevolent as well as self-interested. They need to be able to take some personal pleasure in the satisfaction of the diners quite over and above any expectation of future orders. It is not just that benevolence is the best policy, much as we say, rather more minimally, that honesty is the best policy. They do not doubt that it is, that it is not a matter of being played for a sucker, but is actually the best way to material success. But that is not what they most commonly say. They most commonly say: benevolence is a duty. Full stop. It is that sense of duty, a duty over and above the terms of written contracts, that gives the assurance of the payoff which makes relational contracting viable.

Perhaps one should not overdraw the contrast, however, in view of the fact that the Japanese, who stand out among other capitalist societies for their addition to relational contracts, also stand out as the nation whose businessmen and trade unionists seem to have a more lively sense of their obligated membership in the national community than those of other nations. Japan has fewer free-rider problems in the management of the national economy; patriotism seems to supplement profit-seeking more substantially in, say, the search for export markets. Perhaps the common syndrome is a generalized dutifulness, or to put it in negative form, a relatively low level of individualistic self-assertion. I am reminded of the Japanese scholar and publicist, Nitobe Inazō. In his lectures in the United States in the 1930's, he used to tell the national character story about the international competition for an essay about the elephant. In his version, the Japanese entry was entitled "The Duties and Domestication of the Elephant."

But it seems to me that there is a third element of the Japanese preference for relational contracting besides risk-sharing and long-term advantage on the one hand, and dutifulness on the other. People born and brought up in Japanese society do not much like openly adversarial bargaining relationships, which are inevitably low-trust relationships, because information is hoarded for bargaining advantage and each tries to manipulate the responses of the other in his own interest. Poker is not a favorite Japanese game. Most Japanese feel more comfortable in high-trust relations of friendly give-and-take, in which each side recognizes that he also has some stake in the satisfaction of the other.

The discussion so far has centered on markets in intermediates and capital goods and on relational contracting between enterprises. So far, I have not mentioned labor markets, though the predominance of relational contracting in Japanese labor markets is, of course, much more widely known than its predominance in interfirm trading. By now, every television viewer has heard of the lifetime commitment pattern—the transformation of the employment contract from a short-term spot contract agreement to provide specific services for a specific wage (terminable by one week's or one month's notice on either side) into a long-term commitment to serve as needs may dictate from time to time, with wages negotiated according to criteria of fairness that have precious little to do with any notion of a market rate for the job. The contract is seen, in fact, less as any kind of bilateral bargain than as an act of admission to an enterprise community, wherein benevolence, goodwill, and sincerity are explicitly expected to temper the pursuit of self-interest. The parallel between relational contracting in the intermediates market and such contracting in the labor market is obvious. There can be little doubt that the same cultural values explain the preferred patterns in both fields.

But anyone looking at the competitive strength of the Japanese economy today must also wonder whether this institutionalization of relational contracting, in addition to serving the values of risk-sharing, security, dutifulness, and friendliness, also is conducive to a fourth valued end—namely, economic efficiency. Any economist, at least any economist worth his neoclassical salt, would be likely to scoff at the idea. Just think, he would say, of the market imperfections, of the misallocation and loss of efficiency involved. Think how many inefficient producers are kept out of the bankruptcy courts by all this give-and-take at the expense of the consuming public. Think of the additional barriers to entry against new, more efficient producers.

The Japanese economy is riddled with misallocation. Much of the international dispute about nontariff barriers, for example, has its origin in relational contracting. Take the market for steel mentioned earlier. Brazil and Korea can now land some kinds of steel in Japan more cheaply than Japanese producers can supply it. But very little Brazilian or Korean steel is sold there. Japan can remain pure as the driven snow in GATT (General Agreement on Tariffs and Trade) terms—no trigger prices, minimal tariffs, no quotas—and still have a kind of natural immunity to steel imports. None of the major trading companies would touch Brazilian or Korean steel, especially now that things are going so badly for their customers, the Japanese steel companies. Small importers are willing to handle modest lots. But they will insist on their being landed at backwater warehouses, away from any shipping point for domestic steel, so that the incoming steel is not seen by a Japanese steel company employee. If it were seen, the trucks carrying the imported steel might be followed to their destination, and the purchaser, if he turned out to be a disloyal customer, would be marked down for less than friendly treatment next time a boom brings a seller's market. What distortions, an economist would say. What a conspiracy against the consumer! What a welfare loss involved in sacrificing the benefits of comparative advantage! If the Japanese economy has a good growth record, that can only be despite relational contracting and the consequent loss of efficiency.

And yet there are some good reasons for thinking that it might be because of, not in spite of, relational contracting that Japan has a better growth performance than the rest of us. There is undoubtedly a loss of allocative efficiency. But the countervailing forces that more than outweigh that loss can also be traced to relational contracting. Those countervailing forces are those that are conducive not to allocative efficiency, but to what Harvey Leibenstein calls X-efficiency—the abilities to plan and program, to cooperate without bitchiness in production, to avoid waste of time or materials—capacities that Leibenstein tries systematically to resolve into the constituent elements of selective degrees of rationality and of effort.

To take the case of employment and the lifetime commitment first, the compensatory advantages that go with the disadvantage of inflexible wage costs are reasonably well known. In a career-employment system, people accept that they have to be learning new jobs continually; there can be great flexibility. It makes more sense for firms to invest in training, and the organization is generally more likely to be a learning environment open to new ideas. If a firm's market is declining, it is less likely to respond simply by cutting costs to keep profits up; it is more likely to search desperately for new product lines to keep busy the workers it is committed to employing anyway. Hence a strong growth dynamism will prevail.

As for relational contracting between enterprises, there are three things to be said. First, the relative security of such relations encourages investment in supplying firms. The spread of robots has been especially rapid in Japan's engineering subcontracting firms in recent years, for example. Second, the relationships of trust and mutual dependence make for a more rapid flow of information. In the textile industry, for instance, news of impending changes in final consumer markets is passed more rapidly upstream to weavers and yarn dyers; technical information about the appropriate sizing or finishing for new chemical fibers is passed down more systematically from the fiber firms to the beamers and dyers. Third, a by-product of the system is a general emphasis on quality. What holds the relation together is the sense of mutual obligation. The butcher shows his benevolence by never taking advantage of the fact that the customer doesn't know rump from sirloin. If one side fails to live up to the relational contract ethic, it may be difficult to ditch a supplier because, for circumstances for the moment beyond his control, he is not giving you the best buy. It is perfectly proper to ditch him if he is not giving the best buy and not even trying to match the best buy. The single most obvious indicator of effort is product quality. A supplier who consistently fails to meet quality requirements is in danger of losing even an established relational contract. I know that even sociologists should beware of anecdotal evidence, but single incidents can often illustrate national norms, and I make no apology for offering two:

1. The manager of an automobile parts supply firm said that it was not uncommon for him to be rung up at home in the middle of the night by the night-shift supervisor of the car factory sixty miles away. He might be told that they had already found two defective parts in the latest batch, and unless he could get someone over by dawn, they were sorry, but they'd have to send the whole lot back. And he would then have to find a foreman whom he could rouse and send off into the night.

2. The manager of a pump firm walking me around his factory explains that it is difficult to diagnose defects in the pump castings before machining, though the founders are often aware when things might have gone wrong. "I suspect," he said cheerfully, "that our supplier keeps a little pile of defective castings in the corner of his workshop, and when he's got a good batch that he thinks could stand a bit of rubbish, he throws one or two in."

I leave the reader to guess which is the Japanese and which is the British story.

Another hypothesis emerges: that relational contracting is a phenomenon of affluence, a product, Hobhouse would say, of moral evolution. It is when people become better off and the marketplace haggle gives way to the world of *which*, where best buys are defined more by quality than by price criteria, that relational contracting comes into its own. It does so for two reasons. First, because quality assurance has to depend more on trust. You always know whether the butcher is charging you sixpence or sevenpence. But if you don't know the difference between sirloin and rump, and you think your guests might, then you have to trust your butcher; you have to depend on his benevolence. Also, I suspect, when affluence reduces price pressures, any tendencies to prefer a relationship of friendly stability to the poker-game pleasures of adversarial bargaining, tendencies that might formerly have been suppressed by the anxious concern not to lose a precious penny, are able to assert themselves. Japan's difference from Britain, then, is explained both by the fact that the cultural preferences and suppressed tendencies are stronger, and by the fact that price pressures have been reduced by a much more rapid arrival at affluence, and consequently a greater subjective sense of affluence.

Economists have occasionally noted these trends but have generally treated them as market imperfections, basically lag problems of the long and the short run; in their view, habit always succumbs to the pursuit of profit in the end. And among imperfection problems they have found them less interesting to analyze than other kinds, such as monopoly. Those bold souls among them who have taken abroad the new phenomenon of stagflation and tried to explain the tendency for contraction in demand to lead to a contraction in output, not a fall in price, to increased unemployment but only slow, delayed, and hesitant deceleration in the rate of wage increase, have rarely recognized the importance of a general growth in relational contracting—of the implications for the effectiveness of fiscal and monetary regulators of the fact that more and more deals are being set by criteria of fairness, not by market power. More commonly, they speak of the growth of oligopoly on the one hand, and of trade union monopoly consequent on statutory job protection and higher welfare benefits on the other. They have explained stagflation, in other words, not as the result of creeping benevolence—the diffusion of goodwill and mutual consideration through the economy—but as the result of creeping malevolence, increasing abuse of monopoly power. And the cure that our modern believers in the supreme virtues of the market have for these "rigidities" is a deflation stiff enough to restore the discipline of market forces, to make firms competitive again and force the inefficient out of business, to weaken trade union monopolies and get firms hiring and firing according to their real needs.

But if we think of Japan, a society that has far more developed forms of relational contracting than ours and glories in it, yet nonetheless achieves high growth and technical progress, we might think of a different prescription.

It would run something like this. First, recognize that the growth of relational contracting can provide a very real enhancement of the quality of life. Not many of us who work in a tenured job in the academic career market, for example, would relish a switch to freelance status. I hear few academics offering to surrender their basic salary for the freedom to negotiate their own price for every lecture, or even demanding personally negotiated annual salaries in exchange for tenure and incremental scales. And if you overhear a weaving mill manager on the telephone, in a relaxed and friendly joking negotiation with one of his longstanding customers, you may well wonder how much more than the modest profits he expects would be required to tempt him into the more impersonal cut and thrust of keen auction-market competition.

The second point in the prescription is this. Having recognized that relational contracting is something we cannot expect to go away, and that inevitably a lot of allocative efficiency is going to be lost, try to achieve the advantages of X-efficiency that can compensate for the loss.

Part III: The Company Pattern

C O M P A N I E S are complex entities that are not only made up of many constituent contributors (investors, managers, workers, banks, unions), but depend on managerial strategies for the effective use of technology, human resources, money, marketing skills, and so forth. The ways these are combined in relationship to an evolving competitive environment determine success or failure and establish the levels of risk and return that encourage or discourage investment, and, ultimately, economic growth. In the abstract, the possible combinations and permutations of inputs and strategies making up a company are almost unlimited, but as the following readings indicate, two overriding influences have generated considerable uniformity in the patterns of corporate organization in Japan— namely, market factors and organizational inclinations. Both have produced a company pattern different enough from Western formulas to raise great comparative interest, especially as Japanese companies have emerged as major competitors in world markets.

To understand the interplay of market and organizational factors it helps to adopt a historical perspective. Specifically, at formative times companies create solutions to problems (e.g., capital or labor shortages or labor unrest) that then become institutionalized; that is, they become basic to the corporate formula. Thereafter, even when the old problems give way to new ones, the institutionalized framework, its deep structure, changes rather slowly. In other words, a company's pattern is the product of past problem-solving efforts as well as a response to problems in its immediate environment. One example is company training, which today is universally admired as a strong point of Japanese management. If we look back we see that most Japanese organizations began extensive internal training at a time when they could not fully rely on the education system. The result in this case was felicitous, but historical legacies have resulted in contradictions even within companies recognized as the most efficient in their industries. Certainly, permanent employment is a mixed blessing, and, in an aging population, seniority pay systems are increasingly burdensome. Untangling the historical contributions of culture, organizational legacies, and market influences is an analytic challenge that can only begin with the readings assembled here.

The selections that follow offer many separate perspectives on what is important about Japanese management. If one were to ask these authors, for example, to rank order the significance of financial or personnel or manufacturing strategies in explaining the competitive strength of Japanese management, they would certainly disagree. Yet, they all see distinctively Japanese qualities as important to grasp if we are to comprehend the company framework and on that basis to explain Japan's economic dynamism. The reader is encouraged to note here, in conjunction with the readings in Part II, the sources of flexibility and inflexibility in the system, the ways risks and rewards are allocated and competition and cooperation are structured. The case study of Mazda's escape from bankruptcy should help sharpen these insights.

We know from the Chrysler episode of 1979–80 that high drama ensues when politicians, bankers, labor leaders, and the government all get in the act. There is no fixed scenario for the rescue of large companies in any nation, but action is called for and the ad hoc way self-interests and common interests are joined is inevitably fascinating, for it tells us much about the fundamental commitments, philosophies, and needs of all the parties. A cautionary note: recently, several large companies have been allowed to collapse before being reconstituted, indicating that rescue is no foregone conclusion in Japan.

The following selections focus on the large firm, where permanent employment and postwar prosperity have combined to create what some regard as a distinctively Japanese emphasis on the company as a social community. Included in this pattern are such things as a recognition of common interests and mutual loyalties, heavy socialization and involvement, seniority-based careers and rewards, and enterprise unionism. The interplay of community values and economic rationality induces both managerial tension and much creativity, not to mention eternal academic debate. The reader should not forget, however, that only about one-fourth of Japan's labor force enjoys permanent employment. Smaller firms have different adaptive strategies, and women who leave large firms for marriage or childrearing lose their seniority and permanent status.

21. The Company as Family: Historical Background

Rodney Clark

It is frequently said that Japanese companies are patterned on the family system. In this essay, which is drawn from *The Japanese Company* (1979), anthropologist Rodney Clark traces the historical development of familism as an ideological concept in prewar Japan. He argues that modern labor practices are not actually a continuation of traditional Tokugawa methods, as has been suggested, but a natural development out of Meiji and Taishō labor conditions.

There is an interesting comparison to be made between management ideologies in Japan and America before the war. In Japan, from the very beginning of industrial growth, Confucianism and nationalism made management a collective and ostensibly altruistic activity. The individualistic, profit-motivated entrepreneur had existed in the early Meiji period, probably existed in the 1920's (and certainly exists today), but he did not have the full approval of the community. In the United States, too, by the 1920's, managers were coming to see themselves as harmonious movers of men. But in America, the cooperative management ideology was new and represented a major change from the previous notions of the businessman agonist, the inventor-entrepreneur, and the self-evidently superior victor against the commercial odds, which had held sway in the 1890's and 1900's. Though in America the individual entrepreneur was by 1920 ceasing to dominate business in practice, his robust ideals lived on to reprove timid and temporizing corporate officials. In Japan, there could be unqualified approval for the hard-working, stable, gregarious, sociologically self-conscious fledgling manager, fresh from his law or commerce course. In America, even today, memories of pristine individualism unsettle the collective ideal.

A similar ethic of harmony and cooperation, though of a more factitious kind, pervades the story of the second important development of company personnel policies during the prewar period, the establishment of "familism." There have now been a number of accounts of the rise of familism, many of them designed to refute the suggestion that paternalistic labor practices in modern Japanese companies are a continuation of traditional employment methods. It will only be necessary, therefore, to tell the tale briefly here.

From Rodney Clark, *The Japanese Company* (New Haven, Conn.: Yale University Press, 1979), pp. 37–41. Copyright © 1979 by Rodney Clark. By permission of the publisher.

Between 1868 and 1890, Japan was essentially an agricultural country with one major manufacturing industry: textiles. Cotton spinning and silk reeling, though vital in their contribution to the exports that financed the purchase of foreign machinery and payment for foreign technical advice, constituted only a small part of the national product and employed a tiny fraction of the labor force. A great deal of the production in these industries took place in family workshops. Those establishments big enough and sufficiently well organized to be called factories rarely employed more than thirty or forty workers, so that it was nearly always the case that employees and employers knew each other personally. An overwhelming proportion of the textile workers were women, usually young women brought in from country areas, lured by the prospect of making a little money for themselves or their families before they returned to their villages to marry. Frequently, recruitment took place by agreement between the factory's representatives or agents and family heads and village elders. In these circumstances, where industry was a minority pursuit, where the units of organization were small, where continuity existed between the society of the factory and that of the village, and where the authority of the managers, older, male, and urban, over the workers, young, female, and rural, was so thoroughly in keeping with dispositions in society at large, there was no pressing need for industrialists to justify their prerogatives or plan systematic employment policies.

A number of events occurred between 1890 and 1920 to alter this state of affairs and force employers to develop ideas and practices to support their positions and justify their authority. By the turn of the century, factories were troubled by labor shortages and increases in labor mobility. New industries which employed men rather than subservient young girls came to the fore. The first steps toward the formation of labor unions began to be taken. Throughout the period, there continued to be a campaign for the enactment and then enforcement of labor legislation.

The labor shortage in the textile factories resulted largely from a growing awareness among the peasantry of the often hideous conditions that existed in them and a reluctance to go to factories or to stay in them. Some employers tried to solve the problem by agreeing to restrict competition for workers, but the only sure solution was to make employment conditions more satisfactory. Since so many of the employees were young farm girls, it was quite natural for employers to offer them benefits such as housing, food, and classes in Japanese accomplishments, reconstituting in an industrial setting the kind of paternalism that the girls might have experienced if they had been engaged for domestic service by a village landlord.

In the metal-working and engineering industries, which grew in importance from about 1900, the employees were men and were therefore rather more difficult to control. Skilled workers, who were always in short supply, would frequently move from firm to firm, causing the disruption of work schedules in every factory they left. Employers in these industries were forced to abandon daily wages and to offer their workers the prospects of a career, with better jobs and higher pay after an appropriate length of service, and welfare schemes and profit-related bonuses as further inducements to stay.

If the exigencies of the labor market forced firms to behave in a paternalistic manner, the appearance of labor unions and the controversy over labor legislation challenged managers to produce a coherent defense of their place in industrial society. Spasmodic labor unrest had occurred from the very beginning of the Meiji period, with riots at the notorious mine at Takashima and strikes in textile factories. The frequently appalling conditions in Japanese factories offered every incentive for the development of unions, but they did not come into being until after the Sino-Japanese War of 1894. The government was unsympathetic to them. The Peace Preservation Law of 1900 placed unions in a legal limbo. They were not specifically proscribed, but they were rendered unable to act legally.

The campaign for factory legislation reached its peak at about the time when the first labor unions were forming and being subjected to government harassment. In the story of the factory laws, however, the government and the bureaucracy appear more as heroes than villains. Indeed, the bureaucrats were almost the sole proponents of the laws, the infant labor movement doing surprisingly little to further their establishment. The motives of the bureaucrats were various, but one of them was to improve Japan's standing in the world, for from as early as 1878 the Japanese government had been aware that firms in the West showed care and solicitude for the well-being of their workers.

The rise of the union movement and the imminence of labor legislation evoked a range of similar reactions among industrialists. A few gave more or less limited approval to the new developments. Others professed to welcome them in principle but argued that it was too early to allow them full practical expression, usually because having unions and labor laws would cost industry too much money and make Japanese business uncompetitive. But a common reaction was to assert that the unique circumstances of Japan made Western imports like unions and labor laws unnecessary. In Japan, the relations between managers and employees and between capital and labor were essentially harmonious. Employees loved their masters, just as they had always done, and masters preserved their traditionally benevolent attitudes toward those who worked for them. Industry was pervaded by a spirit (to which unions and laws would surely prove inimical) of mutual understanding, peace, and solicitude, so much so that it was possible to assimilate the factory to the family.

The idea of familism, the epitome of Japanese uniqueness, arose with apparent naturalness out of the circumstances of the time and was, for that reason, a powerfully persuasive doctrine. The metaphor of the family, besides harking back to Tokugawa tradition, was perfectly adapted to interpret employment practices forced on employers by the labor market. The notion of firm-as-family was also consistent with one of the central political concepts of the Meiji period, a concept widely supposed to have remote historical antecedents, but one which was in fact a new garment of old threads: that the Japanese nation itself was a gigantic family with the emperor at its head. Such a well-connected and plausible doctrine as familism, therefore, was able to assert itself over the brash and contentious theories that might have proceeded from some obvious facts: that there were enormous differences in the way managers and workers were treated, that industrial relations were sometimes very bad, or that fraud and speculation were endemic on the stock exchanges. In Japanese industry today, one hears rather less of the particular analogy with the family, largely because the Japanese family itself has changed and no longer constitutes a simple pattern for conduct. There remains, however, an influential ideal of harmony and cooperation in relations among employees and between employees and their firms.

22. Economic Realities and Enterprise Strategies

Peter F. Drucker

A major difference between Japanese and Western businesses can be found in their underlying strategies. Peter F. Drucker argues in this essay that Japanese business strategies—little emphasis on maximizing profit, reliance on outside trading companies, concern with maximizing volume—are rational responses to economic realities that have developed in Japan since the time of the Meiji Restoration.

A great many books and papers have been published in the last few years pointing out, especially to the Western businessman, the differences between the way business is conducted in Japan and in the West. There have been discussions of Japanese personnel policies, of the decision-making process in Japanese business, and of the relationship between business and government. But the area in which Japanese management seems to differ most in behavior from what Western executives are wont to take for granted is the area of business strategy.

Japanese business does not, it seems, put great stress on maximizing profit. Japanese business enterprise also aims at maximizing volume. Increased sales, rather than increased profits, seem to be the first objective. The Western company, American and European, that enters into a joint venture with a Japanese company, invariably reports receipt of a most comprehensive sales plan from its Japanese partner. But rarely does the Japanese partner seem to pay much attention to the profit planning that the Westerner has come to regard as the necessary foundation of rational business strategy.

An understanding of such basic differences in business strategy should contribute greatly to our understanding of Japan and of the Japanese economy, the nature of cultural differences, and the economists' "theory of the firm" that is our model of microeconomics and of economic behavior. The Japanese have built and are running exceedingly successful businesses, yet their basic business strategy not only violates everything a Western executive "knows," but it is incompatible with the economists' (including the Japanese economists') theories of economic behavior and of microeconomics.

It is the thesis of this paper that the business strategy of Japanese enterprise, while indeed different from that of American or European business, is not "mysterious" or "nonrational" or "culturally conditioned." It optimizes, in perfectly rational fashion, the specific structural realities in which Japanese businesses operate, especially those of banking and capital markets and those of wage system and wage structure. These structural realities, in turn, are not the result of Japanese tradition or of Japanese values. They are of recent origin—mid-Meiji at the

From Peter F. Drucker, "Economic Realities and Enterprise Strategies," in Ezra Vogel, ed., *Modern Japanese Organizations and Decision Making* (Berkeley: University of California Press, 1975), pp. 228–44. © 1975 The Regents of the University of California. By permission of the publisher.

earliest. When introduced, they were genuine innovations and not adaptations of new tasks to old institutions or old traditions.

Capital Market, Banking Structure, and the Role of Profit

There is evidence that the Japanese business enterprise puts profits much lower on its scale of values than any Western enterprise. By any of the conventional measurements, the profitability of the Japanese business enterprise appears low. Measured, for instance, as percentage of sales, the most widely used measurement of profitability and profitability objective, Japanese business enterprises, especially large businesses, perform at a much lower rate of profitability than enterprises in similar lines of business in the United States or in Europe. And yet it is also clear that the Japanese economy operates at a higher rate of profit than any Western economy. Japan has, ever since the Meiji period, managed to run its economy at a phenomenally high rate of savings and investments measured as a percentage of total gross national product. This would not be possible unless profits—a major, if not the major, component of capital formation—were consistently very high.

The explanation for this apparent paradox lies in the structure of the Japanese banking system and capital market. As the result primarily of a historical accident—the ascendancy of Iwasaki Yatarō, the founder of Mitsubishi, during the formative years of Japan's modern economy—"profit" is not what the business enterprise shows as such. The profit that matters to the economy is what the banks return, especially the *zaibatsu* (giant economic combine) banks that finance the zaibatsu industries. In the early Meiji years, when Japan started to build her modern economy, banking was already seen as central to economic development. Fukuzawa Yukichi (1835–1901) stressed the need to develop a banking system in his very early writings. And the most brilliant of the young economic leaders in early Meiji government, Shibusawa Eiichi (1840–1931), resigned from one of the most powerful positions in the Finance Ministry at the age of thirty-four to become a banker and thus to serve his nation more productively and forcefully than he could even as a powerful civil servant and government leader.

At that time, the model of banking that dominated the developed world was the English banking system. Fukuzawa Yukichi focused on it in his writing. The early banks, started around 1870, were meant to be joint-stock banks on the English model. But this model of what Americans call the "commercial" bank was not suitable for Japan. The English banking system had been developed before the Industrial Revolution. It was a child of the Commercial Revolution of the late-seventeenth and early-eighteenth centuries and focused on trade, not industry. When industry developed almost a century later, it developed essentially outside the banking structure and without the benefit of the banking structure. Banking remained focused on the commercial, the trading transaction. The English capital market and, following it, the American capital market grew up almost entirely outside the banking system and contributed venture capital directly to local industry.

At the time of early Meiji, a second banking model was being designed. The continental European model, which has become known as the "universal bank," was a deposit bank, unlike the English merchant bank. Its purpose was entrepreneurship: to find and finance industry and to provide venture capital. The aim was to nurse an infant enterprise to the point where its securities would become marketable. At that point the bank would sell off part of its holdings in the enterprise at a substantial capital gain and recoup its investment. The bank, however, would retain sufficient stake in the enterprise to assure for itself the firm's commercial banking business. It would continue to have a controlling voice, since the private investors, with whom the bank had placed the shares of the enterprise, would continue to hold their shares in the custody of the bank and vote their shares through the bank.

This universal bank was the model Japan needed, and the founder of Japanese banking, Shibusawa Eiichi, clearly had this model in mind. Indeed, as a young man shortly before the Meiji Restoration, Shibusawa had spent a year mostly in France—where the idea of the universal bank had originated—and it is highly probable that it was this experience that impressed him with the importance of both banking and business.

The bank that Shibusawa Eiichi founded as Japan's universal bank, the Dai-Ichi Bank, did eventually, within the last few years, become Japan's largest bank. Yet Japanese banking did not follow Shibusawa's logical line, and the reason is one man: Iwasaki Yatarō. Unlike Shibusawa, Iwasaki believed in profit maximization. He also believed strongly that it was unsound to sell shares of enterprises to the general public; an enterprise had to be controlled completely by one man. He grudgingly accepted the need for incorporation, but he made sure that control would remain vested totally in the family head and that the shares owned by other members of the family would be held in what, in effect, was a family voting trust, with the head of the house exercising voting power. As for nonfamily outsiders holding shares, this appeared to him to make management impossible. Iwasaki Yatarō also saw banking as central, as, indeed, any intelligent observer of 1870 Japan must have done. But his idea of a bank was an institution to attract capital for investment in the industries and businesses of the Mitsubishi zaibatsu in such form that the public would in no way acquire title of ownership or control. The public would come in as depositors and not as investors.

As a result, Japanese industry is financed primarily by what legally are bank loans. Economically, most of this money is equity capital. It is not invested in the equity form, however, but in the form of short-term indebtedness. Consequently, Japanese business is legally financed to only about 20 percent of its total investment by equity, that is, by common shares; 80 percent of the investment is in the form of loans. In the United States, the proportion is almost the exact opposite: 30 percent indebtedness and 70 percent equity. On the Continent, the proportion of equity is slightly lower in a large company than it is in the United States, but it rarely falls below 50 percent or so of total capital employment. Where most of the nonequity portion of Japanese capital is in the form of short-term bank loans, the continental European business tends to rely heavily on long-term bonds held by outside investors. In other words, the proportion of money in the form of bank loans is probably no higher in Europe than in the United States and may well be smaller.

The form of financing makes very little difference regarding the total return on the invested capital with which a business has to operate. The cost of capital is remarkably similar, especially in the period since World War II with its international and highly mobile capital market. It can be said that, for the period 1950 to 1970, all business enterprises of any size, whether American, continental European, British, or Japanese, have had to earn 12 percent or so pretax income on total capital invested to earn the cost of capital.

Because of the different structure of banking and capital markets, the strategy needed to earn the cost of capital is totally different in the three areas. A Japanese business must earn enough money to pay the interest on what is legally a bank loan but economically is equity investment in business and industry. The profit in the Japanese economy, the return on venture capital, is essentially the difference between what it costs a Japanese bank to attract and hold deposits and the interest it charges for the loans to industry. Therefore, Japanese banks have traditionally kept interest rates on deposits exceedingly low—in effect nothing. The interest they charge their industrial customers, on the other hand, is rather high and runs at least one-third, if not one-half, above interest rates charged for truly commercial loans. This is, of course, completely legitimate considering that most are not truly commercial loans and therefore include a much larger risk premium. As long as the interest on these loans is secure, the bank is satisfied. Business earnings over and above what is needed to cover the interest charge with a fair safety margin are of no benefit to the bank. The bank's income is fixed, and it therefore exerts little pressure on its customers to increase earnings over and above the interest required.

There is also little reason for the Japanese business executive to try to increase earnings on that fairly small portion of his total capital that is in the form of common shares and legal equity. By old tradition, which is only now beginning to change, companies can only issue additional shares at par value. They cannot, as in the centuries-old Anglo-American business tradition, issue shares at their market value even if the market value is many times the original-issue value. A Japanese business does not acquire the capacity to obtain capital at more advantageous cost if its share price goes up. In effect, successful Japanese enterprises issue new shares as a form of stock dividend, a distribution of earnings, and not as a way to obtain new capital at advantageous cost.

The Japanese business manager, therefore, has little incentive to increase earnings above what is needed to cover the bank's interest charges and earn a modest return on the shares outstanding in the hands of the public—which itself is a post–World War II innovation for the zaibatsu companies. Although his minimum profitability is high for interest charges, this needs qualification. Since legally his profit is paid out as interest on debts, the tax collector does not consider it profit but a deductible business expense. Insofar as the tax is a tax on corporation profits rather than a tax on the consumer as most economists would contend, the Japanese businessman has a decided advantage over his Western competitors. Increasing profits also does not make it possible for him to decrease his dependence on the bank and increase the amount of equity capital he can raise outside in the growing capital market. The tradition that forces him to offer new shares at par shuts this escape hatch.

From the point of view of the Japanese business executive, however, faced as he is by the high cost of the capital on which he depends, minimizing the cost of capital is the most rational business objective. Maximizing profit makes no sense to him: there is no benefit to his company and, incidentally, with stock options being practically unknown in Japanese management, no benefit to him personally. But minimizing the cost of capital—that is, trying to operate the business with the very minimum of borrowed money—is indeed a major rational business objective. His business strategy, therefore, focuses on profit only to the extent to which it represents a minimum requirement. That minimum is quite high by Western standards. It is nonsense to say that the Japanese executive is not profit-conscious. But he is not profit-minded in the sense that profit is an objective. It is a necessity; minimizing the cost of capital is the objective.

The profitability level of the economy is dictated by objective forces, especially by the objective need of an economy for capital. For this reason, the profitability of the Japanese economy—an economy developing from a low base, with poor natural resources, and with a conscious policy of not depending on capital from abroad—has to be very high. And it has been high except during periods of severe economic depression like the early 1920's or the 1930's. But because the true venture capital of the Japanese economy is not investments of the public in equity or even investments of banks in equity but bank loans, the individual Japanese business enterprise does not base its strategy on profit maximization. To do so would be economically irrational. Instead, it bases its strategy on minimizing the cost of capital.

Productivity and the Maximization of Volume

Even if the Japanese business does not aim at profit maximization, it seems to be obsessed by volume. Larger sales, rather than larger profits, are clearly the first objective.

In the West, sales are of course important. And growth, as such, has been seen as good in itself again and again. But the periods in which growth was the most important objective of business have always been few and far between in the West: the 1830's, the 1870's, the 1920's, and the 1960's. Of course, economists and businessmen in the West know of the "economics of scale," but their approach to volume essentially tries to balance the advantages of larger sales against costs and risks. This does not appear to be the typical Japanese attitude. Volume comes first, and questions about its cost come long after, if at all.

Such behavior is completely rational within the structure of the Japanese wage system, which affords automatic increases with seniority and job security until retirement age. But neither Japanese nor Westerners seem conscious of the implications of the Japanese wage system for productivity and for the impact of volume on business results. If wages go up automatically with length of service and independently of job or skill, and if employees have to be kept on the payroll until retirement, then raising volume is the only way to increase productivity rapidly. Not to raise volume is a prescription for rapidly falling productivity and loss of competitive position. Since, by and large, employees in Japan can be hired only for an entrance position (the only significant exceptions have been senior civil servants who move into top management positions in business upon their retirement from government service at age fifty-five), the only way to accommodate expansion of volume is by hiring new people into the entrance grades.

As many students of Japanese organizations have stressed, this practice creates substantial problems. It makes it particularly difficult for a new business to grow fast, which in turn explains in some measure the advantage of a joint venture for a new business. In a joint venture, the established partner can furnish experienced managers, foremen, and skilled workers to a new enterprise, which otherwise would have to staff itself entirely with inexperienced people just entering a career.

The advantages to the Japanese wage system have rarely been considered. Since the beginner is traditionally paid a fraction of what the mature and experienced man receives for the same work, and since most workers, especially rank-and-file, produce pretty much the same regardless of length of service, rapid expansion means that the persons brought in to do the additional work cost only a fraction of what the employees already at work cost, and what the employees doing the same work for the competition cost. Their productivity per man-hour may be somewhat lower than that of experienced employees, though the difference is not particularly great in most routine jobs. But the productivity per unit of wages is as much as three times that of the man who has been on the payroll for twenty-five or thirty years. The business that can expand faster than its competitors, therefore, has a tremendous, almost an unbeatable, advantage in labor costs and productivity. Conversely, with automatic increases in wages with length of service, the business that cannot increase its volume very rapidly finds itself losing productivity.

The objective of maximizing volume, therefore, is completely rational, given Japanese economic realities. In fact, it is the only rational strategy in the situation. The Japanese executive can assume, with considerable probability, that his profitability and his economic results will not be endangered by rapid volume increase even if prices decrease. In other words, he does not need to worry as long as the price he receives covers his present expenses. He knows that the true cost of the additional production is likely to be much lower. In the economist's terms, he knows that incremental revenue pricing, in which the additional volume does not have to cover anything but out-of-pocket expenses, is almost certain to be adequate to prevent a loss and, in fact, obtain a profit.

This is in marked contrast to the position of his Western colleague, who pays primarily for the job rather than for length of service. There, the fact that the new employee is likely to be less productive than the experienced man while still, especially in unionized businesses, receiving the same, or almost the same, wage as the man with seniority on the job, means that additional volume has to produce significantly greater returns to be profitable. This does not rule out incremental revenue pricing, but does limit it to capital-intensive industries, in which capital assets are not adequately utilized. In the Japanese situation, no such limitations apply. Under the Japanese system, labor is, in effect, a capital expenditure and one in which, contrary to all other capital expenses, the fixed charge increases as the "investment" gets older.

Indeed, the much-vaunted rapid increase of Japanese productivity since 1950 represents in substantial part, perhaps as much as half, nonrecurrent shifts in the labor force rather than genuine productivity increases. Japan, during the last twenty years, has been able to move into its modern sector—its large-scale manufacturing and service firms—enormous numbers of young people receiving very low salaries in relation to the average salary. This was the result in part of the tremendous shift of young people from the farm to the city and in part of the short but fairly sharp baby boom Japan underwent in the early 1950's. As a result, Japan went through a period in which the ratio of young employees, whether blue collar, clerks, or managerial (middle school, high school, or university graduates) was unusually high. And while their wages went up very fast, the wage pyramid was highly biased toward the youngest, that is, the cheapest, category and toward the categories with the highest productivity per unit of wages. Since these employees also were very well educated compared with their predecessors, they might well be assumed to have had higher productivity altogether, or at least not to be less productive despite their lack of experience.

This period is at an end. The Japanese birthrate dropped precipitously in the mid-1950's, which means that from now on the number of young men entering the labor force each year will be significantly lower than it was in the 1960's. At the same time, the movement of young, well-educated people from the farm to the city is essentially over (except, perhaps, for young women finishing middle school). In other words, the tremendous availability of young people—those of high productivity per unit of wage—is likely to be replaced by a relative scarcity of young workers in all categories.

23. Allocation of Labor and Capital in Japan and the United States

Imai Ken'ichi and Itami Hiroyuki

This essay, by theoretical economists Imai Ken'ichi and Itami Hiroyuki, examines the widely divergent directions in which Japanese and American business practices have developed. Imai and Itami suggest that differences in labor and capital allocation patterns have led to an entire network of differences in the character of the economic and corporate systems in the two countries.

The Japanese internal labor market and the American internal capital market and their concomitant characteristics shape the different patterns of corporate growth and diversification in the two countries. An oversimplified generalization would be as follows: the Japanese strategy is human-resources-driven, the American strategy capital-driven; the Japanese strategy is capabilities-driven, the American strategy demand-driven.

First, let us consider labor allocation. Japanese labor allocation has at least

From Imai Ken'ichi and Itami Hiroyuki, "Organizational and Market Principles in the Japanese and American Firm" (unpublished paper). By permission of the authors.

three characteristics that differ from those of the United States labor market. They are (1) low labor mobility, (2) limited ports of entry for new employees, and (3) the low profile of labor unions (which are mostly enterprise unions rather than industry or trade unions). The third point may need clarification. What we mean is that, unlike American labor unions, which conduct industrywide bargaining and are sometimes closed shop, Japanese labor unions play a less active role in marketwide labor allocation. Japanese enterprise unions certainly play a major role in wage determination and job determination within the firm, but not throughout an industry or in the labor market as a whole.

Ports of entry to Japanese firms from the external labor market are more limited than in the United States along two dimensions. Especially among college graduates, mid-career ports of entry are very few at best. Most hiring is done at the time of graduation from school. The second dimension is the central control over all hiring held by a firm's personnel department. In this sense, there is only one port of entry to any company, namely through the personnel department, whereas in the United States, each division, or even each manager in some cases, functions as an employer with hiring authority. In other words, because ports of entry are limited in Japan, workers pay great attention to getting their first job and are extremely cautious about changing jobs. Ports of entry in the United States, on the other hand, are multiple and decentralized, making job changing a more casual and frequent phenomenon.

Low labor mobility and limited ports of entry imply that internal labor allocation and reallocation has to be done more actively in Japan for the firm to cope with changed demand conditions and changing technology. Just as labor adjustment through external labor markets is less practiced in Japan, the development of internal labor markets is more extensive. Workers often move from one job category to another in the firm without much constraint from the union. This occurs both as a regular part of career development and irregularly as a part of internal labor adjustments to changing demand and technology. Divisions bid for internally allocated labor to the central personnel department, a process that is responsive to changes in business conditions.

As a buffer for business fluctuations, many Japanese firms rely on subcontractors more than United States firms for supplies of parts, intermediate goods, and labor services. This subcontracting amounts to the firms' labor adjustment mechanism. When a recession hits, the firm can first cut back on subcontracted work instead of laying off its core workers. In this sense, temporary and part-time workers are simply one form of subcontractors.

The personnel department of a Japanese firm functions as the operator of this extensive internal labor market, governing its port of entry and its adjustment mechanisms. As one can imagine, the power and relative status of personnel managers is much higher in Japan than in America.

In sum, the external market is more weighty in the United States labor allocation picture, whereas the organization plays a more major role in Japan. External markets are efficient in a rationalist sense, but they are prone to be inequitable. Internal markets are more equitable, but prone to be inefficient. The American labor market has thus seen the infiltration of various organization-like principles of allocation into its free-market-based resource allocation mechanism. One example is strong industrywide trade unions to protect the collective interests of workers in one trade. Another example is the closed shop. This certainly limits the freedom of entry into labor transactions by each individual worker. A third example is government regulation, standards, and oversight.

In contrast, we can see in Japan the infiltration of more free-market-like principles into the internal labor allocation system. The flexible movement of workers across job boundaries, often at their own initiative, is an example. Bidding for labor by divisions when it becomes rather fluid is another example. Widespread use of subcontracting can also be seen as a way to make the membership pool of internal labor transactions less fixed, for it opens the internal market to specified outsiders.

In simple terms, the net effect is this: In the United States, labor allocation and reallocation occurs by workers crossing the firm-market boundary more often, but occupational boundaries less often, than in Japan. In Japan, workers tend to stay within the firm-market boundary but cross occupational boundaries more frequently than in the United States.

As has been well documented, there are three major characteristics of Japanese corporate finance that set it apart from corporate finance in the United States. They are (1) a heavier reliance on bank loans, (2) less internal financing, and (3) less dependence on the equity market.

Heavy reliance on bank loans naturally leads to extensive and deep involvement by the banks in market capital allocation. Moreover, the number of significant banks is much smaller than in the United States. There are only 13 city banks, which control 52 percent of Japan's total bank lending to corporations. The capital they control originates with investors who have few alternatives to bank deposits. Thus, in a very rough sketch of Japanese capital allocation, its major feature would be that banks gather most of their capital from individuals and then allocate it to borrowing firms. Perhaps as a natural outgrowth, highly intimate and long-term relationships emerge between banks and firms. It is quite usual for a firm to have one lead bank that acts as the de facto leader of the banks that lend money to the firm. The lead bank monitors the firm's operations and performance with much greater care than other lenders and often shoulders a major responsibility when the firm gets into critical trouble.

The Japanese equity market and corporate bond markets have been much less developed than in the United States. And in that market as well, the Japanese banks have been major players. Unlike American banks, the Japanese banks can (and do) hold equity in their client firms. This makes the bank-firm relationship even tighter.

All this suggests that capital transactions between a Japanese bank and a borrowing firm are not typically an arm's-length market transaction. The intimate and long-term relationship between the lender and the borrower and frequent information flows associated with it make transactions "quasi-organizational" or "quasi-internal." Clearly, organizational elements creep into what starts out as a free market transaction. The institutional framework of the Japanese capital market suggests that this has occurred on a relatively large scale.

Financing within a business "group" (such as the Mitsui or Sumitomo group) is a very good example. There are six very large business groups in Japan, each having a major city bank as one of their leaders. In the postwar era, business groups are not conglomerates with central authority, but rather a group is a loosely connected group of firms (typically with a common history of association in the past) which often act together for their collective interest. The member firms get their major share of financing from the lead bank of the group. Clearly, this capital transaction is not a pure arm's-length market transaction.

The fact that internal financing plays a much larger role in the financial structure of American firms seems to indicate that the internal capital market within firms is much better developed in the United States. That is, serious efforts to apply principles of internal capital allocation are a distinct feature. This is a necessity in American firms in order to cope with the failures of organizational mechanisms to manage a large pool of internal capital, a pool separate from the external capital market.

There is much supporting evidence for the assertion that internal capital markets are more developed in the United States. For example, American firms place more emphasis on ROI (return on investment) in internal capital allocation than do Japanese firms. ROI-based systems of allocation look somewhat like price mechanisms. The techniques for internal capital allocation such as PPM (product portfolio management), which assumes the headquarter's centralized power to collect capital from various divisions and reallocate it according to a given criteria (quite often financial), are also much more widespread in the United States. The chief financial officer (a very central actor in the firm) acts like an auctioneer in this internal capital market. Naturally, his status within the management hierarchy of the firm is high.

In Japan, partly because financing for capital projects is often done through the banks (i.e., the external market), central coordination of internal capital flows is less important. On a project-by-project basis, capital quite often flows between the divisions and the banks (even though these transactions have to go through the headquarter's finance department). The status of Japanese chief financial officers has been in general that of a chief borrowing strategist, rather than that of a chief auctioneer of internal capital flow, and their internal status has not been as high as in the United States. Further evidence of Japan's less developed internal capital market is the nonexistence of conglomerates in Japan. Reputedly, one of the major reasons for their existence in the United States is as a response to and an advance means of developing a large internal capital market.

In sum, capital allocation in the United States crosses the firm-market boundary less often and within-firm divisional boundaries more often than in Japan. If we compare the market (external) and the divisional (internal) boundaries for capital and labor, we find that the American-Japanese differences in capital allocation are the complete reverse of the differences in labor allocation. Even the overall weight of each in the system is reversed. The market's weight is greater in the United States for labor, in Japan for capital. Within the American firm, the weight of capital allocation is greater than in Japan, whereas the weight of labor allocation is less. Numerous other important differences between the two societies' economic and corporate systems follow from these basic distinctions.

Perhaps the most important benefit of a well-developed internal labor market is that it serves to enlarge each employee's firm-specific skills and know-how. Employees in a typical Japanese firm (both white collar and blue collar) tend to be given more extensive training than in the United States and to be periodically transferred to various jobs within the firm to expand the range of their skills, experience, and personal relationships within the firm. Such internal development of individual capabilities is the norm and the strength of the Japanese internal labor market.

With this norm and strength, a Japanese company seeking diversification is bound to follow a strategy that takes it into areas related to the firm's existing core skills, capabilities, market connections, and interfirm relationships. Firms seek to utilize internally developed capabilities. If some new capability is required as part of this advance, the Japanese company will try to develop it internally. It follows that diversification cannot reach too far beyond existing lines of business.

Two other factors reinforce this tendency: the firm's decision-making process and its relationship to the external capital market. Japanese companies' decision-making process tends to be characterized by bottom-up plan generation and consensus-oriented approval of such plans. Typically, a diversification plan is prepared at the middle-management level and channeled upward through the firm's organizational hierarchy, with much informal communication occurring between different hierarchical levels to arrive at a consensus. As the plan moves upward through the organizational hierarchy, its contents are reviewed at each level, approved after adjustments are made, and in turn submitted upward. No drastic diversification plan is likely to come out of this process. People will propose things they know well. Consensus is easy to obtain for those things that many in the hierarchy know well.

The second reinforcing factor is the bankers' close involvement in the firm's external financing. A plan to enter areas unrelated to the firm's existing capabilities is usually hard to sell to the outside bankers. A group's bank sees the group as a diversified whole and is quite familiar with the particular capabilities of each member firm.

Even a prospective new product with a very large potential demand is unlikely to be approved unless it is in some way relevant to the firm's existing businesses and accumulated capabilities. Even if middle management were to put forth such a proposal, it would not be accepted by top management. Of course, there are some cases of diversification into unrelated areas based on decisions made by top management alone, but even then the practice of trusting outside consultants to plan the new project and recruiting new employees from outside to run the new business (both often done in the United States) are very uncommon in Japan. Plans have to be created by an in-house project team, and the firm's employees will be reassigned to the new business as feasible.

What, then, is the likely pattern of diversification in American firms, with their restricted internal mobility of labor and their well-developed internal capital allocation mechanisms? It is important to note that capital, unlike labor, is inanimate and does not embody or accumulate skills and know-how. It is firm-specific only in the sense that it is at management's total disposal and invested in accordance with corporate strategy. This means that there are fewer limits on its application. For example, geographical expansion as a multinational corporation is a form of diversification much more easily entered into by American firms. Geographical diversification is attractive, because it involves the geographical extension of its accumulated inanimate resources in search of the best ROI. If labor is needed at overseas localities, the firm can find it there. Furthermore, many of the risks of multinationalization, such as unforeseen political upheavals in host countries, can be absorbed by the combination of the firm's internal capital market and the relative ease of personnel flow between it and the external labor market in the host country.

At the same time, the American firm tends to diversify into businesses that are very much unrelated to its main product lines. The many American conglomerates typify this. In sharp contrast to multinationalization, the conglomerate transforms its resources by adding new ones quite unrelated to its existing portfolio. But both the conglomerate and the multinational corporation have a similar strategic logic in the sense that they are both highly demand-driven rather than capabilities-driven. Even if a firm's capabilities are highly specialized and involve a particular set of skills, its diversification strategy may not try to exploit these; rather, it will seek new markets solely because of the prospects for future demand.

In fact, in the now-famous product portfolio management model, strategy is mainly derived from assessments of future demand prospects and the need to achieve a dynamic balancing of internal cash flows. A new field for diversification is selected by this strategy as if management were picking stocks for an investment portfolio. Capital required for the selected diversification plan is supplied by the firm's internal capital market, which is at management's own discretion. Corporate takeovers, which are very uncommon in Japan, are in this sense just one kind of option. Creation of a new business is another. Competent personnel to run the new business are then recruited from the external labor market. In short, the resources needed for implementing a diversification plan are often procured from the outside; it is primarily capital that comes from the inside.

The success of this American kind of diversification depends to a large extent on how good the strategic planning is. If the corporate strategy anticipates the future correctly, corporate sales will grow, and the firm's resources and capabilities may undergo a qualitative improvement with the injection of new (outside) blood to stimulate further growth. If the original strategic projection proves mistaken, however, there remains little margin for fine tuning or integration with the firm's other businesses to cope with the problem. The results can be traumatic. A typical Japanese diversification, on the other hand, allows the firm more room to adapt or fine-tune the new business to environmental changes, because its strategy tends to keep the new business close to its existing businesses. Internal capabilities are close by to help. In a sense, then, one can expect medium performance for the Japanese approach to diversification and either very high or very low performance for the American.

However, the success of this Japanese type of corporate strategy is premised on several conditions. The first is that changes in demand not be too abrupt, but rather at a rate that permits fine tuning, such as product differentiation and improvements in an existing product line. The second condition is that the economy continue to grow at a certain speed, creating a stable level of long-run growth for firms. Sustained growth is important because it invigorates the firm's internal labor market and reduces the need for layoffs. Unless these conditions are fulfilled, the Japanese firm's diversification strategy will run into problems.

24. Debt and Equity Financing: Implications

Daniel I. Okimoto

A number of studies support the widely held belief that differences in corporate financing methods in Japan and the United States have led to differences in business strategies. In this selection, taken from *Competitive Edge* (1984), Stanford University political scientist Daniel I. Okimoto analyzes the implications of these different methods for Japanese and American companies in general and the semiconductor industry in particular. He concludes that both systems have functioned well in the past and that present trends suggest growing similarities between the two.

It is a widely held belief that indirect bank financing gives Japanese companies greater leeway to pursue long-term strategies in world competition. In the United States, reliance on equity financing is said to lead to preoccupation with high returns on equity (ROE), strict monitoring and controls over investments, and an obsession with high stock valuation. Presumably, this inclines United States companies toward short-term goals and quarterly profit earnings that keep stockholders happy and works against the profit-forsaking, market-share approach that is considered essential for staying power and competitiveness. By contrast, Japanese firms are said to come under much weaker return-on-investment (ROI) and stockholder pressures. Presumably, this permits them to invest heavily in new plant and equipment, price products aggressively, incur sustained losses, and expand long-term market share.

Data from a Chase National Bank study seem to substantiate these stereotypes. The study reveals that Japanese semiconductor producers operate on lower profit margins and lower capital turnover ratios than United States companies. In fact, Japanese semiconductor firms show an average rate of return on capital that falls below their cost of capital. United States firms also appear to fall slightly below the breakeven point, though, according to the Chase study, their rates of return have roughly equaled their cost of capital. If Japanese competition forces United States rates below the breakeven point, the Chase study warns, this will damage stock prices and the industry's access to equity capital. Here, again, Japan's financial system appears to bestow substantial competitive advantages on its semiconductor producers. But is this the case?

From Daniel I. Okimoto et al., *Competitive Edge: The Semiconductor Industry in the U.S. and Japan* (Stanford, Calif.: Stanford University Press, 1984), pp. 207–13. By permission of the publisher.

Itami Hiroyuki has written a book that analyzes questions of capital utilization, comparing Japanese and American companies in three sectors. Itami's findings also appear to substantiate important aspects of the foregoing portrayal, but the implications drawn are significantly different.

Itami finds that Japanese firms use capital less efficiently than United States companies, partly because Japanese management is less concerned about earning a high return on investment. The need to maximize short-term profit or to show hefty quarterly earnings is not a major concern. Not that Japanese companies disdain "filthy lucre"; in markets as competitive as Japan's, companies have to be concerned with profits. It is just that the system of indirect, external financing permits greater slack in the management of liquid assets.

Not surprisingly, the ratios of value added to both sales and total assets fall substantially below those of United States firms. The low level of value added is largely a function of less complete vertical integration (with extensive networks of subsidiaries, contractors, and distributors) and higher price-to-cost ratios (i.e., prices closer to costs). The price-to-cost ratio reflects the intensity of competition in Japan, particularly where price, not product function or quality, determines consumer choices. Itami thinks that price competition is excessive because Japanese companies do not choose their product portfolios wisely. Contrary to stereotypes of exemplary planning, Japanese corporations seem somewhat deficient in systematic product strategies. Many appear to follow a one-set principle, producing one of everything simply because their competitors are. There is a haphazardness about the whole process, with little or no market analysis or strategic evaluation of how products fit into an overall portfolio. A better selection of products would raise value added and relieve pricing pressures, Itami believes.

Why are Japanese managers, otherwise noted for their adaptability, so backward in the area of strategic planning, especially in view of the seemingly favorable leeway for the pursuit of long-term strategy made possible by debt financing? Itami links the portfolio problem to rigidities caused by Japan's lifetime employment system. Once facilities are built to produce certain goods, closing them down becomes difficult since the livelihood of permanent employees is at stake. An effective product strategy requires flexibility to retreat quickly from product lines of only marginal value added. Here, again, we see that the complex institution of permanent employment brings with it advantages as well as drawbacks for Japan's industrial system.

With capital abundantly available, Japanese firms traditionally invest heavily in new plant and equipment as a means of improving product quality and lowering production costs. Such investments are mainly responsible for steep rises in labor productivity over the years. Companies compete intensely in the capital investment arena, because that extra "edge" acquired through labor-reducing mechanization can be converted into significant gains in the marketplace, and no one wants to be left behind. The availability of capital allows companies to enter the race and to stay in it over a sustained distance. One can expect this dynamic to continue driving Japan's semiconductor companies, just as it has other industries. Climbing capital intensity in the semiconductor industry seems to play to one of Japan's systemic strengths.

On the basis of an admittedly limited sample, not directly focused on the semiconductor industry (but including several semiconductor manufacturers), Itami provides evidence that seems to validate some of the commonly held notions about corporate financing in Japan:

1. Capital is plentiful and relatively cheap.
2. Bank borrowing relieves pressures for high ROI.
3. Capital intensity is high but value added is low.
4. United States firms outperform Japanese companies with respect to returns on assets (ROA) and capital productivity.
5. Japanese firms compete fiercely in capital investments.
6. Products are priced closer to costs.
7. Japanese firms place less emphasis on stock market valuation.
8. Japanese companies feel less compelled to maximize short-term profits and price/earnings ratios.

At first glance, these conclusions appear to lend credence to the notion that Japanese companies take a farsighted approach to strategy, free of the short-term myopia caused by ROI imperatives. But Itami offers no evidence to confirm this view. America's capital market does not stop companies from following long-term, market-share strategies. Certainly no one is accusing American Microsystems, Inc. (AMI), Hewlett-Packard, or IBM of strategic myopia. Although pressures to maximize short-term profits and ROI are undoubtedly more strongly felt in American companies, and although such pressures can lead to an unhealthy preoccupation with short-term profits, the behavior of United States semiconductor manufacturers defies facile generalizations, particularly those based on what might be called "financial determinism." The strategy of a number of leading United States semiconductor companies would have to be described as long-term, adaptable, and market-share-oriented. How else could one explain the high and sustained capital investments, the extension into overseas markets, the commitment to quality control, the support for university-based research and manpower training, the bold new attempts to coordinate research activities, or the new programs for future generation technologies such as the Defense Department's Supercomputer Project? Short-term objectives (such as profits) need not be incompatible with long-term goals (such as market share). Strategic plans can be broken down into a series of objectives, the accomplishment of which in sequence advances the company ever closer to its long-term goals.

Nor does heavy debt financing necessarily force Japanese corporations to devise farsighted plans. Itami suggests that Japanese companies are not as adept as their American counterparts in managing money efficiently or in conceptualizing and implementing strategic plans, at least in the area of product portfolio management. Others have also debunked the myth of Japanese management's "genius" for long-term planning. Ohmae Ken'ichi observes that the "stunning Japanese successes in the auto, semiconductor, and consumer electronics markets have taken place over the long haul, but have occurred primarily because of a determined focus on short-term, incremental gains." The structural determinism underlying the view that differences in corporate finance compel United States firms to follow a short-term strategy of profit maximization while Japanese firms pursue a long-term strategy of market share simplifies what is in fact a very complex set of circumstances on both sides.

This is not to deny that debt financing gives Japanese companies more slack to tolerate some sacrifice of short-term profit. There are noteworthy examples of a willingness to absorb early losses in order to break into a new product line or new industries—semiconductors being but one case in point. Such persistence is generally more difficult under stricter ROI guidelines.

Itami's study suggests perhaps that the system of debt financing inadvertently breeds inefficiency (in somewhat the same manner that military contracts and procurement almost guarantee some measure of waste in the United States). Japanese companies tend to forgo the use of standard American methods of financial analysis—ROI, discounted cash flow, and so on—though they do try to ensure through regular monitoring that sufficient money is available before new investments are made. Other costs that emerge out of Japan's structure of corporate financing include a penchant for overinvestment, excess capacity, excess competition, corporate vulnerabilities during recession, high bankruptcy rates, merger and capital acquisition difficulties, and the need for administrative guidance and government coordination. Whether the advantages of lower capital costs and more flexible capital utilization outweigh such disadvantages is not altogether clear.

In trying to understand and assess the costs and benefits of Japan's financial system, it would be well to remember the postwar context within which it evolved. Heavy debt financing grew out of an era of rapid growth and financial insulation—when Japan's equities and bond markets were underdeveloped. To finance their growth, Japanese companies had no choice but to rely on banks as their primary source of capital. Had the capital market offered a fuller range of instruments, the "banking-industrial complex" might not have developed in the way it has. But it did not, and the momentum of high-speed growth deepened bank-company ties and consolidated the system of external indirect financing. For years, the whole system was considered fragile, susceptible to collapse in the face of the first severe crisis. But full-speed growth allowed the system to operate effectively and with surprising stability.

The onset of a period of slow growth following the oil crisis altered the foundations of Japan's economy. Heavy debt financing no longer functioned as well as it had prior to 1973. It was, in many ways, ill-suited to an era of sluggish growth, high unemployment, and future uncertainty. The dramatic shift away from debt financing is no doubt a reflection of the transformation that has taken place in the wake of the oil shock. The trend seems likely to continue as long as growth rates stay sluggish. Some companies with very low debt financing—for example, Sony and Matsushita—are managing very well under harsh business conditions. The internationalization of Japan's financial system will no doubt accelerate the trend toward greater equity financing. Thus, American and Japanese patterns of financing seem to be edging closer together, though it will be a long time, if ever, before there is convergence.

Both American and Japanese financial systems seem to be functioning satisfactorily—albeit in different ways—to meet the escalating needs of their semiconductor industries. Both industries enjoy ready access to capital, on comparatively favorable terms, mostly through internal financing, but also from direct and indirect external sources. Japanese corporations can draw on a variety of strengths inherent in Japan's financial system, including sound macroeconomic policies, extraordinary rates of capital formation, close banking-business relations, and effective mechanisms of risk diffusion and reduction. Such formidable strengths in the financial infrastructure are reflected in tangible advantages for Japanese corporations, such as lower costs of capital, greater capital availability, lower transaction costs, and fuller information on which to base decisions. The nature of corporate financing in Japan also appears to ease the kinds of pressures to maximize short-term profits and ROI that lie at the core of American management concerns.

This is not to say, however, that Japanese firms enjoy financial advantages of such magnitude that they will turn out to be decisive. There are costs associated with Japanese-style financing that have already been pointed out, such as the burdens of heavy debt-servicing, which render companies vulnerable to fluctuations in interest rates and downturns in the business cycle. Such costs are by no means insignificant. Nor should anyone lose sight of the fact that Japan's financial system is undergoing change—in response, especially, to the powerful forces of internationalization. If the economy is fully opened up, this will probably mean that some of the advantages that Japanese semiconductor companies have enjoyed, such as low and stable interest rates, will be diminished. In anticipation of such changes, a number of Japanese semiconductor manufacturers are acting already to decrease their dependence on bank lending and increase their proportion of equity financing. Just how far and how quickly such trends proceed is a matter that bears close monitoring, particularly since financial considerations have become so important to the United States–Japan semiconductor competition.

25. Japanese Policies: Past and Future

Murakami Yasusuke

In this selection, taken from an article published in 1982, economic theorist Murakami Yasusuke provides an overview of the Japanese business, financial, and administrative systems. Murakami describes the characteristics of the pre-oil-crisis period, noting that in recent years most of these characteristics have disappeared. He argues that, in the future, structural and institutional changes will require the development of new industrial and government policies.

Long-Run Orientation of Japanese Firms

In the pre-oil-crisis Japanese economy, a firm's long-run orientation was not so much a characteristic inherent in Japanese culture as a product of a certain mixture of three economic environments—that is, the borrowable technology, the risk-reducing financial system, and the Japanese employment system, particularly in-

From Yasusuke Murakami, "Toward a Socioinstitutional Explanation of Japan's Economic Performance," in Kozo Yamamura, ed., *Policy and Trade Issues of the Japanese Economy* (Seattle: University of Washington Press, 1982), pp. 6–9, 38–44. By permission of the publisher.

trafirm job mobility. As of today, the first advantage has disappeared, and the second is, as I will discuss later, disappearing. These two changes seem cogent enough to conclude that Japanese firms can no longer operate on a decreasing long-run average cost curve. Leading industries before the oil crisis, such as steel, automobiles, electric appliances, and petrochemicals, are now facing an increasing long-run average cost situation just like others that are not latecomers.

This change will imply that in those hitherto leading industries the market mechanism is likely to be more stable or, in other words, less prey to excessive competition. During the growth period, administrative guidance to curb the investment race or to introduce a recession cartel was justifiable. From now on, however, continuation of such a policy stance is likely to cause a downturn toward inefficiency and stagnation in those formerly vigorous industries. In a similar vein, the "down-pouring" of Japanese exports will become not only increasingly difficult (owing to international friction), but also less urgently needed by major Japanese industries. Economically speaking, there will hereafter be no powerful reason why Japanese firms should be particularly different from their Western counterparts.

While this paper cannot analyze the Japanese employment system, a good guess is that sociologically Japanese firms will remain considerably different and retain most features of the Japanese employment system, because of inertia and because group orientation is changing but not disappearing. Recently many Japanese have seemed to be seeking a panacea in this system. I agree with them to the extent that one of the system's features, intrafirm job mobility, has greatly contributed to the dynamism of Japanese firms. However, this feature is, in essence, capable of adjustment but not of creating anything new, so that by itself it cannot be a miracle medicine for continued vigor.

In my opinion, group-oriented Japanese management and individual-oriented Western (or rather Anglo-American) management are now on quite equal footing, facing the following challenges in the coming decades: (1) how to deal with a short-term impact (such as the oil crisis) without causing a long-term adverse aftereffect (such as a wage-price spiral or a productivity decline); (2) how to create consummatory (intrinsically satisfying) work, or jobs for women or the aged; (3) how to innovate in a truly creative way; (4) and how to make adjustments or even provide leadership in interindustrial restructuring.

Concerning the capability of the two types of firms to meet these challenges, there seems to be a preconception. An average view might be that a Japanese firm is better for (1) and part of (2), because it showed a better performance during the oil crisis stagflation and it also succeeded in keeping the work ethic alive. On the other hand, a Western firm might excel in (3) and (4), because a creative individual is better rewarded and interfirm mobility of workers is higher. However, it seems that this popular view is only a preconception. An opposite conclusion about each of the four issues can be worked out, depending on what premises one adopts, though this paper has to leave this interesting intellectual experiment untried. My interim answer is that neither their success during the rapid growth period nor their praiseworthy performance during the oil crisis guarantees the superior performance of Japanese firms in the future.

The Japanese Financial System

In the early 1970's, many signs of change emerged in the Japanese financial system, including explosive expansion of the marketing of bonds with repurchase agreements (*gensaki* market), an internationalization of financial markets, and a frequent revision of deposit interest rates. After the oil crisis, further important changes appeared, such as huge national bond issues, a much-delayed development of consumer loans (mainly housing loans), and the introduction of negotiable certificates of deposit.

These changes were mainly due to two factors. First, the government Finance Ministry and Bank of Japan had to acknowledge and respond to increasing complaints about the unfairness of regulations from various interested parties, such as securities companies, corporate investors (mainly trust banks and insurance companies), households, and most notably the outside world. This was an indication that the government could no longer hold in check the voices of various related interests by a catch-up growth dictum. Actually, a constitutional suit was filed during the post-oil-crisis inflation against the government because of the unfair depreciation of household savings caused by the regulation of interest rates. Second, an excess supply of loanable funds seems to have occurred for the first time in the postwar period, because the sudden deceleration of growth triggered by the oil crisis created a sharp reduction in private investment and therefore in the demand for loanable funds, while household savings and the supply of funds remained strong. Indirect evidence of excess supply is the fact that the city banks became, for the first time since the war, seriously interested in lending to consumers. The situation changed from a dominance of excess demand to that of excess supply.

The postwar Japanese financial system symbolized by an artificially low interest rate policy is going to die a natural death. Two conditions are inimical to its survival. First, household savings in Japan will remain strong, and asset-holding behavior will be more sensitive to the interest rate. Therefore, if the Japanese system still tries to peg the deposit interest rate at an artificially low level, a huge amount of assets will shift from deposits to other forms, as foretold by an explosive increase in postal savings compared to an increase in bank deposits. Since the average Japanese household's financial assets are now comparable to those in the United States, there is no reason why only the Japanese household should stick to assets in the form of deposits. Second, the internationalization of the financial system will liberalize, particularly, the bond market. Yields on foreign yen-denominated issues are now liberalized, and only one-third of each issue is assigned to the banks. The rest is, via securities companies, placed with the smaller-scale financial institutions and households. Under this new development, it will soon be difficult to retain control of yen-denominated bonds issued by the Japanese. Third, the large amounts of national bonds issued after the oil crisis to finance increased deficit spending will work in favor of liberalization of the interest rate. Since all central government deposits are concentrated in the Bank of Japan, the banks cannot resort to a compensatory deposit practice against the purchase of national bonds at artificially low nominal yields. National bonds will have to be issued at the market rate. Therefore, a secondary market for outstanding national bonds will develop and be open to the general public. The many changes now occurring need not all be detailed here. All these signs obviously indicate that the growth-oriented Japanese financial system is gradually coming to an end.

Administrative Regulation

The crux of administrative regulation in postwar Japan was the building of a consensus for voluntary compliance in each industry. There were two mainstays for this key practice. First, the nationwide consensus about catch-up growth worked as an ultimate rationale for industrywide agreements. This once paramount consensus is, however, now fading among the Japanese. Second, voluntary compliance was buttressed by a miscellany of rewards and penalties, most of which were justified as incentives for economic growth. Quite a few of them are now being repealed, and their legitimacy is visibly in decline. The original mainstays of consensus building are deteriorating. On the other hand, the experience of industrywide guidance and consultation accumulated over a quarter century seems to have created a kind of symbiosis between each industry (represented by the industry association) and the particular branch of government in charge. Thus, it may not be unreasonable to suspect that such a close relationship will primarily come to serve each industry's parochial interest as well as each administrative branch's sectional consideration. We cannot rely solely on Japanese bureaucrats' elitist morals and intelligence to avoid this hangover of growth-oriented regulation.

In fact, there are a number of catalysts to give rise to such industrywide protectionist practices. As one example, international trade conflicts are nurturing government-led cartels, such as the trigger price system in the steel industry and the voluntary trade restrictions in the automobile industry. For another example, expanding large-scale overseas projects are necessitating government loans and administrative guidance to foreign countries as well as to Japanese firms involved in the projects (as exemplified by Iran Petro-Chemical, many industrial plants in China, and various mining investments all over the world). These recent developments are some of the most important politico-economic events in post-oil-crisis Japan, and they might imply that the interests specific to each industry or ministry are getting too deeply involved in international politics and are increasingly difficult to coordinate with national interests.

An inherent problem in the bilevel structure of the Japanese political economy is the potential unfairness between industries compared to the substantive fairness within each industry. As long as the Japanese economy was rapidly growing and all industries were more or less prosperous, interindustrial differences did not matter much. However, in the coming post–Pax Americana period, when the economy will grow slowly and the second wave of technological innovation will not yet have come, conflicts in interindustrial interests are likely to be intense, beyond the control of implicit administrative guidance, which has now lost most of the persuasiveness that was based on catch-up strategy. Many labor-intensive industries, let alone conventional agriculture, will have to be rationalized and probably abandoned, and even hitherto leading industries, such as steel, will face competition from the newly developing countries. In these days of flexible exchange rates, the increasing productivity of export industries will imply a greater burden on the industries directly dependent on imported resources. All this will intensify the need for constant interindustrial restructuring and will therefore require above all a fair rule between industries. In particular, the rule should be acceptable to the foreign companies that will appear more and more often on the Japanese scene. The Japanese industrial policy up to now, in effect, is likely to be less workable and less beneficial to the national interest, except possibly in such potentially innovative industries as the development of new energy sources, large-scale integrated circuits and their application, new communication systems, and biological engineering, in which the benefits of decreasing long-run average cost might remain.

In postwar Japan, the bilevel, loosely institutionalized, politico-economic system has proved effective in achieving the national consensual target of catch-up growth. However, most of the prerequisites for this system are now fading. Because of the achieved material affluence, the consensus for catch-up growth no longer exists, and average Japanese are getting less instrumental and more consummatory. Their desire to increase consumption will diminish, and they will be increasingly motivated to hold more assets. In the years to come, macroeconomic policies, in terms of aggregate demand or the labor supply, will be as difficult to put into practice in Japan as in other industrial countries. Yet a more serious challenge will come from the more structural or more institutional problems. At the start of rapid economic growth, many people were concerned that industrial growth would cause internal conflicts and societal division similar to a class struggle. Their apprehensions were apparently unfounded. However, new types of structural friction now seem to be emerging—for example, the younger people versus the older people, female versus male, the hitherto leading industries versus the new innovative industries, the export-oriented industries versus the industries dependent on imported resources. The old network of government regulation and the philosophy behind it seem to be, in many respects, ill-fitted to solve this new set of structural issues.

Above all, the Japanese economy will be internationalized, in many senses of the word. The flow of commodities, capital, and even people will be liberalized in and out of Japan. The Tokyo market is likely to be one of the major financial centers of the world. Overseas investment will increase and automatically affect Japan's foreign policies. The commitment as well as the responsibility for international politics will inevitably increase. The past introverted, almost ethnocentric, economic policies should be abandoned, and a new set of policy stances as well as an institutional setting linked with them should be reformulated and implemented. These challenges might be regarded apprehensively by the established industries and branches of government. However, they only mean that the Japanese economy will be on an equal footing with other industrial countries of comparable magnitude. Even in this context, Japanese characteristics might be incorporated in a beneficial way—in the form, for example, of a new Japanese employment system. However, such an attempt should never perpetuate the specific socio-institutional framework that was effective only in the particular historical experience of the rapid economic growth period.

26. People Management Is What It's All About

Thomas J. Nevins

Thomas J. Nevins asserts in this article, which appeared in *Look Japan* in 1980, that Japanese companies differ most notably from those of the West in their use of manpower. He describes some of the features of Japanese employment and labor policies and their implications for business practices. Nevins is President of TMT Inc., a personnel consulting and executive search firm he founded in Tokyo in 1978, and the author of *Labor Pains and the Gaijin Boss* (1984).

The most important key to Japan's strength is the way it effectively employs and makes the most of its people through good manpower, labor relations, and personnel policies. Teamwork and organization is Japan's secret. If you stop and think about it, people are really about all Japan has. Look at what it has done with people and people management.

Everybody's in the Union Together

To put the system, which most Western businessmen are now quite familiar with, in readily identifiable terms, the Japanese enterprise union means that all employees, whether blue collar workers or white collar university graduates, are in the union together from the time they enter the company to their late thirties or early forties when they become *kanrishoku* (administrators) or reach a certain *kachō* (section head) class management level. Dues are paid directly to the enterprise union, and no national or outside industrial union representatives sit in on collective bargaining sessions.

The worker's allegiance is to his company rather than to the trade or national union, because there is no such thing as a cross-company union hiring hall or union seniority to protect the worker should he lose his job with one company. Lack of strong outside union influence, trade-union-imposed seniority and work rules, and competing union jurisdictions within one company also makes for easy job restructuring to adapt to technological innovation or automation and rationalization of work process and methods.

Some might wonder why a person would work so hard if his job is guaranteed by lifetime employment.

When a Japanese enters a company directly after school, he knows that he is there for life. He doesn't have the option of leaving, finding an equally good job, and starting all over should he not handle his responsibilities or himself well. His fate becomes one and the same with his company's prosperity, and every man's

From Thomas J. Nevins, "People Management Is What It's All About," *Look Japan*, July 19, 1980. By permission of the author.

contribution from the beginning reflects on his cash wages and future performance, the size of his lump-sum retirement allowance, and most importantly, his job security.

Unlike Western companies, Japanese companies suffer no disincentive effect from bringing in management talent from the outside to block promotions and stifle ambition. From the beginning, the positions are there to be filled. An employee knows approximately when they will be filled and against whom in his "entering class" he will be competing.

Because supervisor and subordinate work within an arm's length of each other and enjoy a constant rapport and healthy give-and-take exchange, there is also probably more polite disagreement and critical advice expressed by the Japanese subordinate than by his Western counterpart. There are decidedly fewer arguments and ruptures in personal and working relationships. Even company directors positioned on the board will rarely sit in their private rooms, preferring instead to take a desk in the big room that squeezes anywhere from twenty to two hundred people together.

Worker Participation in Small Groups and Quality Control

Within Japanese organizations, worker participation better mobilizes human resources and potential to contribute to and achieve organizational goals. The Japanese style is basically worker participation in shop-floor decision making, designed to create a degree of self-management and self-innovative capacity in the line departments and sections. A lot has been done with zero-defect programs, quality-control circles, workers independently setting targets or devising proposals and suggesting them to management, company-initiated MI (Management Improvement), campaigns to create brighter and better workshops, and JEL (Job Enlargement) assembly methods.

With Japan's population aging even faster than populations in most other advanced industrial nations, a lot of trailblazing efforts taken with the cooperation of labor and management have been greatly successful in creating and establishing maintenance and service subsidiaries, or even whole factories, exclusively for the useful employment of the surplus of old- and middle-aged workers.

Worker participation begun in the 1960's has done much toward cutting defects, increasing attendance, enhancing the self-development of workers through skill acquisition and cultivation of leadership qualities, and boosting worker morale or a sense of worth in doing (*yarigai*) and a sense of fulfillment in living (*ikigai*). The great majority of Japanese companies have such programs.

When it comes to quality control, American management assumes that workers know where the defect or quality problems are and that only pecuniary rewards will draw out the information. Japanese management assumes that no one knows what the problems are and that they must be solved together. Nowadays there are very few full-time quality assurance personnel in Japan. Quality control is becoming the job of every employee.

These patterns and practices have elements of universality and could be transferred more conscientiously into the Western business context. The enterprise union is not just a prototype that worked well in Japan's special circumstances.

This creation of an internal labor market may be the model most appropriate in meeting the purposes of labor and management at our present advanced stage of capitalism.

In the modern capitalist countries, capitalists themselves have mellowed and overall social values and conscience are such that what was very real exploitation of the working man even thirty years ago will no longer take place. Institutions and regulations that did not exist or had not taken root earlier now check management and protect the workers. Management is more sophisticated. It knows that the earlier exploitation and blind, stubborn refusal to recognize unions or bargain in good faith merely was the fertilizer for equally unreasonable and uncooperative labor and an open invitation to hostile outside union organizing forces.

There would be tremendous benefits in bringing about a restructuring of the horizontal labor market into an internal labor market, with the bargaining unit limited to parties knowledgeable of, and sensitive to, the corporation's profit picture and the specific conditions and needs of workers within a given firm.

With the more internalized labor markets of Japan and a more humanized approach and commitment to sustaining employment, employers are accustomed and willing to train the unskilled and will usually reap the benefits. In Japan, unemployment is generally said to be about 2 percent. More significant is that percentage of the workforce that is widely recognized to be underemployed. These underemployed, however, are not on public welfare doles requiring support with income and corporate tax dollars. They are at least partially productive and contribute to the economy as active consumers.

27. The Education of a Japanese Banker

Thomas P. Rohlen

Many large Japanese companies include meditation and military exercises in their training programs. In this essay, Stanford anthropologist Thomas P. Rohlen describes a training program for bank employees in which he participated. He analyzes the value of such programs for both the employees and their companies, suggesting that the programs themselves sprang from a need for Japanese in the postwar period to reestablish native roots in the face of the severe cultural upheavals of the Occupation.

The Zen priest, a long wooden paddle in his hand, strolled through the group of Japanese bank trainees, stopping here and there to whack across the back those whose determination had waned. Although the purpose of meditation, "to preserve the unity of spirit and body . . . to teach the power of spiritual concentration," had been explained to us, we felt little tranquility. We fidgeted and twitched, our discomfort etched on our faces. Leg muscles ached from the unfa-

From Thomas P. Rohlen, "The Education of a Japanese Banker," *Human Nature Magazine*, vol. 1, no. 1 (Jan. 1978), pp. 22–30. By permission of the author.

miliar lotus position, stomachs churned with hunger, and anxiety grew with each loud thwack. My own awareness of the progress of the priest down the line made the prescribed counting to ten over and over again an impossible task.

After a full hour of meditation, we marched into an adjoining mess room and sat, again in the lotus position, at long, low, narrow tables. First a thin soup was served, then a gray, lumpy rice gruel. Seconds were offered but most of us, despite nagging hunger, refused extra food. Next a priest poured hot water into one of our two bowls. We were told to rinse them in succession with the same water until only one contained warm water and residue. This awful stuff the priest ordered us to drink in one gulp. Except for a few breaks, including a six-hour period for sleep, we continued to meditate for the next day and a half.

Stability, security, and opportunity for advancement are the obvious reasons that induce employees of large firms to endure such harsh training practices as long meditation sessions, grueling marathon walks, and even bathing in icy waterfalls. According to recent estimates made by the Industrial Training Association, approximately one-third of all Japanese companies with 1,000 or more employees include these or similar practices in their training programs. Why should a bank be interested in teaching its new employees anything more than the necessary technical and bureaucratic skills?

Some might pass these training practices off as publicity stunts or as evidence of a peculiar twist in the traditional Japanese character that will disappear as the Japanese adopt Western ways. But companies rarely advertise what they are doing, and even top executives from such corporations as Japan Air Lines and Matsushita Electric (Panasonic in the United States) may join their recruits in these painful exercises.

This group had begun its rigorous indoctrination approximately five weeks before, when new employees from throughout the region gathered at the bank's training institute. Upon their arrival, the trainees received two simple uniforms, gray for study and white for athletics. For the next three months, we would live together in dormitories that were part of the training institute, a large, modern, four-story building.

The first night we gathered in the gym and practiced close-order military drill in preparation for a two-day trip to a Japanese army camp. There we did more marching under the direction of a sergeant. Wearing cast-off army fatigues, the trainees—fat and thin, strong and weak, fit and unfit—sweated their way over obstacle courses and later took the Japanese army physical-fitness test. We were told that a large company with thousands of people to coordinate required a high degree of order and discipline and that the military was the best organization to teach us this. To my surprise, the recruits accepted this explanation. Thereafter, no one felt imposed upon by activities "unbecoming to a banker." In fact, during breaks, the recruits took great pleasure in saluting one another.

On a later trip to the former Naval Officer Candidate School at Edajima, now a museum dedicated to the kamikaze, the Japanese suicide pilots of World War II, the same theme was repeated. After we had looked at the diaries and other personal effects of the kamikaze, the director of the museum lectured us on the lessons the suicide pilots provided for the youth of peaceful, modern Japan. "Nobody wishes to experience unpleasant things," he explained, "but unpleasant things are part of life, and nothing of significance can be achieved without suffering. Today's individualism ignores this fact and easily becomes empty egoism. The men of Edajima had the kinds of individualism and independence that focus on the mission to serve one's country, not on the pursuit of pleasure." As he related tales of individual suicide pilots and the tragedy of flying off on a warm spring day never to return, members of the audience, sitting straight in their chairs, silently wept.

Late during the second month of our training we were taken to a youth center in rural Japan, and from there, early in the morning, sent to beg for work in a small market town. We were instructed to go singly from house to house offering to work without pay. Further, we were forbidden to volunteer more than our names and that we were willing to be of help. In Japan, where strangers usually ignore each other and any conversation between them is apt to be hurried, impolite, and marked by suspicion, to refuse such an offer is normal. It was with considerable trepidation, then, that the trainees approached houses. Some walked four or five blocks in small groups before one of them mustered the courage to knock on a door.

Most trainees suffered two or three polite rejections before being taken in, and those who met hostile refusals found it difficult to go on. In the end, however, everyone found work in a house or a shop. We were all glad to help and overjoyed at no longer having to approach strangers. Some worked in the fields, others sold toys, delivered groceries, or pumped gas. One recruit even worked at a roadhouse mixing cocktails and swapping stories with customers until an instructor discovered him, reprimanded him for finding inappropriate work, and sent him on. Since we were told not to return until late afternoon, we spent most of the day at our various tasks.

When we returned, the instructors divided us into small groups and directed us to discuss the meaning of work. After a number of fruitless abstract discussions, we turned to relating the day's events. The instructors expected this, and at a certain point they introduced highly pointed questions. Does the satisfaction of work depend on money? Is satisfaction a matter of suitable employment? What makes work enjoyable and meaningful?

The day's experiences had primed us to see answers that we would otherwise not have accepted. Neither money nor suitability seemed critical. We had just done menial tasks without any pay and enjoyed them. We had developed a liking for the people who were kind enough to take in strangers, and in gratitude for our acceptance, we had labored with diligence and zeal. The recruits generally agreed in the course of the discussion that the enjoyment of work has more to do with a person's attitude toward his task than with the kind of work performed. We had learned our lesson: work is intrinsically neither good nor bad, satisfying nor unsatisfying, appropriate nor inappropriate. Whether a job will be a joy or a drudgery depends on one's outlook. Since the bank must assign dull, methodical tasks to many of its employees, it finds this lesson of significant value.

Between such memorable exercises as Zen meditation and itinerant labor, we studied banking operations and followed a concentrated routine of daily activities. Life at the institute was organized, from the exercises and dormitory cleanup at half past six every morning to the recreational games on Saturday night. Each day was filled with 14 hours of supervised activity; only Sundays were free. Even our grooming, posture, and language were constantly under scrutiny. In each stairwell, for example, a mirror was hung—to remind us of our appearance. We mastered the elaborate phrases of polite Japanese, a necessary task for those of us used to the coarse and informal manners of students. One evening we practiced the correct ways to bow.

The program placed much emphasis on learning cooperation. Living together day and night for three months was expected to teach us this, but many little exercises were also arranged. For instance, we wore slippers everywhere in the institute, except in one large room covered with straw mats. The first time all 120 of us entered this room, our slippers were left at the door in a messy heap. The instructors took us back to the door and showed us how to line up the slippers before going inside. "So much of cooperation is like this," we were told. "A bit of foresight, a bit of self-control, and a concern for others are all that is required."

On a number of occasions executives came to give us lectures, comparing work done for the bank to work done for society. They explained that the bank performs a critical and necessary function for the whole national economy; the work of every employee is thus linked to the peace and prosperity of all Japan. "When she was troubled and poor, the homeland was militaristic," we were told, "but economic success has freed her from the need for military expansion." We were also encouraged to appreciate the number of shopkeepers in the province who were able to stay in business thanks to our loans. "Low interest rates are possible when banks are efficient and carefully managed," the executives pointed out. The basic message was clear: because the company serves the public interest, good workers are good citizens.

Not everything we did, however, was sober and serious. We went on an overnight camp-out and several hikes. We had bonfires around which we sang and presented funny skits, and sometimes we played games and folk danced at night. In fact, after working as tellers for a few weeks, most trainees looked back at their training with nostalgia.

In contrast to the men's training, the two-week program for women, all high school graduates, was directly related to their jobs in the bank and to the expectation that they would leave within a few years. The women were taught the same office routines as the men but were not asked to run marathons or to offer service in private homes. Instead, office etiquette, including serving tea and arranging flowers, was stressed. A representative of the women's liberation movement would be outraged by the sex-role stereotyping. A special theme emphasized in the course of the women's training was the value of bank work in preparing to be a wife and mother. It was said, for example, that proper etiquette and polite language would make a woman cultivated, charming, and graceful, and thus a more attractive wife and an exemplary mother. Similarly, record-keeping techniques would help a wife and mother maintain the family budget.

The high point of the men's training, the last special event and the one the trainees had heard about and discussed long before entering the program, was the 25-mile marathon walk. The program was simple enough. The trainees were to walk the first nine miles together in a single body. The second nine miles were to be covered with each squad walking as a unit, and the last seven miles were to be walked alone and in silence. Our instructions were to take as much time as we needed, as long as we completed the entire 25 miles. The course was set around a large public park in the middle of the city. The training staff would also walk the distance, but going in the opposite direction.

When we began, the day was fresh and cool. It seemed as though we were beginning a pleasant stroll. Walking together in one large group, the recruits talked, joked, and paid very little attention to the walk itself. The miles passed quickly and pleasantly, and the severe physical hardship we had been expecting seemed remote.

Forming small groups for the second nine miles, we were reminded not to compete. But we had not gone far before each group, discovering squads close before and behind, began to escalate the pace. The trainees found themselves walking fast, so fast that those with shorter legs occasionally had to run to keep up. The sweat poured from us, but our pace did not slacken. We had been instructed not to take any refreshment, but a dozen or so young men from the bank were stationed along the route to tempt us with offers of cold drinks. By the end of the second nine miles the toll was obvious. Stiff legs, blisters, headaches, and heat prostration afflicted many of the walkers. Some lay under a tree by the finish line sucking salt tablets. By that time it was nearly noon, and the park baked under the heat of a June sun.

Any gratification the leaders found in their victory was soon forgotten. No congratulations and no rest awaited them. Squads were instructed to break up and continue walking, this time in single file and in silence. Soon a long line of slowly moving trainees stretched along the circumference of the course. Having already covered 18 miles, the last nine at a grueling pace, we found the excitement and clamor of competition gone. We pushed forward, each individual alone in a quiet world, confronted with the sweep of his own thoughts and feelings.

I was to become acutely aware of every sort of pain. Great blisters had formed on the soles of my feet; my legs, back, and neck ached; at times I had a sense of delirium. The thirst I had expected to be so severe seemed insignificant compared to these other afflictions. After finishing each lap, instead of feeling encouraged, I plunged into despair over the laps remaining. My awareness of the world around me, including the spectators in the park and the bank employees tempting me with refreshments, dropped almost to zero. Head down, I trudged forward. Each step was more painful than the one before. The image of an old prospector lost on the desert kept recurring in my mind, and the temptation to stop and lie down in the lush grass was tremendous. Near the end I could walk no more than a minute or two at a stretch.

The others seemed to be doing the same. But it was hard to be aware of them for very long. For some reason I was heartened to discover that six or eight of the trainees had fainted. They were prostrate under a shady tree, receiving medical attention. I too wanted to lie there, and yet I was encouraged that I had not fallen. "I was stronger, I could make it." Despite my feverish state, I was able to examine my response to this test of endurance. The content of several training lectures came back to me. I could see that I was weak, easily tempted, and inclined to quit.

To finish I would need willpower, what the Japanese call spiritual strength. I was angered and amused to realize how cleverly this exercise had been conceived. I vowed never again to get involved in such a situation.

Yet, within days, the memory of the physical pain had dimmed, and like all the other trainees, I took great pride in my accomplishment. My completion of the 25-mile course was proof that I could do anything to which I set my mind.

Many Americans and Europeans would object to this kind of training as authoritarian. In the Western view, a company has no place teaching anything other than whatever skills are required by the job. But in Japan, such company training is accepted by most people. We must grasp the reasons for this attitude if we are to understand the different contexts of work in the two cultures. Individualistic Americans value independence from work organizations. We view the employment relationship as essentially contractual. We exchange set amounts of time and skill for pay.

Work in Japan, especially work for a large company, is conceived of somewhat differently. As the bank's trainees are told during their entrance ceremony, taking a job at a bank is like joining a large family. As in a family, the individual's well-being is closely tied to the prosperity of the group. As in a family, those not fulfilling their roles receive understanding and retraining. Unlike a job in the United States, a job in Japan involves no implicit contract; there is, instead, a mutual adoption for life—or at least until retirement.

Other Japanese business practices also seem familylike. Dormitories for bachelors, apartments for married couples, vacation villas, stipends for child care, and so on, are all part of the employee's fringe benefits. Just as workers are often expected to put in extra hours without overtime pay, so the company offers extra benefits. The paycheck is still basic, of course, but other benefits are important, especially as symbols of the special relationship between employer and employee. Employees not only work long hours together, they also socialize almost to the point of excluding outside relationships. Once every few months, after the normal 10-hour workday, a meeting and party are held for the staff at each branch. After bank officers discuss the past record and future aims of the branch, food and beer are served. Inevitably, while the men continue drinking, a round of solo singing begins. Some giggle their way through a tune, while with more beer others gain the courage to sing or tell stories instead, but each employee is expected to take his turn. Around nine o'clock the women leave for home, and the men, at the invitation of the chief, retire to a local bar for a few more hours.

Large Japanese companies are distinctly different from the contract-based, machinelike work organization familiar to Westerners. Where we maintain order by separating the employee's personal life from his business life, the Japanese incorporate the two into one grand system. In this light, the rigorous training programs for new employees make sense. By participating in the programs, recruits learn the values of the "family" they are about to enter, values that in many ways conflict with those found in other parts of Japanese society.

Such extensive company training is *not* traditional. It represents an attempt by the companies to undo the cultural changes brought on by education reforms imposed by the American Occupation after World War II and the Westernization of popular culture. After several decades of distinctly Japanese nationalism, the country was forced to reverse its course in 1945. This left a deep sense of cultural contradiction that continues to influence Japan to this day. To business leaders like the bank's president, postwar changes in society and education seem basically foreign and threatening. Company training programs are aimed at exorcising these foreign influences. They may not be able to challenge the educational system or the mass media, but they can try to counter their influence among new recruits to the company. Thus, while essentially modern developments, employee training programs incorporate many traditional Japanese practices.

Americans have not experienced the shock of a drastic cultural reversal, so American businesses have never experienced the need to develop such extensive training programs. Our system of work organization remains consistent with the attitudes and behavior patterns with which we are socialized. The individualism that so threatens Japanese organization is assumed by our own type of corporate organization. A basic key to the dynamics of Japanese society is the character of its organizations, whereas an important key to American business dynamics lies in our stress on individual initiative.

The Japanese experience reflects a major issue in Western society today, the meaning of work. Our pay may be better and our working hours shorter than ever before, yet we ask, "Is the work relevant? Is it satisfying?" American businessmen are concerned with what they see as a steady deterioration of the work ethic: rising worker dissatisfaction, plagues of absenteeism at many factories, frequent wildcat strikes. Perhaps, as we learned during the bank's exercise in begging for work, the problem lies not in the work itself but in the attitude toward work. If the official motivations are only money and self-interest, then prosperity will surely undermine commitment and open the door to cynicism. While the bank might appear to control too great a portion of the lives of its employees, it also supplements their motivation by promoting a deep sense of affiliation that appears to be both personally rewarding and economically efficient. Often this element seems lacking in our society today.

28. Working Women in Japan

Alice H. Cook and Hayashi Hiroko

How do women fare in the Japanese work force? In this selection, Alice H. Cook and Hayashi Hiroko argue that although in Japan an unusually high proportion of women are employed, their income and work careers suffer because they are treated as temporary or part-time employees. Cook is Professor Emerita at the New York State School of Industrial and Labor Relations, Cornell University, and specializes in labor relations; Hayashi teaches law at Kumamoto University of Commerce and specializes in the law of workers' compensation. The essay is drawn from their book, *Working Women in Japan*, which was published in 1980.

From Alice H. Cook and Hiroko Hayashi, *Working Women in Japan: Discrimination, Resistance, and Reform* (Ithaca: New York State School of Industrial and Labor Relations, Cornell University, 1980), pp. 1–91. By permission of the publisher.

Japan's labor force has a higher percentage of women working than any other noncommunist country. Its figures rival those of Sweden and Finland and have remained remarkably steady at 50 to 51 percent of women fifteen years of age and over from 1955 to 1975. Many norms that are used to describe the nature and scope of women's work in the national economies of the industrial nations, however, do not apply to Japan. Whereas in many countries, women work after leaving school and until the birth of their first or second child, then remain at home for a few years caring for children and return to work either part or full time, the Japanese employment system makes such a pattern very difficult for women to follow without great loss in both status and income. In most countries, a close, positive correlation exists between a woman's level of education and an uninterrupted or only briefly interrupted work life. In Japan, again because of the employment system, women college graduates have the greatest difficulty in finding and keeping employment and in receiving wages commensurate with their education. Like many other industrial countries, Japan has established in its law the principle of equal pay for the sexes. As in other countries, the discrepancies between men's and women's earnings are wide, but in Japan they grow wider with the length of employment. Indeed, given the traditional views that most Japanese, male and female, hold about women's roles in the family and at work, the Japanese employment system probably exploits women more extensively than is the case in any other industrialized country.

In spite of their high rate of labor market activity, women cannot be said to be really a part of the permanent employment system. To be sure, they start off at close to the same rate as men, but very quickly the gap between their earnings and those of men opens up and widens. Women are restricted to a narrow range of occupations, all considered auxiliary and, with very few exceptions such as teaching, low-paid. Women are promoted much more slowly than men, when they move upward in skill or scope at all.

Women receive little or no on-the-job training. The employer does not expect them to remain with him more than a few years, for he and they understand that the women will marry in their middle twenties and that when they do, their main interest will presumably no longer be their work but their homes and their children. Because no employer expects them to do other than follow this pattern, he justifies giving them less training and wants them to retire when they marry or have their first or second child, or when they reach the age of twenty-seven to thirty. This practice is euphemistically referred to as "early retirement." The employer genuflects in the direction of the established retirement system, in that a woman "retiring" at this point receives a lump-sum payment representing her acquired rights in the company's retirement system, which are based on the number of years she has worked. The employer may go further and collude with her to write her up as unemployed so that she can draw unemployment insurance. That monthly income together with her lump-sum payment constitute a kind of paternal dowry from the firm on the occasion of her marriage or the birth of her child.

As recently as ten or fifteen years ago, women "retiring" in this way usually did not return to the labor force unless they were widowed or their husbands became incapacitated. Now more than half the women thirty to thirty-nine years of age and 64 percent of those between forty and forty-nine are working. In fact, the percentage of those working after forty is almost as high as that of women in the premarital years; in 1970, the actual numbers of older women working considerably exceeded the numbers of younger ones—an indication of the aging of the Japanese population as a whole.

But, clearly, women returning to work after ten years' or so absence from the labor market are not reemployed in the upper level of the economy as "permanent" workers. By "retiring," they have given up all claims to returning to their former places of employment. A glance at the nature of their work and their location in the labor market shows that they are working in small companies, or as unpaid family members, or in the large companies as "temporary" or "part-time" workers at low wages, often uninsured and without fringe benefits or private pensions—certainly with no hope of promotion or improvement in their circumstances.

Nothing better illustrates women's unequal status than their wages. Although women's total cash earnings increased 16.1 times while men's rose 12.7 times between 1955 and 1978, women earned 56.2 percent of what men did in 1978.

Although women's years at work have increased considerably in the last decade, their work life remains much shorter than that of men. A good deal of this extended work life is a product of the growing tendency on the part of women to return to work at middle age, but these women can rarely hope for permanent employment at this age and instead work most frequently as part-time or casual workers, meaning that they fall outside the private benefit system and not infrequently are unreported to the public system as well. In addition, retirement at the end of a continuous work career may be not simply five years earlier than for men but ten or more years earlier.

Pensions in Japan, as in many other countries, are of two kinds: a national social security monthly payment based on insurance to which the worker contributes throughout his or her working life, and, particularly in the upper level of the economy, a sum paid by the firm. In Japan, this latter sum is usually based on years of work with the company, accumulated at the rate of about 2 percent of annual earnings and paid as a lump sum on retirement. Under both systems, Japanese women suffer by reason of their low wages. But even more, when they must retire—not just five years but often as much as 25 years—earlier than men, they have little to fall back on. The lump sum they have accumulated by retirement from a firm, not as large as a pension, is treated as a kind of wedding or birth present and as such is a substantial "gift."

Most companies, including public ones, set a general retirement age of fifty-five. The unions have been urging, with some insistence, retirement at sixty, and in many companies they have succeeded in pushing the age upward toward that limit. But wherever it is set, no one assumes that it will apply to the managers at the top or to the women at the bottom. And, indeed, men who are capable of continuing to work after fifty-five are usually reemployed after retirement for another four or five years, but at a lower salary than they received under the seniority system. The reason for early retirement is obviously rooted in the seniority wage system; it is a device for unloading older workers before they become unbearably expensive.

As for women, often their employment contracts or the companies' agreements with the unions call for their retirement on marriage, or at childbirth, or at no later than thirty years of age. Even when companies set older retirement ages for women, these limits usually fall five to ten years earlier than men's, and it is most unusual for a company to continue to employ a woman past her retirement, no matter what her age.

Companies justify early retirement procedures by pointing out that women are for the most part doing "supplementary" work, or work that does not need to be carried on further, or work for which an inexperienced younger woman can readily be found. They contend that women contribute too little to the company to justify retaining them when their salaries under the seniority-education system must increase every year without accompanying increases in productivity. They also point to the protective legislation that requires them to give maternity leave when women become pregnant, and they note the other protections that must be accorded to pregnant women, all of which make them less efficient and more expensive to the company. Moreover, they believe that when a woman has a home, this becomes the primary focus of interest, and working efficiency necessarily drops.

When women endeavor to resist company regulations or customary practices that would force their early retirement, companies sometimes respond by making their life on the job so difficult that the women give up the struggle and accept dismissal or "retirement." For example, persons who refuse to accept transfers to inconvenient or distant places—and transfer is often a form of discipline imposed on these women—are guilty of disobeying supervisors' orders and thus make themselves liable to disciplinary dismissal.

Action toward improving conditions of women is going ahead along at least three lines: (1) issues of harassment, downgrading, equal job opportunity, and job assignment are still being brought before the courts; (2) the Socialist Party, the Democratic Socialist Party, and the Communist Party have each presented a bill that would provide equal job opportunity similar to that provided by the British and United States antidiscrimination and equal job opportunity laws; (3) the staff of the planning and policy commission in the Prime Minister's Office issues studies of women's present status and initiates programs that both voluntary organizations and government bureaus are urged to implement. The government has undertaken a number of programs to implement the recommendations of the Labor Standards Law Research Society.

To the extent that litigation has become a way out of discrimination for Japanese working women, it will continue to be used and is worthy of note, by persons outside Japan as well as inside, as a gauge of the degree and nature of women's discontent and exploitation.

On the whole, the unions have not been active in these cases. Their indifference is a product of a variety of factors. First, union contracts are never written for units larger than the single firm; very often they are written for just a single plant or branch (only in the public corporations are they national in scope). The national federation, and often the national union, has no power or influence over the content of these contracts and only rarely has a record of what their contents are. Hence, many contracts are written in agreement with the company's discriminatory policy, and no national body is in a position to impose sanctions or discipline, even if it would.

Second, union leaders by and large share the societal views about women at work. They believe that women are and should be only transitorily in the labor market and that, as short-term or part-time workers, their concerns are of secondary importance to those of the genuinely lifetime male employees.

What is largely lacking as a force to propel government initiatives more rapidly along is a massive women's movement such as exists in a number of Western countries. A dedicated corps of women lawyers, journalists, academics, legislators, and public servants raise the issues and publicize them. A number of outraged women carry cases to court independently and are supported by ad hoc groups of supporters who raise the money to pay their costs and to sustain them, often through years of litigation. The national unions and their federations, which might supply the mass base, the money, the power, and the momentum to attack problems, on behalf not only of disadvantaged individuals but of women categorically, are unable and even unwilling to act concertedly on these issues.

Working women in Japan will at best make slow progress toward equality. The amazing thing is that they keep at it and that on at least some of their issues, the courts find in their behalf.

29. Permanent Employment Policies in Times of Recession

Thomas P. Rohlen

It is a commonplace that Japanese companies espouse a system of lifetime employment. What does this mean in actual practice? In this essay, Thomas P. Rohlen looks at the way the lifetime employment system operates in times of recession, pointing out the mechanisms available to reduce labor costs while maintaining the job security of regular employees.

The recession of 1973–77 has made it much easier to sort out fact from fiction concerning what is called "permanent employment" in Japan. The importance and durability of the principle of job security for regular employees has definitely been confirmed by company, union, and government policies, yet this is but part of a larger story. The significant limits to its application have been more clearly manifested than ever before, and a fascinating complex of alternative mechanisms for reducing labor costs has been revealed.

Following the oil shock of late 1973, Japan experienced its worst postwar recession. The index of production for manufacturing dropped by 11.5 percent in just 14 months beginning in November 1973. Despite such cutbacks, manufacturers' inventories piled up precariously.

Personnel reductions in manufacturing over the four years from the end of 1973

From Thomas P. Rohlen, " 'Permanent Employment' Faces Recession, Slow Growth, and an Aging Work Force," *Journal of Japanese Studies*, vol. 5, no. 2 (1979), pp. 235–72. Copyright © 1979 Society for Japanese Studies. By permission of the author and the publisher.

Table 29.1.   Decline in Employment in Manufacturing,
1974–1975
(In percentages)

Country	Male	Female
Japan	2%	11%
United States	8	8
West Germany	8	9

SOURCE: Sōrifu (Prime Minister's Office), *Rōdō Hakusho* (White Paper on Labor), 1978.

to the end of 1977 totaled more than one million, a decline of nearly 10 percent. The rate of reduction differed considerably for different categories of employees. During the first two years of recession, for example, the number of women employed in manufacturing experienced a very rapid decline, followed by a partial recovery during the next two years, whereas the number of males declined slowly but the decrease continued over the entire period. A similar pattern can be seen in the rates of decrease for part-time and regular employees. During the early stage, part-time workers were cut heavily, while the number of regular workers declined much more slowly but for a longer period. By midway in the recession, some industries were adding part-time workers while continuing to cut their numbers of regular employees.

In the Japanese system, two groups of permanent employees always have relatively high turnover rates: young women (approaching marriage) and older men (approaching retirement). In the recession, both groups were pressed by the management of troubled firms to leave early. In the case of retiring men, management cut back drastically on the numbers rehired as temporary employees after their formal retirement. As a result, older men began to swell the ranks of the unemployed.

The turnover rate for women in the twenty-three to thirty age range is normally quite high, despite the fact that most enjoy permanent employee status. They leave companies at the time of marriage or pregnancy with few exceptions, and thus by freezing the hiring of young women, companies can easily make reductions in their female work force of better than 10 percent per year. The ratio of women to men employed varies considerably, however, and only some industries are in a position to benefit greatly from this source of flexibility.

No aspect of the Japanese employment system distinguishes it more from the system in the United States and Western Europe than the role played by women (see Table 29.1). Should anyone doubt the influence of permanent employment in Japan, he need only look at these figures to find powerful evidence of its great significance where *male* employees are concerned. Just the opposite could be said of women, yet the fact is that precisely because permanent employment is a burden, cutting the number of male employees is far more important in the long run. They, not women, are expensive (thanks to seniority pay); once a recession has been weathered, it is very useful to reestablish a thick cushion of female and temporary employees in preparation for the next downturn. Females constitute the short-term safety valve, while the core of permanent males must be cut to achieve long-term efficiency.

Table 29.2. *Rate of Increase in Female Applications for Unemployment Insurance, 1973 and 1975*

Country	Number of women		Percentage increase
	1973 (thousands)	1975 (thousands)	
Japan	240	340	41%
United States	2,064	3,445	66
West Germany	124	452	262

SOURCE: Sōrifu (Prime Minister's Office), *Rōdō Hakusho* (White Paper on Labor), 1978.

Few Japanese women, despite leaving or losing work in great numbers, applied for unemployment compensation. This is also very different from what occurred in the United States and West Germany (see Table 29.2). These figures are remarkable when we note that overall female employment (including manufacturing) actually increased in Germany and the United States during the period, and only in Japan did female employment decline. Apparently, leaving work to marry or to return to homemaking or to farming does not appear to Japanese women as sufficient reason to have themselves listed as unemployed. The weak development in Japan of the idea of careers for women is reflected clearly in this phenomenon.

A survey of the nation's 250 top manufacturing and commercial companies conducted by the Industrial Labor Research Institute, which focused on their personnel adjustments between March 1974 and March 1978, is particularly instructive. One hundred eighty-five companies (75 percent) had reduced employment over the period. The average rate of reduction amounted to 12.6 percent, or more than 1,000 people per company. One in five companies had cut employment by 20 percent or more. Differences between industries and sectors were quite marked, with cuts of 25 percent being common for electric appliance makers (Fuji Electric, for example, pared away 5,500 jobs out of a total of 20,300), textiles, and aluminum smelting, while increases in employment were limited to such particular industries as auto manufacturing, electric power, computers, and mining.

How these reductions were achieved was also investigated. Of the 185 firms cutting employment, 71 percent stopped hiring "mid-career" applicants, 64 percent set up voluntary early retirement plans, 43 percent stopped hiring new graduates, 41 percent laid off part-time workers and temporary workers, 39 percent introduced special holidays, and 38 percent transferred workers to subsidiaries and related companies.

Industries in serious trouble could hardly rely on trimming their workforce by a simple combination of a hiring freeze and the reduction of marginal workers. A hiring freeze reduces employment slowly, especially in industries with proportionally few women. Steel, shipbuilding, and other heavy industries faced with the necessity of cutting their labor force by 20 to 50 percent began to transfer factory workers to sales and service divisions or to loan them to other companies.

Tōyō Kōgyō, the faltering auto manufacturer, for example, sent production workers to its sales affiliate, assigning them the sobering task of learning to be car salesmen overnight. The larger and more diversified the company, of course, the more opportunities there are available for this kind of internal adjustment. Ties to other firms within an industrial or financial "group" were also utilized. Workers "loaned" out from troubled companies almost invariably went to other companies of the same group. Mitsubishi Heavy Industries, for example, sent 3,720 employees (4.5 percent of its total labor force) to 110 other Mitsubishi firms. A flow of workers from the ailing steel and shipbuilding industries to automakers was effected in this manner.

Finding "volunteers" was exceptionally trying for both unions and management, not to mention the employees involved. The critical point, however, is that the union agreement and volunteers were forthcoming. The capacity of unions in large firms to assume a pragmatic perspective and the willingness of management to painstakingly explore solutions short of layoff and termination are illustrated in these arrangements.

The terms of transfer typically required that the company being relieved of workers assume a larger proportion of the transferees' salaries, remain responsible for their welfare and conduct, and promise to take them back after a specified loan period, usually six months to one year. Even in their new workplaces, transferees continued to wear the uniforms of their old companies, and much ado was made over the fact that they were expected to work hard and well as representatives of their home companies. Undoubtedly, loan arrangements benefited host companies, too. In the auto industry, for example, besides solving immediate needs for additional labor, the temporary nature of loaned workers meant retained flexibility of staffing as a sales slowdown was expected. Hard bargaining between union and management was required to shape such arrangements, and negotiations were held almost continually in many companies.

The government also encouraged companies not to dismiss regular employees. By paying a subsidy to firms in qualifying industries, which is described as a payment of part of the allowances that companies are required by law to pay when they temporarily furlough workers, the government, in effect, pays companies to furlough but not dismiss employees. Taxpayer-subsidized permanent employment is the result. With government assistance, the temporary furlough-with-pay approach becomes quite practical, and of course it keeps unemployment from rising steeply.

Just how much unemployment would result if this subsidy was not available is hard to estimate, but it is clear that, in 1975, just under three million workers were furloughed for short periods (an average of ten days) and their allowances paid in part (50 to 66 percent) by the government. Had even one-quarter of these people joined the unemployment lists, Japan's unemployment rate in the 1975–76 period would have gone from 1.4 to 3.1 percent, which, adjusted for the differences between Japanese and United States unemployment accounting and structural systems, would have put Japanese unemployment at around 5 percent by United States standards.

In times of serious trouble, the managerial commitment to company economic survival naturally supersedes its commitment to the principle of permanent employment. Unions make job tenure their highest priority, of course, and this sets the stage for a terrific showdown whenever companies are faced with the necessity of severe reductions. The government, no doubt with much urging from business, has instituted a costly form of subsidy to help avoid this kind of conflict.

Before jumping to the conclusion that permanent employment is simply a creation of government policy based on the willingness of taxpayers to pay for the preservation of this principle and the social and economic stability associated with it (a kind of national employment insurance system for regular employees), we would be wise to consider what happened to profits in the recession. They dropped more steeply in Japan than in other industrial countries in 1974. Three major factors were involved: excess inventories, heavy fixed debt, and a limited capacity to reduce employment costs. The point is that while the government is willing to subsidize a few seriously troubled industries, the rest must pay for the short-term preservation of permanent employment out of profits. The downward pressure of this recession affected the wages of regular employees in a quite delayed fashion, leaving the cost burden to be borne by marginal workers, government, and corporate profits. All paid heavily, while, in contrast, the standard of living and consumption patterns of regular workers showed no adverse effects. The service sector in Japan and the individual savings rate increased dramatically from 1974 to 1978.

Reductions in Japanese employment as measured against the decrease in production were not as rapid, as "elastic," as the response in the United States. They were, however, on a par with the responses in leading European countries. Therefore, by comparative standards, it is the American—not the Japanese—employment system that appears "unique" in this regard.

The Japanese response of finding as many ad hoc and temporary adjustment measures as possible and using them in combination to cut costs without challenging the principle of permanent employment until "natural attrition" (i.e., the results of a hiring freeze) and economic recovery close the gap between employment and production must be regarded as filled with risk. Profit levels in 1974 decreased far below what would have been tolerable levels in the United States, but even so, significant levels of assistance from the government, banks, and related firms were needed in many instances. The risk was spread rather broadly in the case of larger firms possessing group relationships, underlining a set of points already on the books about Japanese companies compared with American ones— namely, their greater flexibility regarding profits, the greater extent of government and bank guarantees, and the risk-sharing qualities of interdependent company groupings. Union-management talks were also conducted on a nearly continuous basis in hard-hit companies so that adjustments would be accepted.

The Japanese response also appears more humane, and it works to preserve organizational morale, but at the same time it is more complicated, hectic, and harrowing for management. A more severe or prolonged recession might have brought the entire system, the healthy firms as well as the troubled ones, to its knees.

30. Productivity Changes in Japan, 1960-1980

Ohta Hajime

Compared to the productivity of the United States and other Western industrial nations from 1960 to 1980, Japan's productivity growth (and especially, in this article, labor productivity growth) has been high. In this selection, which is taken from a United States–Japan Trade Council report of 1980, Ohta Hajime examines some of the factors that have contributed to Japanese growth, focusing on the roles of capital formation, improved technology, and individual workers. He notes that within the twenty-year period, there have been a number of stages during which the Japanese economic system has had to adapt to new business conditions.

Productivity is defined as output (or value added) per unit of factors of production, such as labor, capital stock, and resources including oil. However, this report will focus largely on labor productivity because it is a major determinant of the standard of living. The rate of change in labor productivity fluctuates with business cycles because employment adjustments normally lags behind production adjustment. During the early stages of a business upswing, production expands rapidly while the workforce remains static, resulting in an increase in productivity. But, at a later stage of the business cycle, productivity increases slow down. To understand productivity changes, it is helpful to look at the economy over the last two decades.

Productivity Changes in the Last Two Decades

Productivity gains in Japan, particularly in the manufacturing sector, have surpassed those of other industrialized countries. Average productivity growth between 1960 and 1973 was 10.7 percent, compared with 3.6 percent for the United States, 5.9 percent for West Germany, and 3.5 percent for Great Britain. In the post-oil-crisis period, the average growth rate fell to 5.3 percent in Japan, 2.3 percent in the United States, 3.7 percent in West Germany, and 0.8 percent in Great Britain. In 1978, it increased again to 8.5 percent in Japan, while the United States recorded 1.9 percent, West Germany 2.7 percent, and Great Britain 1.0 percent. In short, labor productivity in Japan more than quadrupled from 1960 to 1978 (or an annual average increase of 8.2 percent), as compared with less than double in the United States (or an annual average increase of 3.4 percent) and a low annual average of 3.2 percent in Great Britain.

Gross national product growth per worker (GNP/Employment) has shown a similar development. The average growth rate for Japan between 1963 and 1973 was 8.7 percent and decreased to 3.5 percent between 1973 and 1980. On the

From Hajime Ohta, "Productivity Growth in Japan—The Last Twenty Years," United States–Japan Trade Council Report, no. 39, Oct. 10, 1980. By permission of the publisher.

other hand, corresponding figures between 1963 and 1973 for the United States, West Germany, and Great Britain were 2.2 percent, 4.6 percent, and 3.0 percent, and for 1973 to 1980 were 0, 3.1 percent, and 0.4 percent, respectively. The poor productivity (GNP/Employment) performance of recent years in some countries is partially related to rapid employment growth, as the Organization for Economic Cooperation and Development (OECD) suggests in its *Economic Outlook* of July 1980. In this context, it must be noted that zero or minus growth of productivity does not necessarily mean zero growth or declining growth of per capita GNP. Nor does it mean either zero or declining growth of GNP or income per family, but instead may reflect the absorption of a spouse or an additional family member into the labor force.

The United States continues to enjoy the highest level of productivity among the major industrialized nations because of the strength of its agriculture, high technology, and defense-related industries, as well as its vigorous service sector. In addition to low productivity growth in the late 1960's and 1970's, declining figures in the United States since 1977 have raised the level of concern. Although many factors contribute, those most often cited are lower increases in equipment ratio per worker (low capital formation), poor technological development (lower research and development [R&D] investment to GNP ratio), demographic changes (composition of workforce and mobility), as well as changes in industrial structure and economic overregulation. Conversely, these same factors explain why Japan's labor productivity growth has been higher. A brief review will show the effects of increases in capital stock, the contribution of technology, and the role of the individual worker.

Role of Capital Formation

Investment in capital equipment per Japanese worker increased at a higher rate than in other industrial countries owing to persistently high private investment activities in the rapidly expanding economy. For instance, in the 1960's, the ratio of private capital investment to GNP averaged 18 percent, 5–10 percent higher than in other developed countries. Gross investment was close to 40 percent of GNP from the mid-1960's to the early 1970's. Because the Japanese economy started from scratch, a sharp rise in capital equipment rate per worker was understandable. Opinion favored high growth rates. Business optimism resulted in economic development with enormous capital investment, high productivity, rising income for workers, high rates of consumption, steady growth of savings, and rising exports. However, it should not be overlooked that some production facilities that were installed in the early postwar period had already been replaced by the late 1960's and 1970's, notably steel plants.

Labor productivity corresponds to changes in the capacity utilization rate and output coefficient (output per unit of production capacity). Compared with the United States, however, these factors seem to have played an insignificant role in improving productivity in Japan. The large increase in labor productivity improvement in the 1960's and the early 1970's is largely attributable to the increase in capital investment that resulted in more equipment per worker. The steel, nonferrous metal, petrochemical, and shipbuilding industries all achieved large increases in equipment ratio per worker, thanks to rapid and sizable capital investment. This achievement was enhanced by economies of scale and by increasing world trade. Increased domestic demand and external demand (exports) supported the production expansion.

Productivity gains began to slow down after the 1973 oil crisis. The economy entered a period of slow growth. As private business investment slowed, the rate of capital stock increase per worker also declined. Substantial excess production capacity caused by falling demand forced a drop in capacity utilization and adjustments to capital stock. As a result, productivity dropped in 1974 and 1975. With new efforts to streamline the excessive labor force and the recovery of a satisfactory capacity-utilization ratio, productivity recovered in 1976 and 1977. After 1978, the economic expansion resumed, and the capacity-utilization ratio rose; capital investment resumed, and higher labor productivity growth was achieved.

Role of Improved Technology

It is generally believed that improved technology is the most important contribution to productivity after capital stock increases. Investment in plants and equipment raises productivity, but technologies embodied in the new capital contribute further to the growth of productivity. In this context, the rapid growth of capital stock in the postwar period generally made possible the smooth introduction of the newest technology into production facilities, and this is reflected in the younger vintage of production machinery in Japan. It is estimated that the average age of plants and equipment in the Japanese manufacturing sector was at the lowest level in the early 1970's (about six and a half years). Earlier, in the mid-1960's, it was nine years old. Plants and equipment in the United States have been between 10 and 11 years old. Currently, the difference between the two is narrower; the average vintage of capital stock in Japan is about eight years, the result of stagnant investment during the post-oil-crisis period, while that of the United States is now between nine and 10 years, according to a Ministry of International Trade and Industry (MITI) white paper of 1980.

The slowing down of investment since the oil crisis indicates the relative importance of technology to productivity growth. It is well known that after World War II, Japanese companies imported technologies and sophisticated machinery developed in the United States and other countries, adapting and sometimes improving them. Recently, however, Japan's sophisticated industries have begun to develop their own technology. The gap between United States and Japanese technology is considered to have disappeared between 1970 and 1973. (But there still remains a gap between United States and Japanese aggregate output.) According to a recent MITI survey, 31.5 percent of Japanese firms indicate that their technological level is higher than their overseas competitors', and 56.8 percent consider it comparable to foreign competitors'. This technological development seems to have been incorporated in the rationalization investment (i.e., investment to conserve energy, resources, and manpower) of the second half of the 1970's. This is partly a result of increasing R&D investment (a 15–20 percent annual increase in the last decade). These investments should be separated from those designed to expand production capacity, although the latter undoubtedly embodied the newest technologies available.

The MITI white paper of 1980 estimates that capital increases in the 1960's contributed most heavily to increases in production. In the 1970's, labor made a minus contribution, but the importance of technology and other factors rose. Chemicals, textiles, metal products, and industries including electric, electronics, and transportation enjoyed a relatively high input of technology. Development and use of machines such as numerical control equipment computers and new production techniques including industrial robots have been responsible for this growth.

The Human Element

The absorption of workers into higher-productivity jobs has promoted average labor productivity until recent years. Reallocation has occurred in shifts from rural areas to urban areas, agricultural sectors to manufacturing sectors, within manufacturing sectors, and within individual corporations. Through this process, the substantial underutilization of the human element was reduced to a low level by the 1970's. Employment of better-educated workers has also helped. What about the quality of labor and management? Typically, we hear that Japanese are hard workers. Although there is no way to compare Japanese and American workers, several relevant points must be made. Labor productivity is jeopardized by industrial disputes. Lost workdays per 1,000 employees in Japan totaled 36, compared to 455 in the United States; the number of disputes registered 1,517 in Japan and 4,300 in the United States. Japanese labor management practices, such as lifetime employment, unions organized by company, and wages by seniority, could contribute to this difference. Social values and perceptions toward work, family structure, and motivation might also be important considerations.

Moreover, unless workers fully understand the function of new equipment and master its operation, its installation will not ensure high productivity. Employees themselves contribute significantly to productivity by improving methods and techniques, inventing shortcuts, and assuring quality control. Intensive and thorough communication between management and labor improves the quality of work and increases productivity. Management itself lists high-quality workers as one of the contributing factors to the improvement of productivity. According to the same MITI white paper, those factors also include stable labor-management relations, wage-price stability, competition between companies, and efficient management. Business executives consider wage-price stability important because price increases will be inevitable if wages increase more than productivity, and a vicious cycle of declining demand and decreasing labor productivity will result. Competition among companies tends to push up labor productivity as firms strive to reduce costs. MITI believes that the degree of concentration in the manufacturing industry in Japan has not risen, while it has generally gone up in the United States and Europe. Another factor often thought by Americans to promote Japanese productivity growth is the high leverage of the Japanese company. The importance of this factor, however, can be overemphasized, as is evident from the many successful American corporations. Many Japanese firms, as well, have succeeded without heavy borrowing.

Higher oil prices produced both inflation and deflation in oil-importing countries. An increase in oil productivity through more efficient use of oil is one way to moderate this unfavorable impact. Until the 1973 oil crisis, oil productivity decreased as the use of oil penetrated into both energy and nonenergy sectors of the economy. It was only natural to make abundant use of readily available and inexpensive oil. After 1974, however, oil prices surged; demand declined, particularly in industries faced with shrinking demand. Higher oil prices provided the incentive for reduction of energy input per unit product in the chemical and iron and steel industries and promoted the substitution of alternative energy sources in the iron, steel, cement, paper, and pulp industries. At the same time, basic material manufacturing sectors have become less active, and less energy-consuming industries (processing and assembly industries which are engaged in exports, such as cars and machinery) have expanded. Thus, higher energy prices and expectations of persistent increases in the future have promoted industrial and trade structural changes to achieve higher energy productivity.

This energy saving in the industrial sector is reflected in the elasticity coefficient of oil consumption to GNP. The coefficient was 1.0–1.2 before 1973 but has since fallen rather sharply (0.25 between 1974 and 1979). Real GNP rose between 1973 and 1979 by 27 percent, while oil consumption remained basically the same (257 million kiloliters in 1973 and 259 million kiloliters in 1978).

Post-Oil-Crisis Productivity and Inflation

As with productivity, a variety of factors contribute to inflation. The problems are related. Productivity must rise if inflation is to be fundamentally reduced. Simply to criticize wage increases that are higher than productivity gains ignores the fact that excessive demand, seller monopolies or limited competition, and government regulations all may induce price hikes. In these circumstances, the government is basically at fault. Nevertheless, consistent productivity growth will act to ease pressures for price increases. When figures for productivity, wages, and wage costs are compared, productivity is an important determinant in containing wage costs.

Let us examine wage costs in the Japanese manufacturing sector after the oil crisis. In 1974 and 1975, particularly in 1974, wage costs were up more than 30 percent because of sharp salary increases in the face of a reduction of real income and a sharp decline in productivity. Another wage cost increase came in 1977 and early 1978, when productivity gains were exceeded by wage hikes. But in 1976, when productivity gains were substantial, wage costs were stable and even declined slightly. After the second half of 1978, wage costs fell steadily, reflecting substantial productivity growth and slower wage hikes against relatively stable consumer prices. In the United States, wage costs showed a drop in 1976, when productivity expanded significantly. Except for that year, wage costs rose continuously, reflecting slower productivity gains—or zero growth—and constant wage hikes.

It is clear that in circumstances of imported inflation (e.g., oil price hikes), wage cost increases that are higher than productivity gains inevitably cause a shrinkage in corporate profit. Thus, capital investment slows down, employment adjustment takes place, and unemployment goes up. At the same time, pressure for price hikes intensifies. At a time of excess demand caused by stimulative economic policies, or when competition is limited in the market for a variety of reasons including import restrictions, stagflation becomes inevitable. Generally speaking, this is what happened during the 1973 post-oil-crisis period in most oil-importing countries, including Japan. The Japanese economy's performance during this time was poor compared to that of most other industrial countries in terms of such indicators as growth rate, price, and external balance. However, since the second oil crisis, fundamentals have improved and compare favorably with those of other countries. Productivity gains in labor and oil have undoubtedly contributed to this change, together with other factors including flexible wages, competitive markets, and anti-inflationary economic policy, although there is no assurance that this will continue.

31. The Mazda Turnaround

Richard Pascale and Thomas P. Rohlen

In 1975, Tōyō Kōgyō, the manufacturer of the Mazda automobile, was on the brink of bankruptcy. Because of the company's importance as an employer in the Hiroshima area, its failure would have contributed to a general economic collapse in that region. By 1980, however, Tōyō Kōgyō had changed direction, and its recovery was well under way. In this essay, Richard Pascale and Thomas P. Rohlen describe the complicated interplay between economically significant events and institutional and cultural factors that made possible the company's turnaround. The study, based on fieldwork in Hiroshima in September 1982, first appeared in the *Journal of Japanese Studies* in 1983. Pascale is a consultant and a lecturer at the Graduate School of Business, Stanford; Rohlen teaches anthropology at Stanford.

Two years after the Arab oil embargo of November 1973, Tōyō Kōgyō (hereafter TK), the maker of Mazda automobiles, declared a 17.3 billion yen ($70 million) loss. New car registration dropped 22 percent in Japan in 1975. Exacerbating these problems, the industry had earlier accepted labor demands for a 30 percent increase in nominal wages. Thus, costs were pushed up just as sinking demand preclosed further increases in prices.

TK was hit harder than its competitors. Mazda registrations in Japan fell 31 percent in contrast to Honda (-5 percent), Toyota (-6 percent), and Nissan

Revised from Richard Pascale and Thomas P. Rohlen, "The Mazda Turnaround," *Journal of Japanese Studies*, vol. 9, no. 2 (Summer 1983), pp. 219–63. By permission of the authors and the publisher.

(− 26 percent). TK's inventories piled up precariously, peaking at 140,000 unsold vehicles. The reasons for TK's particular vulnerability were numerous.

1. The Wankel (rotary) engine was less fuel-efficient than conventional engines at a time of extreme emphasis on fuel economy and conservation.

2. TK was more dependent on exports than its Japanese competitors, and its confrontation with the United States Environmental Protection Agency had precipitated a particularly steep revenue shortfall in the United States market. Plummeting sales and the rotary engine's tarnished image triggered dealer defections in the United States and a general weakening of the distribution network.

3. TK had not cut back production when its competition did. Consequently, inventories piled up, precipitating a severe cash-flow problem.

4. TK was the highest-cost producer in Japan, averaging only 19 automobiles per employee annually against a Japanese industry average of 30. TK had previously concealed this problem by offering lower dealer margins. Now, in a time of crisis, this strategy further weakened its dealer network.

The company was on the brink of bankruptcy. With 37,000 direct employees in 1974 (and an additional 23,000 people employed by dependent suppliers), TK accounted for one-quarter of the total manufacturing employment of the Hiroshima area. Since Hiroshima's other major industry, shipbuilding, was unalterably in steep decline, the regional economy faced virtual collapse if the automaker failed. Management faced the classic challenge of troubled companies: cutting costs, boosting sales, trying to keep ahead of cash flow, holding creditors in place, and retaining the loyalty of suppliers and dealers. This article outlines the crucial steps taken to meet the challenge. What emerges is a detailed portrait of the interplay between economically significant events and institutional and cultural factors.

TK's turnaround was dramatic. By 1980, debt had been reduced dramatically. Cash and deposits had grown by 100 billion yen. Revenues from sales had more than doubled, and, most critically, the production per employee ratio had gone from 19 to 43 vehicles per year. As a result of these improvements, profits had doubled from their pre-oil-shock levels. Yet this is a complex story.

The Pre-Crisis Situation

Management

Founded as Tōyō Cork Industries in 1920 by Matsuda Jujiro, founder and first president, TK produced its first motor vehicle in 1931. The founder was a strong, autocratic manager, who resembled many other start-up entrepreneurs. Over the next forty-five years, his style of management was passed from grandfather to father to son, the personality of the firm continuing intact over three generations despite extraordinary increases in the company's size, sales, and complexity.

TK diversified beyond automobiles into rock drills and precision measuring instruments; during World War II it also manufactured rifles. When the world's first atomic bomb exploded over Hiroshima on August 5, 1945, fate smiled on the young company: its facilities were located on the sheltered side of the only hill in the river delta in which Hiroshima is situated. While the city was devastated, TK's facilities were left intact. When Jujiro's son, Tsuneji, was installed as president in 1951, TK had become Japan's leading truckmaker.

Throughout the 1950's, while TK focused on its established position as a truck manufacturer, Toyota and Nissan expanded into the larger and more lucrative passenger car market. In the early 1960's Matsuda Tsuneji saw the implications of having neglected the passenger car market, but by then TK was a late entrant; the firm needed a viable means of closing the gap. With characteristic Matsuda flair, TK hung its fate on the rotary engine.

Matsuda signed a technical agreement with Audi NSU-Wankel of West Germany in 1961. Six years later, after redesigning the engine in practically every respect, TK succeeded where General Motors had failed, when it introduced the first commercially successful rotary engine in automotive history. In 1970, when third-generation Matsuda Kenji took over from his father as president, Mazda launched its United States campaign, where the powerful but quiet rotary engine was an immediate hit. By 1973, 70 percent of Mazda's sales were exports, as contrasted to roughly 40 percent for Nissan and Toyota.

Mazda's export success concealed a variety of weaknesses that would contribute to the unforeseen crisis of 1975. First, the success of the family's bold product decisions had created an aura of invincibility. The firm's initiatives depended almost entirely upon the thinking of the Matsuda currently in charge. The company was primarily product-driven. Furthermore, the company had always recruited the cream of engineering talent, but within the managerial ranks a domineering family style tended to cultivate yes-men. Ideas and initiatives from below did not flow upward. A wide variety of manufacturing improvements, essential to long-term success, were neglected. Yearly model updates were ignored. Even major model changes were irregular and were introduced at six-to-eight-year intervals— far longer than those at Nissan or Toyota. Few pressures were put on suppliers to reduce costs or improve facilities. Information and control systems did not keep up with the growth of the company. Inventories were high and cost controls seriously lacking. The pace on the assembly line relaxed to the point that workers could go to the toilet while on the line without needing a replacement.

The oil crisis of 1973 didn't *cause* TK's problems; it simply *exposed* them. After United States government tests showed Mazda's rotary engine getting only 10 miles per gallon in city driving, Mazda's American sales dropped 60 percent in one year. Furthermore, Matsuda Kenji would not acknowledge the oil crisis as a long-term problem. For 12 agonizing months, TK continued to mire itself in difficulty and debt. Middle management was paralyzed. Accustomed to direction from the top and constrained by presidential outbursts, executives below Matsuda's level could not bring about a change of course, despite considerable below-the-surface consternation.

Dealer Relations

The relations with dealers had greatly deteriorated by 1975. In Japan, TK sold its passenger cars through a network of 114 "independent" dealers. Each dealer had an exclusive territory in which it operated a set of new car sales offices and used car lots. None of these dealers was cross-franchised with other auto manufacturers. Thus, while in ownership and management the dealers were independent, they were quite dependent on TK in such crucial matters as the product's competitiveness, new product development, and marketing policy.

This tight and exclusive arrangement is characteristic of auto retailing in Japan, but not in the United States. When TK faltered in North America, some dealers bailed out and others used their cross-franchised arrangements to protect their interests. No such shifts were possible in Japan, although individual car salesmen (reliant to some degree on commissions) began to leave Mazda dealers in significant numbers in 1974 and 1975.

It is important to grasp the differences in automotive retailing between Japan and the United States. United States salesmen work a showroom, handling several makes of new and many kinds of used cars simultaneously. The customer comes to them. An American car salesman averages eight to ten car sales per month. In Japan, sales are largely conducted door-to-door. Because space is at a premium, showrooms and lots are small and scattered. Outlets are quite labor-intensive. A seasoned car salesman sells four to five cars per month. Ironically, in an industry in which the Japanese have the highest levels of manufacturing productivity in the world, the distribution productivity is comparatively low. Finally, auto sales volume in Japan varies in direct relationship to the number of salesmen in the field.

TK's dealers had more than an inkling of the company's precarious situation in 1975. Their inventories of unsold cars had been growing from late 1973. The company was booking its auto shipments to dealers as "sales." The dealers carried the inventory but made payment to TK only upon an actual retail sale. By mid-1975, 140,000 cars in excess of normal inventory were sitting on dealer lots and at Mazda transshipment centers (including those for export). Domestic sales, which had been running about 18,000 a month in 1973, had declined to 11,000 per month in 1974. At that rate, if the factory closed down entirely, it would still take more than a year just to get the inventories to normal levels.

The situation was made tolerable to the dealers by TK's willingness to accept very long-term promissory notes, which in effect constituted an agreement to demand payment only when the cars were actually sold. The 11–12 percent interest on these notes was the dealers' responsibility, however, and this was destroying their margins.

Dealers had many other grounds for complaint. The company offered poor incentives; the development of new models was erratic; dealers felt the company was out of touch with consumer desires. Production was not geared to dealer orders, but rather dealers had to accept whatever came off the line. Such problems are especially serious in cases of exclusive ties within a hierarchical system. Since Japan's economy appears to have many arrangements of this type, it is, theoretically at least, more vulnerable to poor upward communication from market to manufacturer.

As sales slumped in 1974 and 1975, TK continued to produce too many cars that did not gain customer acceptance. To salesmen it seemed that the company was refusing to face up to reality. During 1974, an estimated 20 percent left their jobs with Mazda dealers and many were not replaced. Sales threatened to slip even further as the manpower to generate sales decreased. A vicious circle was growing, in which rising inventories, eroding dealer margins, TK management inflexibility, and loss of sales force all led in a common, destructive direction.

Supplier Relations

Approximately 70 percent of the total manufacturing cost of a Mazda comes in the purchase of materials and parts. Thus, it is external to the company. Fundamentally, Japanese auto companies are planners, assemblers, and marketers of autos. The company's suppliers can be divided, for purposes of explanation, into (1) material suppliers, (2) direct subcontractors in the Hiroshima area, and (3) component suppliers. The first group consists largely of steel manufacturers selling through trading companies.

The second group includes about ninety smaller companies that are closely tied to TK. They belong to an association known as the Tōyukai (Friends of Tōyō Kōgyō), whose members are all located in Hiroshima and whose major common function is to produce everything from body stamping work to seat manufacturing according to TK designs. Many Tōyukai members sell only to TK, and nearly all sell 50 percent or more of their production to the automaker. As in the case of dealers, Tōyukai suppliers are very tightly linked to the company. Their dependence on its policies and business fortune has been nearly total for many years.

Costs of materials account for about 18 percent of total purchasing costs in manufacturing. Payments to Tōyukai subcontractors account for another 26 percent. The largest group of suppliers in terms of their role in the manufacturing cost structure are the components makers, who account for 56 percent of total external manufacturing costs. Some of these firms produce according to either TK designs or to jointly developed designs, and several sell more than 50 percent of their production to the company. Most, however, such as battery and headlight makers, sell to other auto companies in Japan. They have something of an arm's-length relationship with the company, and its success is of less consequence to their survival.

Relationships with most suppliers have complex histories. More than half the external manufacturing input comes from suppliers who must work very closely with TK in such matters as production planning, product design, engineering, and finance. In many cases, TK actually purchases the materials for fabrication by its subcontractors. The situation with the closely related suppliers involved several kinds of inefficiencies in the period prior to 1974. It appears that suppliers were dealt with in a patronizing manner that simultaneously protected them, made them subservient, and prevented them from making much progress in productivity. The automaker had access to its suppliers' books. This allowed its purchasing department to set prices that granted suppliers a reasonable profit. Such a financially based arrangement was cozy as long as Mazdas sold well, but it did not pressure suppliers to seek greater manufacturing efficiencies. "It was an old-style ('wet') kind of relationship," states one supplier, with each side asking favors at times and neither side introducing the kind of discipline that would have forced rapid progress. Top officials spent time entertaining suppliers but no time working with them to strengthen their common business. Suppliers with questions or suggestions felt they were rarely heard. The Tōyukai was an association in name only as far as the suppliers were concerned, since there was no leadership in the group to help it meet competition.

In sum, in its relationships with both dealers and suppliers, TK's superior position in the overall business grouping had led to an aloofness and a lack of good two-way communication. Top management failed to exercise progressive leadership, and it sought to balance and rebalance its subordinate firms' interests without forcing the whole system to be more competitive in the fundamentals of product attractiveness and manufacturing cost.

To be successful in such a "typically Japanese" structure, management must shape the meaning of hierarchy to realize interdependence. It must achieve overall coordination by establishing two-way communication, something that depends on a spirit of mutuality and trust. Yet the company's early success had masked the fact that its structure was imbued with a patronizing spirit that undermined good communication.

The Union

As is typical in Japan, all regular employees except middle and senior management belong to the labor union. Like other unions in the Japanese auto industry, the TK union recognizes that the company must prosper if wage increases and job security are to be assured. On the other hand, and again like other auto unions, it has a history of aggressively pursuing the interests of its workers through the use and threatened use of strikes. Ichihara Hayato, the union's president, explained, "Our union has always negotiated with strong support from the members. We would take a strike vote and go in with a threatening posture. The members supported a union that fought hard with management for the gains it achieved . . . and management typically responded to our strike threats with a conciliatory attitude."

Yet management was not fully open with the union when the company's problems became serious. The two sides sat down on a regular basis to talk about the company's results, but the excess of inventory and the financial difficulties were not seriously examined. "We knew there were serious problems, and we had been urging management to reduce its debt level for some time, but our opinions were ignored," says Ichihara.

As a result of greatly increased inventory profits, continuing economic prosperity, and high inflation in 1973, nominal wages in Japanese manufacturing increased by a monumental 30 percent in 1974. Planning for the 1974 wage settlements had largely been concluded by the time of the oil shock of November 1973. A company in trouble, TK should have been in serious discussion with its union throughout 1974, but not until November 1974, a year after the first oil embargo, did management acknowledge to the union's leadership the extent of its problems. Wage costs represented 19 percent of the total internal manufacturing costs of a car at TK. Given permanent employment, massive layoffs were out of the question, but other, less severe adjustments were possible. In its relations with the union, TK's management displayed the same lack of leadership and openness already noted in dealer and supplier relations. It seriously underestimated the severity of the company's problems and moved to remedy them too late to allow for normal adjustments.

Central to this pattern was the character of Matsuda Kenji. He apparently resisted advice from nearly everyone, including his bankers, who were increasingly alarmed. TK's location, far from Osaka and Tokyo, may partly explain its independent spirit, but Matsuda's behavior was something more. His status as a leading citizen of Hiroshima and his family's central historical role in creating and building the company made him nearly invulnerable to pressure until it was certain the company would fail. Only in early 1975 did the Sumitomo Bank send in a top manager and Matsuda's role begin to diminish.

The Turnaround

The Sumitomo Bank

TK's two major lenders were the Sumitomo Bank and the Sumitomo Trust Bank; the former was the company's lead bank. Hiroshima Bank was next among the top lenders and also a principal lender to many of the company's local suppliers. In all, 73 lending institutions were financing the company in 1975.

It is evident that for about a year the Sumitomo Bank knew of TK's problems, and yet it did not or could not take major corrective action. By early 1974, the bank had placed two officers within TK to familiarize themselves with the company's financial condition. This was certainly noticed by all those close to the situation, yet no overt actions or statements from the financial community occurred. By late 1974, however, sensing the magnitude of the problems, and with an exposure of $234 million, the bank abruptly altered its role. The head of its Tokyo office, Murai Tsutomo, was designated to lead a team of seven resident Sumitomo executives who would supervise the automaker's affairs. In a sense, the bank put the company in quasi-receivership status but without any involvement from courts or lawyers.

In December 1974, the bank made its first public statement about TK's problems. It called a meeting of all the lenders and announced categorically that it would stand by the automaker. It expressed confidence that the company could be put back on a healthy business footing. As proof of its confidence, the bank said that Sumitomo Trust Company would carry any new loans needed to tide TK over its immediate problems. This no doubt came as a relief to the other financial institutions involved. It served to consolidate and strengthen a general resolve among the lenders, and not one called a loan or refused to turn over their existing credits as they came due.

The Sumitomo group also contributed in smaller, less conspicuous ways. The bank, the trust bank, and the Sumitomo Marine and Fire Insurance Company switched their auto purchases entirely to Mazda, and they asked all Sumitomo group companies to do what they could to purchase more cars and trucks from the company. TK sources estimate that the 600-member Sumitomo group purchased 3,000 vehicles per year (or 18,000 vehicles over the six years 1975–81)—a conservative guess, given the total size of the group.

Key lenders, especially Hiroshima Bank, aided the recovery in yet another way by supporting the suppliers during the critical period when their orders were down and cash flow was very tight. Especially critical here was the banks' willingness to carry the lengthened (and theoretically quite insecure) promissory notes TK was issuing to its suppliers. Without Sumitomo's willingness to back up the entire system, the financial safety net would have quickly collapsed.

The National Government

The fact that the government in Tokyo made no loans or loan guarantees has been pointed out as illustrating a basic difference between the Japanese approach and the Chrysler "bailout." The Japanese government did play an indirect role that relied primarily on the private sector, and it is also clear that Japanese bankers did not hold out for government loan guarantees. But this is not to say that the government chose to depend solely on market mechanisms. Rather, it followed a strategy separate from either of the extremes usually contemplated by Americans.

There is little doubt that the government played a key role in the decision that Sumitomo Bank would preserve TK. The economy had not faced such economic uncertainty in two decades. The government could not allow Hiroshima to enter a depression that would affect the morale and confidence of the nation. A former senior official of the Finance Ministry has remarked to the authors that while the ministry would allow almost any industrial company to go under, it would never permit the collapse of Japan's largest banks and trading companies. Sumitomo Bank, by this perspective, was working with an implicit government guarantee. Such a guarantee is quite outside the public, legal domain and requires no explicit invocation. It does not imply that the Finance Ministry would have compensated Sumitomo directly for any losses. Rather, presumably the ministry would have cared for the bank and restored it to health by granting it special business favors (e.g., shifting larger portions of the government's cash account to Sumitomo). It was such an understanding, confirmed by close, private consultation, that was part of the background for the bank's energetic response to TK's problems.

It is also interesting that the national Diet, and especially the Diet members from Hiroshima prefecture, are described by the company as playing no significant role in generating pressure for a rescue effort. Legislative involvement in business affairs brings forth a particular kind of lobbying and publicity. This was not the kind of publicity or involvement Sumitomo or TK wanted. Undoubtedly, political allies in Tokyo helped smooth the way for support, but none of this ever reached the public or caused a national debate as in the Chrysler case.

While the Ministry of Trade and Industry (MITI) viewed the country's auto industry as overcrowded and due for an adjustment, its reaction was one of support. In early 1975, a vice-minister traveled to Hiroshima to visit the company and announced to the press his ministry's full support. Company and Sumitomo Bank officials do not credit MITI with a significant role, but one director of a competing auto firm says that MITI officials cautioned his company against taking advantage of TK's problems in the marketplace—specifically urging dealer restraint in exploiting Mazda's rotary engine's fuel inefficiencies. In addition, MITI explicitly directed TK's large suppliers to continue their dealings on "normal terms." MITI also "counseled" the media to curtail press coverage that might have significantly damaged consumer confidence.

One minor legislative move was made to help TK nationally. A bill was submitted to the Diet to reduce the licensing fees for new passenger cars that met certain stiff emission standards. Only Mazdas and Hondas could pass the test. This was viewed by all as a legislative sleight-of-hand to help Mazda sales. Testimony took months and when the bill finally passed, it made little difference to Mazda sales.

In sum, the crucial part played by the government was bureaucratic, implicit, and private. Its readiness to stand behind a leading financial institution was the ultimate strength of the safety net lying below the company. Such a commitment is fully tested only in a widespread recession, but instances like TK illustrate the way the government can "leverage" its commitment to stability by encouraging private sector banks to take responsibility and initiative for problem cases. Bankruptcy risks are partly a product of public confidence. As confidence is established, the banker's risk is reduced. The government and the lead bank are crucial in managing this attitudinal environment. If we envisage Japan as a set of concentric circles (with the government at the center, the top ten or so banking and trading firms in the next circle, larger companies like TK in the third circle, and so forth, out to much smaller supplier firms), then we find bankruptcies in Japan are numerous indeed, but they rarely affect companies tied into those in the inner circles. Japan has an implicit social policy of protecting the inner circles, it appears, and the crucial government job is one of allocating scarce resources to maintain core stability without sacrificing the growth of overall economic efficiency. In this task, the core private sector institutions are key allies. This is not a legal or legislated arrangement, but one that has evolved historically. It seems evident that market forces can work differently within each circle of the system, leaving considerable room for flexibility and ad hoc arrangements in the government's response to each case.

Management

Murai Tsutomo, a Sumitomo Bank executive with no prior manufacturing experience, was selected to head the bank's management team. Murai had been carefully selected from a number of possible candidates. In addition to having experience with a prior rescue situation, he came from Japan's southernmost island, Kyushu, and had a style and personality that "fit" Hiroshima. Four executives accompanied Murai. They were placed in charge of the marketing, finance, and cost-control functions. When they first arrived, many Hiroshima people resisted their involvement, viewing them as an "occupying force." For a time, employees derisively named TK "Sumitomo Auto."

Murai's style is worth noting in detail. As he tells it:

I wanted to have Tōyō Kōgyō employees understand my personality and create an atmosphere of openness. For example, I looked for opportunities to drink with younger people and, when I had time, I looked up union officials out on the shop floor and joined them in a cup of coffee. I accepted lots of invitations for dinner. I wanted to reduce any feeling of hesitancy toward me. Once, after some employees went fishing, I talked them into coming over to my apartment to cook their catch. In an incident that became famous, I was walking from one bar to another one night with a journalist when a bunch of younger employees unhesitatingly greeted me, and I replied, "There are too many of you to buy drinks." Everyone had a good laugh, and the surprised journalist wrote about the new openness at TK.

I spent almost no time by myself. My secretary worked on the principle of scheduling as many meetings as possible. I spent a lot of time with Hiroshima business leaders, with the press, and with managers and workers at the education and training center. In two years, I met with every manager personally and with at least 2,000 of our hourly employees.

I worked 16-hour days. Around ten o'clock at night, I'd begin to work on the drafts of speeches I'd be making the following day. I did my thinking and reading at midnight—worrying over the abacus. When you are absorbed in something, you cease eating and sleeping. I lived alone in Hiroshima for the entire time, but my wife came from Osaka to host foreign visitors and to join me in serving as a go-between in TK marriages. I saw her perhaps once a week over the four years.

Murai's approach was to keep a low executive profile and to utilize the energies and talents of TK's own managers. It is important to bear in mind that, from Murai's arrival in December 1974 until late 1978, when Matsuda Kenji was forced to formally resign, all efforts toward change were made in the presence of Matsuda. Murai enlisted some of the best and brightest middle managers to spearhead actual changes. He put a bright and intensely likeable executive in charge of cost reduction and created a task force to ascertain the facts of TK's predicament. His task force established systems and key indicators through which the executive committee could take informed action and make long-term capital development plans. Murai found there was no database upon which to make such decisions.

Murai placed plant manager and production specialist Yamasaki Yoshiki, fifty-eight years old, in charge of the production streamlining effort. Throughout 1976 and 1977, Yamasaki persisted in efforts to improve the production process. Production efficiency began to increase. Vehicles produced per worker increased to 34 per worker by late 1977. Yamasaki's record and legitimacy as a career TK employee made him an ideal candidate for the presidency when Matsuda resigned. He had come up through the ranks and had the loyalty and confidence of the other employees.

Despite Murai's efforts, Matsuda's obstinacy created many barriers to change. This situation finally led to an orchestrated effort involving the bank and leaders of the Hiroshima business community to convince Matsuda to step down. Matsuda's departure allowed Yamasaki to be named president and legitimized many of the latest efforts toward shared decision making and decentralization. One executive recalls, "Whereas in Matsuda Kenji's tenure, Mr. Murai was always pushing one step ahead, as soon as Mr. Yamasaki became president, Mr. Murai stepped into a 'one-step-behind' position."

Despite progress on other fronts, TK's relations with its dealers remained poor until Matsuda's departure. Yamasaki's very first move as president was to call a dealer conference. For three days, 16 hours a day, he listened to grievances. At the conclusion, with tears in his eyes, he committed the company to a number of significant changes, including increasing dealer margins from 16 percent to 21 percent (to be competitive with other Japanese manufacturers). He also agreed not to produce cars unless dealers ordered them. For many dealers, this was the first time in forty years that they had met with the president. This fact, and Yamasaki's ability to listen sincerely, began to erode dealer cynicism.

It is well to remember that Yamasaki had virtually no sales experience. His entire career was in manufacturing. Yet, upon assuming the presidency at the age of sixty, he devoted more than 50 percent of his time during the first year to sales problems, most of it in the field. He personally visited all 114 dealerships, and Murai traveled with him. Yamasaki made a practice of insisting that his host, the dealer, sit in the seat of the honored guest. This, too, symbolized TK's commitment to change.

Yamasaki is striking for his friendly demeanor and warm, open manner. He is a listener. In his subordinates' view, his management style embraces two interesting techniques—management by sampling and triangulation on key details. Yamasaki turns up at meetings or on the factory floor at any time of the day or night. Talking to workers, observing, grasping the gist of a management discussion, he effectively takes "core samples" throughout his organization.

Yamasaki encountered many entrenched beliefs among first-line management. Initiating a job-rotation program, he had two-thirds of TK's section chiefs rotated to new positions during his first year as president. "Too many people had stayed in one job too long," he states. "The reshuffle changed their ways of looking at problems." Yamasaki inaugurated extensive education and training of supervisory people to focus their attention on process efficiencies. More specifically, this training was aimed at getting supervisors to understand which activities created value and which did not (e.g., bringing a component from a pile to the assembly-line creates no value; attaching the component to the car adds value). TK's training staff created a toy model-building game based on teams of six to eight foremen. Each team chose a production strategy and established procedures to try to produce the most units with the highest quality. Teams decided everything about how they would produce their cars and were then judged on a complex set of criteria, including the cost of their tools, time, quality and so forth. In this way, shop floor supervisors were trained to focus on efficiency and quality. The training stressed teamwork, analysis, and participative problem solving.

Under Yamasaki, TK also instituted "walking rally" training—a nighttime contest in which teams learned to navigate through a city in a fixed time span without the aid of watches. Self-Defense Force training (including marching and obstacle courses), Zen meditation, and a marathon 50-kilometer mountain climb up Mount Oro were also required of male employees. Explains the Director of Training, "The underlying purpose was to train intensively enough to build each employee's character. Character provides the basis for individual day-to-day capability."

The Union

Earlier in 1974, employees had read in the paper that their company had put its two large office buildings in Tokyo and Osaka up for sale. Yet no public financial announcements were made, and employees were not initially enlisted in an effort to correct the problem. By November, however, there was simply not enough cash available to pay the full December bonus. Abruptly, the atmosphere became tense.

The union was asked to accept a postponement of 60 percent of the end-of-the-year bonus and to approve a plan whereby the employees would be dispatched to dealers to help boost sales, filling the breach created by departing salesmen. The pressures on the union were enormous once the problems were made clear, for the company's survival was of crucial concern to everyone in Hiroshima. The union's members would have no other jobs awaiting them if TK went under. Still, much hard bargaining ensued. The union demanded and received management's promise that there would be no lay-offs. Without agreement on this crucial principle, the negotiations would have foundered. This is an essential point in grasping the labor-relations aspect of Mazda's turnaround: once job security and the company's survival were tied inextricably together by the reconfirmation of permanent employment, union and management were inclined to move along a relatively cooperative path.

The union accepted a rescheduling of bonus payments: one-quarter of the payment was to be postponed for six weeks, one-quarter for 12 weeks. Rescheduling alleviated a critical cash flow problem by shifting approximately $7 million into the first quarter of 1976.

This formula was followed for the three following bonus payments in the next 18 months. Alone, this change would hardly have solved the company's problems. Its significance lay in the fact that a fundamental agreement between labor and management and subsequent union membership approval of that agreement was accomplished in just three weeks. Worker acceptance, furthermore, was facilitated by the union's efforts to arrange bridge loans from its credit union for members who could not meet personal payments as a result of the bonus postponement. As the union president explains:

TK is a crucial part of the Hiroshima economy. If it fails, we lose our jobs and so do many of our neighbors. We had no choice but to do our part. There would have been immediate public disapproval and great dissension in the union if we had resisted management's proposals, even though the company's problems were primarily management's responsibility.

The Dispatched-Worker Program

At the time of the bonus rescheduling, President Matsuda also asked the union for approval of a plan to send several thousand employees to dealers, where they would learn to sell the company's cars. They would retain all their seniority and other privileges. The dealers would pay each dispatched worker a partial salary and cover local housing costs; the company would pay remaining wages, bonuses, and benefits. Dispatched workers would serve for six-to-twelve-month intervals; families would stay behind. A special two-week sales training course would be established to facilitate worker adjustment to the new jobs.

The plan seemed full of potential for exploitation. It relegated seasoned industrial and white collar workers to the role of temporary migrant laborers in an unknown occupational field, and it took them far from the protection of their union. The union was reluctant to approve the plan without strong assurances that (1) the program would be voluntary; (2) appropriate living and working conditions would be guaranteed; and (3) no career would be penalized if an individual did not succeed as a salesman. With these preconditions met, the union was induced to explain to the rank and file how the program would benefit the company, given that there were simply not enough orders coming in to justify the number of TK employees. The union was granted the right to independently monitor all aspects of the program, interviewing each volunteer before final selection, visiting dispatched workers at the dealerships, and checking the personnel files of those who had served as salesmen.

The plan proved to be an ingenious move from the company's point of view. It reduced annual labor costs by roughly $7,600 per dispatched worker, while helping to fill the gap created by the departure of salesmen. The fact that auto retailing in Japan is so labor-intensive made the program sensible. A dispatched worker had to sell only 1.5 cars per month for the dealer to recover his costs, yet even this level of accomplishment required inexperienced people to work hard calling door to door. Many dealers were skeptical at last. In the first analysis dealers, like the unions, had no choice. The average dispatched worker actually sold two cars per month. With the incentives the dealers received on incremental sales increases, the results proved satisfactory to the dealers, who continued to utilize dispatched workers right through 1981.

The dispatched-worker program evolved over time. Initially it was a hastily put-together arrangement in which workers rotated in and out of sales in less than a year, insufficient time to become fully effective. Beginning in 1978, workers (and their families) were sent out for two years, with an optional third year. More than 8,000 workers participated before 1978. At its peak, 2,900 employees were serving as salesmen and another 450 as service mechanics. By the end about half of TK's employees had spent time as dispatched workers. Again, this program alone did not save the company, but it had an immediate effect and, in combination with other cost-reduction efforts, it proved to be a significant contribution to the entire course of recovery.

Obviously, had TK's workers been unwilling to go, the program would have failed and led to union-management conflict. Had they seen the program as oppressive, they also could have sabotaged it by simply not selling cars. But did they really volunteer? Some workers actually did step forward of their own free will, but most were quite reluctant. There was no flood of volunteers. Managers and foremen had to actively recruit "volunteers," and there was a good deal of peer pressure to take one's turn once the program got rolling. The first volunteers almost everywhere were more senior people, including many middle managers and foremen. This seems contrary to practical reasoning since (1) they were the ones least inclined to leave their families; (2) they were the least dispensable to their workplaces; and (3) being middle-aged, they would be the slowest to learn a new kind of work. Yet, as the leaders of their work groups and the ones expected to be the most responsible, they were under the greatest obligation. They were the ones to set the example.

Proportionally, more went from the white collar than the blue collar ranks, but there was a general balance from department to department thanks to the administration's guiding hand. Nearly every section was expected to supply volunteers. Managers were allocated targets for their recruitment efforts. Once the flow out and back was established, group pressure worked to keep up the supply. As time passed, those who had not stepped forward came to feel a degree of shame for not having sacrificed as their colleagues had. While it is clear that this sacrifice was far from a spontaneous outpouring of company loyalty, it was the product of the strong sense of common interest and collegial responsibility. Japanese culture and the Japanese orientation toward the employing company provided the base of obligation that fostered acquiescence in the plan. The results, however, were not simple to achieve, or just a product of Japanese values. A great deal of management effort and union cooperation were required.

Production Improvements and Quality Teams

TK first endeavored to come to grips with its manufacturing deficiencies soon after Murai's arrival. With Yamasaki spearheading the effort, many of the old givens of production were reexamined. For two years prior to becoming president himself, Yamasaki analyzed factory operations. He detected an elegance (i.e., expensive excess) that the company could ill afford. The factory had expensive, built-in safeguards against failure. Among the luxuries, Yamasaki ruefully recalls the large parts inventories on the factory floor that ranged up to a week's supply. Large inventories absorbed capital and space and encouraged workers to operate less efficiently. "If the level of a river is very high, it is difficult to see the many rocks underneath," says Yamasaki, adding, "It is necessary to reduce the water level to find the rocks."

Yamasaki brought needed efficiencies to the assembly line. Machine maintenance improved, so that downtime fell by 50–60 hours per month. Despite TK's massive debt, automation was introduced throughout the engine plant assembly line. Imitating Toyota's *Kanban* system, inventory was reduced to a half day for most parts. Parts floats were reduced from a 6.8 days' supply to one of 2.5 days' supply. The reliability of machinery and the quality of workmanship were enhanced. These improvements in production methods and processes occurred as the level of floats came down. Specific examples illustrate these programs:

Shortening of changeover time for dies and cutters:

Stamping dies	40 minutes to 10 minutes
Ring gear cutter	390 minutes to 13 minutes
Die-casting machine	90 minutes to 4 minutes

Machining of steering knuckles:

Number of workers	11 to 14
Number of floats	1,000 to 60

Machining of timing gear case and cover:

Number of workers	10 to 7
Number of floats	650 to 0

Float reduction brought other problems to the surface, creating a sequence of problem-solving challenges. The quality control program addressed these challenges. In fact, its name creates a false impression, for at its core, it fostered group problem solving based on careful statistical analysis and time-and-motion study. All of this entailed intense involvement by workers and their first-line supervisors. By 1978, all supervisors had been retrained and rotated through different jobs to stimulate their perception of problems.

At TK, as at other Japanese auto companies, the system of worker group participation had been established years before, but it lacked vitality. Yamasaki revitalized these groups. In all, 2,000 different groups were established with seven or eight members apiece. Their focus was on productivity and quality control. Voluntarily organized, these quality circles met two or three times a month to discuss immediate common concerns. As of September 1981, the company had 1,600 circles in operation. While workers alone solved only 15 percent of the issues raised in their circles (help from engineers and management was required to solve the rest), it was the capacity of these sessions to define problems and opportunities that contributed immensely to TK's results. In 1979, 600,000 employee suggestions (22 per capita) saved TK approximately $11 million. In 1982, 1.8 million suggestions were generated, for a remarkable rate of 65 per capita. About 60 percent of these suggestions were adopted.

The Suppliers' Contributions

Prior to Murai's involvement, suppliers were seen to be of great importance in TK's overall cost position, but management exercised little direct control over them. Recall that 70 percent of manufacturing costs were external. As an emergency measure, beginning in late 1974 and continuing through 1977, payment terms to suppliers were lengthened from the usual 180 days to 210 days. This was not a popular move with suppliers, who were simultaneously suffering from declining demand, nor was it an act of leadership on the automaker's part. It was simply a crisis move that few suppliers could oppose. Given the size of TK's annual purchasing budget (about $1.4 billion), however, a one-month extension significantly improved its cash flow and reduced interest payments. These costs were actually spread out among the suppliers. In turn, the suppliers generally passed on some of the risk by discounting the notes with banks or by making sales through a trading firm. The financial framework was a safety net common to both the central manufacturer and its suppliers.

Where the commitment to TK was likely to give way first was among those large components suppliers whose size, diversity, and breadth of customers would allow them to drop the automaker's business as too risky. In 1975–76, a study was made of one such supplier located in Kansai. The company did 15–20 percent of its total business with TK, and it was expected to make significant investments for tooling changes as new models came along. This supplier stationed its second-highest executive in Hiroshima for long periods of time in 1975, in order to assess on a daily basis the risk factor in continuing to do business with TK. As this executive explained, his company did not want to go bankrupt with TK, but it felt it had to stick by the firm as long as possible. It was affiliated with the Sumitomo group and its loyalty would eventually be rewarded.

Upon Murai's arrival, supplier relationships began to change, but with Yamasaki as president, TK adopted a more aggressive stance. Yamasaki asked for significant price reductions, proposing a two-year program. Supplier prices had already been rolled back an average of 2 percent on an ad hoc one-year basis in 1976. In June 1977, the new schedule outlined step reductions every six months, totaling between 12 and 17 percent. The plan had separate targets for different categories of suppliers. TK proposed to work with each supplier to achieve these goals through more productive manufacturing processes and better coordination of design work to lower costs. Some TK engineers had been working with suppliers, and the results were impressive. Anticipating greater supplier cost savings than price reductions, the scheduled price cuts were the company's way of sharing the gains. TK also stated that if cost reductions proved difficult to achieve, the company would be flexible on a case-by-case basis. In this way, the company began playing a leadership role for its production system.

The cost reductions scheduled did not come primarily from heavy investments in labor-saving equipment. Rather, the gains came from small process improvements of many kinds achieved over many months of examination and adjustment. These kinds of changes, in turn, would allow small but continuous reductions in the supplier labor force. At times, as many as 250 TK engineers were working full time with suppliers in pursuit of improved manufacturing.

On the basis of results available, Yamasaki's program was a significant success, accomplishing an average reduction of about 14 percent in supplier prices over two and a half years. The Tōyukai Association suppliers' workforce, to cite a key example, was reduced from 23,000 to 17,000 between 1974 and 1981, despite an increase in annual auto production of half a million vehicles. Within the Tōyukai, productivity increased 220 percent, while the wage level increased 68 percent during the 1976–80 period. Profits and dealer margins improved greatly as a result, and the suppliers themselves gained from both increased sales and shorter payment terms.

Most media commentary on Japanese auto manufacturing has implied that robots and other capital equipment have provided a great advantage. Ironically, the truth of the matter is that the great majority of labor-saving innovations involved little capital expenditure. Most innovations at TK had been initiated at the shop-floor level through the interaction of plant management and workers. TK sources confirm that fully 80 percent of the improved productivity came from small, incremental improvements in processes and quality control. Spot checks with plant floor people confirmed this estimate. Even though its plant and equipment were old by the standards of the Japanese auto industry, TK chose to focus on incremental process improvements; management realized how much slack there was in the system.

The fact that 70 percent of the cost of manufacturing was external made this program the single most crucial one in putting TK back on a sound footing. It did not produce quick savings, but it laid a new competitive foundation. Especially remarkable is the fact that it was accomplished in the face of inflationary pressures and in a Japanese industry already highly efficient by world standards.

Labor Costs

The principle of permanent employment was explicitly reaffirmed in the November 1975 agreement with the union in exchange for cooperation in delaying bonus payments and dispatching workers to the dealers. Management thus faced a long, uphill effort to cut labor costs and increase productivity. A number of separate adjustments were involved. First, hiring was virtually frozen beginning in the spring of 1976 to allow natural attrition to lower the level of total employment. Second, restraint in wage and bonus increases was required. Third, efforts were undertaken to improve manufacturing productivity so that TK labor force reductions could continue over the long term without undermining plant efficiency or product quality.

Before the oil crisis, the natural attrition rate was about 11 percent. This was a turnover rate high enough to reduce total numbers quickly, but most voluntary departures were of young, lower-salaried workers. In 1973, even before the financial crisis, the company was replacing only one of every five departing workers, which meant a 10 percent reduction in workforce annually. From 1976 through 1978, management initiated a nearly complete hiring freeze. But because of the recession and the tight job market, the company's attrition rate had declined by then to only 6 percent. On the other hand, production was picking up during this period, and thus, despite the slower rates of workforce reduction, high rates of labor productivity could be maintained. From 1975 to 1979, TK reduced its workforce by 27 percent.

Nearly all the reduction occurred among factory workers. The number of office workers declined only 2 percent from 1974, whereas the blue-collar workforce had declined by 18 percent. Or, put another way, 82 percent of the total reduction in the workforce took place on the factory side of the organization. Much of this remarkable imbalance can be explained by two converging factors:

1. The attrition rate among young males (high school graduates) working in the factory was very high, whereas the attrition rate for male university graduates working in engineering, sales, and administration was very low. New male high school graduates left the company at the rate of 16 percent their first year, for example, whereas the rate for university graduates was 1 percent.

2. Improvements in manufacturing efficiencies were regularly achieved, but office efficiency was neither targeted nor improved as effectively.

These two factors shaped the resulting patterns in which productivity increases in manufacturing greatly exceeded those in white-collar areas. The units of production per factory employee ratio moved from 33 vehicles in 1974 to 75 in 1981. Factory productivity had more than doubled in seven years.

Negotiated restraint in the rate of increase of wages and bonuses was another targeted source of savings. By comparing TK's wage increases with those for the Japanese auto industry as a whole, we can assess the contribution of this factor. Regarding the reputed flexibility of enterprise unionism in Japan, the picture is actually quite mixed. Although the union adopted a cooperative approach to the dispatched worker program, it was far less flexible in the matter of wages.

From 1974 to 1978, the total TK-industry difference in base pay increases amounts to only 6,539 yen, which comes to about a 1.5 cents per hour difference. Compare this with a difference of several dollars an hour in the Chrysler case. Bonus payments, however, present a different story. Rates of bonus increase were significantly below industry average rates in 1975, 1976, 1977, and 1978. Thus most of the difference in total pay between the company and the industry stems from decreases in the rate of increase in the bonus. At its maximum point below the industry averages (1976), TK employees earned only $436 less per year than their counterparts at other auto firms. This means an hourly differential of 18 cents.

The contention that the Japanese wage system is very flexible because the bonus is tied to the profitability of the company is not confirmed. While TK's union accepted reduced rates of bonus increase and were thus somewhat flexible on a short-term basis, union members came out of the whole affair with their income virtually intact because pay increases stayed in line with industry averages.

It is well worth noting that once the company was healthy again, union members were given a share of "the profits" in terms of increases in wages and bonuses above the industry average from 1978 on. It appears that their cooperation during the crisis was rewarded. When questioned about wage negotiations during the period, management underscored its wish not to gain great concessions at the expense of the workers' livelihood and morale. Reducing the head count was the preferred method, since "it was the employees who had to turn the company around."

Conclusions

Just as the company's cash flow, sales, and production problems in 1974 revealed underlying weaknesses in management and leadership, so the many programs that contributed to improving cash flow, production efficiencies, and sales rested primarily on managerial changes that unlocked the potential strength of the organization's thousands of employees.

Full recovery took a number of years. In the rescue stage, improving cash flow and firming up credit lines were the two most immediate challenges. Sumitomo Bank, with the government as a shadow partner, played the pivotal role with its bold action virtually guaranteeing the company's debts. The bank, the suppliers, and the union all contributed to improving cash flow and they did so quickly. What is most striking is how important the supplier relationship was to TK even in resolving the cash flow crisis. By comparison, bonus sacrifices by the union do not seem particularly significant. The already suffering dealers were only asked to accept the dispatched workers and to cover a portion of their wages.

As we turn to the second phase of the turnaround, a variety of cost-cutting programs take center stage. The overall process took five years, with the major efforts aimed at reducing direct labor costs and bringing down the prices of materials and parts supplied by vendors. The impossibility of layoffs made gradual long-term efforts to reduce labor costs (via natural attrition) the only viable avenue to a competitive cost structure.

Supplier price reductions and decreases in the TK workforce stand out as the significant elements of this effort. More than 85 percent of the total cost savings were generated by these two programs, each of which involved a gradual reduction of head count as efficiencies were achieved. The relative insignificance of wage and bonus restraint in the total picture also emerges clearly in this comparison, accounting for less than 5 percent of the total savings. The dispatched worker program, while not inconsequential, was also a relatively small contributor.

Indeed, the heart of the cost-cutting story is undeniably the capacity of engineers, foremen, and shop floor production workers to continually generate new efficiencies of many kinds in both TK's and suppliers' plants over a four-year period. Neither heavy capital outlays nor brilliant ideas accomplished this feat. Rather, the effort was a matter of discovering the potential of existing plant and equipment. It was employee dedication, skill, and a capacity to cooperate at lower levels of the organization that proved most crucial in putting the company's production on a solid competitive footing. Management directed and facilitated this process, but only thousands of hardworking people realized the goals. To what can this effort be attributed? In our estimation, both management and the quality of human resources were crucial. The Japanese willingness and capacity to make such changes is the cornerstone of the country's postwar manufacturing success, not only in turnaround situations but in successful companies of all kinds. Here, at the microeconomic level, culture and society as sources of efficient cooperation play a large role in differentiating one country from another.

How do we evaluate the influence of permanent employment in this overall pattern? It forces management to take a longer-term view of cost-cutting measures, as it endures the risky wait for attrition. And it forces management to take seriously the potential of average workers to make a difference. Compared to American turnaround situations, Japanese companies in trouble are apt to find themselves long on people and about equally strapped for cash—although cash flow remains a problem longer because of the inability to institute layoffs. Using people well thus becomes a necessary skill of Japanese management in such crises. The TK story also suggests that labor cooperation has a good deal to do with the way management structures its turnaround efforts. The support of union leaders, the talents of lower-level management, and the basic abilities of production workers all come into play as additional factors shaping the success of such an approach. Clearly, permanent employment encourages a sense of long-term mutual interest upon which greater effort and better communication can be achieved.

Yet in the smaller firms, the notable cost reductions passed on to TK were not accomplished in a context of job security similar to that in TK itself. We do not know how many people were laid off by these firms as they too sought to remain solvent in the crisis and as they improved productivity in cooperation with the Mazda engineers, but unquestionably it is at this level that jobs are more readily cut in downturns and that a sizable proportion of the workforce is untenured. It is important to recognize that part-timers, rehired retirees, temporaries, and other non-core workers at this level in the structure serve to cushion the job security of TK regular workers.

Ironically, the long-term effort at improving labor productivity led to a significant reduction in blue-collar jobs. About a 30 percent decline was experienced by the TK "group" in manufacturing employment. Using its increased profits, furthermore, the company has been completing a new, highly automated plant that will contribute to productivity gains and further reductions in the amount of labor input per unit. The union's membership experiences wage gains in all this, but the union has declined in size. In this sense, permanent employment is a factor causing companies in prosperous industries to aggressively seek labor productivity increases in an ongoing (if unstable) alliance with unions that are trading a decrease in the number of jobs for an increase in the standard of living. The alliance has proved dynamic and viable to date.

Improved sales were important to the turnaround, too. TK's sales rebounded quickly enough after 1974 to facilitate the productivity improvements that we have just considered. One factor sustaining domestic sales in 1975 was the absence of damaging news coverage that might have eroded consumer confidence. Second, the Japanese dealers held their course—having few alternatives but to increase their efforts to sell Mazdas. The dispatched-worker program contributed incremental sales of 400,800 vehicles, enough to liquidate three times the excess inventory on hand at the end of 1975. Friendly institutions in Hiroshima and the Sumitomo group purchased perhaps 40,000 additional autos. As important as these factors were, perhaps the most significant element of the sales story was the development of two immensely popular new models: the GLC/Familia (the third-greatest-selling model in Japanese auto history) and the RX-7 sports car. Both models were conceived during Matsuda Kenji's tenure, but they were developed in remarkably short periods thanks to the inspired atmosphere of trying to save the company. A project-team approach allowed the company to create new designs tailored to the customer's needs and dreams. The design process, in other words, was a product of the new management style and, as on the production side, this new style unlocked great energy and initiative.

TK's dependence on exports also meant that the favorable exchange rate over the period contributed a good deal to sales buoyancy, and this in turn raises the question of government involvement, for despite its hands-off policy toward TK, the government did play a role in keeping the yen relatively weak during the time of the company's recovery. Just the reverse can be noted of the Chrysler bailout, where direct government assistance was coupled with an adverse exchange rate.

The TK story contains many of the best and many of the worst qualities of Japanese business practices. Before 1975, it was a one-man company with weak supplier and dealer relations and little mutuality in management's treatment of the union. Furthermore, as the crisis mounted in 1973 and 1974, little was done to reverse this situation at a time when trust and open communication were most needed. The company possessed few of the attributes of Japanese management so widely praised of late, yet it was very Japanese in an older sense. It was autocratically run and secretive. Communication was almost entirely top-down. Paternalistic practices were notable and patron-client relationships were quite prominent. In other words, "wet" and "feudalistic" qualities were much in evidence, as they were throughout prewar Japanese industry.

It is remarkable, then, that things held together so well. Despite a generally poor economic situation, seven other automakers competing fiercely for the domestic market, declining Mazda popularity, and high production costs, the commitment of all parties held firm. The safety net of relations proved to be very constant and flexible in its response to the needs of the mother company. It is also remarkable how fundamental improvements in the entire system were gradually accomplished which did much more than just float the company off the rocks. Costs were cut to such a degree, for example, that Mazda is now a leading international competitor.

What explains the strength of the safety net? Three things: (1) the immediate and firm commitment to the company of the government and Sumitomo group; (2) the "We're all in the same boat" response of dealers, suppliers, workers, and people in the Hiroshima region; (3) the latent readiness to pull together and sacrifice for a long-term common goal on the part of those involved. All three are factors that *in degree* distinguish Japan from the United States.

The strength of the safety net raises the question of risk. It is widely appreciated that assessment of risk in Japan is less a matter of weighing a company's balance sheet and assets and more a matter of appraising its network of support and the quality of its management. This is because risk is shared in Japan beyond the confines of a stockholder/management set. The tendency to exclusive, close business ties both reflects and explains this characteristic.

Other questions immediately come to mind. How does the government view market forces in such circumstances? Does the system surrounding large Japanese companies spread the risk so effectively that market forces are comparatively weaker than in comparable cases in other countries? If so, does the cost of capital reflect this in Japan? Is there a middle ground between "bailing out" a troubled company and "letting the market work," a concept that we in the West have trouble grasping and analyzing because of the polarities of our thinking about the workings of an economy? There are no clear answers to these questions at present, but this case cannot be fully analyzed without considering them.

At the heart of such crises lie the meaning and limits of interdependence as a social quality. Independence and dependence, freedom and constraint, superordination and subordination, these are alternative qualities of relationships, and

Japanese economic ties can be judged within these dimensions. But there is a static arbitrariness and shallowness in the insights gained by such an approach. The challenge in understanding Japan, as we see it, is to grasp the underlying dynamics of interdependence as an institutional and cultural starting point. A process approach, centered on leadership and management skills and considering the relational system's response to varying pressures and opportunities, appears to be a more fruitful avenue for study. The TK turnaround is a lesson in managing interdependence.

It is also a lesson in the economic significance of such fundamental, but seemingly intangible, characteristics of a population as attitudes, work habits, cooperation, commitment, and skills—matters of national character and culture. Interest rates, industrial policy, trade barriers, and the like are undoubtedly important factors in a comparative history of economic growth, but only managers and workers build cars and other products. Their capacity to pull together in a crisis is a crucial measure of a society's strength.

Part IV: Government Institutions and Policy Making

J A P A N ' S pace-setting rate of economic growth has overshadowed the equally remarkable performance of its political system. Japan's record of stable and effective governance has to be considered at least as impressive an achievement as its economic recovery and growth. Indeed, the two—politics and economics—are closely interconnected. Over the postwar years, Japan's political system, with its pro-business orientation, has provided an unusually supportive environment within which the economy has flourished. If the political system had been less stable, the economy might not have grown as rapidly or adapted as well as it has.

By almost any standard of comparison, Japan has to be considered among the world's most stable democracies. In no other large industrial nation has a single political party dominated both houses of parliament for virtually the entire postwar period. Single-party organizations, in coalition with smaller parties, have held onto the reins of power for fairly long stretches of time in such European countries as Italy; but only Japan's Liberal-Democratic Party (LDP) has managed to rule as majority party without having been forced to enter into coalition arrangements.

What makes the LDP's long domination especially noteworthy is that it has continued despite all the changes wrought by accelerated economic growth. Within only a generation's time, Japanese society has undergone a major metamorphosis. The labor force, once heavily concentrated in agriculture, is now overwhelmingly involved in manufacturing and the services sector; the primary sector, which accounted for 48.3 percent of the workforce in 1950, now employs only 8.8 percent. As excess farm workers have found employment in manufacturing and service sectors, large numbers of Japanese have migrated from the countryside to metropolitan and urban centers.

In addition to fundamental shifts in employment and urban patterns, postwar Japan has also undergone dramatic demographic change. Life expectancy has increased by 25 years: for Japanese males, from 50.1 years in 1947 to 74.5 years in 1984; for Japanese women, from 54.0 in 1947 to 80.2 in 1984. This has had the effect of expanding the number of Japanese over sixty-five from about 5 percent of the population to more than 12 percent. As a result, in one generation's time, Japan has gone from being one of the youngest to being one of the oldest populations in the world. This demographic revolution has had, and will continue to have, far-reaching consequences for Japan. It has forced the LDP, among other things, to upgrade its social security and national health insurance policies.

How has Japan's political system maintained such an even keel during this period of far-reaching social change? Why haven't the structural transformations led to wrenching political realignments? What coalition of support groups have kept the LDP continuously in power? How have the government bureaucracies managed to retain substantial power over policy making? These are just a few of the questions discussed in the readings in this section.

How does Japan's political economy, which seems so different from anything in the West, look in comparative perspective? Are the models we use to describe Western democracies appropriate or accurate? Should Japan be called "elitist"? Or is it more properly labeled "pluralist"? Is it governed, as some have maintained, by a "ruling triad" of the LDP, the bureaucracy, and big business? Is the widely used term "Japan, Inc.," the best shorthand description of what makes Japan unique?

One of the most intriguing, and controversial, questions concerning Japan's political economy is the importance ascribed to the role of the state. Some scholars, like Chalmers Johnson, believe the bureaucratic state (specifically, the Ministry of International Trade and Industry, or MITI) is the dominant actor in Japan, more dominant than either the legislative branch or the private sector. Such terms as "Japan, Inc." and "developmental state" convey a sense of its pivotal position. The conventional wisdom, in fact, is that the administrative state is what holds Japan's political economy together. It is thought to be more powerful than that in any other advanced industrial country—stronger certainly than America's or Great Britain's and more dominant than even France's.

Indeed, Japan is one of the few countries in the world that appears to have found a relatively effective formula for administering a coherent industrial policy. Almost everywhere else, including Great Britain, Italy, France, and other European countries, the attempt to upgrade specific industries or individual companies through the instrument of industrial policy has failed. Why has it succeeded in Japan? The answer seems to reside in the structure of Japan's political system, which features MITI's broad scope of authority over most manufacturing sectors, its relative insulation from politicized pressures, and its ability to reach a binding consensus with producer groups. Such features make it possible for MITI to administer a comparatively effective industrial policy, which includes measures tailored to fit the differing needs of both sunset (structurally depressed) industries and sunrise (rapidly growing) industries.

Japan's reliance on industrial policy has had international repercussions. Business and government leaders in other countries have complained that Japanese industrial policy has fostered unfair trade practices, practices that violate the letter and spirit of GATT (General Agreement on Trade and Tariffs). By encouraging huge capital investments in manufacturing facilities (for strategic industries such as steel and semiconductors), Japanese industrial policy has led to extended production runs, which have spilled over into export deluges overseas. Moreover, the benefits of mass production for domestic and overseas markets make it exceedingly difficult for foreign companies to compete in Japan. Infant industry protection and anti-recession cartels, two other instruments of industrial policy, help keep the doors to Japanese markets tightly shut.

Many government and business leaders in Japan take issue with these criticisms. They maintain that the chain of negative repercussions allegedly set off by Japanese industrial policy is exaggerated. Anti-recession cartels and infant industry protection, to begin with, no longer exist, and they point out that a "capital investments race" takes place in most rapidly expanding sectors, including those that lie outside the scope of industrial targeting. This implies that the construction of manufacturing capacity is not a by-product of industrial policy, but rather reflects much deeper forces at work within the industrial system. Japan's defenders argue that the problem of large trade surpluses emerges out of the crucible of macroeconomic forces, such as national savings-to-consumption ratios, not out of industrial policies.

How accurate is the perception that the Japanese state is the most powerful in the advanced industrial world? In one of the readings that follow (Okimoto's "Japan, the Societal State"), the answer given runs counter to the conventional wisdom. It argues that the Japanese state has never had, historically, a universalistic foundation on which to base its legitimacy. Its extraordinary power in the postwar period has come from two factors: the legacy of the Occupation and the capacity of government and business to reach consensus on industrial goals. This argument holds that the Japanese state, by itself, is not endowed with the kind of authority that simply overwhelms private opposition. Rather, its power appears thus embedded in the structure of public-private sector interdependence and is dependent on its capacity to work in close coordination with the private sector.

Within the structure of extensive interdependence, the state is, of course, indispensable; it serves such crucial functions as communication, coordination, collective goal-setting, resource mobilization, conflict resolution, and interest aggregation. But in order to fulfill these responsibilities, the Japanese state must be able to persuade, not coerce, private entities to comply voluntarily with its directives. How does it secure this compliance? Some, including Okimoto, say this is achieved by consulting widely with private sector groups, taking their views and interest fully into account, and arriving at a carefully crafted consensus. The readings in this section explore the character of this process and raise questions about the nature of political power, as exercised by the Japanese state—how power emerges more out of a complex network of relationships and voluntary arrangements, and less out of a framework of legal authority or the threat of coercive sanctions.

32. Liberal-Democratic Party Dominance in the Diet

Daniel I. Okimoto

Despite the existence of a number of opposition parties in Japan, the Liberal-Democratic Party (LDP) has controlled the government almost without interruption since the end of World War II. In this selection, drawn from *Between MITI and the Market* (forthcoming), Stanford political scientist Daniel Okimoto analyzes the factors in the Japanese political system and within the LDP that have allowed this continual domination.

The most remarkable feature of Japan's political regime is the monopolization of majority power in the Diet (parliament) by the Liberal Democratic Party (LDP) for almost the entire postwar period. No party in any of the world's large industrial democracies comes close to matching this record. The unprecedented feat has had a profound impact on the structure and processes of Japanese politics. It has given rise to a party system almost totally dominated by a single party, in which interest aggregation is structured largely by the political exchange between the LDP and interest groups in its support coalition, within the functional boundaries of the individual bureaucracies.

The LDP's monopoly of power is also remarkable when viewed against the background of the fundamental changes that have taken place in Japan's socioeconomic structure: it has survived profound changes in demographic composition, industrial structure, and occupational distribution, as well as business cycles, external shocks, and the transformation of the international system. The LDP has presided over nothing less than an industrial revolution. The revolution has had far-reaching socioeconomic ramifications, some of which (such as steep increases in real income) have helped maintain the LDP in power, while others (such as the contraction of the primary sector) have eroded its base of support.

Japan's system of electoral districting is structured so that voters in rural and semirural urban constituencies have had a greater voice in election returns than their counterparts in metropolitan districts. Although eligible voters in the agricultural sector represented only about 20 percent of the national electorate in 1976, the rural and semiurban districts decided about 30 percent of the seats in the Lower House.

In the 1982 election, for example, a vote cast in the rural 5th District of Hyōgō

From Daniel I. Okimoto, *Between MITI and the Market: Japanese Industrial Policy for High Technology* (Stanford, Calif.: Stanford University Press, forthcoming). By permission of the publisher.

Table 32.1.   Distribution of Seats in the Lower House,
1987

Party	Number of seats
Liberal-Democratic Party (LD)	302
Japan Socialist Party (JSP)	85
Kōmeitō	56
Democratic-Socialist Party (DSP)	26
Japan Communist Party (JCP)	26
New Liberal Club	6
Social-Democratic League	4
Independents	7

SOURCE: Japanese Information Service.

Prefecture carried more than three times the weight of a vote cast in the urban 4th District of Chiba Prefecture; that is, a candidate from Hyōgō's 5th District won a seat with only 81,375 votes, compared to the 321,351 it took to win one in the 4th District of Chiba. Thus, Japan's system of election districting has allowed agriculture to be disproportionately represented relative to its population. The egregious imbalance, which calls into question the constitutionality of election districting, has continued with only cosmetic adjustments (adding some seats to the metropolitan and urban districts). The tyranny of the status quo is reflected in the resistance of the two largest parties, the LDP and JSP (Japan Socialist Party), to plans for radical reapportionment; both parties benefit greatly from the current imbalance.

The LDP (as well as the JSP) has had its strongest base of support in rural and semiurban districts, with the small opposition parties—the JCP (Japan Communist Party), Kōmeitō, and DSP (Democratic-Socialist Party)—faring best in the large metropolitan districts. If one vote carried the same weight in metropolitan precincts that it does in the rural districts, the small opposition parties would be in a position to claim significantly more seats in the Diet, without any change in their percentage of votes. As it is, only 25 districts out of 130 can be classified as "purely" metropolitan. Ishikawa Masumi points out that, although the population concentrated in these metropolitan precincts—Tokyo, Yokohama, Osaka, Nagoya, Kyoto, and Kobe—represents more than 40 percent of the national total, the number of representatives these areas elect to the Diet comes to only 100 out of 511, or less than 20 percent.

Through shrewd campaign strategy, the LDP can usually capture a stable share of seats from the metropolitan districts. This is due to the high percentage of "dead" votes cast for opposition party candidates (that is, votes cast for candidates who fail to be elected) in the metropolitan precincts. By minimizing its number of "dead" votes, the LDP is usually able to win around one-third of the seats from the 25 metropolitan districts. Hence, the power of the agricultural sector far exceeds its demographic size, to say nothing of its economic output. According to Kenzo Hemmi, "The LDP has been able to remain in power for so long because, and only because, it has enjoyed support in rural districts."

The LDP has managed to hold its Diet majority in spite of the steady falloff in its percentage of votes, beginning in the late 1950's and "bottoming out" two de-

Table 32.2. *Opposition Parties and Support Groups*

Opposition party	Main support group
Japan Socialist Party	Sōhyō labor union
Democratic-Socialist Party	Dōmei labor union
Kōmeitō	Soka Gakkai
Japan Communist Party	Communist Party

cades later. In 1984, following a serious election setback, the LDP clung to a bare majority, with 258 seats out of 511 in the Lower House. Still, the 258 seats represented more than twice that of the largest opposition party, the JSP, more than three times that of the second-largest opposition party, the Kōmeitō, and nearly ten times that of the JCP. Indeed, the largest LDP faction, with more than 60 members of the Lower House, is bigger than any one of the opposition parties except the JSP. Slim as the LDP's majority was in 1984, with only two seats over the threshold of 256, the numbers fail to communicate the true dominance of the ruling conservative party. The New Liberal Club, an LDP offshoot, and some of the Independents work closely enough with the LDP that they can almost be considered de facto members of the ruling party. Moreover, top leaders in the LDP maintain fairly close behind-the-scenes ties with members of the DSP and the Kōmeitō, the third- and fourth-ranking parties, blurring the boundaries between conservative and opposition camps. Even if the LDP eventually loses its parliamentary majority, as political soothsayers have been predicting since the late 1950's, it will still be in a position to enter into a formal coalition with one or more of the opposition parties.

None of the opposition parties is big enough to be within range of unseating the LDP. Because of deep divisions within the opposition ranks, there is no realistic possibility that an all-opposition coalition can be formed. The differences dividing, say, the Kōmeitō or Democratic-Socialists, on the one hand, from the Communists, on the other, are far deeper than those separating the Kōmeitō and Democratic-Socialists from the LDP. Although opposition leaders have often talked about forming a united front, the talk has never amounted to anything more than wishful thinking. About the best the Kōmeitō, DSP, and JSP have managed to do is agree not to compete against one another in a few election districts.

Party weaknesses and deep schisms within the opposition camp have thus helped the LDP stay in power. In fact, by 1987, LDP strength was back to over 300 seats (see Table 32.1). Even voters who are disgruntled with the LDP feel there are no viable alternatives. In their eyes, not one of the opposition parties appears ready to step in and assume the reins of government. In sharp contrast to the LDP, most of the "progressive" parties depend on support from a single, narrowly based, relatively closed interest group; indeed, so strong are the ties of dependence that the opposition parties tend to be viewed as mere "captives" of their particularistic support groups (see Table 32.2). To survive in Japan's monopolistic political marketplace, opposition parties simply have to maintain the organizational, electoral, and financial backing of their respective support groups; failure to do so would be tantamount to political suicide. Yet dependence comes at a high price. It stands in the way of attempts to broaden the base of popular support beyond the narrow confines of parent organizations. Nearly all opposition parties are thus stuck with the image of being captive to some special interest. The encompassing nature of the LDP's grand coalition could hardly pose a more striking contrast. The LDP is not only free of domination by a single interest group, but its support coalition consists of groups so diverse that, on certain issues, their interests actually conflict. Being the only party with a broad base of national support places the LDP in a very advantageous position. It has benefited from the fragmentation of the opposition camp and the limited support base of each opposition party. And it has fully exploited the powers that come with incumbency to consolidate the hegemonic structure of Japan's political system.

Japan's one-party-dominant system rests on the LDP's broad base of electoral support, which covers a diverse cross section of society—from farmers to big business executives and small-to-medium entrepreneurs. The LDP even picks up votes from rank-and-file members of organizations like Dōmei, which is formally aligned with the DSP. The electoral base of the LDP's support coalition thus spans nearly all segments of society (at least in some measure), cutting across what are often deep-seated cleavages in other countries: young and old, labor- and capital-intensive industries, primary and manufacturing sectors, rural and urban, big and small business, management and labor. Although the proportion of those represented from each category differs, of course, the LDP's is truly a "grand coalition," especially in terms of the spectrum of interests represented.

The inclusiveness of the LDP's ruling coalition parallels and plays off against inclusiveness at the administrative and bureaucratic level. Virtually all interest groups in Japan fall under the jurisdiction of one government bureaucracy or another. The political and bureaucratic isomorphism simplifies interactions between the legislative and administrative branches. Instead of having to divide their time evenly between conservative and opposition camps, Japanese bureaucrats can concentrate on working with key LDP leaders who head LDP policy committees or belong to various informal caucuses (*giin renmei*) and policy support groups (*zoku*). Because ad hoc LDP policy groups cover the full range of economic activities, the inclusive, hegemonic structure functions fairly smoothly to aggregate interests with respect to bread-and-butter policies.

Political and administrative inclusiveness is made possible by the relative cohesiveness and homogeneity of Japanese society, especially the comparative absence of deeply rooted cleavages. There are few permanent schisms based on class, ideology, religion, region, race, history, ethnicity, or language. The religious schisms between clericalism and anticlericalism historically observable in France and Italy, for example, have no counterpart in Japan. The traditional antagonism between labor and management, perhaps the most salient political cleavage in the West, is muted in Japan by the company-based nature of labor organization. The homogeneity of Japanese society has facilitated LDP efforts to encapsulate support from a very broad socioeconomic cross section, and, exploiting the powers of incumbency, to reward loyal adherents. Its ability to hold together, and even extend, a diverse coalition of interests has also been greatly enhanced by the positive political consequences of sustained economic growth, notably steep increases in real income for the Japanese people, combined with equitable distribution of that increased income.

33. The Liberal-Democratic Party's "Grand Coalition"

Daniel I. Okimoto

The Liberal-Democratic Party (LDP) is a broadly based party, which manages to provide support for business interests without alienating its other support groups. In this selection, Stanford political scientist Daniel Okimoto argues that the LDP maintains two different kinds of relationships with its constituencies: a politicized, pork-barrel relationship with the labor-intensive sector of society, and a more distant, bureaucratically mediated relationship with the business sector.

How has the Japanese government managed to sustain a climate so favorable to business interests without succumbing to parochial pressures from interest groups or to partisan politicking? An analysis of the LDP's "grand coalition" of support, and the nature of its interactions with its support groups, tells us a great deal about Japan's political economy.

The LDP draws support, in varying degrees, from nearly all sectors of society, but its interactions with two broad groups deserve special mention: (1) the "labor-intensive" sectors of society—farmers, fishermen, small–medium entrepreneurs, retailers, doctors, those in the service sector, the elderly, and so on—from which the LDP receives votes; and (2) big businesses—the large corporations at the heart of Japan's industrial development—from which it receives financial support. The gerrymandered election system, which allows nonmetropolitan districts to be heavily overrepresented in the Diet, has given rise to a situation in which powerful interest groups, such as agriculture, fishing, and other primary-sector occupations, have provided the electoral base for the LDP, which, in turn, has converted voter support into pursuit of rapid industrial growth.

From 1952 to 1972, the LDP focused much of its political energy on satisfying its traditional support groups, using the prerogatives of incumbency to direct subsidies, public works contracts, and favorable public policies to labor-intensive, largely nonmanufacturing sectors of society in return for votes. The LDP's relationship with these labor-intensive groups has been particularistic, symbiotic, politicized, and unabashedly based on the pork barrel. Not surprisingly, the government ministries in charge of regulating these interest groups, such as the Ministry of Agriculture and Forestry and the Construction Ministry, have been among the most highly politicized. The LDP used its power to buy off these electorally salient sectors by earmarking large sums from the General Accounts Budget (e.g., for rice price subsidies) and by passing generous tax packages (as for medical doctors). Consequently, the labor-intensive sectors, particularly those left behind in

From Daniel I. Okimoto, *Between MITI and the Market: Japanese Industrial Policy for High Technology* (Stanford, Calif.: Stanford University Press, forthcoming). By permission of the publisher.

the processes of industrial development, received the benefits of a continual redistribution of income, and the gap between the "backward sectors" (e.g., the countryside) and the "rapidly advancing sectors" (e.g., the metropolitan areas) never grew large enough to threaten political or social stability. Of course, such stability has come at a price—witness parochial interest-group lobbying, political favoritism, corruption, and egregious examples of economic inefficiency in the primary and service sectors. But the damage has tended to be contained within single-issue domains, and the most blatant forms of pork barreling and petty politicization have not spilled over into and contaminated government-business relations in the manufacturing sectors.

The LDP's relationship with the capital-intensive manufacturing sector has been of a sharply different nature: more distant, less particularistic, less politicized, and more formally mediated by the powerful economic bureaucracies who have jealously guarded their prerogatives against interest-group and LDP encroachments. With the LDP's attention heavily absorbed in the politics of the non-manufacturing sectors, the Ministry of International Trade and Industry (MITI) and the Finance Ministry have managed to maintain firm control over policies related to the industrial economy. The LDP has been content to let MITI run the industrial economy, because MITI has demonstrated exceptional competence, and the LDP has obtained what it has really wanted—namely, large financial contributions from big business. Japanese industrial policy has therefore enjoyed a degree of insulation from both LDP interference and parochial interest-group lobbying that must be considered extraordinary among postwar industrial states.

Several reasons can be cited to explain this situation. Aside from the peculiarities of Japan's electoral districting, already alluded to, perhaps the most critical factor has been MITI's capacity to forge general consensus with industry. Not only are broad objectives agreed upon within the framework of a long-term industrial vision, but concrete policy measures are also worked out between specific MITI divisions and bureaus (*genkyoku*) and individual industrial sectors. The LDP may try to influence MITI on behalf of special interest groups during the formative stages of policy deliberations, but once an agreement has been reached, LDP members have little opportunity to intervene.

MITI and industry are able to arrive at consensus because: (1) a relationship of trust has been built over years of interaction; (2) industry understands that MITI adopts policies in the general interests of industrial sectors and the economy as a whole; (3) MITI's track record over the postwar period inspires confidence; (4) MITI's unusually broad scope of authority compels it to act on behalf of collective interests; (5) industry has had very little to complain about with respect to industrial policies; and (6) MITI has studiously avoided having to rely on legislative action and the law. MITI bureaucrats firmly believe that the fiercely competitive nature of Japan's company-centered industrial economy seems to depend on active mediation and coordination on the part of a neutral entity, government, which acts in the national interest. Both MITI and industry prefer that the use of law be kept to a minimum; administrative guidance is one means of sidestepping legislative interference.

34. The Exchange of Political Goods and Services

Daniel I. Okimoto

In this selection, political scientist Daniel Okimoto argues that the political transactions of the Liberal-Democratic Party (LDP) with its support groups can be divided into four different types, according to the group involved, its relation to the LDP, and its corresponding government bureaucracy. The essay was taken from *Between MITI and the Market*.

The dynamics of the Liberal-Democratic Party's (LDP's) interactions with its interest coalition, and with the bureaucracy in turn, provide the essential materials for constructing a model of the Japanese policy-making processes, which are called here segmented political configurations. The model explains why there are striking variations across sectors in the degree to which Japanese industrial policy is politicized. It helps us to understand why industrial policies for the manufacturing and high-technology sectors under the Ministry of International Trade and Industry (MITI) have been relatively free from political interference, while those for agriculture and construction tend to be shaped by political considerations. The theory is based on the fundamental concept that political transactions involving the exchange of political goods and services serve as the driving force behind the nexus binding the LDP to the various interest groups that make up its support coalition. Such transactions take place under a single-party-dominant political system, within the framework of jurisdictional boundaries worked out between individual bureaucracies.

Over decades of single-party rule, political exchanges have become relatively routinized. The inability of opposition parties to pose a realistic alternative to single-party rule has been of great significance. It has meant that most interest groups in the LDP's grand coalition have had no choice but to depend on the LDP, operating within an institutional framework of policy segmentation. Out of the complex interplay between groups in the LDP's grand coalition, the LDP itself, and the bureaucracies has emerged a model of political exchange. The LDP's grand coalition can be divided into the following four types, based on the nature of the political goods and services exchanged:

1. *Clientelistic Votes.* The LDP receives votes from clientelistic support groups in exchange for favorable legislation, subsidies, generous tax treatment, and other advantages. Private interests that take part in the exchange include traditional LDP support groups—agriculture, small-scale enterprises, health professions, heads of local postal services, etc. The bureaucracies involved include Ag-

From Daniel I. Okimoto, *Between MITI and the Market: Japanese Industrial Policy for High Technology* (Stanford, Calif.: Stanford University Press, forthcoming). By permission of the publisher.

riculture and Forestry, Small and Medium Enterprise Agency (part of MITI), Post and Telecommunications, and Welfare.

2. *Reciprocal (Pork-Barrel) Patronage.* The spoils of public expenditures (public works, procurements, subsidies) are recycled back to the LDP in the form of financial contributions. The relationship is one of reciprocal patronage. Involved interest groups include a variety of traditional LDP supporters—local interests, construction, transportation, defense industries. Recycling also takes place in the regulatory arena, with regulated industries contributing to the LDP in return for acceptable regulatory policies (transportation, telecommunications, electrical power utilities). The bureaucracies involved include Construction, Transportation, Post and Telecommunications, Local Autonomy, and Defense.

3. *Untied Financial Support.* Various interest groups—big business, banking and financial institutions, etc.—give the LDP financial support, untied to specific expenditures or public policy favors. It can be understood as a general exchange, one based on the broad benefits the business community receives from having a pro-business party in power. Big businesses' willingness to contribute what are usually large sums—in spite of the public goods nature of the contribution—can perhaps be understood as a kind of insurance premium charged to those most capable of paying. The bureaucracies under whose jurisdiction these donors fall are MITI and the Finance Ministry and various divisions or bureaus in other ministries.

4. *Generalized Voter Support.* As the size of groups in Type 1 above shrink with economic maturation, the LDP has had to win support from a much broader and more diffuse cross section of voters: white-collar salarymen, housewives, young residents in metropolitan areas, the self-employed. These groups tend not to be politically well organized, to identify themselves only weakly (and conditionally) with the LDP, and to vote on the basis of broad policy concerns (such as welfare, pollution, and the overall health of the economy). The LDP tries to appeal to them through the crafting of public policies aimed at improving the overall quality of life. Given the diffuseness of the groups and their concerns, no single set of ministries can be identified as principally in charge.

The four types of political exchange can be viewed hierarchically in terms of levels of politicization and the closeness of ties between the LDP interest groups and bureaucratic agencies: Type 1 is the most politicized, with the closest adhesion between the LDP, the interest groups, and the ministries; the degree of politicization and adhesion declines a bit in Type 2; Type 3 is significantly freer of politicized interference; relations between members of this interest configuration are more at arm's length; Type 4 is the loosest, most diffuse, and least stable of all the LDP–interest group–bureaucracy configurations.

35. Liberal-Democratic Party Factions

Daniel I. Okimoto

The Liberal-Democratic Party (LDP), which has been dominant in Japan since World War II, is not a monolithic party representing only one interest group. Its power derives from a complex balance of factional interests. In this essay, taken from *Between MITI and the Market*, political scientist Daniel Okimoto examines the political mechanisms that have given rise to these factions and the use the LDP makes of them.

In spite of its long reign of power, the Liberal-Democratic Party (LDP) is not tightly knit or organizationally strong. Lacking a broad base of grass-roots support, with only 2.57 million dues-paying members, the LDP has had to rely on individual Diet representatives to mobilize voter support through their own personal organizations, called *kōenkai*, in rural and semi-urban districts. The LDP is often described as a federation of semiautonomous factions, constantly jockeying for power and advantage within the party. In 1983, there were six factions, ranging in size from Tanaka Kakuei's, the largest, with 107 members, to the smallest with only 13.

Factions arise out of a combination of conditions, perhaps the most important being Japan's unusual system of multicandidacy election districts. In each district represented in the Lower House, anywhere from three to five seats are open, with each registered voter holding the right to cast only a single vote. This system places the political parties in a dilemma. Each party must decide how many candidates to run in a given district, taking into account not only its base of voter support relative to the number of seats available, but, more important, its best estimates of how the vote will break down for each of its candidates. If the LDP errs in its campaign strategy, one candidate may wind up garnering the lion's share of the votes, far in excess of the minimum number needed to win, and other LDP candidates will suffer. Or if the LDP runs too many candidates in one district, it might fracture the party's support base in such a way that no LDP candidate wins.

The system is one that places a premium on careful campaign calculations. What each party tries to do is cut down its percentage of "wasted" or "dead" votes—that is, votes cast for party candidates who are not elected. Unlike the Federal Republic of Germany's system of proportional representation, Japan's multiseat electoral system lends itself to potentially large disparities in terms of the total votes received by a particular party compared to the total number of seats won. This disparity in the ratio of votes to seats is, in fact, one reason the LDP has managed to maintain itself in power as majority party even though it receives much less than 50 percent of the votes cast.

In the rural districts, which overrepresent the farm population, only 20 percent

From Daniel I. Okimoto, *Between MITI and the Market: Japanese Industrial Policy for High Technology* (Stanford, Calif.: Stanford University Press, forthcoming). By permission of the publisher.

of the votes cast are "dead." The LDP and the Japan Socialist Party (JSP) have a lock on the majority of rural and semi-urban seats, making it very difficult for the Japan Communist Party (JCP), Kōmeitō, and the Democratic-Socialist Party (DSP) to expand their rural district footholds. The largest number of dead votes are cast in the metropolitan districts, which are underrepresented in the Lower House. These are the districts where the JCP, Kōmeitō, and the DSP are strongest. Even in these opposition strongholds, the LDP can count on winning its share of seats and still keep the percentage of wasted votes within a tolerable range by carefully limiting the number of candidates it chooses to run.

Japan's multicandidacy system thus gives rise to a situation in which LDP candidates wind up running as aggressively against each other as against candidates from other parties. It cannot help but foster fierce intraparty competition. Out of the crucible of this intense struggle for power emerges the phenomenon of LDP factions. Not all parties operating within the same multiseat constituency system face factional problems. The JCP and Kōmeitō, for example, have been able to avoid LDP-type factions because of the greater degree to which they are centralized party organizations. The multiseat, single-vote constituency system is but one structural factor, albeit a central one, that has given rise to LDP factions.

Supporting the hypothesis that LDP factions are structurally related to the multiseat constituency system is the fact that there are very few districts that elect more than one member from the same faction. In 1983, only ten districts out of the 130 in the Lower House, or less than 8 percent of all constituencies, had two representatives hailing from the same LDP faction. LDP factions compete fiercely against one another but manage to avoid internecine warfare by staying out of precincts where fellow faction members already have a base. The idea is to expand at the expense of rival factions and opposition parties, not at the expense of fellow faction members. Indeed, multiseat districts are the central battlegrounds in which the ongoing struggle between rival factions is carried out.

Although the existence of factions decentralizes and disperses power, it also concentrates power among a small group of faction bosses. In order to become Prime Minister, a politician usually has to be boss of a major faction, someone capable of collecting enough contributions to sustain his own faction and of securing enough support from others (in exchange for promises of cabinet and party posts) to win the party nomination. This narrows the field to a tiny handful of candidates—less than a half dozen in theory, but normally no more than two or three in practice—which makes the succession process less chaotic and more predictable than might be the case otherwise. These leaders are capable of making on-the-spot decisions that have a crucial bearing on the country's well-being. When the party or country faces a serious problem, it is perfectly acceptable for a small elite of faction leaders and elder statesmen to circumvent standard procedures and make quick decisions; extraordinary circumstances warrant unusual steps. From the point of view of the Ministry of International Trade and Industry (MITI), the concentration of power is an advantage if it expedites the sometimes unwieldy and almost always time-consuming processes of building a consensus within the LDP.

Factions are thus a mechanism for orderly competition within the accepted rules of the game. Just as organizational ties structure Japan's market economy, so too human relations, informal networks, factions, and seniority criteria impose order and predictability on political competition within the LDP. As in the case of extra-market institutions in the private sector, the imposition of organizational mechanisms (factions) on the freewheeling political marketplace has had the curious effect of intensifying competition on the one hand, while curbing its excesses on the other. It has also created opportunities for lateral entry from the outside while reinforcing the power of the status quo. By breaking down the undifferentiated mass of LDP Diet members into smaller subunits, factions serve to decentralize the hierarchy of party authority, diversify the channels of communication, and facilitate the mobilization of party resources.

In some respects, centralized management of the party is complicated, and internal decision making is rendered more time-consuming by factional decentralization. However, LDP factions should not be viewed as rigid, mutually exclusive units; if they were, the party would be hopelessly fragmented and incapable of acting in unison to achieve collective goals. Like *keiretsu* groups of affiliated business firms, which are sufficiently loose-knit to permit considerable interaction across keiretsu boundaries, LDP factions leave ample slack for individual members to cross factional boundaries and forge close ties with members of other factions.

Although faction members are expected to close ranks during intraparty elections or after a consensus has been reached, they are not bound to take a particular position with respect to specific policy issues. Most belong to one or more of the very large (and always growing) number of informal policy study groups that flourish within the LDP and link members from all factions. Because factions do not divide along ideological or policy lines, differences of opinion on specific issues do not threaten the fabric of party unity. Functioning within a consensual system, free from ideological cleavages, LDP factions have infused the party with a healthy dose of pluralism, which has helped the party escape the extremes of iron-handed rule or stultifying stagnancy.

36. Bureaucrats and Politicians: Shifting Influence

Inoguchi Takashi

It is generally acknowledged that government bureaucrats—and particularly officials in the Finance Ministry and the Ministry of International Trade and Industry (MITI)—were responsible for the policies that brought about Japan's extremely rapid postwar economic recovery and growth. In this selection, written in 1983, Inoguchi Takashi discusses the shift in influence from bureaucrats to politicians that has taken place since the 1960's. Inoguchi writes about Japan's political economy; he teaches political science at the Institute of Oriental Culture at Tokyo University.

From Takashi Inoguchi, *Essays in Japan's Political Economy*, II (Tokyo: Institute of Oriental Culture, University of Tokyo, 1983), pp. 188–89. By permission of the author.

The image of bureaucratic dominance in the decision-making process that prevailed during the 1940's, 1950's, and 1960's has changed. When asked, "Who do you think is most influential in determining national policies in Japan today?" both bureaucrats and politicians answer in favor of the political parties, meaning the Liberal-Democratic Party (LDP). More precisely, 46.1 percent of the bureaucrats answer "the political parties," and only 42.9 percent view themselves as more influential. On the other hand, 55.6 percent of the politicians view themselves as more influential, and only 35.6 respond "the administrative bureaucrats." Among the LDP Diet members, 68 percent answer "the political parties" and only 30 percent "the administrative bureaucrats." Clearly, there has been a shift in the respective influence and importance of the major actors—politicians, bureaucrats, and interest groups.

The Finance Ministry's long adherence to a balanced budget policy was gradually broken by intense political pressure from the ruling party in the early 1960's and more dramatically by the 1965–1966 recession. Since then, government bonds have been issued regularly, which became a major problem after the first oil shock in 1973. In the late 1960's and early 1970's, however, government bonds played a constructive role, because they assisted the expansion of education, medical care, and social welfare programs, as well as the consolidation of the domestic social infrastructure in public housing, public works, and environmental regulation.

During the years that Tanaka Kakuei was prime minister (1972–74), political pressure was so intense that the Finance Ministry's draft budget was rejected and expanded considerably to incorporate various demands from the politicians. Since the first oil crisis, the central government's deficits have accumulated massively, and government bonds have been issued at an alarming rate. As of 1982, the total amount of accumulated bonds was 93 trillion yen, which is equivalent to approximately one-third of Japan's gross national product. When the economy was vigorously expanding, government bonds could be issued without negatively affecting the nation's economy, at least in the long term. Since the oil crisis, however, with the persistence of stagflation and recurrent recessions, reductions in bond issues without revenue increases seriously disturbs the economy. With a huge volume of bonds assigned to commercial banks and security firms for sale, the Finance Ministry has become more vulnerable to pressure from banks and high-income-bracket private interests. The LDP's policy committees have grown into very powerful bodies because politicians, long affiliated with and specializing in one or two committees, have acquired considerable legislative expertise and lobbying connections. In terms of knowledge and competence, some of these politicians surpass the bureaucrats, whose assignments are normally changed every two or three years.

37. Ex-Bureaucrats in the Liberal-Democratic Party

Daniel I. Okimoto

More than any other political party, the Liberal-Democratic Party (LDP) has benefited from an influx of experienced, knowledgeable former government officials. In this selection, taken from *Between MITI and the Market*, political scientist Daniel Okimoto analyzes the attraction of the LDP for these ex-bureaucrats and the contribution they make to their party.

More ex-bureaucrats can be found in the Japanese Diet than in the legislative branch of any other country. Of all the Liberal-Democratic Party (LDP) representatives elected to the Lower House since 1955, 21 percent have come from the higher civil service. Ex-bureaucrats represent the second-largest of all occupational groups in the LDP, second only to local politicians (those hailing from elected office in prefectural or city assemblies), who as a group account for 26 percent of all LDP representatives. Considering the very small number of higher civil servants leaving the bureaucracy each year—not more than several hundred—the 21 percent figure is statistically quite astonishing.

Equally astonishing is the fact that virtually all bureaucrats moving into the legislative branch enter as representatives of the LDP. Only 2 percent of all Japan Socialist Party (JSP) Lower House representatives since 1955, 1 percent for the Kōmeitō since 1967, and 3 percent for the Democratic Socialist Party (DSP) since 1960 have hailed from bureaucratic backgrounds. The inability of progressive parties to recruit ex-bureaucrats goes back to the immediate aftermath of World War II, when progressive parties were at the zenith of their power, and no one predicted that the LDP would dominate for such a lengthy period. The ex-bureaucrats did not simply gravitate to the LDP because it happened to be the party in power. There were other factors at work.

In 1947, when the JSP held the reins of a coalition government for a momentary interlude of less than a year, JSP leader Nishio Suehiro tried in vain to persuade Satō Eisaku, Ikeda Hayato, and other retiring civil servants to run for the Diet as socialist candidates. Instead, they decided to run as Liberal and Democratic Party candidates. Even though the JSP was in power and socialist doctrines were in vogue in academic circles, the civil servants running for office viewed the JSP as rigid, doctrinaire, and closed—in short, not a party suited to their tastes. The JSP's reliance on labor unions and the importance placed on union experience for rising within the JSP ranks also diminished the civil servants' prospects for up-

From Daniel I. Okimoto, *Between MITI and the Market: Japanese Industrial Policy for High Technology* (Stanford, Calif.: Stanford University Press, forthcoming). By permission of the publisher.

ward advancement. Not only did they sense a basic incompatibility; they also did not foresee a bright future for the JSP or other opposition parties. If they were going to enter the world of politics, they reasoned, better the Liberal or Democratic Party (prior to the merger of the two into the LDP, as it is known today) than any other party.

For the LDP, the large influx of ex-bureaucrats began in the late 1940's, when Prime Minister Yoshida Shigeru recruited many of the country's top retiring civil servants, including Ikeda Hayato, Satō Eisaku, Fukuda Takeo, and Ōhira Masayoshi, who all later went on to become Prime Minister. In the 1949 election, more than 50 former bureaucrats were persuaded to run for Lower House seats; more than 30 of them were elected. Many joined the Yoshida faction, forming the nucleus of the famous "Yoshida School." The Yoshida School, comprising the colorful leader's many disciples, became the LDP's "conservative mainstream," providing Japan with the leadership it needed during the formative period of its postwar reconstruction and laying down the basic policy orientation that carried Japan to its present position.

For the JSP, the most popular occupational route to a seat in the Lower House is through organized labor. A large proportion (37 percent) of all JSP representatives since 1955 have come up through the labor union ranks. The contrasting patterns of LDP and JSP recruitment—one from the higher civil service, the other from organized labor—could hardly be more stark. The DSP is similarly dependent on candidates with labor union experience. More than a quarter of its representatives have served in private sector labor unions (which tend to be less militant than the public sector unions that support the JSP). For the Japan Communist Party (JCP), only 10 percent have come up through the labor union hierarchy, with none from the higher civil service, and 34 percent from within the Communist Party itself. Similarly, 32 percent of Kōmeitō representatives have risen from within the party itself or from the Soka Gakkai, the religious organization with which the party is closely affiliated. Not surprisingly, the JCP and Kōmeitō, the two parties with the highest percentage of internal recruitment, happen to be the most centralized, tightly organized, and probably least open, in terms of being inbred and not closely tied to outside organizations. The one route of recruitment to the Lower House common to all parties is local government, which is either the largest or second-largest occupational category for all parties except the JCP (see Table 37.1).

The contrast between LDP ex-bureaucrats and JSP ex-labor-union-officials is even sharper in the Upper House, where national constituencies account for 49 out of 125 seats. To win in national, as opposed to local, election districts, Upper House candidates often require the backing of organizations that have national networks, which some of the bureaucracies and labor unions can provide. Typically, more than 40 percent of all LDP Upper House members come from bureaucratic backgrounds, whereas more than 60 percent of all JSP members come from labor union backgrounds. This suggests that, in terms of personnel, the two largest parties pose so sharp a contrast—the higher civil service vs. the public sector labor unions—that it comes close to being a class distinction. The cleavage reveals fundamental differences in the network of groups with which the two leading parties are closely connected.

Table 37.1.   *Occupational Backgrounds of Members of Lower House, Japanese Diet*
(In percentages)

Occupational background	Political party				
	Liberal-Democratic	Japan Socialist	Kōmeitō	Democratic-Socialist	Japan Communist
ALL POSTWAR MEMBERS[a]	$N = 732$	$N = 362$	$N = 98$	$N = 90$	$N = 90$
University graduates	74%	44%	49%	59%	54%
University of Tokyo graduates	29	10	2	13	20
Local politicians[b]	26	26	46	33	14
High bureaucrats[c]	21	2	1	3	0
Business executives	15	3	0	4	1
Politicians' staff	11	1	2	4	0
Lawyers	4	3	2	5	21
Functionaries of political parties or organizations	1	14	32	10	34
Union officials	0	37	1	27	10
ELECTED IN 1983	$N = 258$	$N = 111$	$N = 58$	$N = 37$	$N = 26$
University graduates	83%	44%	57%	73%	69%
University of Tokyo graduates	29	4	3	16	31
Local politicians[b]	26	33	36	35	23
High bureaucrats[c]	20	0	2	3	0
Business executives	16	1	0	5	0
Politicians' staff	19	2	2	5	0
Lawyers	3	3	3	0	31
Functionaries of political parties or organizations	1	7	41	11	23
Union officials	0	44	30	0	7

SOURCE: Fukui Haruhiro, "The Liberal Democratic Party Revisited," *Journal of Japanese Studies*, vol. 10, no. 2 (Summer 1984), p. 393.
[a]All party members ever serving in the Lower House since the founding of their respective parties: for LDP, 1955; JSP, 1955; Kōmeitō, 1967; DSP, 1960; and JCP, 1946.
[b]Former elected local politicians, primarily former prefectural assemblymen.
[c]Former senior officials in central government ministries and agencies.

The ramifications from the influx of former bureaucrats into the LDP but not the opposition parties have been far-reaching. There is no doubt that it has extended the LDP's longevity as the majority party in power. The higher civil service has served as the LDP's most fertile source of leadership talent. The majority of Japan's postwar prime ministers come out of the higher civil service, and a disproportionate percentage of her most influential faction leaders have also had training in the bureaucracies. Moreover, looking at all cabinets from 1948 to 1977, we should note that 183 out of 425 cabinet members, or an amazing 43 percent, have been ex-bureaucrats. The fact that nearly half of all LDP cabinet members have been ex-bureaucrats bespeaks the disproportionate power they have wielded within the ruling conservative party.

With entrance to the higher civil service based on meritocratic criteria—specifically, a very rigorous set of examinations—the bureaucrats who have won seats in the Diet represent the country's "best and brightest." Quite apart from native ability, they have given the ruling conservative party leadership ability, based on firsthand experience in public administration, intimate knowledge of the policy-making processes, access to the best available information, and extensive contacts with elites in both public and private sectors.

It is hard to imagine how the LDP might have fared without this influx of bureaucratic talent. What would have happened if, instead of the LDP's commandeering all the ex-bureaucrats, the opposition parties had succeeded in attracting their share? While this is pure speculation, of course, the likelihood is that Japan's postwar political history would have turned out very differently. LDP leadership would not have been as effective, nor would the party have been able to stay in power for so long. The LDP's unchallenged capacity to recruit top talent from the higher civil service has made a very significant difference.

More specifically, the large influx of higher civil servants has led to the consolidation of ties between the LDP and the various ministries. The marriage between the LDP and the bureaucracies has turned out to be one of the LDP's greatest assets. It has joined the bureaucracy's administrative skills and technical know-how with the LDP's constitutional authority and public mandate. This union has allowed both sides to benefit mightily, as has the country at large, from the comparative effectiveness of public policies and the stability of the political system. In addition to the incalculable, indirect benefits of effective public administration, the LDP-bureaucratic nexus has permitted the ruling conservative party to exploit the formidable prerogatives of incumbency to keep itself in power, serving the vast array of interest groups in its grand coalition.

With so many ex-bureaucrats in the fold, the LDP maintains extensive channels of communication with all the ministries, especially those that are functionally crucial (like Finance) or politically central (like Agriculture and Forestry). The LDP hears vital news before other parties and is on the receiving end of far more information. Much of it is transmitted informally, through the network of personal relationships that exist between ex-bureaucrats (or LDP cabinet ministers) and the various ministries. Being shut out of this insiders' loop makes it harder for the opposition parties to participate as fully in the public policy-making process as the LDP. Lacking the same nucleus of former bureaucrats, the opposition parties have had trouble winning the public's confidence in their ability to govern the country. Here, in image as well as reality, is an example of the extraordinary advantage of having a large core of former bureaucrats in the LDP's ranks, working in close cooperation with the higher civil service.

38. Dispute Resolution in Contemporary Japan

Kawashima Takeyoshi and Noda Yosiyuki

Misunderstandings frequently arise between Japanese and Westerners because of differences in their approach to the settlement of disputes. In this essay, drawn from two articles published in 1976, Kawashima Takeyoshi and Noda Yosiyuki discuss the Japanese understanding of the concepts of right, adjudication, and contract.

In Japan, there is a strong expectation that a dispute should not and will not arise; even when one does occur, it is to be solved by mutual understanding. Thus, there is no raison d'être for the majority rule that is so widespread in other modern societies; instead, the principle of rule by consensus prevails.

It is obvious that a judicial decision does not fit and even endangers relationships. When people are socially organized in small groups, and when subordination of individual desires in favor of group agreement is idealized, the group's stability and the security of individual members are threatened by attempts to regulate conduct by universalistic standards. The impact is greater when such an effort is reinforced by an organized political power. Furthermore, the litigious process, in which both parties seek to justify their position by objective standards, and the emergence of a judicial decision based thereon tend to convert situational interests into firmly consolidated and independent ones. Because of the resulting disorganization of traditional social groups, resort to litigation has been condemned as morally wrong, subversive, and rebellious.

The Conception of Law Among the Japanese

The term "right" is generally defined as a legally protected interest. The Romans insisted on their rights as interests protected by the law. But the fact that something is protected by the law implies that it is protected by an objective standard. It therefore follows that the rights of all people are to be protected equally by an objective standard called law. So, when one asserts his right, he implicitly assumes the existence of law; therefore, he must be prepared to accept the assumption that other persons can also assert their rights on the basis of the same law. In other words, in order for a given concept of right to be valid, it must be applicable to others just as it is applicable to him.

In Japan, the concept of right did not exist until the end of the Tokugawa period. Early in the Meiji period (1867–1912), a man named Mitsukuri Rinshō, who was commissioned to translate the French Civil Code, racked his brain to find a Japa-

The first three paragraphs are from Takeyoshi Kawashima, "Dispute Resolution in Contemporary Japan," p. 278, and the remainder from Yosiyuki Noda, "The Character of the Japanese People and their Concept of Law," pp. 304–10, both in Hideo Tanaka, ed., *The Japanese Legal System* (Tokyo: University of Tokyo Press, 1976). By permission of the publisher and the authors.

nese equivalent of *droit* and finally came up with a Japanese coinage *kenri*. This episode serves to show that the concept of right was first introduced only in the early years of the Meiji period. The concept still has a long and tortuous way to go before taking firm root in this country.

Next, let us examine the Japanese concept of adjudication. We seek to establish a harmonious situation with which both parties are neither satisfied nor dissatisfied, where there is no loser or winner. This is the ideal we expect of adjudication. In Japan, we have a story called *Sambō Ichiryō Zon* (All three lost one pound each). This is a story about a trial during the Tokugawa period that illustrates the Japanese concept of adjudication. One day, so the story goes, a plasterer picked up a purse on the road containing three *ryō*. (A ryō is an old Japanese gold coin.) The purse also contained a piece of paper identifying a certain carpenter as its owner. The plasterer took the trouble of locating the carpenter to return the purse. For all his pains, the plasterer was told by the carpenter: "Since the purse elected to slip out of my pocket, I don't want such ungrateful money. Go away with the money." The plasterer insisted that the money belonged to the carpenter. Thereupon a brawl started, and finally they agreed to take the case to arbitration by the Lord Ōoka of Echizen. Having heard the story from both sides, the lord added one ryō to the three ryō, split the sum in two, handed two ryō to each party, and announced: "My good men, this is my decision. The plasterer could have gained three ryō if he had walked away as the carpenter told him to do. By this decision, he will end up with two ryō, so he is to lose one ryō. The carpenter could have recovered all three ryō if he had accepted the plasterer's kindness with a good grace. Instead, he refused to accept the purse. By this decision, he is to lose one ryō. I also have to contribute one ryō. So, each of the three of us is to end up with one ryō less." Of course, this is just a fiction, but still it is suggestive of a notion of the function of a lawsuit that is peculiar to the Japanese.

This is, in a sense, a really ingenious settlement of the dispute. Everybody came out as neither a winner nor a loser. Even the judge went out of his way to contribute one ryō in the interest of all-around amicability. The standards of law had no role to play here. Incoherent though it may seem to us students of law, such a decision appeals to the Japanese as demonstrating the most humane consideration. We Japanese tend to feel uncomfortable with a black-or-white type of adjudication. If a Japanese loses in a lawsuit, being of emotional inclination, he is bound to be embittered against the winner, and even against the judge. We do not want to leave the embers of a grudge smoldering. We would rather pay a small price, if such a price rounds off the sharp edges, and let bygones be bygones. This explains why a large majority of cases that are brought to court are settled through compromise. This is very indicative of the peculiar character of the Japanese.

Last, let us consider the Japanese conception of contract. Westerners view social life, basically, as a struggle. In order to resolve struggles in a peaceful manner, they need to have effective communication between holders of conflicting views and interests. They believe that social coherence has to be built on contracts. One source from which they derive their concept of contracts is the Hebrew concept, which found its way to European countries along with Christianity. For the Hebrews, the contract, or *berith* as they called it, between God and man was basic to their lives. To them, violation of the contract was tantamount to a breach of their duty to pay homage to God. Therefore, they could not violate the contract without experiencing a deep sense of guilt, and this mentality governed their attitude toward ordinary contracts. Westerners inherited this mentality, and even today they are very serious about honoring contracts.

By contrast, the Japanese way of life has been such that we did not need the kind of contract that Westerners developed in order to form a community. From the early days of our history, we Japanese were agrarian people and settled ourselves in large numbers in a given locality as tillers of land. We therefore felt no particular need for a contract. In order to cooperate among ourselves, we did not need a contract whose violation invoked sanctions. People got together and talked things over to enlist the cooperation of their neighbors. This tradition has bred in the minds of the Japanese a very easy-going attitude toward contracts. We Japanese do not go so far as to consider a breach of contract to be a virtue, but we are certainly not very serious about honoring contracts. One might say that a breach of contract is not often accompanied by a sense of guilt. In fact, we view contracts in such a light-hearted manner that a contract is often regarded as a sort of tentative agreement (which may be revised as the circumstances change). If a party to a contract is subsequently urged by the other party to perform his contractual obligations to the letter, he considers such a demand to be an inhumane act.

Given the difference in the cultural backgrounds, it is not surprising that Europeans find it difficult to understand the Japanese concept of contract. For instance, contracts drawn up by large Japanese trading companies invariably contain a "good-faith" or "amicability" clause. Typical of these is a clause which states that "in case a dispute arises between the parties hereto with respect to their rights and obligations under this contract, the parties hereto shall discuss the matter among themselves with good faith." This seems to indicate that the contract sets forth only a tentative agreement, and if something goes wrong, the parties should renegotiate the terms and conditions of the contract. By contrast, once the parties have agreed on the specific terms and conditions of the contract, Europeans think that they are entitled to take the other party to court if the latter fails to perform his contractual obligations. This is often a source of misunderstanding between Japanese and Westerners in relation to contracts they sign. The Japanese assumes that even if he does not perform his part of the contract, it just will not happen that the other party will immediately take an action for the enforcement of the contract. The Westerner, on the other hand, thinks it simply a matter of course that he can proceed in such a manner to enforce the contract as it is written. The difference between Japanese and Westerners in their concepts of contract has caused a number of sad misunderstandings.

39. The Role of Law and Lawyers in Japanese Society

Tanaka Hideo

> Because Japanese approach the resolution of disputes differently from Westerners, the role of the law has evolved differently in Japanese society. In this selection, taken from an article published in 1976, Tanaka Hideo analyzes this role, arguing that there is a tendency to avoid the use of lawyers unless a situation arises that makes their employment unavoidable. Tanaka is a professor at the University of Tokyo.

Japan has a system of courts no less refined than those of Western nations, at least so far as its formal structure is concerned. Nor is she deficient in the system governing her legal profession. The manner in which these systems function in Japan, however, is quite different from that of their counterparts in Western nations. Put simply, many matters in Western nations that are dealt with within the framework of the regular machinery of law are left in Japan to work themselves out outside this machinery. This peculiarity has been pointed out time and again by lawyers from foreign countries while visiting in Japan.

Number of Lawsuits

The number of civil suits brought before the Japanese courts is far smaller than those of other countries. The number of civil suits brought before the courts of a country is determined by a number of factors, chief among which are the ways the country's social system functions and the substance of the various rules incorporated into its legal system. Nevertheless, the fact is that the number of civil suits per capita brought before the courts in Japan is roughly between one-twentieth and one-tenth of the figures for suits per capita in the common law countries of the United States and Great Britain. Even if we also include the number of cases brought to conciliation proceedings in Japan, the difference remains large, between one-sixteenth and one-eighth. These figures serve to show the extent to which the courts are remote from the everyday life of the populace.

It is significant that there is an even larger difference in the number of cases per capita involving small claims. This dramatizes the fact that Japanese people resort to court actions to protect their rights far less easily and readily than people in other countries.

Limited Sphere of Activities of Practicing Attorneys

Even where a large number of disputes are settled out of court in a given system, one would have less cause to worry if these disputes were settled in a manner

From Hideo Tanaka, "The Role of Law and Lawyers in Japanese Society," in Hideo Tanaka, ed., *The Japanese Legal System* (Tokyo: University of Tokyo Press, 1976), pp. 254–61. By permission of the publisher and the author.

not repugnant to the policies embodied in the laws, through the intermediacy of qualified attorneys. But the situation prevailing in Japan is a far cry from such a system of dispute resolution. In Japan, the role of attorneys is confined, with a few isolated exceptions, to lawsuits and areas directly related to lawsuits. They play a minor role in the area of preventive law. Even among those corporations which retain attorneys on a general retainer basis, few seek the advice of their attorneys on matters not directly related to lawsuits, such as the drawing up of contracts. Indeed, not very many seek an attorney's advice even when drafting a standard-form contract. Even rarer are ordinary private citizens who go to an attorney for his advice before drawing up a will or who consult an attorney on the purchase or sale of a piece of real estate.

In fact, the activities of attorneys in Japan do not even cover the entire range of areas directly associated with lawsuits. Even in relatively serious cases, which are heard in the first instance by district courts, the number of cases in which both the plaintiff and the defendant were represented by an attorney accounted for only about 40 percent. Furthermore, in about one-third of the appellate hearings, either the plaintiff or the defendant elected to argue his own case without resort to the advice of an attorney.

By contrast, there are countries where representation by an attorney is mandatory in all lawsuits (except in minor cases). Even in the United Kingdom and the United States, where representation by an attorney in civil cases is not mandatory, all cases except minor ones are in fact presented and argued by attorneys, so much so that cases in which parties to appellate hearings are not represented by attorneys are extremely rare. It is indeed peculiar to Japan that a large number of cases are argued by the party himself without the benefit of the expert advice of an attorney. Lack of legal knowledge on the part of the parties not only hampers the efficient conduct of trials and hearings but also gives rise to a deplorable situation where the parties fail to protect their interests sufficiently.

Law-Consciousness of the Japanese People

In order to put these phenomena into a proper perspective, one must delve into the law-consciousness of the Japanese people.

When a dispute arises between two parties, not very many Japanese view the dispute in terms of rights and obligations. Nor does it occur to them, when they fail to work out a solution between themselves, that the best approach to the dispute is to take the matter to the court. Instead, the traditional value of "harmony" (*wa*) prevails upon them. To their minds, settlement of disputes without arguing their points of view in a reasoned way and without fighting out their cases to the finish in court is of supreme virtue. (Compromise in the Japanese political world is another manifestation of this spirit. In reaching a political compromise, Japanese often shelve their principles and work out a compromise by "adding their contentions and dividing the sum by two.")

Of course, the smaller the number of actual disputes, the better. Few would praise a suit-happy person who insisted on continuing to dispute with others for the sake of disputing, even when there was room for a reasonable compromise. The traditional Japanese spirit of harmony, however, does not inculcate a concept of settlement based on a reasoned compromise between the parties and incorporating a clear notion of one's rights. By the same token, only in a very small number of instances is a detailed arrangement made between parties in advance for the purpose of preventing disputes from arising later. Even corporations, which are supposed to embody the modern rationalistic spirit, often fail to consult their attorneys until a dispute reaches a stage where it defies solution short of litigation in the courts. Even today, there are many Japanese who would hesitate to knock on the door of a law office, even after circumstances have led them there and left them little alternative.

40. The Way of the Bureaucrat

Suzuta Atsuyuki

In the Tokugawa Period, Bushido, or the way of the warrior, provided a code of values and action for the samurai. Suzuta Atsuyuki suggests that, for better or worse, an equally rigid code determines the values and actions of postwar Japanese bureaucrats. The article appeared in *Japan Echo* in 1978. Suzuta is a senior editorial writer for *Mainichi Shimbun*, one of Japan's leading daily newspapers.

The Unwritten Law of the Self-Styled Rat Pack

Early summer is musical chairs season at the central government offices in Tokyo's Kasumigaseki district. It is a time of transfers, a time of reassigning the bureaucracy's innumerable directors, deputy directors, and on up to vice-ministers. It is, in effect, a time for reshuffling the lineup of the elite bureaucracy that actually governs Japan.

It is also a time of retirements. Some people leave Kasumigaseki pleased; others leave with regret. Into the places they have vacated flows another generation of bureaucrats imbued with a sense of mission. Yet their expressions betray an unusual pallor this year. Although foresight and political neutrality are the Japanese bureaucrat's raisons d'être, today's bureaucracy has proved itself somewhat less than foresighted, as it has lost economic control during the shift from rapid to slower growth, has failed to prevent a prolonged recession, and has been unable to deflect the yen's appreciation and other pressures from overseas. Moreover, as the government and opposition parties have become more equally represented in the Diet, the bureaucracy has also been dragged into politics. This wavering foresight and political neutrality has given rise to a pervasive sense of frustration.

Despite this, the bureaucratic system and its governing code remain fundamentally unshaken. Changes may be taking place outside, but the bureaucracy rolls on. There is a mood of grim confidence within the bureaucracy that even if the opposition should come to power, it will have to come to terms with the bureaucracy

From Atsuyuki Suzuta, "The Way of the Bureaucrat," *Japan Echo*, vol. 5, no. 3 (1978), pp. 42–53. By permission of the publisher.

before it will be able to do anything. Even the Supreme Commander for the Allied Powers was unable to reorganize the bureaucracy after World War II. Japan's bureaucracy has a strong instinct of self-preservation. While it may be being drawn into the political fray, it also knows how to use politics to further its own ends. The bureaucracy may seem to be under siege, yet it is very much alive and well in Kasumigaseki.

It was the Finance Ministry bureaucracy that laid the foundations for the rapid-growth economy and the doubling of Japan's national income, just as it was the Ministry of International Trade and Industry (MITI) bureaucracy that rehabilitated Japanese industry from the devastating aftermath of the war, directed the nation's productive energies into heavy industry, and stimulated industry to enhance its international competitiveness. Indeed, the bureaucracy well deserves its accolades for having turned Japan into the second largest economic force in the free world so quickly. At the height of its success, the elite bureaucrats walked tall, and they might well have been likened to lions and tigers.

But the last few years have been ones of ignominious failure for the bureaucracy. When the yen was revalued upward, the Finance Ministry mindlessly staked Japan's reputation on preserving an impossible exchange rate of 360 yen to the dollar, making Japan the laughingstock of the world. It also misread the effects of accelerated excess liquidity. Taken completely by surprise by the oil crisis, MITI flailed about furiously but ineffectively, too panicked to devise any real policy response to this emergency. MITI was unable even to control the petroleum industry, over which it has nominal jurisdiction, and finally resorted to accusing the industry of being "the root of all evil." This was a startling display of MITI incompetence and impotence. With all the world able to see how helpless the bureaucratic giant was, political intervention became more widespread and public scorn more pronounced. The bureaucrats themselves suffered a drastic loss of confidence.

Think Elite

The warped psychology of the bureaucrat calls to mind Bushido, the way of the warrior. As illustrated by the old saw that "the samurai betrays no weakness even when starving," true devotion to one's lord is defined as the ability to endure. Devotion to the lord is akin to love, and the endurance expected of a loyal samurai is similar to that of a burning love that goes unspoken unto death. This is an ideal that the average person would find it most difficult to comprehend, yet it is this abstruse Bushido that was the ruling code of samurai society. The elite think differently from the common people, they make their own rules, and they constitute a special social order of their own. Although the warrior class and Bushido were officially abolished shortly after the Meiji Restoration of 1868, Bushido lives on in its spiritual heirs within the bureaucracy.

Let us look first at how the tradition is perpetuated. The Finance Ministry, MITI, and the other major government agencies each hire a couple of dozen college graduates every year. These are the fledgling bureaucrats who have scored well on the upper-grade civil service examination. During the initial training period, they are introduced to the workings of their ministry. They are told, for ex-

ample, that it is highly irregular to leave work at quitting time and that it is not uncommon to work until midnight or even to spend the night at the office when the
budget is being drawn up. If they work in the Budget Bureau of the Finance Ministry, they should also forget about Sundays and holidays from September through
December. The conscientious worker will easily put in 200 hours of overtime a
month.

All the important work of a given division is done by the career bureaucrats,
that elite group of directors and top deputy directors who have passed the upper-
grade civil service examinations. It is the division director's top deputies who bear
the brunt of the load. The white-haired, noncareer assistants play only a supporting role. Even the way the young deputy directors are addressed is different. It is
also these young careerist division directors and deputy directors who do the ministry's negotiating with other ministries; it is they who attend the important conferences within their own ministries. When they go drinking, they generally go
with their own kind, with newcomers permitted an occasional whiff of this
camaraderie.

During budget season, these Budget Bureau deputy directors cannot go home
even to take a pregnant wife to the hospital. In fact, one division director at MITI
lost his wife to the year-end budget wars. He was working every day until after
midnight drawing up the budget requirements for a national project when his wife
came down with pneumonia. Her illness was not discovered until it was too late.
The bureau director and vice-minister paid her the highest homage of grief at the
funeral. As a true bureaucrat's wife, she had been "killed in action." It was a
home-front death during the bureaucracy's most important campaign, the battle of
the budget. Extreme though it is, this incident is indicative of the expectation that
the bureaucrat will be willing to sacrifice all for the state.

There has recently been an increase in the divorce rate in the Finance Ministry,
MITI, and other major government offices. Some divorces undoubtedly stem
from incompatibility and other causes, yet it is not hard to guess that the sacrifice
of home to bureaucracy is also a factor.

Most of these bureaucrats marry after they have completed their initial training
period, and the overwhelming majority are arranged marriages, almost always to
women introduced by the director of the Secretarial Division or one of the young
man's other superiors at the ministry. A major reason for this preponderance of arranged marriages is that the young bureaucrat is too busy learning his trade to in-
dulge in courtship.

The brides are usually from rich or powerful families seeking elite husbands for
their daughters. Such offers literally pour into the ministry's Secretarial Division
from Diet members, former ministry employees, and influential businessmen
who have an in with the ministry. As a result, the young man ends up marrying
someone from an established, well-connected family.

Never Yield Jurisdiction

It is also while the young man is a divisional deputy director that he is initiated
into the rules of bureaucratic warfare. Two of the most important points here are
logical precision and behind-the-scenes maneuvering to effect adjustments, com-

promises, and disposition of problems. The deputy director must first develop his proficiency in logic. The higher up he goes in the ranks, the more amenable he will be to compromise and working things out, but he must first learn to argue them out with logic.

The various ministries are forever coming up with new policy initiatives. We should establish a public corporation for energy stockpiling. We should build a second national theater. Most of these ideas originate with the divisional deputy directors, who are also charged with giving the ideas the necessary logical defenses to enable them to make their way through the bureau and ministry debates until they emerge in the form of new policy initiatives and budget requests.

On the receiving end of these requests is the Finance Ministry, where their first hearing is, appropriately, at the divisional deputy director level. Even granting the need for stable energy supplies, won't this proposal profit only the oil companies? What do we need another national theater for? Arguments are examined up, down, inside out, and sideways in a debate neither side can afford to lose.

The logic has to be impeccable and soundly structured, for it will soon be cut to shreds if it is not. The petitioning deputy director is exhorted to be three times better prepared on his subject than the defending Finance Ministry deputy director, while the Budget Bureau man has to be thoroughly versed in his subject if he expects to make any cuts in the budget request.

Hand in hand with logic must go a close familiarity with the practical side of the issue. For example, there are tales of the deputy director assigned to review Defense Agency budget requests who traveled to the central fish market to pinpoint a discrepancy in the agency's calculation of food expenses, and who knew the cost of raising a piglet down to the last yen so well that he was able to draw up a list of regional differential coefficients from Hokkaido in the north to Kyushu in the south. Nothing goes unchecked, no matter how small. As well as being a mark of the elite bureaucrat's perfectionism, this is also a reflection of the iron rule that every bureaucrat's logic must be impeccable. Arguments are built with logical precision on the basis of accurate facts and figures to resist the many demands of politicians and special interest groups. Although considerably buffeted of late by politics, this remains the very basis of the way of the bureaucrat.

One other rule of bureaucratic warfare is the absolute injunction against yielding jurisdiction under any circumstances. This rule applies not only to division deputy directors but all the way up through division and bureau directors to the vice-minister himself. For example, Prime Minister Fukuda Takeo last year proposed the creation of an Energy Ministry. Taken aback, MITI countered that energy policy is so inextricably linked to industrial and trade policies that to separate them would seriously impair the functioning of Japanese economic policy. These rationalizations aside, the real reason for MITI's opposition was that separating energy policy would weaken MITI authority within the government. Everyone from Vice-Minister Toshinobu Wada on down was mobilized to prevail upon the Miki and Nakasone factions within the Liberal-Democratic Party (LDP) to derail the Prime Minister's plan, with the divisional directors and deputy directors responsible for providing the logical underpinnings of this assault upon the proposed Energy Ministry.

Keeping the Political-Favor Balance Sheet

When one goes beyond the divisional deputy director level, political contracts add a new dimension to the traditional bureaucratic considerations.

One of the most famous Finance Ministry stories about this involves the late Murakami Kotarō when he was director of the Budget Bureau. At that time, the Finance Ministry, fearing that politically inspired bloating of the budget would result in Japan's having the same lock-step budgetary rigidity that hobbled West Germany, was impelled to launch a campaign for maintaining budget flexibility. In the midst of this campaign, Murakami was visited by a leading government-party politician lobbying on behalf of one of his special interest groups seeking a budget allocation. After hearing him out, Murakami told the politician flatly that his arguments would not wash and that there was no money for his cause. "Well," said the politician, "couldn't you at least repay a favor?" To which Murakami retorted, "If you'll look at the balance sheet, I think you'll find I'm already several up on you." Ministry bureaucrats who overheard this exchange later expressed surprised admiration that even such a straight-arrow type as Murakami had a political-favor tally sheet.

For the Finance Ministry bureaucrat, making room in the budget for a politician's pet program would constitute a "loan" on this sheet, while a "debt" would be such things as a politician's going out of his way to help the budget through the Diet. Although criticized by the mass media as "collusion," adroit manipulation of these favors is an essential part of bureaucratic life.

Since the Diet consists of the elected representatives of the people and thus may be assumed to reflect the public will, and since the government party may logically be thought to reflect the people's desires by virtue of its majority representation, it is difficult for the bureaucracy to act overtly counter to the government party's wishes. However, the government party today is actually a loose confederation of pressure groups and vested interests, and to blindly follow its dictates would lead to major injustices in the administration of public policy and would impair the national consensus. Thus the bureaucrat must also have a conscience, and it is the mission of the technocratic bureaucracy to reconcile the demands of politics with the demands of conscience as best it can.

Just look at the inefficient and time-wasting way the Diet is run, with its endless rounds of dull questions on trivial points. The government officials who are called upon to answer these interpellations, far from considering the Diet to reflect the national will, do so with a sense of despair over the political process.

Yet this is not to imply that the bureaucracy is helpless in the face of political intrusions. When a political demand is unacceptable, the astute bureaucrat personally explains why it is impossible to those who have been pressuring him, before turning them down. Even when the political pressures are unrelenting, the politicians themselves are incapable of drawing up the necessary legislation for fitting something new into the system. As a result, the actual formulation of legislation is entrusted to the bureaucracy, offering ample opportunity for modifying the impact of the change.

For example, both government and opposition parties pushed hard in the Diet for passage of a small-business market protection law, but MITI opposed the law as detrimental to consumer interests. In the end, the politicians prevailed and the law was enacted, but in considerably altered form, for the MITI bureaucrats, charged with overseeing the entire industrial structure, were unwilling to single out the small-business sector as a particularly weak element demanding special protection.

The Short-Lived Cicada

The life of the high bureaucratic official has been aptly likened to the life of the cicada. The cicada, it will be recalled, lives seven years underground as a nymph before emerging for an adult life of only several days' duration. The bureaucrat spends fifteen to twenty years as an administrative assistant and divisional deputy director and in other embryo posts before becoming a division director. Then he must stick it out for almost another decade before becoming a bureau director. Although there are those who would say a bureau director is also an adult cicada, since only three or four people in any given class attain this rank, the real prize is the post of vice-minister. This is granted to at most one person from each entering class, and even then he has but a year or two to fly before his short life as an adult cicada ends.

It is also a rule of the bureaucracy that everyone who does not make bureau director or vice-minister must leave the ministry when it is clear he has been passed over. The bureaucratic structure is pyramidal in form, and it needs constant infusions of new talent if it is to retain the organizational vitality to respond to the changing times. Indeed, this up-or-out rule is one of the factors accounting for the Japanese bureaucracy's vaunted excellence, but it is uncompromisingly harsh on those who do not make the grade.

In theory, personnel decisions are to be made by the Cabinet, but the bureaucratic code neither waits on the ministerial pleasure nor brooks ministerial interference. The bureaucracy's leaders are chosen from within the bureaucracy itself. This is the rule, even if not always the practice.

When Prime Minister Fukuda was Minister of Finance, he prevailed upon Sumita Satoshi (now president of the Export-Import Bank of Japan), who is also from Gumma Prefecture, to stay on an extra year as vice-minister. Both Sumita and the other people at the ministry had expected his vice-ministership to be the usual one-year term, but Fukuda specifically asked him to stay. Thus, although there was considerable grumbling about this interference in the ministry's internal affairs, Fukuda insisted, and Sumita spent another year as vice-minister.

Aware of these dangers to its tight-knit structure, the bureaucracy has built in numerous barriers to block such interference. When Finance Minister Ichimanda Hisato wanted to dismiss Vice-Minister Hirata Keiichirō (former president of the Industrial Relocation and Coal Production Areas Promotion Corporation) in 1955, for instance, the man next in line for the vice-ministership, Morinaga Teiichirō (now president of the Bank of Japan), said, "If Hirata goes, I go," and mobilized the entire ministry behind Hirata. As a result, Ichimanda was stalemated and Hirata stayed.

The personnel decisions on vice-ministers and bureau directors are made within the ministry, drawing upon information and reports collected by the minister's secretariat from ministry employees past and present, as well as from outside sources.

While the way of the bureaucrat is a demanding code, it also provides due rewards for those who cooperate for its preservation. In fact, arranging such rewards for predecessors and underlings alike is one of the biggest jobs of the vice-minister and chief of the secretariat. Every effort is made to establish new public corporations or, barring that, new associations or centers where deserving people can be placed. These efforts are also paralleled by the exploitation of the ministry's jurisdiction over certain industrial sectors to find suitable employment for people there. Such attention to the needs of the people who have supported the bureaucracy is essential to the bureaucracy's survival. Moreover, the various public corporations are like extensions of the ministries themselves, and the ministries both seek their cooperation in facilitating policy implementation and throw work their way so that they may grow stronger. In these ways are the cooperative relationships between present and former ministry employees reinforced.

Signs of Impending Change

Thus far, we have focused upon the way of the bureaucrat, as seen in the lives of elite career bureaucrats. Now let us look at how this bureaucratic code is changing.

There are several signs of impending change. For one thing, the bureaucratic mentality is adapting in response to the opposition parties' increasing influence within the Diet, and a number of young bureaucrats have already formed study groups in anticipation of a coalition government. The bureaucracy has long been politically oriented, and it has not been uncommon for bureaucrats frustrated at the limits of their own power to cross over into elective politics. However, this tendency has been accelerating at all ministries. This is partly because the political parties are turning to the ministries for their talent, but still more it is because bureaucrats looking at the political landscape have been unable to suppress their own misgivings and have thus decided to go into politics while they are still young.

Although the overwhelming bulk of these bureaucrats-turned-politician join the ruling Liberal-Democratic Party, recent years have seen increasing numbers going into the opposition New Liberal Club, Democratic-Socialist Party, and Japan Socialist Party as disenchantment with the LDP has grown. At the same time, the younger bureaucrats are forming the nuclei of study groups bringing together both bureaucrats and nonbureaucrats to study what policy responses are appropriate to these frustrating times.

Last year, the opposition parties forced a revision of the budget to include a provision for a tax cut. This was for the bureaucracy an all-too-vivid illustration of the closer balance between government and opposition political forces, as the Budget Committee fell under the control of an increasingly powerful opposition. At this time, the Finance Ministry leadership called an elite huddle and announced, "No matter what political changes may take place, only the bureaucracy has the ability to assess the economy in its entirety and to formulate policy." They added, confidently, that the people would never stand by and allow the politicians to distort the perfect policies formulated by the bureaucracy.

This attitude is illustrative of an attempt to regroup and rebuild around the technocrats' proven record and abilities. There are even some who complain that all the politicians are after is applause, and that now is the time for the bureaucracy to speak out in forthright opposition to this grandstanding before Japan's national priorities get more badly skewed. Newly appointed Vice-Minister of Finance Ōkura Masataka, previously director of the Tax Bureau, has said bluntly, "Tax cuts are no longer a valid policy. We need tax increases to regain fiscal integrity, and we should not be afraid to say so." The bureaucracy has come to the conclusion that politics is too important to be left to the politicians, and it appears to be gearing up to take a more prominent role.

Nevertheless, I am highly skeptical of whether these elite bureaucrats will be able to make the necessary changes in their thinking as long as they remain bound by the traditional bureaucratic code. Even conceding their technocratic ability, they will not be able to save the nation if their underlying philosophy is warped. The current bureaucratic frustration offers an excellent opportunity for the bureaucrats to reexamine their own assumptions, to abandon their elitist contempt for the public, and to learn to work truly with and for the people, if they only will.

41. New Support for the Liberal-Democratic Party

Murakami Yasusuke

In spite of scandals, factional struggles, and economic crises in recent years, the Liberal-Democratic Party (LDP) has not only retained its power but actually increased its support. In this selection, which is drawn from the *Journal of Japanese Studies* (1982), Murakami Yasusuke examines the possible reasons for this resurgence, concluding that the LDP has become an interest-oriented catchall party. Murakami is a professor at Tokyo University who has written about economics and sociology.

There has recently been a marked resurgence of the Liberal-Democratic Party (LDP). The LDP resurgence appears all the more remarkable when we consider what has happened to it during recent years. The oil crisis seemed to wreak havoc on the economy; the incumbent party leader, Premier Tanaka Kakuei, was forced to resign and was indicted in the "Lockheed scandal"; young dissidents left the LDP to form a new party (New Liberal Club); and a series of factional struggles

From Yasusuke Murakami, "The Age of New Middle Mass Politics: The Case of Japan," *Journal of Japanese Studies*, vol. 8, no. 1 (Winter 1982), pp. 59–72. Copyright © 1982 Society for Japanese Studies. By permission of the author and the publisher.

finally led to the passing of a nonconfidence motion against Premier Ōhira Masayoshi. Some potent factor has worked to overshadow these disgraceful events, but what is that factor?

One often-mentioned possibility is a "revival of conservatism" or a reemergence of tradition-oriented conservatism. "Traditional elements" in postwar Japanese society have played, and still play, a unique, often beneficial role in the process of rapid economic growth. Moreover, most recent Japanese newspapers and magazines are full of long-delayed reactions to the antinationalist and antiindigenous arguments that have dominated most postwar intellectual controversies. Thus, one hypothesis is as follows:

The tradition-orientation hypothesis: The crisis conditions of the late 1970's, the oil crisis, the mounting trade conflicts, and the increasing Russian military threat in East Asia stirred the Japanese out of their complacency resulting from material affluence, leading to a reemergence of tradition-oriented conservatism among Japanese voters.

However, there is also a second hypothesis:

The interest-orientation hypothesis: In the 1970's, the LDP virtually converted itself into an "interest-oriented catchall party" in order to widen its base of support.

Each of these two hypotheses cannot be entirely false; each might explain some part of the political behavior of the Japanese. Yet it is of crucial importance to judge which trend will be dominant, because that will determine the policies to be taken by the LDP as well as the opposition parties.

In order to distinguish the two hypotheses, we may focus on the problem of party loyalty. If the LDP increases the voters' support by appealing to their interest-orientation, their loyalty to the LDP on average will decline because their support is based on calculations of self-interest. On the other hand, if the voters' support is based on tradition-oriented conservatism, their loyalty will increase because tradition-orientation is, in essence, an emotional attachment to something more deeply rooted than economic interests—the indigenous Japanese norms, the country itself, and the party that represents them. Therefore, the degree of party loyalty to the LDP will mirror whether the voters are becoming more tradition-oriented or more interest-oriented. For example, if tradition-oriented conservatism is really reviving among Japanese voters, we might surmise that the voters' loyalty to the LDP will increase, compared to, say, the early 1970's.

Two methods seem available. First, we may compare actual election outcomes with pre-election forecasts. If the outcome is far from any pre-election forecast, we may infer that the voters are unpredictable, volatile, and therefore not loyal to the party in question. Second, if the opinion polls ask relevant questions, we may break down the supporters into, for example, active and passive groups. If the ratio of passive supporters is increasing, we may say the voters are becoming less loyal.

For the first test, we can refer to the results of two recent national (Lower House) elections in 1979 and 1980. As Japanese postelection commentaries agreed, these two elections were unpredictable in their outcomes. In 1979, all opinion polls indicated there would be a big increase in the LDP vote; for example, a Jiji Tsūshinsha survey showed nearly a 5 percent increase in LDP support from the previous election year of 1976. The conservative resurgence seemed all too visible, so that most pre-election forecasts were optimistic about the prospects of the LDP. Nevertheless, the actual outcome turned out to be stunningly contrary to predictions. The number of LDP seats actually decreased to a slim two-seat majority, and the percentage of LDP votes (out of the total votes cast) increased by far less than expected, resulting in what was seen in the press as a "big defeat for the LDP." The 1980 election outcome was again a great surprise. This time the opinion surveys showed only a small increase in LDP support and more forecasts were for a status quo result; half the observers thought there would be an end to single-party government. In fact, the form a coalition government might take was discussed seriously for the first time in thirty years. However, the outcome stunned all forecasters. The percentage of LDP votes increased by more than 3 percent, and the number of LDP seats increased by 7 percent, providing the LDP with its largest majority since 1969. There is no denying that some technical or short-run factors, such as election strategies, weather, and so on, contributed to this unexpected victory. However, the very fact that the voters became so sensitive to such minor factors seems to suggest declining party loyalty. Thus, this first test tends to refute the tradition-orientation hypothesis.

For the second test, let us draw on two NHK opinion surveys conducted in 1973 and 1978, because they were of large enough scale to supply ample information about cross-relations among many questions. According to these surveys, LDP support *significantly* increased from 34.3 percent in 1973 to 38.2 percent in 1978. If we include the NLC (New Liberal Club), created in 1976 as an offshoot of the LDP, the combined support for conservatives rose from 34.3 percent to 39.6 percent. On the other hand, the support for the major ideology-based opposition parties fell significantly: Japan Socialist Party (JSP) support fell from 19.8 percent to 14.1 percent, and Japan Communist Party (JCP) support from 4.2 percent to 2.1 percent. The number of respondents indicating they did not support any particular party increased from 31.6 percent to 33.8 percent. The trend is obvious: a conservative resurgence and a decline in opposition-of-principle parties.

This survey is useful because it asked a follow-up question of those who did not indicate any particular party support: "If you had to support a party, isn't there one you could possibly choose?" Those who chose some party in response to this question can be called "passive supporters," while those who already showed party support before this follow-up question can be called "active supporters." In the five-year period from 1973 to 1978, passive support for the LDP increased from 7.2 percent (of total respondents, as in other percentage figures in this paragraph) to 9.1 percent, and the NLC passive support was 2.1 percent in 1978 (the NLC did not exist in 1973, and its core members then belonged to the LDP). On the other hand, passive support for the JSP decreased from 6 percent to 5 percent, and that of the JCP fell from 2.3 percent to 0.9 percent. These changes are all statistically significant. Thus, the composition of passive supporters changed remarkably. In 1973, the LDP passive support of 7.2 percent was smaller than the passive support of the JSP and JCP combined (8.3 percent), but in 1978, the conservative passive support of 11.2 percent (inclusive of the NLC) was nearly twice as large as the JSP and JCP passive support of 5.9 percent. Floating votes were definitely moving from the ideological opposition parties to the conservative parties.

It was once conventional wisdom in Japan that floating votes were mainly urban and proprogressive or anticonservative, while the LDP was a party of rural loyalists. This seems to be quickly changing, as floating votes are defecting from the ideology-based opposition parties. This change is, however, a mixed blessing for the LDP, because the basis of conservative support is now becoming less solid, though it has substantially broadened. There is one corollary that is related to the effects of voter turnout. If the turnout is low and passive voters do not come to the voting booth, the losers will now be those parties that are relying increasingly on floating voters; those are now the LDP and the JSP. A good example is the 1979 Lower House election, in which the JSP lost a large number of seats and the LDP also lost one seat, contrary to the prediction made based on pre-election polls. Voter turnout was at an all-time low of 67.9 percent. Commentaries referred to two factors: cold and rainy weather, and Prime Minister Ōhira's speech alluding to the possibility of raising taxes (though later in the campaign he had virtually revoked this pledge).

The situation was reversed in the 1980 election. The possible LDP loss of majority control was widely discussed during the campaign. Passive supporters could appreciate the risk of a radical system change. The turnout rate was one of the highest in recent decades, at 74.5 percent. The result was a stable majority for the LDP and a retention of the same number of JSP seats. Two parties with strong core supporters, the Kōmeitō and the JCP, lost a large number of seats.

In the final analysis, recent elections were decided not so much by the choice of parties as by the choice of whether or not to vote. When the majority is threatened, interest-oriented voters return to vote for their immediate choice, the LDP. All these actions are consistent with our "interest-orientation hypothesis." The wide variation of election outcomes compared to opinion poll results, the increasing sensitivity of voters to minor issues, and the strong opposition to any change in the existing regime are all evidence of the change in the nature of the LDP toward an interest-oriented catchall party.

The changes in the LDP's policy stance in the last ten years seem to support our hypothesis. From the early 1970's, the LDP strengthened the social welfare system, established antipollution policies, and attempted to improve the environment in the cities, all through a substantial increase in public expenditures. In the first half of the 1970's, an important step was thus taken toward "big government" in terms of public expenditure. In responding to the oil crisis and subsequent stagflation, the LDP government put a priority on employment, forcing industries to make a sacrifice. The result was a striking decrease in the profits of most industries. The party also made an effort to form a nationwide grass-roots organization, which boosted the number of LDP members to more than two million. While all this may not have been done consciously or willingly on the part of LDP politicians, the net result was to attract strongly those parts of the voting population not previously wooed by the LDP. Reacting to the political needs created by socioeconomic change, the LDP became transformed into an interest-oriented catchall party.

The LDP's urban policy is a good example. The early 1970's saw an end of the population flow into the megalopolitan areas, and the aforementioned increase in public expenditure for the cities was thus able to make a significant improvement in the urban environment. This effect was felt gradually by urban residents in the late 1970's, though it escaped the general attention it deserved because of the overshadowing issue of the post-oil-crisis stagflation. The NHK survey gives some evidence of this improvement. Answers to the question, "How satisfied are you with your present life?" showed a significant increase from 1973 to 1978 in the level of satisfaction, particularly in those groups which previously had not favored the LDP: urban residents, people under thirty-five, white-collar workers, and students. An increase in satisfaction was greater among wage and salary earners than among farmers, the self-employed, or managers.

The change in the composition of LDP support paralleled this change in satisfaction. A significant increase in *active* LDP support came from a good mixture of the traditional base and the new base: residents of big cities and villages, high school graduates, people aged thirty-five to forty-four, skilled workers, the self-employed, and housewives. A new trend was more evident in the significant increase in *passive* LDP support found in residents of middle-sized cities, college graduates, people twenty-five to thirty-nine, and unskilled workers. The NLC attracted its main support from suburban residents, people under twenty-nine, and students. Thus, the conservative support from the groups that had previously been against the LDP such as the urban, the young, and the employed significantly increased from 1973 to 1978, and this new support tended to be passive in nature.

The election results themselves may be worth mentioning. Some evidence can be gathered by examining the breakdown by electoral districts of LDP votes in the recent elections. Compared to previous elections in 1976 and 1979, the 1980 election showed an increase in LDP votes, particularly in urban precincts. Newspaper opinion surveys taken just before every election suggested that the increase in LDP votes was probably due to an increase in younger supporters and supporters among wage and salary earners, confirming the findings from the NHK survey data.

All in all, the NHK survey, as well as factor analyses of it, seems supportive of our hypothesis that the recent LDP resurgence has been due to its successful conversion to an interest-oriented catchall party. In the political context of the future, one that will include the development of interest-oriented catchall parties, the meaning of "interest" will—and also should—be understood in increasingly wider terms and not just the narrow economic sense. In order to cope with future major issues, each interest-oriented party will have to transcend the interest group politics we used to know in the past, by reaching out for an integral social philosophy without invoking the old class ideology or simple-minded liberalism. The tasks are so enormous that we can see no easy future.

However, it seems likely that no class society will reemerge, because the trend toward political equality is unlikely to be reversed, and no foreseeable cultural trend is likely to legitimize any explicit class hierarchy. It is indeed conceivable that the existence of the present alignments will be endangered if economic progress is halted (as some may suggest, owing to shortages of energy resources or environmental disruptions) and/or international order is broken down (as some fear, by large-scale warfare). However, a probable consequence of these crises will be not so much a class society as mass society in the conventional sense, that is, an emotion-ridden society that could be manipulated by an ultramodern charismatic leader or group. More concretely, an embargo of energy resources or food supplies, another country's closed-door policy to Japanese exports, sizable military incidents in East Asia, or any combination of these might possibly give rise to an excessively nationalistic, even ethnocentric government. However, this type of radical swing is by far less likely to occur than in the 1930's because of greater international understanding and coordination and because of greater equality in the distribution of material affluence. Present-day Japanese society is more fluid and amorphous than any other society in history. Nevertheless, this is probably only a form of transition from the industrial society we have had up to now to a future society which we will some day call a "transindustrial society."

42. Japanese Political Economy Today: The Patterned Pluralist Model

Ellis S. Krauss and Muramatsu Michio

To explain the distinctiveness of Japan's political economy, several models have been advanced, such as "Japan, Inc." Political scientists Ellis Krauss and Muramatsu Michio feel such models are misleading and, in a paper written for this volume, propose their own concept of "patterned pluralism."

The models of politics and political economy that are applied to Japan seem woefully inadequate to characterize the Japanese system. We suspect that some of the most popular models—those emphasizing the overwhelming power of the bureaucracy, or the harmonious cooperation of a close-knit power elite comprising the bureaucracy, top Liberal-Democratic Party leaders, and big business executives in working together to dominate policy making to their own advantage, for example—were probably only partial reflections of the description of the system that has emerged in the last decade and a half.

At the same time, models that have been applied elsewhere, such as the classic pluralist model originally developed to describe the Anglo-American democracies, seem inadequate to describe the much more structured situation in Japan, where there is a permanent dominant party, a powerful government bureaucracy, and relatively institutionalized relationships between interest groups and bureaucracy and party. Yet corporatist models that are today so popular among political scientists for analyzing some European systems appear only partially to capture the dynamics of the Japanese system. Political parties play too great a role, and some interest sectors are more autonomous and conflictual with government today.

We suggest that our problems in characterizing the Japanese political economy today arise because all these characterizations are partially true, and because the Japanese system is not completely like any other. Rather, we propose that the political economy that has developed over the postwar period under the conservative ruling coalition and its flexible and responsive conservative policy line may best be called a system of *patterned pluralism.*

In this type of system, access is open because the dominant party's social-interest coalition is wide, and because the government bureaucracy is inclusionary and also has strong ties to interest groups. Influence in the system has relatively wide distribution because the ruling coalition is flexible and must remain so to perpetuate its dominance in the face of social change and challenge from an opposition that has not been completely delegitimized.

The system's processes and direction are pluralistic in fundamental ways: influence is widely distributed, not concentrated, there are many points of access for interest groups to the policy-making process, and although interest groups are definitely tied to the government, there are also elements of autonomy and conflict with the government.

Yet we are not dealing here with pluralism in the classic sense, a pluralism in which policy making is merely the outcome of an open-ended equilibrium between competing pressure groups' lobbying activities on a relatively weak government. In patterned pluralism the government and its bureaucracy are strong, but the boundaries between the state and society have become blurred by the integration of social groups into the government and by the intermediation of political parties between social-interest groups and the government. The government is not weak, it is just *penetrated* by societal and semi-linkage organizations such as political parties. Lobbying activities and coalitions are not open-ended because interest groups are also in relatively constant alliances with the same parties and bureaucratic agencies.

Essentially, the pluralism is patterned and mitigated by three basic elements that structure the otherwise pure pluralist relationships and prevent alliances and policy outcomes from being completely fluid or changeable on every issue:

1. There is a dominant party perennially in power.

2. There is an ideological cleavage between that party with its interest group allies and the opposition parties with their own interest group allies.

3. The bureaucracy remains the pivot of the policy-making process, with coalitions forming around the particular ministry in a specific policy-making area.

Consequently, policy making on nonideological issues pits relatively fixed alliances of certain interest groups and elements within the dominant party and the government against other, similar coalitions when the issue crosses subgovernment boundaries. Issues within these boundaries are sometimes handled more cooperatively and consensually, usually with the bureaucratic agency providing the crucial coordinating arena. In these cases, the opposition plays a peripheral role in the policy-making process. But when a controversial issue arises that involves basic ideological divisions over policy, the ruling coalition party, the bureaucracy, and their interest group allies clash with a mobilized opposition and its sympathizers.

A patterned pluralist system like Japan's, we would suggest, is most likely to arise in nations that modernize relatively late and that have experienced mass democratization and economic growth only recently. Late modernizers have two characteristics essential for the later development of patterned pluralism, characteristics that retain some viability into the democratization period of the late twentieth century. First, they usually have a strong bureaucracy, partly inherited from traditional society and partly developed for the purpose of leading the nation toward modernization. Second, delayed but rapid modernization and the strengthened power of the state that emerges as industrialization progresses creates an opposition characterized by resistance to the governing power on the basis of ideology and principle.

Thus, patterned pluralism arises in late modernizers that must adapt traditions of strong government bureaucracy and state power to an increasingly pluralistic society with democratic and consumer-oriented values, to a differentiated and powerful interest group structure, and to a viable, if not powerful, principled opposition.

Patterned pluralism may be contrasted with the "interest group liberalism" found in the United States. In systems of the American type, institutionalized democratic pluralism centered on politicians and interest groups has to be reconciled with the later growth of bureaucracy in the modern state. Here, too, we find the growth of subgovernments, but the role of the bureaucracy remains less well developed and subgovernmental policy making continues to pivot around the politician–interest group axis. Conversely, the particular mixture of dominant party, pluralist competition and relationships, bureaucratic power, and corporatist elements that characterize patterned pluralism represents the adaptation of a late-modernizing, bureaucratic state to an affluent, consumer-oriented society with increasingly institutionalized democratic norms. Policy making in patterned pluralist states is characterized by the central role that the bureaucratic arena and procedures continue to play in that system. The bureaucracy, rather than politicians and interest groups, represents the pivot around which policy making alliances are formed on particular issues.

In the later stages of patterned pluralism we are witnessing today, the patterned elements remain but decline in strength. The dominant party's role in policy making increases vis-à-vis the bureaucracy, the ideological polarization between government and opposition diminishes, and some major interest groups acquire the resources and incentives to become less reliant on government. As these developments unfold, the pluralist elements and tendencies in the system become more obvious.

43. Japan, the Societal State

Daniel I. Okimoto

In this selection, drawn from *Between MITI and the Market*, political scientist Daniel Okimoto defines in theoretical terms the Japanese conception of the state. He suggests that, in contrast to the Western idea of government as an "administrative appendage," the Japanese state should be seen in terms of its central position within a societal network.

The Japanese State

Many keen students of Japan, from Robert Bellah to Maruyama Masao and Nakane Chie, have stressed the overriding importance of the state in relation to the structure of society. Bellah characterizes Japan as a society in which the collectivity, be it the family, corporation, or nation-state, takes priority over its individual members, and the polity (broadly defined) is given primacy over other sectors of society. The emphasis on the polity and on political values means that Japan is oriented toward the achievement of collective goals, with a value system based on performance, particularism, and loyalty.

The state's central role is to function as guardian of the public welfare. That its responsibility is to serve the public by advancing the interests of the largest and most important collectivity—not its individual parts—is reflected in the enormous symbolic (though not always functional) importance attached to the head of the group, be it the father, corporation president, or chairman of a business association. State and society form mutually reinforcing parts of a whole. The state is not, as in some Western countries, simply an administrative appendage, superimposed on society with the responsibility of allocating resources, laying down equitable rules and norms, and adjudicating conflict through the operation of the legal apparatus.

Perhaps the closest Western equivalent to the Japanese state is the concept of the "organic state," which emerges from a time-honored philosophical tradition stretching all the way back to Aristotle. In Aristotle's view, the political community (*polis*) takes priority over individual citizens because the whole is of greater importance than the sum of its constituent parts. The state's central mission—indeed, its moral obligation—is to use its authority to advance the common good of the political community as a whole.

This moral obligation provides the normative underpinnings for a highly interventionist, if not authoritarian, state. Although there is no intrinsic reason why groups in the private sector cannot play vigorous roles, the organic state's attitude toward interest-maximizing private organizations is a far cry from Adam Smith's unshakeable faith in the benefits of freewheeling politico-economic competition.

From Daniel I. Okimoto, *Between MITI and the Market: Japanese Industrial Policy for High Technology* (Stanford, Calif.: Stanford University Press, forthcoming). By permission of the publisher.

Because the behavior of selfish interest groups can damage the welfare of the political community as a whole, the organic state bears the responsibility for stepping in and keeping private actors from tearing apart the fabric of society. It is no accident, therefore, that corporatist and authoritarian states have sprung up from the philosophical soil of organic statism, especially in the Iberian countries and Latin America.

The concept of the organic state is similar in some respects to the concept of the Japanese state. Both function within the framework of a collective community that takes priority over its constituent parts. Both symbolize, and have the functional responsibility to reaffirm, the basic solidarity of the national collectivity. Both are expected to steer private groups away from the pursuit of the narrow self-interest that tends to undermine long-term collective objectives and national goals. Harmony, unity, pragmatism, and national interests constitute overriding values for both.

There are, however, some basic differences between the Japanese state and the Western concept of the organic state. One is the absence of universalistic principles underpinning the legitimacy of the Japanese state. Without a foundation of universalistic principles on which to base its *raison d'être*, the Japanese state has had problems establishing a higher ground as the basis for exercising autonomous power. It has had either to stand on its record of superior performance, or, failing that, to fall back on particularistic values to undergird its authority. There have been times, though these are the exception rather than the rule, when the Japanese state has converted its particularistic underpinnings into coercive regimes. The period of prewar militarism, 1931–45, is probably the best-known, and most extreme, example. What the military regime did was to practice repression at home and aggression abroad, using ultranationalism to buttress its power. But it can be argued that the prewar military state was never able to establish a stable base of legitimacy, and that its emergence is attributable to the concatenation of "abnormal" developments at home and abroad.

The Meiji (1868–1912) and early postwar (1952–78) periods provide two more "normal" and intriguing eras of stable governance from above. Unlike the prewar military regime, the Meiji and early postwar states established a strong basis of legitimacy to justify policies of government intervention. And if Japan's performance during these two periods is measured by standard economic indicators, these two cases of rapid growth under the auspices of what Chalmers Johnson calls the "developmental state" can be highly evaluated. Do the two examples prove that Japan is a statist society? Or were the Meiji and early postwar experiences historical aberrations?

Bellah and Johnson (as well as all believers in the notion of "Japan, Inc.") would take the first position—that the Japanese state is intrinsically powerful; but an argument can be made in support of the latter interpretation, since the Meiji and postwar periods are among the few instances in the long history of Japan in which the state has played a dominant role. In both instances, the power wielded by the Japanese state can be explained by the convergence of extraordinary circumstances—the threat of foreign domination, potentially crippling industrial backwardness, the perception of national crisis, and the urgency of a latecomer's catch-up efforts—all of which provided the essential backdrop for the assertion of strong, centralized authority. For most other stretches of Japan's two-thousand-year history, however, state power had been circumscribed by the absence of a legitimizing system of universalistic principles and by the diffusion of power in Japanese society.

By contrast, the philosophical tradition of organic statism is rooted in universalistic values associated with Aristotle, Roman law, and Catholic social thought. Curiously, this universalistic grounding at once limits and strengthens state power. It is limiting in the sense that the organic state is itself accountable by strict standards of behavior, based on such universally applicable values as democratic representation and legal justice. It is reinforcing in that state authority carries the powerful weight of universalistic values behind it. On balance, the net effect has been to strengthen the hand of authoritarian states.

State and Society

Because the Japanese state today is stable and actively involved in the management of the country's economy, the notion that it has traditionally had problems establishing an independent base of authority may be hard to believe. The statist model is, after all, the reigning paradigm for contemporary Japan's political economy. How can the notion of a state historically lacking in universalistic legitimacy and autonomy be reconciled with abundant evidence of a vigorously active, if not dominant, state? Perhaps the conundrum can be cleared up by placing the state in its broad, societal context.

If the state's authority is circumscribed, what is the source of its power? The answer can be found in a number of distinctive historical and institutional characteristics: the legacy of the Allied Occupation, a broad national consensus supporting industrial catch-up, the clampdown on militant labor and its organization into enterprise unions, the emphasis on *wa* (harmony) as an integrative principle of social organization, and the structure of Japanese society, which provides the framework within which the state functions. In *Japanese Society*, Nakane Chie characterizes Japan as a "frame society," composed of numerous vertically organized groups locked in fierce competition, with only weak horizontal links holding the groups together. Japanese society thus calls for, and facilitates, central coordination by a neutral entity, the state:

Characteristics of Japanese society assist in the development of the state political organization. Competing clusters, in view of the difficulty of reaching agreement or consensus between clusters, have a diminished authority in dealings with the state administration. Competition and hostile relations between civil powers facilitate the acceptance of state power; [because groups are] organized vertically, once the state's administrative authority is accepted, it can be transmitted without obstruction down the vertical line of a group's internal organization (p. 102).

Although Nakane underestimates the strength of horizontal ties, she calls attention to the pivotal role played by the state in aggregating competing private interests through the vehicle of consensus formation. Consensus is an effective means of coordination not only in homogeneous countries like Japan, but also in socially fragmented countries like the Netherlands. But because consensus is not always readily reached by rivalrous groups, some central authority—the state—must act to bring it about.

In Japan, the task of forging consensus or mediating private conflicts is facilitated enormously by the emphasis placed on *wa* (harmony). All individuals and groups with a claim to authority invoke wa to buttress their capacity to take binding action. For the Japanese state, especially, the concept of wa provides an indispensable source of power. The state would have an infinitely harder time fulfilling its oversight functions if the principle of wa did not carry such strong normative weight.

Effective power thus hinges largely on the state's capacity to achieve harmony—in terms of collective interests and national goals—amidst the cacophony of dissonant private interests. Consensus, the most common manifestation of wa, is the concrete means by which Japan reaches agreement within the private sector and between the private sector and government. As neutral mediator and as guardian of the public interest, the state is usually involved in coordinating the processes of consensus formation; and consensus, painstakingly arrived at, provides legitimation for state intervention in the activities of the market economy.

In taking vigorous action, the Japanese state seldom brandishes the threat of legal sanctions to bring recalcitrant groups into line. The exercise of naked power is considered neither desirable nor effective, particularly as a frequently used instrument of governance. Rather, the state prefers to rely on its ability to (1) maintain an aura of strict neutrality in relation to competing interest groups; (2) keep the trust of groups with which it works; and (3) use persuasion and incentives to steer the private sector in desired directions. The state's capacity to persuade the private interests to take voluntaristic action—which, the state usually argues, lies in their long-term, collective interests anyway—is the secret of its effectiveness. The state's capacity to wield power emerges, in short, out of the structure of its working relationship with other groups in society, particularly private corporations. Its power is far from absolute.

Perhaps Japan can be characterized as a "network," a "relational," or "societal" state in the sense that government power is intertwined with that of the private sector. It hinges on its capacity to work in concert with the private sector, with each side making an effort to take into account the needs and objectives of the other. Political power in Japan is thus exercised through a complex process of public-private sector interaction, involving subtle give-and-take, not frontal confrontations which would result in the forcible imposition of one side's will on the other.

In terms of the state's capacity to impose its will on society, the power of authoritarian states in Latin America and in parts of the Third World far exceeds that of Japan. Indeed, throughout Japan's long history, the central government has almost never wielded absolute power. Even during the heyday of prewar military rule, military cliques never had the absolute power of fascist regimes in Germany or Spain.

If state power is defined solely in terms of confrontational clout, even the American government might be considered stronger than its Japanese counterpart: consider, for example, the many cases of U.S. government enforcement in the regulatory, antitrust, equal opportunity, and national security arenas (the last involving, for example, controls over the export of dual-purpose technology). Differences in the exercise of power by the American and Japanese governments can be seen not only in the contrasts between America's arm's-length, legalistic style and Japan's close-up, cooperative approach, but also in the frequency of, and reliance upon, confrontational coercion in the United States, as opposed to persuasion, painstaking negotiation, and mutual accommodation in Japan.

To be effective, the Japanese government must maintain close working relations with the private sector, since mutual trust is the *sine qua non* of cooperation and compliance. This implies that the state, like a parent, has to have the best interests of the private sector at heart, even when it seeks to reconcile parochial private interests with collective goals. It must listen to the views of private companies, taking them fully into account when formulating public policies—but without becoming merely the puppet of powerful private interests. For a "societal state" like Japan's to assume a strongly pro-business posture is, therefore, hardly surprising. This stance is perfectly in keeping with the way Japanese society is structured, and the way political power is exercised.

44. Market Rationality vs. Plan Rationality

Chalmers Johnson

In this selection Chalmers Johnson, a political scientist at the University of California, Berkeley, compares the operation of the United States economy, as an example of market rationality, to the operation of the Japanese economy, as an example of plan rationality. Johnson suggests that active government intervention and protection made possible the change in industrial structure that occurred in Japan during the 1960's, which in turn brought about Japan's "economic miracle." The essay is adapted from his study of the Ministry of International Trade and Industry (MITI) published in 1982.

Nowhere is the prevalent and peculiarly Western preference for binary modes of thought more apparent than in the field of political economy. In modern times Max Weber began the practice with his distinction between a "market economy" and a "planned economy." Some recent analogues are Ralf Dahrendorf's distinction between "market rationality" and "plan rationality," Ronald Dore's distinction between "market-oriented systems" and "organization-oriented systems," and George A. Kelly's distinction between a "rule-governed state" and a "purpose-governed state." I shall make use of several of these distinctions later, but first I must stress that, for purposes of the present discussion, the right-hand component of these pairs is not the Soviet-type command economy. Economies of the Soviet type are not plan-rational but plan-ideological. In the Soviet Union and

From Chalmers Johnson, *MITI and the Japanese Miracle: The Growth of Industrial Policy, 1925–1975* (Stanford, Calif.: Stanford University Press, 1982), pp. 18–31. By permission of the publisher.

its dependencies and emulators, state ownership of the means of production, state planning, and bureaucratic goal-setting are not rational means to a developmental goal (even if they may once have been); they are fundamental values in themselves, not to be challenged by evidence of either inefficiency or ineffectiveness. In the sense I am using the term here, Japan is plan-rational and the command economies are not; in fact, the history of Japan since 1925 offers numerous illustrations of why the command economy is not plan-rational, a lesson the Japanese learned well.

At the most basic level, the distinction between market and plan refers to differing conceptions of the functions of the state in economic affairs. The state as an institution is as old as organized human society. Until approximately the nineteenth century, states everywhere performed more or less the same functions, functions that make large-scale social organization possible but that individuals or families or villages cannot perform for themselves. These functions include defense, road building, water conservancy, the minting of coins, and the administration of justice. Following the Industrial Revolution, the state began to take on new functions. In the states that were the first to industrialize, the state itself had little to do with the new forms of economic activity, but toward the end of the nineteenth century the state took on regulatory functions in the interest of maintaining competition, consumer protection, and so forth.

In states that were late to industrialize, the state itself led the industrialization drive; that is, it took on developmental functions. These two differing orientations toward private economic activities—the regulatory orientation and the developmental orientation—produced two different kinds of government-business relationships. The United States is a good example of a state in which the regulatory orientation predominates; Japan is a good example of a state in which the developmental orientation predominates. A regulatory, or market-rational, state concerns itself with the forms and procedures—the rules, if you will—of economic competition, but it does not concern itself with substantive matters. For example, the United States government has many regulations concerning the antitrust implications of the size of firms, but it does not concern itself with which industries ought to exist and which industries are no longer needed. The developmental or plan-rational state, by contrast, has as its dominant feature precisely the setting of such substantive social and economic goals.

Another way to make this distinction is to consider a state's priorities in economic policy. In the plan-rational state, the government will give greatest precedence to industrial policy—that is, to a concern for promoting the structure of domestic industry that will enhance the nation's international competitiveness. The very existence of an industrial policy implies a strategic or goal-oriented approach to the economy. On the other hand, the market-rational state usually will not even have an industrial policy (or, at any rate, will not recognize it as such). Instead, both its domestic and foreign economic policy, including its trade policy, will stress rules and reciprocal concessions (although perhaps influenced by some goals that are not industrially specific, goals such as price stability or full employment). Its trade policy will normally be subordinate to general foreign policy, being used more often to cement political relationships than to obtain strictly economic advantages.

These various distinctions are useful because they draw our attention to Japan's emergence, following the Meiji Restoration of 1868, as a developmental, plan-rational state whose economic orientation was keyed to industrial policy. By contrast, the United States, from about the same period, took the regulatory, market-rational path keyed to foreign policy. In modern times, Japan has always put emphasis on an overarching, nationally supported goal for its economy rather than on the particular procedures that are to govern economic activity. Only during the 1970's did Japan begin to shift to a somewhat regulatory, foreign-policy orientation, just as America began to show early signs of a new developmental, industrial-policy orientation. But the Japanese system remains plan-rational, and the American system is still basically market-rational.

This can be seen most clearly by looking at the differences between the two systems in terms of economic and political decision making. In Japan, the developmental, strategic quality of economic policy is reflected within the government in the high position of the so-called economic bureaucrats—that is, the officials of the Finance, International Trade and Industry, Agriculture and Forestry, Construction, and Transportation ministries, plus the Economic Planning Agency. These official agencies attract the most talented graduates of the best universities in the country, and the positions of higher-level officials in these ministries have been and still are the most prestigious in the society. Although it is influenced by pressure groups and political claimants, the elite bureaucracy of Japan makes most major decisions, drafts virtually all legislation, controls the national budget, and is the source of all major policy innovations in the system. Equally important, upon their retirement, which is usually between the ages of fifty and fifty-five, these bureaucrats move from the government to powerful positions in private enterprise, banking, the political world, and the numerous public corporations—a direction of elite mobility that is directly opposite to that which prevails in the United States. The existence of a powerful, talented, and prestige-laden economic bureaucracy is a natural corollary of plan rationality.

In market-rational systems such as the United States, public service does not normally attract the most capable talent, and national decision making is dominated by elected members of the professional class, who are usually lawyers, rather than by the bureaucracy. The movement of elites is not from government to the private sector but vice versa, usually through political appointment, which is much more extensive than in Japan. The real equivalent of the Japanese Ministry of International Trade and Industry (MITI) in the United States is not the Department of Commerce but the Department of Defense, which by its very nature and functions shares MITI's strategic, goal-oriented outlook. In fact, the pejorative connotations in the United States of terms such as "Japan, Inc." are similar to those surrounding the domestic expression "military-industrial complex," referring to a close working relationship between government and business to solve problems of national defense.

Another way to highlight the differences between plan rationality and market rationality is to look at some of the trade-offs involved in each approach. First, the most important evaluative standard in market rationality is efficiency. But in plan rationality, this takes lower precedence than effectiveness. Both Americans and Japanese tend to get the meanings of efficiency and effectiveness mixed up. Americans often and understandably criticize their official bureaucracy for its inefficiency, failing to note that efficiency is not a good evaluative standard for bureaucracy. Effectiveness is the proper standard of evaluation of goal-oriented strategic activities. On the other hand, Japanese continue to tolerate their wildly inefficient and even inappropriate agricultural structure, at least in part because it is mildly effective: it provides food that does not have to be imported.

Second, both types of systems are concerned with "externalities," or what Milton Friedman has called "neighborhood effects"—an example would be such unpriced social costs of production as pollution. In this instance, however, the plan-rational system has much greater difficulty than the market-rational system in identifying and shifting its sights to respond to effects external to the national goal. The position of the plan-rational system is like that of a military organization: a general is judged by whether he wins or loses. It would be good if he would also employ an economy of violence (be efficient), but that is not as important as results. Accordingly, Japan persisted with high-speed industrial growth long after the evidence of very serious environmental damage had become common knowledge. On the other hand, when the plan-rational system finally shifts its goals to give priority to a problem such as industrial pollution, it will commonly be more effective than the market-rational system, as can be seen in the comparison between the Japanese and the American handling of pollution in the 1970's.

Third, the plan-rational system depends upon the existence of a widely agreed-upon set of overarching goals for the society, such as high-speed growth. When such a consensus exists, the plan-rational system will outperform the market-rational system on the same benchmark, such as growth of the gross national product (GNP), as long as growth of GNP is the goal of the plan-rational system. But when a consensus does not exist, when there is confusion or conflict over the overarching goal in a plan-rational economy, it will appear to be quite adrift, incapable of coming to grips with basic problems and unable to place responsibility for failures. Japan has experienced this kind of drift when unexpected developments suddenly upset its consensus, as during the "Nixon shocks" of 1971 and after the oil shock of 1973. Generally speaking, the great strength of the plan-rational system lies in its effectiveness in dealing with routine problems, whereas the great strength of the market-rational system lies in its effectiveness in dealing with critical problems. In the latter case, the emphasis on rules, procedures, and executive responsibility helps to promote action when problems of an unfamiliar or unknown magnitude arise.

Fourth, since decision making is centered in different bodies in the two systems—in an elite bureaucracy in one and in a parliamentary assembly in the other—the process of policy change will be manifested in quite different ways. In the plan-rational system, change will be marked by internal bureaucratic disputes, factional infighting, and conflict between ministries. In the market-rational system, change will be marked by strenuous parliamentary contests over new legislation and by election battles. For example, the shift in Japan during the late 1960's and throughout the 1970's from protectionism to liberalization was most clearly signaled by factional infighting within MITI between the "domestic faction" and the "international faction." The surest sign that the Japanese government was moving in a more open, free-trade direction was precisely the fact that the key ministry in this sector came to be dominated by internationalistic bureaucrats. Americans are sometimes confused by Japanese economic policy because they pay too much attention to what politicians say and because they do not know much about the bureaucracy, whereas Japanese have occasionally given too much weight to the statements of American bureaucrats and have not paid enough attention to congressmen and their extensive staffs.

Looked at historically, modern Japan began to be plan-rational and developmental in 1868. After about a decade and a half of experimentation with direct state operation of economic enterprises, it discovered the most obvious pitfalls of plan rationality: corruption, bureaucratism, and ineffective monopolies. Japan was and remained plan-rational, but it had no ideological commitment to state ownership of the economy. Its main criterion was the rational one of effectiveness in meeting the goals of development. Thus, Meiji Japan began to shift away from state entrepreneurship to collaboration with privately owned enterprises, favoring those enterprises that were capable of rapidly adopting new technologies and that were committed to the national goals of economic development and military strength. From this shift developed the collaborative relationship between the government and big business in Japan. In the prewar era, this collaboration took the form of close governmental ties to the *zaibatsu* (privately owned industrial empires). The government induced the zaibatsu to go into areas where it felt development was needed. For their part, the zaibatsu pioneered the commercialization of modern technologies in Japan, and they achieved economies of scale in manufacturing and banking that were on a par with those of the rest of the industrial world. There were many important results of this collaboration, including the development of a marked dualism between large, advanced enterprises and small, backward enterprises. But perhaps the most important result was the introduction of a needed measure of competition into the plan-rational system.

What difference does industrial policy make? It is very difficult to do cost-benefit analyses of the effects of industrial policy, not least because some of the unintended effects may include bureaucratic red tape, oligopoly, a politically dangerous blurring of what is public and what is private, and corruption. Professional quantitative economists seem to avoid the concept on grounds that they do not need it to explain economic events.

I cannot prove that a particular Japanese industry would not or could not have grown and developed at all without the government's industrial policy. What I believe can be shown are the differences between the course of development of a particular industry without governmental policies (its imaginary or "policy-off" trajectory) and its course of development with the aid of governmental policies (its real or "policy-on" trajectory). It is possible to calculate quantitatively, if not retrospectively, how, for example, foreign currency quotas and controlled trade suppress potential domestic demand to the level of the supply capacity of an infant domestic industry; how high tariffs suppress the price competitiveness of a foreign industry to the level of a domestic industry; how low purchasing power of consumers is raised through targeted tax measures and consumer-credit schemes, thereby allowing them to buy the products of new industries; how an industry borrows capital in excess of its borrowing capacity from governmental and government-guaranteed banks in order to expand production and bring down unit costs; how efficiency is raised through the accelerated depreciation of specified new machinery investments; and how tax incentives for exports function to enlarge external markets at the point of domestic sales saturation. Kodama Fumio has calculated mathematically the gaps between the real trajectory and the policy-off trajectory of the Japanese automobile industry during its infant, growing, and stable phases (the data are not yet available, of course, for a future declining phase). His measures are also tools for analyzing the appropriateness and effectiveness of the various governmental policies for the automobile industry during these phases.

The controversy over industrial policy will not soon end, nor is it my intention to resolve it here. The important point is that virtually all Japanese analysts, including those deeply hostile to MITI, believe that the government was the inspiration and the cause of the movement to heavy and chemical industries that took place during the 1950's, regardless of how one measures the costs and benefits of this movement.

This shift of "industrial structure" was the operative mechanism of the economic miracle. Did the government in general, or MITI in particular, cause it to occur? Or, to put it more carefully, did the government accelerate it and give it the direction it took? Perhaps the best answer currently available is a comparative appraisal: three of the countries with which Japan can most profitably be compared (France, Germany, and Italy) shared some or all of Japan's initial advantages—e.g., flexible labor supplies, a very favorable (in fact, even more favorable) international environment, the possibility of rebuilding an industrial structure using the most advanced techniques. Yet other conditions were very dissimilar. The most crucial difference was perhaps in the field of economic policies. Japan's government exercised a much greater degree of both intervention and protection than did any of its Western European counterparts; and this brings Japan closer to the experience of another set of countries—the centrally planned economies.

45. Procartel Policy: The Advantages

Kozo Yamamura

In this selection, which first appeared in 1982, University of Washington economist Kozo Yamamura outlines the advantages derived from Japan's tolerance of cartels. Yamamura suggests that such government protection is no longer necessary to the Japanese economy.

Japan's lax antimonopoly policy has provided its industries with a relative advantage over American and other Western industries in international competition. Many segments of Japanese export-oriented industries—for example, steel, shipbuilding, chemicals, and machinery—have been shielded from the vagaries of the market forces by sanctioned collusion.

From Kozo Yamamura, "Success That Soured: Administrative Guidance and Cartels in Japan," in Kozo Yamamura, ed., *Policy and Trade Issues of the Japanese Economy: American and Japanese Perspectives* (Seattle: University of Washington Press, 1982), pp. 100–101. By permission of the publisher.

In contrast, in the United States, where antitrust statutes are enforced more vigorously, firms cannot seek refuge in times of recession. In making investments, they cannot enjoy the reduced risks of coordinated investment under the guidance of governmental agencies. Thus, the advantages gained by Japanese firms can be substantial, in periods of both rapid and slower growth. In the former, capacity increases are achieved more quickly, because the effects of excess capacity can be cushioned. Once an industry achieves higher productivity and larger capacity, it is easier for it to retain its competitive ability and to improve itself further, especially if the government also becomes increasingly involved.

Other international competitive advantages are even more obvious. In times of recession, a Japanese industry protected by a cartel can rebound in the international market as soon as market conditions improve. The same industry in the United States may succumb by going bankrupt or being forced to reduce productive capacity too rapidly to reenter the international market competitively. This is precisely the advantage Ministry of International Trade and Industry (MITI) officials use to justify their procartel policy. In earlier years, they justified guidance cartels on the grounds that such cartels prevented the "loss of productive capacity that is needed for international competition." This was basically the argument MITI officials used, for example, in successfully advocating the Designated Recession Industries Stabilization Act of 1978.

In the 1950's, and even in the 1960's, such a policy was easy to justify. The advantage enjoyed by the protected industries helped the Japanese economy to grow, benefiting many people. Today, however, we should ask why cartels are still needed to protect some industries while Japanese industry as a whole is so successful in world markets. We should ask why Japan continues to permit such cartels, when, in effect, they provide subsidies from the national coffers and consumers so that selected recession industries can compete internationally.

46. Japanese Industrial Policy: International Repercussions

Kozo Yamamura

Economist Kozo Yamamura argues in this selection that Japanese governmental policy encourages coordinated export drives as a means of alleviating domestic economic problems. The essay is drawn from *Policy and Trade Issues of the Japanese Economy* (1982).

Ministry of International Trade and Industry (MITI) policies have provided an important justification for the export drive of Japanese firms, as many knowledgeable Japanese economists (and even businessmen) readily recognize. Yet one

From Kozo Yamamura, "Success That Soured: Administrative Guidance and Cartels in Japan," in Kozo Yamamura, ed., *Policy and Trade Issues of the Japanese Economy: American and Japanese Perspectives* (Seattle: University of Washington Press, 1982), pp. 99–100. By permission of the publisher.

result of the MITI policies has been to increase an industry's capacity beyond what is prudent. At the same time, the reduction in total excess capacity is slower than it would be if no collusion were permitted. This means that firms have a great incentive to increase exports in order to make full use of the industry's large capacity and to absorb the burden of high fixed costs.

This is only part of the reason for what the Japanese aptly call a "concentrated downpouring of exports," which occurs because new technology tends to be adopted at about the same time by all firms in an industry (often aided by MITI). At about the same time, the desire to increase exports also matures for all the firms in an industry. The more extensive the policy inducements—whether subsidies, low-cost loans, effective guidance cartels, or specific laws—the stronger and more pronounced the export drive will be. Of course, domestic recessions intensify this drive, as does misjudgment (typically overestimation) by MITI and the industries of the growth of domestic demand. The periods of sudden, and at times sustained, Japanese export drives into American and other markets can easily be identified. Beginning with the "dollar blouses" of the mid-1950's, influxes of radios, tape recorders, television sets, various steel and chemical products, and other goods have occurred during the past thirty years.

One must be aware that not all industries engage in export drives induced directly or indirectly by MITI. A rapid increase in exports can take place independently of any policy inducement. Nevertheless, the point here is that the Japanese policy accentuates product cycles. Any export drive in the 1980's will more severely strain economic and political relations between Japan and her major importers than in the past.

47. The Costs of Japanese Industrial Policy

Daniel I. Okimoto

Stanford University political scientist Daniel Okimoto argues in this selection that the economic costs of Japan's state intervention in industrial policy are relatively low. Costs do exist, however: there are large areas of economic inefficiency and instances of substantial mistakes in policy judgment. The article is taken from Okimoto's *Between MITI and the Market*.

Since antitrust violations are prosecuted with less vigor in Japan and broader use is made of industrial policy, one might suspect that the economic costs of state intervention are much higher in Japan than in the United States. Industrial policy making is, after all, susceptible to political pressures, and when government intervention is driven by politicized forces, the overall costs in terms of economic inefficiency are almost always substantial. But even though the costs of Japanese

From Daniel I. Okimoto, *Between MITI and the Market: Japanese Industrial Policy for High Technology* (Stanford, Calif.: Stanford University Press, forthcoming). By permission of the publisher.

industrial policy are significant, the aggregate costs of United States government intervention (even without an explicit industrial policy) are probably higher, taking into account the negative consequences of all the disincentives to economic efficiency—trade barriers, discriminatory tax treatment, regulations, subsidies, and so forth. And, of course, the economic costs in such European countries as England are higher still.

The reasons for the Japanese anomaly—namely, extensive state intervention through the vehicle of industrial policy, yet comparatively limited damage to economic efficiency—can be summarized in terms of six factors:

1. the conscious crafting of industrial policies on the principle of enhancing efficiency and international competitiveness;

2. effective mechanisms of interest aggregation through the Ministry of International Trade and Industry (MITI);

3. the long dominance of the pro-business Liberal-Democratic Party;

4. the insulation of large segments of the manufacturing sectors from parochial political interference;

5. sound macroeconomic management; and

6. the strengths of the private sector.

The first four factors give the Japanese government exceptional strengths in converting private interests into comparatively unpoliticized policy outputs, often based on some economic (rather than purely political) rationale. The last two factors diminish the need for more extensive microindustrial intervention. Thanks largely to these six factors, the costs of Japanese industrial policy have been comparatively well contained.

To say that the economic costs of Japanese industrial policy are not as high as might be expected, however, is not to assert that they are negligible. One of the great myths enshrouding Japanese industrial policy is that it has been nearly error-free and costless. Nothing could be further from the truth. One need not look far to find pockets of conspicuous inefficiency in the Japanese economy. Agriculture and livestock are probably the best known, but others include sugar refining, confectioneries, tobacco, public transportation (especially railways), construction, space, defense, health services, some areas of pharmaceuticals, segments of financing, and the service sector. Of course, only some of these industries fall into the domain of MITI's industrial policy, which is the focus of this essay; the root problem in most of the above cases is that parochial lobbies have managed to secure political control over the policy arenas of direct relevance to their vested interests. But one can also find striking examples of economic inefficiency created by political expediency even in the domain of MITI industrial policy (though, as already implied, MITI is far more successful at protecting public policy from dominance by parochial politics than other ministries such as Construction, Welfare, Agriculture, Transportation, and Postal and Telecommunications). The coal industry is but one example. Owing to the coal industry's political influence in certain regions of Japan (Hokkaido, Kyushu, and areas on Honshu such as Ibaraki prefecture), MITI has been funneling large subsidies to the coal industry for decades. The subsidies cannot be justified on economic grounds, but politics prevents MITI from abolishing them. Similarly, MITI provides handsome subsidies to Japan's textile industry. Who winds up paying the bill for such economically unjustified industrial policy? The taxpayer.

The power of politically efficacious interest groups is also evident in Japan's retail network for consumer durables, an overextended and highly inefficient sector. This network is dominated by a national honeycomb of small mom-and-pop stores located in residential neighborhoods, often in the home of the proprietor. Large retail chains, offering a broad selection of goods at discount prices, also can be found in the big metropolitan districts, but they are relatively few in number. Small shops account for 99.7 percent of all retail stores and nearly 80 percent of total sales. Small shopowners have virtual veto power over proposals to establish large discount outlets in their neighborhoods. Hence the push to set up national networks of large discount stores, which gained momentum during the late 1960's and early 1970's, has been aborted by MITI's protective treatment of small retail interests.

MITI officials contend that, though they would like to streamline the inefficient retail distribution sector, their hands are tied by regulatory laws passed by politicians eager to win the votes of mom-and-pop storekeepers. Virtually all political parties rally around the banner of small shopowners, regardless of the costs in economic inefficiency. Although such protection may help absorb excess labor and distribute income more equitably, it clearly runs counter to market forces, perpetuates inefficiency, exacerbates inflationary pressures, and erects de facto barriers against the import of foreign products (since few small shops carry any foreign-made goods). Hence the economic costs of Japanese industrial policy in the retail distribution sector are substantial, and they contradict MITI's professed commitment to the principle of market efficiency.

The myth of MITI omniscience is also belied by costly mistakes that have been made. Consider, for example, the strategy of industrial catch-up in the petrochemical industry. In the mid-1960's, MITI's ambitious plan to create a world-class petrochemical industry seemed like a sound and far-sighted idea. The petrochemical industry looked like a sure winner, a high-growth industry capable of yielding high value added and certain to move Japan's industrial structure to the next logical phase of comparative advantage. If Japanese companies invested heavily in new plant facilities, the country seemed poised to seize a significant share of the world market and to expand that share steadily over time. MITI tried to facilitate the industry's rapid development by providing, among other things, favorable incentives for heavy capital investments.

Notwithstanding MITI's image of never making mistakes, this vision failed to materialize as planned. The first oil crisis hit not long after a major expansion of new plant capacity. As the costs of energy spiraled upward, Japan's petrochemical industry—utterly dependent on imported oil—found itself caught in a terrible squeeze, hard pressed to cut costs deeply enough to compete with foreign manufacturers. Moreover, the recession into which the world was plunged left Japan's petrochemical industry saddled with large idle and excess capacity. So intractable were the problems that disquieting questions were raised concerning not only the petrochemical industry's short-term capacity to ride out the recession, but also its long-term, competitive staying power.

Here was a case where Japanese industrial policy led directly to serious structural problems, which required other policy measures—applied over a sustained period—to correct. Not that a decentralized market system would have averted this error; the oil embargo by the Organization of Petroleum Exporting Countries (OPEC) caught everyone by surprise, including the United States. The point is that Japanese industrial policy exacerbated the costs by pushing ahead with the expansion of new plant facilities at a faster pace than would have been the case under a laissez-faire system.

Part V: Issues for the Future

A S W E H E A D into the waning years of the twentieth century, Japan finds itself at a crucial turning point in its modern history. Having completed the tasks of postwar recovery and latecomer industrial catchup, Japan now faces the challenge of adapting to fundamental changes in both the domestic and the international environments. The spread of economic interdependence also means that the interaction between domestic and international systems is expanding in scope and impact. With what is now the world's second-largest economy, Japan's role in the international system is itself undergoing change; the rest of the world looks to Japan to assume responsibility for global stability and prosperity commensurate with its rise as an economic power.

At home, Japan is going through a complex transition, occasioned by the convergence of three forces: the evolutionary processes of maturation, mounting foreign pressures, and proliferating ties of international interdependence. Specific examples of the changes under way include the aging of its population, the possible erosion of Japan's work ethic and traditional values, the transition to a postindustrial economy, the need to demonstrate the capacity to innovate at the frontiers of technology, educational reforms, pressures to deregulate and internationalize domestic capital markets, trade conflicts, and a reexamination of Japan's defense policies.

The aging of the population is perhaps the most striking example of the maturation process at home. Since the end of World War II, Japan has undergone what can only be called a "demographic revolution"; having one of the youngest populations in the world in 1945, it now has one of the oldest. The number of Japanese sixty-five and over has more than doubled, jumping from roughly 5 percent in 1950 to over 12 percent in 1986. It is expected to exceed 15 percent by the year 2000 and will break the 20 percent mark by the year 2040. Life expectancy for Japanese males has increased from 65.3 years (in 1960) to 74.8 in 1984; in the U.S., the figure is 71.6 years, in Sweden 73.6. Japanese women can expect to live for 80.4 years, a steep rise from the life expectancy of 70.1 years in 1960, and longer than the 78.8 years for American women and 79.6 years in Sweden.

The speed with which Japan's population is aging is bound to have far-reaching ramifications. It will increase the number of retired people in the workforce, strain welfare programs, alter social, residential, and consumer patterns, reduce household savings, affect electoral and political behavior, and compound pressures for an expansion of government expenditures in such areas as social security. Will the relatively lean Japanese government, with its low rates of taxes and expenditures, grow fat, or at least significantly fatter? How will the aging affect political stability?

The structure of the Japanese economy is also changing, as labor, capital, and production shift away from the heavy manufacturing industries, which served as the pillars of Japan's smokestack economy during the 1960's. Labor and capital are shifting steadily to the knowledge-intensive and service sectors of a high technology economy. With the shift from heavy manufacturing to high technology, will Japan continue to enjoy the competitive success it has known in the past? This question, which is of great concern not only to the Japanese themselves but also to their economic competitors, leads to another: Will the Japanese be able to innovate in key areas of high technology? As Japan moves to the forefront of leading-edge technology, and as the newly industrializing countries (NIC's) of Asia close in on Japan from behind, the Japanese will have to rely increasingly on technological breakthroughs to sustain their lead position.

Whether Japan will be able to compete at the technological frontiers is not entirely clear. To date at least, apart from process technology, where it has excelled, Japan has been considered a technological follower and incremental adaptor. The organization of its industrial system, while well-suited for latecomer catch-up, is widely seen to pose problems for state-of-the-art innovation. Is this the case? Or are Western perceptions either inaccurate or out-of-date? Several readings in this section provide insights into these questions.

As economic interdependence with the rest of the world increases, Japan is also facing the reality of severe conflicts with other countries and strong external pressures for change, particularly on matters related to trade. In 1985, Japan ran an overall trade surplus of $55 billion while the United States incurred a deficit of $124 billion. Japan accumulated most of its surplus with the United States ($39 billion) and the European Community ($11 billion). Not surprisingly, Japan's trade conflicts are most severe with the United States and Europe, which maintain that their deficits in merchandise trade can be attributed, in significant measure, to Japan's closed market and unfair trade practices.

In response, many Japanese (and some Western scholars) argue that the trade imbalance cannot be blamed on import barriers or unfair trade practices. It is an outcropping, they say, of much deeper-seated forces at work, especially national differences in savings and consumption, differential rates of growth, exchange rate misalignments, and productivity differentials. The implication of this argument is that the imbalance will persist, even with the removal of all artificial impediments to trade, unless such underlying factors as the savings rate either rises in the United States, or falls in Japan (as it may do because of Japan's aging population). Thus Japan and its trading partners may simply have to live with continuing international conflicts, as an unavoidable by-product of Japan's growing size, competitiveness, and economic interdependence.

Japanese leaders are reviewing their options for alleviating trade conflicts. One option, put forward by the Maekawa Committee (whose report is included in this section), is to transform the structure of Japan's economy from an export-oriented economy to one more reliant on domestic demand. The transformation, if undertaken, would have the positive effects of moderating the compulsion to export and expanding the demand for foreign imports. Over the long term, Japan's huge trade surpluses would be brought into better balance and trade-related conflicts with other countries would be alleviated. But such a transformation would take time, and there is no assurance that the desired outcomes would be achieved.

One unavoidable consequence of greater international interdependence is the greater likelihood of conflict—but another is increased opportunities for cooperation. Consider, for example, the trade issue. Although economic interdependence can generate serious frictions, it can also strengthen the kind of international links—capital flows, direct overseas investments, joint ventures, and such—that offset and reduce the level of frictions. In 1985, Japan sent $64 billion to foreign countries as capital outflows, as purchases of foreign securities, loans, and direct foreign investments. Japan has become, in fact, the world's largest net creditor nation, another side of ramifying interdependence.

As its power and influence continue to grow, will Japan continue to adhere to its postwar policy of separating economic from politico-military power? Will Japan maintain its low military profile when no other economically powerful nation in modern history has done so? What are the Japanese themselves thinking? How do they view their national identity in the face of changes in the domestic and international systems? Is nationalism becoming a problem?

The defense issue is itself part of the general question of whether, and to what extent, Japan will assume a larger role in the international system. Will it take more initiatives designed to bolster international regimes? Will it play a bigger role in efforts to stabilize exchange rates? Or will it define its national interests so narrowly as to limit its international role, which one of the readings in this section considers its ultimate vulnerability?

Japan stands at a historical crossroad. How it responds to the complicated array of changes and challenges that lie ahead remains to be seen. Will Japan in the twenty-first century look and behave very differently? Will other countries continue to feel threatened by Japan? Probably the only safe predictions are that forces from the outside world will increasingly impinge on Japanese institutions and policies, and that developments within Japan, in turn, will have a progressively greater impact on the well-being of other countries—not to mention the future shape of the international system.

48. The Impact of Aging

Ikeuchi Masato

The aging of Japan's population is creating new problems in all parts of Japanese society. In the following selection, which is drawn from The Japan Economic Journal *of March 1, 1981, Ikeuchi Masato examines this aging trend and its effects. Ikeuchi is economic analysis editor for the* Nihon Keizai Shimbun, *a newspaper similar to the* Wall Street Journal.

The Japanese have now become the world's longest-living people—an occasion for real celebration. One cannot, however, be totally blind to the serious problems posed by the sharp rise in the average age of the population, not only for individuals and homes, but also for corporations and the country as a whole.

The average age of the Japanese people stood at only 44.25 years for males and 44.73 years for females as late as 1911, or merely seventy years ago. It is from about 1947 that the average age of the Japanese started curving upward dramatically. There are two primary reasons for this. One is a sharp decline in deaths caused by killer diseases like tuberculosis and typhoid, and the other is an equally marked drop in newborn deaths because of the rapid popularization of hospitals as the places for giving birth. The years after 1955 saw another major factor added in the form of a spectacular improvement in the Japanese people's living conditions and nutrition standards as a result of the nation's high economic growth.

As a result, as of 1979, the Japanese people's average age zoomed to 73.46 years for males and 78.89 years for females. These figures are high enough to place Japan first among countries with a population of more than ten million. Japan's figures are even higher than those of Sweden, the erstwhile pacesetter in this field. Population experts predict that the Japanese people's life expectancy will continue to grow; by the year 2000, it will reach 77.45 for males and 82.94 years for females.

On the other hand, the number of babies has been in decline. While in the prewar years families with five or six children were not at all rare, the average number of children per family now is only slightly higher than two. The birthrate has been slipping constantly. In the baby-boom period immediately following World War II, as many as 2,600,000 infants were born in a single year. A clever writer has aptly referred to this baby-boom generation as the "generation of massed-up

From Masato Ikeuchi, "Aging of the Population Is Due to Have Big Impact on All Phases of Society," *The Japan Economic Journal*, Mar. 1, 1981. By permission of the author.

people." In 1979, however, the total number of newborn babies was 1,650,000, about one million less than in the baby-boom period.

This two-pronged development—the growing life expectancy and the steady decline in the number of babies—has brought about a drastic change in Japan's population structure and the "senilization" of Japanese society. Rapid aging of society is a common development in advanced countries. In Japan's case, however, there are two conspicuously different phenomena. One is the extraordinary speed with which the society is aging. According to an estimate by the Population Problems Research Institute, Japan took only 43 years for the old-age population (people over sixty-five years) to increase from 5 percent to 12 percent of the entire population. The comparable figures for other advanced nations stand at 105 years for Sweden, 170 years for France, and 60 years for Great Britain. Furthermore, according to a survey by the Ministry of Welfare, at its peak in 2020 the old-age population of Japan will reach 18.8 percent. The corresponding figures are estimated at 14.1 percent for Great Britain (in 1980), 16.1 percent for Sweden (in 1990), and 13.7 percent for France (in 2000). In other words, Japan exceeds all other advanced countries not only in the speed with which the aging of the society is progressing, but also in the percentage of the elderly in the entire population. The aging-related problems Japan is facing now are therefore far tougher than those confronting other countries.

Up to some thirty years ago, the Japanese people were resigned to dying at around fifty years of age. Today, however, many live to be seventy, while people in their eighties are not exactly a rarity. For salaried men and women, life after compulsory retirement is steadily getting longer, and they have to worry increasingly about their economic security, health, and personal affairs. Above all, they have to find something worth living for. In order not to be caught unprepared at the time of retirement, Japanese salaried men and women must start planning for their later lives at a very early stage in their careers. Many families will come to have two old-age generations, and even four-generation families will make their debut. To cope with this development, drastic modifications will become necessary in housing and other facilities.

There is a growing movement among Japanese corporations to extend compulsory retirement ages in the face of the steadily rising age of their workers. The biggest problem involved here is the inevitable rise in personnel costs. In all probability, seniority wage systems will become more and more eroded, if only for reasons of cost. Corporations will be required to strike a delicate balance between young workers (who will be frustrated by a slowdown in promotions because of continued employment of old-age workers) and their older counterparts (who will demand jobs to which they can really devote themselves). Whether corporations can do this or not will have a serious bearing on their future.

Japan's old-age population (aged over sixty-five) topped ten million in 1979. According to an estimate by the Ministry of Welfare, the figure will grow to 13,900,000 by 1990 and to 19,000,000 by 2000. By 2020, it will reach 26,000,000, or 18.8 percent of the nation's entire population. This sharp increase in the old-age population is bound to greatly increase old-age welfare outlays by the central and local governments. Who is going to bear such welfare burdens? The ratio of the productive-age population (people aged fifteen to sixty-four) to the old-age population now stands at 7.5 to 1; in other words, 7.5 productive-age workers are now supporting one old person. In ten years, the ratio will fall to 6.2 to 1; in twenty years, to 4.5 to 1; in forty years, it will sink to 3.3 to 1, or less than half what it is now.

To make matters worse, the energy situation is expected to become extremely difficult in the next forty years, and the economy will be restricted to very slow growth. On the other hand, taxes and social security levies on working people are bound to increase steadily. As a matter of fact, tax increases are already becoming an inevitable necessity from the government's point of view, while tax reductions are becoming a must from the taxpayers'.

Cushioning the impact of an aging society should be foremost in the minds of those who look for solutions to such pressing problems as the optimum size of government, the development of Japanese-style welfare, methods of energy saving, and ways to reform the industrial structure.

49. The Path to Big Government

Noguchi Yukio

In this article, published in 1982, Noguchi Yukio asserts that an inevitable increase in public expenditure is under way in Japan. He suggests that unless the government begins to reallocate its resources intelligently, existing government-business relationships will be damaged, and the result will be chaos rather than an improvement in Japanese life.

According to a recent estimate by the Ministry of Welfare, the ratio of social security contributions to national income must be increased from its present level of 5.35 percent in 1977 to 12.35 percent in the year 2000. Other sources of funds must also be increased. No improvements over the present system are assumed in the above estimate. The need for increases will occur automatically through maturing of the pension system and demographic change.

In principle, an overall increase in the financial burden could be avoided. First, downgrading the benefits or changing the conditions of payment (for example, by raising the eligible age) may be considered. Second, by cutting expenditures that are not urgent, it would be possible to accommodate the remaining expenditures without significantly increasing the burden. Third, by discontinuing some of the present FILP programs (Fiscal Investment and Loan Program), the resulting surplus could be allocated to purchase bonds issued through the General Accounts budget, which would also prevent an increase in the burden. The problem is whether such radical changes in the present fiscal structure could be made.

It might be argued that, although the burden increase is significant, the result-

From Yukio Noguchi, "The Path to Big Government," in Kozo Yamamura, ed., *Policy and Trade Issues of the Japanese Economy: American and Japanese Perspectives* (Seattle: University of Washington Press, 1982), pp. 139–42. By permission of the publisher.

ing level would roughly be the same as, or even lower than, that of European countries, so that it does not imply a doomsday. This is true as far as the preceding discussion is concerned, but the following must be noted. First, the estimate of needed social security expenditures is very likely an underestimate, especially for medical expenses. The estimate reflects only demographic changes. Other factors, such as improvements in medical treatments or relative increases in medical costs, also increase medical expenses.

There are still other factors that inflate public expenditure. One is defense. The present level of defense expenditure is extremely low compared to that of other countries, especially in its ratio of GNP (gross national product). It would not be surprising, therefore, if defense expenditures in the near future increased to twice or even three times their present level. The other factor is economic cooperation. Although Japan's aid to developing nations has improved remarkably in recent years, not only in absolute amount but also in ratio to GNP, it is still regarded as insufficient in terms of the latter measure (in 1978, Japan's figure was 0.23 percent, far lower than the official objective of 0.7 percent). Again, it would not be surprising if a considerable increase took place in the near future (the Ministry of Finance has recently agreed to double such aid within the next five years).

If all these factors are taken into account it is possible that the ratio of taxes and social security contribution to national income will increase to around 50 percent. It is important to note that most of the factors that contribute to inflating the government's share of income are already present in the existing fiscal structure.

What are the implications of an increase in the government's share? First, the government-business relationship will no longer be peaceful. The present relationship is not full of tension—businessmen seem to accept, although not unconditionally, increases in taxes. Such a peaceful relationship cannot be expected to continue if taxes and social security contributions are increased drastically. Attempts to increase taxes will certainly meet strong opposition; if they fail, deficits will again increase, and this might bring inflationary pressures into the economy. If taxes are successfully increased, the private sector's vigor will be considerably weakened.

Second, the principle of self-reliance will be lost, and dependence on government for everything will become popular. If this atmosphere prevails, it will fundamentally destroy the vitality of Japanese society.

Third, the allocation of public resources to new areas of social demands, such as urban development and redevelopment, will continue to be extremely difficult. As is frequently pointed out, Japan's level of social overhead capital in large cities is considerably lower than that of Western countries. It is quite probable that this situation cannot be improved in the future.

The future, as presented here, is admittedly a gloomy one. My basic reason for choosing this gloomy picture is large organizations' strong inertia in making decisions and their inability to adapt to a changing environment. It may be argued that societal structure is adaptive and that a kind of negative feedback may work to prevent society from running off in a dangerous direction. I do not necessarily deny such a possibility, but I am not sure that such a mechanism would in fact work in the near future.

Finally, I wish to consider the international aspects of this problem. It is most important for public finance in Japan that the present public policies be reexamined and a way found to reallocate resources for new areas of social needs such as urban development. This is virtually the only area in which substantial new domestic demand will be found in the future. Without realizing this demand, it would be difficult to change the Japanese industrial structure from its export orientation to domestic-demand orientation. If substantial resource reallocation can be realized in this respect, there will be important implications for Japan's future industrial structure and its export performance.

Furthermore, it can be argued that the international competitiveness of Japanese exports is supported by the workers' poor living standard (a variant of the social dumping thesis). In fact, although the nominal wage has increased remarkably, its purchasing power for housing has been reduced. If such a situation is to be improved, huge investments must be made in urban infrastructures, and if such a reallocation of resources were realized, Japan's export performance would change significantly.

50. Japanese Nationality: The Rising Debate

Kenneth Pyle

Now that Japan's postwar recovery is complete, what should its future role in the world be? In this essay, drawn from the *Journal of Japanese Studies*, University of Washington historian Kenneth Pyle describes the national debate currently taking place in Japan on this subject.

Since the late 1970's, a national debate on Japan's future role in the world has been in full swing. Conducted primarily in the general interest magazines, it has all the usual trappings of political debates, including its share of passion, personalities, and pettiness. If we put aside the finer distinctions of this debate and concentrate here on the broader outlines of the alternatives being proposed, it is possible to discern four major approaches or schools of thought with regard to Japan's future role in the world: (1) the progressive; (2) the liberal-realist; (3) the mercantilist; and (4) the new nationalist. We must emphasize that these are ideal types or general categories and that many well-known Japanese will not fit neatly into these categories. In fact, leaders of the Liberal-Democratic Party borrow freely from the rhetoric and ideas of all four approaches as suits their convenience. All of which is to suggest that we are dealing with modes of thought that are very much in the mainstream of thinking about Japan's future.

The finest hour of the progressives was the postwar reform era. Their ideas emerged out of wartime disillusion, revulsion from Japanese nationalism, and

From Kenneth Pyle, "The Future of Japanese Nationality: An Essay in Contemporary History," *Journal of Japanese Studies*, vol. 8, no. 2 (Summer 1982), pp. 242–63. Copyright © Society for Japanese Studies. By permission of the author and the publisher.

profound distrust of traditional state power. They took their stand in support of the new postwar democratic order, and, above all, in support of the role that the Constitution envisioned for Japan in the world. Progressives argued that it was Japan's unique mission in the postwar world to demonstrate that a modern industrial nation could exist without arming itself, that Japan could show the way to a new world, in which national sovereignty would be forsworn, and that nation-states, which were artificial creations, would disappear, allowing the naturally harmonious impulses of the world's societies to usher in a peaceful international order. The Japanese people, having been victimized by a reactionary leadership that indoctrinated them in an artificial nationalism, had shown the demented course of the modern nation-state by its aggressions in Asia. As victims of the advent of atomic weapons, the Japanese people could argue convincingly that wars were ever more destructive, that a new age in international affairs was accordingly at hand, and the sovereign prerogative to go to war must be renounced. No other nation embraced the liberal hope of the future world order with the enthusiasm of Japan, for no other nation's recent experiences seemed to bear out so compellingly the costs of the old ways.

This view had deep and profound appeal. It provided a new orientation, an idealistic mission that would expiate the sins of the past. Moreover, it provided a justification for rejecting world politics and devoting national energies entirely to rebuilding the national livelihood. By the late 1970's, however, a "siege psychology" was showing that the new world order was not coming to pass, and that Japan's national interests, now vastly greater than two decades earlier, were hostage to power politics.

Another troublesome problem of the progressives, however, was that the values and institutions they espoused were attacked as not being the products of Japan's own history and traditions. They were imposed. Initially, the progressive position rested on a highly critical evaluation of Japanese politics and society. In recent years, as national self-confidence has grown, the progressive position has had less appeal, and there has been a discernible effort by progressives to reconcile the postwar system and its values with indigenous traditions.

It is apparent that the progressives have far less influence over Japanese opinion now than was the case in the 1960's. Their radical critique of Japanese society, so popular in the early postwar period, lost its cutting edge in the aftermath of Japan's rapid economic growth and the consequent pride felt in Japanese social values and institutions. Until the mid-1960's, approximately 80 percent of the opinion leaders were of the progressive persuasion, but now this situation has been reversed, and 80 percent are of center or conservative leanings. Affluence has undermined the appeal of socialism, writes Ijiri Kazuo, editorial writer of the *Nihon keizai shimbun*, explaining that the overwhelming majority of the Japanese people are not persuaded by theories of conflicting class interest: "The leftist intellectuals have not been able to cope with the sweeping changes that have occurred in the masses themselves over the past twenty years or so." Moreover, traditional intellectual influences have been replaced by the leadership of "middle-class intellectuals," by which Ijiri means editorial writers, columnists in the media, bureaucrats, and businessmen, who lack the depth and background of academic intellectuals but who are more in tune with middle-class values. Ijiri points to surveys showing that 90 percent of the Japanese people now regard themselves as middle-class. Intellectuals of the progressive persuasion have failed to provide values consonant with the real conditions of economic growth. Middle-class intellectuals, on the other hand, address themselves to the tastes and interests of this broad middle class. Above all, their writings often dwell on Japanese character and traditions and feed the appetite for self-reflection.

A second approach to Japan's role in the world is what we may call the liberal-realist school of thought. It charted its position in part by opposing the progressive vision of an unarmed and neutral Japan. The realists believed that the institution of the nation-state was not about to disappear, that the strength of nationalist feelings was unabated, and that a competition of national interests within an environment constantly approaching international anarchy was the only realistic way of understanding international politics. Because the realist school tends to see Japan's national interest in a cooperative defense relationship with the liberal democracies, one can trace its roots to the prewar pro-Anglo-American groups whose moderate views of foreign policy and domestic reform were overwhelmed after 1931. While this school seeks a democratic order, it does not make the radical critique of Japanese society that progressives have made. Nor does it have the progressives' distrust of traditional state power. In fact, typically, many of the proponents of this school have identified with liberal conservatives in the government.

A representative par excellence of this school is Inoki Masamichi, scholar of international communism, former President of the National Defense Academy, and now head of a research institute for peace and security. Inoki has been a steady critic of what he calls the "utopian pacifist viewpoint" for many years. He has criticized the progressives for failing to make moral distinctions between the communist countries and the liberal democracies. Inoki opposes a massive rearmament but advocates a steady and significant increase in defense expenditure in cooperation with the Western allies. In the light of the new attitudes and conditions in Japan, the views of realists like Inoki receive a more respectful hearing now than probably at any time since 1945.

Inoki recently served as chairman of the Comprehensive National Security Study Group, an advisory committee appointed by the late Prime Minister Ōhira Masayoshi, which issued its report in July 1980. It represents probably the clearest statement of the realists' position to date. The report argues that "the world is not a peaceful world at present, nor is there any possibility that it will become a peaceful world in the foreseeable future." An intelligent approach to securing Japan's interests requires a joint effort with the Western allies. Japan must overcome the incongruity between its economic power and political weakness by accepting international responsibilities more commensurate with its economic strength. The role of "economic giant and political dwarf" must be replaced by an activist foreign policy and a substantial defense establishment that would cooperate with the Western allies in the maintenance and management of the international system. The Korean Peninsula, Southeast Asia, and the Middle East are areas where Japan must contribute politically to stability. The report acknowledges that strains with the allied nations are serious and likely to grow. Japanese-American cooperation will be difficult during the 1980's, when Japan's per capita gross national product

(GNP) will likely overtake that of the United States; "Japanese manufactured products will by and large be more competitive on the international market, and Japanese exports will continue to expand faster than United States exports. In this sense, the positions of the two economies are being reversed, and this itself will entail difficult psychological problems." Though appointed by the Prime Minister and hence basically friendly to sections of the Liberal-Democratic Party, the Study Group criticizes the government for its political expedience and its lack of candor and leadership in developing a new defense policy. The report concludes with the hope that it will serve as a catalyst for a vigorous national debate and for the formation of a consensus in favor of an active political and strategic role in the world.

At the heart of the realists' argument is their rejection of what we might call the notion of Japanese exceptionalism. Few aspects of Japan's foreign policy draw as sharp criticism from the realists as the contention that Japan is—in the words of former Foreign Minister Miyazawa Kiichi—"a special country," which, owing to its exceptional historical experiences and constitutional restraints, is kept from normal participation in international politics. Realists are repelled by justifications of Japan's withdrawn international behavior that rely on Article 9 of the Constitution, the nuclear "allergy," the three nonnuclear principles, the postwar legacy of pacifism, and other such extraordinary explanations. They "violate international common sense," writes Sase Masamori, a professor at the National Defense University and one of the most vocal realists. To have a policy of reliance on the American nuclear umbrella and at the same time refuse to allow nuclear weapons to be installed in or even pass through Japan, to speak of a United States–Japan alliance but to deny its military implications, he writes, violates international common sense. It may appear that Japan is trying to shirk military efforts. The critic Fukuda Tsuneari recalls Foreign Minister Miyazawa visiting the White House to reconfirm the American obligation to defend Japan. Yet, he writes, neither Miyazawa nor anyone else in the government had told the Japanese people that they themselves had an obligation to defend Japan. To behave like an "international eccentric," says Sase, is to invite scorn; to wander through international society "peddling one's special national characteristics" is to risk diplomatic isolation.

Realists have reason to be pleased. The very fact of an intense national debate on defense issues bespeaks an increased public awareness of the choices Japan is likely to have to make in its foreign policy. At the same time, however, the torrent of congratulatory literature, both at home and abroad, has brought to the surface a highly popular sense of national self-assurance. This could represent difficulties for the realist. Their problem could be their very respectability, moderation, and balance. Their desire to make common cause with the Western liberal democracies could lose its appeal if nationalism eroded the institutions of economic and political cooperation among the allies.

A third mode of thought that we may discern in the cacophony of voices evoked by the debate and the newfound self-confidence is what we may call the mercantilist view. The proponents of this school argue that a dispassionate analysis of Japan's geopolitical position, its resource endowments, and the structure of its economy leads inexorably to a conclusion that Japan's national interest is properly seen as a great trading nation—as Venice or the Netherlands was in the past. This school of thought is particularly interesting since it most closely corresponds to the role that Japan has actually been playing in the international system since at least the mid-1960's. Kosaka Masataka, one of the country's influential political scientists, in an article in *Chuō Kōron*, entitled "Japan as a Maritime Nation," defined the national purpose in these terms. In November 1975, in the same journal, Kosaka elaborated his view. Japan should act the role of a merchant in the world community—a middleman taking advantage of commercial relations and avoiding involvement in international politics. "A trading nation does not go to war," he writes, "neither does it make supreme efforts to bring peace. It simply takes advantage of international relations created by stronger nations. This can also be said of our economic activities. In the most basic sense, we do not create things. We live by purchasing primary products and semifinished products and processing them. That is to say, we live by utilizing other people's production." Kosaka emphasizes that this is not a popular role in the international order, since it is regarded as selfish and even immoral. Particularly with the United States it causes problems, because "Japan has enjoyed both the advantages of being an ally and the benefits of noninvolvement." With the breakdown of the Bretton Woods system and the oil crisis, Kosaka foresees difficult times, as "politics and economics become more intertwined with the economic policies of nations." He believes that Japan could adapt to the new circumstances and survive as a trading nation if it could manage its crisis of spirit. That is, holding firmly to no clear principles, but merely pursuing commercial advantage, the danger is that the Japanese people might lose their self-respect. This is a crisis, he writes, that all trading nations face. "A trading nation has wide relations with many alien civilizations, makes differing use of various different principles of behavior, and manages to harmonize them with each other." This, however, tends to weaken the self-confidence and identity of the persons engaged in the operation. They gradually come to lose sight of what they really value and even of who they really are.

Amaya Naohiro, the former Vice-Minister of the Ministry of International Trade and Industry (MITI), has become the most outspoken and flamboyant advocate of the mercantilist role. In a series of widely discussed articles marked by their color and candor, Amaya draws analogies from Japan's history to illustrate the role of a merchant nation, which he hopes Japan will pursue in a consistent and thoroughgoing manner. He likens international society to Tokugawa Japan, when society was divided into four functional classes: samurai, peasants, artisans, and merchants. The United States and the Soviet Union fulfill the roles of samurai, while Japan bases itself on commerce and industry; Third World countries are peasant societies. International society is a jungle, and it is necessary for the merchant to act with great circumspection. The nation has conducted itself for some time as if it were an international trading firm, he writes, but it has not wholeheartedly acknowledged this role and pursued it singlemindedly. Amaya wants the Japanese to show the ability, shrewdness, and self-discipline of the sixteenth-century merchant princes of Hakata and Sakai, whose adroit maneuvering in the midst of a samurai-dominated society allowed them to prosper. "In the sixteenth-century world of turmoil and warfare, they accepted their difficult destiny, living unarmed or with only light arms." By the end of the Tokugawa period, Amaya points out, merchants were so powerful that Honda Toshiaki remarked, "In appearance all of Japan belongs to the samurai, but in reality it is owned by the merchants." What is required is to stay the course, to put aside the samurai's pride of principle, and to cultivate the tradesman's information-gathering and planning ability, his tact and art of flattery.

What Amaya most fears is lack of self-discipline in the merchant's role and rebirth of an emotional nationalism, which he calls "soap nationalism," since it has the emotional character of a soap opera. Amaya himself feels victimized by soap nationalism because of the role he played in reaching a settlement of the Japanese-American automobile dispute in the spring of 1981, which resulted in the decision to restrain export of autos to the United States.

Through Amaya's writings runs a strain of pessimism over whether, with rising nationalism in Japan and protectionism in Europe and the United States, the mercantile diplomacy he advocates can be sustained. He concludes that if efforts as a merchant country appear unable to guarantee Japan's security, then the time will have arrived to become a samurai country.

Amaya's formulation of the purely merchant role for Japan has elicited sharp criticism from many quarters. The foreign affairs commentator Itō Ken'ichi calls it a "kowtow foreign policy" and an "unprincipled foreign policy" that would not be respected or trusted by foreign countries. Moreover, Itō argues that the exclusive concern with preserving Japan's economic interests is already creating a spiritual malaise among the Japanese people, since it causes them to sacrifice the self-respect that comes from adherence to a clear set of moral values. Similarly, the head of the Foreign Ministry's Policy Planning Division, Ōta Hiroshi, writes that the "merchant nation thesis" was possible for Japan in the past when American political and economic power maintained a world order in which Japan was free to concentrate its efforts entirely on economic gain. Both writers, however, hold that the decline of American power and the expansion of Japan's global interests make it impossible any longer to separate politics and economics in the way Amaya's metaphor suggests, and that Japan must join in a greater cooperative effort to ensure the security interest of the industrial democracies.

The kind of approach Amaya advocates leaves Japan open to deep resentments and strong criticism from abroad. The business economist James C. Abegglen, ordinarily a defender of Japan's international position, recently wrote, "All of Japan's interactions with the rest of the world in trade, investment, aid, and defense can be interpreted as those of a country acting purely in self-interest, with regard only to consequences for itself." He criticizes Japan for selfishly "refusing to undertake initiatives in international policy." The answer of Amaya's critics is that, in addition to creating a damaging image of Japan internationally as a country that is narrowly self-centered, refusal to become involved in political-strategic issues leaves Japan subject to the will of other countries.

A fourth school of thought in this grand national debate about the future of Japan is what we may call the new nationalism. It is characterized by the same recognition of the continuing role of power in the world and by the profound contempt for the progressives' attitude on this question that characterizes the liberal-realist school. It shares the realist belief that a competition of national interests within an environment constantly verging on "international anarchy" is the only realistic way of understanding international politics. The new nationalists likewise reject continued reliance on Japan's extraordinary and peculiar postwar political status. More resolutely than the liberal realists, they reject important aspects of the postwar order, for in sharp contrast with the realists, they do not see a shared community of interest and values with the Western democracies that would impel them to cooperate in an alliance framework. In this they are more akin to the economic nationalism of the mercantile school. As Shimizu Ikutarō, undoubtedly the new nationalist who has attracted the most attention, writes, "On the one hand, Japan must encourage friendly relations with America, the Soviet Union, and all other countries, but at the same time we must not forget for an instant that Japan is alone. In the end we can only rely on Japan and the Japanese." Shimizu, observing the decline in American power and world commitment, believes that Japan cannot rely on the American deterrent in an emergency. As a consequence, the nationalists seek more than a modest buildup of arms. "If Japan acquired military power commensurate with its economic power," writes Shimizu, "countries that fully appreciate the meaning of military power would not overlook this. They would defer; they would act with caution; and in time they would show respect."

Pressing on relentlessly to his most dramatic point, Shimizu observes that the nuclear powers, "even though they do not use their weapons, are able to instill fear in those countries that do not have them. A country like Japan that does not possess nuclear weapons and is afraid of them will be easy game for the nuclear powers. Putting political pressure on Japan would be like twisting a baby's arm." Japan, in short, must "exercise the nuclear option."

Shimizu's essay sent a shudder through Japanese society. Yet, there was a certain fascination with it. Unlike the right-wing nationalists, whose sound trucks in downtown Tokyo are readily ignored, or Mishima Yukio's bizarre suicide, which can be dismissed as another personal aberration, Shimizu has to be taken seriously. He is a respected intellectual, a leading theoretician of postwar progressivism, and is often said to be a barometer of the changing political climate in Japan. More than any other writer, he confronts directly and insistently the contradictions and incongruities that trouble Japan's postwar order, and he advocates clear and decisive resolutions that touch deep and ambivalent emotions.

Predictably, Shimizu has been excoriated by progressives for his apostasy. But the realists, too, have written sharp and thoughtful responses to his ideas. They are appalled not just by his more favorable view of prewar institutions and values, his sweeping rejection of the postwar order, his proposal for an all-out military buildup, and his independent course in foreign affairs. They see his ideas as raising the specter of militarism and therefore coloring attitudes toward their own proposals for a modest rearmament. Inoki Masamichi writes plaintively that Shimizu's about-face threatens to confirm his worst fears: that the "utopian pacifism" of postwar Japan might give way to "utopian militarism." Becoming a military superpower, Shimizu's critics hold, will lead to greater rather than less insecurity. Japan will be diplomatically isolated from the West, the object of suspicion among Asian countries, and, owing to its concentrated urban population, highly vulnerable in a conflict between nuclear powers. His critics invariably accuse him of advocating ideas that will lead to a repetition of the disaster that befell Imperial Japan.

The confidence of the new nationalists that Japan is capable of an independent role in world politics is supported by the immense pride in Japan's socioeconomic and technological achievements. The most vocal of the nationalists in this regard is Nakagawa Yatsuhiro, whose prolific writings are characterized by a boldness and bombast that appeal to a mass audience. Demanding that Japan play "a positive role on the world stage," he calls Japan, in the title of a recent book, "the ultra-advanced country." By his calculations, the average Japanese worker in 1978 had an after-tax income at least 1.4–2.0 times what his American counterpart earned. Nakagawa stresses the role of the bureaucracy in promoting the livelihood of the people, because he wants to reverse the distrust of the Japanese state that has prevailed since 1945. He argues that MITI, the Labor Ministry, the Ministry of Agriculture and Forestry, and other government agencies are devoted to the Japanese workers' welfare. In fact, "in everything but name, Japan has turned itself into a textbook example of a socialist country." In describing Japan as "the workers' paradise," Nakagawa considers welfare payments, income, health care, diet, housing, and education. In these categories, he contends that Japan has outstripped Western countries and has done this without high taxes and in an extraordinarily egalitarian setting.

There is nothing in this present debate over the future character of the Japanese nation to lead one to expect that it will come to a set of conclusions, and that the nation will, as a consequence, adopt new policies and move in a new direction. Some would argue that "immobilist" traditions in Japanese foreign policy making would preclude such internally generated decisive departures. What this debate does suggest, however, is a new fluidity of opinion about the future, the recognition of a new international environment for Japan, an awareness of new potentialities and the consideration of new alternatives and opinions, and a groping for a new definition of Japanese nationality.

At the heart of the debate is the issue of Japanese exceptionalism. Everyone involved agrees that Japan has been an exceptional nation-state since World War II, but the issue is: Can and should Japan continue as an "extraordinary" nation? Or should and must it conform to new international conditions and become an "ordinary" nation? Of the four general modes of thought that we have considered, two favor continuation of the exceptional characteristics of the postwar state, and two oppose continuation. Progressivism believes it is Japan's unique "mission" to show the way to a new world. Mercantilism calculates it in Japan's shrewd self-interest to maintain its "incongruous" nature. On the other hand, liberal realism sees diplomatic isolation resulting from Japan's "eccentric" behavior. Finally, new nationalism believes that Japan will be at the mercy of the power of other countries as long as it continues as an "abnormal" country.

It is evident that the future course of the nation will be critically determined by its international political-economic environment and, in particular, the fate of the free-trade order and of the coherence of the Western alliance. It is also apparent that running through the debates about the future is an emergent new sense of nationality.

51. Economic Structural Change

Murakami Yasusuke

In this selection, published in 1982, University of Tokyo professor Murakami Yasusuke outlines the factors operating in the international economic environment that are causing the Japanese economy to undergo a radical structural change.

Like other industrial economies, the Japanese economy is facing external environments that are different from those it faced ten years ago. The differences may be summarized as follows. First, there is no more readily available technology for Japanese industries to borrow. The first wave of technological progress after World War II is fading away, and the second wave, if there is one, will be based on mechatronic and biological engineering. In this possible second wave, Japanese industries will no longer have the advantage of being a latecomer. Second, the international economic system will be far less stable than in the 1950's and 1960's, the ideal of free trade will falter, and protectionism will be invoked more readily and frequently. As the Japanese share of total world trade is close to 10 percent, it will be increasingly difficult for Japanese exports to grow faster than world trade. In particular, the outpouring of exports will no longer be a means to ease a recession. And, third, energy resources, particularly petroleum, will be increasingly costly. Because the Japanese economy is heavily reliant on imported oil, this problem will indeed be serious. From the viewpoint of competitiveness between industrial economies, however, the impact of an oil price hike will be a mixed blessing for the Japanese economy. Owing to this impact, the Japanese economy will indeed fluctuate more than other economies in terms of output and prices; it will also have greater incentive to conserve oil and, more generally, to rationalize the whole industrial structure, as was indicated by the performance of the Japanese economy during the past two oil crises. This third issue may not be so fatal to the Japanese economy as it first appeared.

All these new basic external economic conditions of the coming decade will slow down economic growth and force the Japanese economy to change its structure radically.

From Yasusuke Murakami, "Toward a Socioinstitutional Explanation of Japan's Economic Performance," in Kozo Yamamura, ed., *Policy and Trade Issues of the Japanese Economy: American and Japanese Perspectives* (Seattle: University of Washington Press, 1982), pp. 39–40. By permission of the publisher.

52. Education for the Fifth Generation

Edward A. Feigenbaum and Pamela McCorduck

Computer science programs in Japanese universities are notably poor. In this selection, Edward A. Feigenbaum and Pamela McCorduck argue that the universities are not so much educational institutions that train young people for future professions as access routes to employment. Preferring to train their own personnel, companies look for people who are hardworking and flexible enough to adapt to new situations and new technology. It is these qualities that the Japanese educational system fosters. The essay is drawn from *The Fifth Generation* (1983).

Japanese universities are not educational institutions so much as gates to the professions. The particular university a young Japanese attends will have a crucial influence on his future professional opportunities, and so he aims to enter the "best" university he can, though "best" doesn't mean the same in Japan as it does in the West. Because the university he attends is so important, a Japanese student undergoes excruciating pressures in preparation for college entrance exams during his secondary school years (and for the very ambitious, even during primary school years).

The pecking order among the universities for science and engineering runs roughly this way: at the top are the major national universities, beginning with Tokyo, followed by Kyoto, and then Osaka. In a second tier, there are the private universities, not only lower in the order by tradition, but in fact often skating near the edge of financial ruin, depending as they must for their existence solely on student tuitions. This ranking doesn't necessarily match the facts; a first-rate department might very well exist at what is perceived as a second-rate school—indeed, little pockets of excellence are a constant surprise in otherwise shabby educational enterprises. Nevertheless, everybody behaves as if the pecking order is valid, both students at entrance and employers at exit.

Upon graduation, the former students typically move into lifetime employment with a firm or government agency, and any further education they receive comes there. In fact, employer-supplied education is considerable. Firms routinely bring in top instructors, including American professors, and invest two to three years in the education of their new employees, an investment of time—and a great deal of money—in which they feel confident, knowing that the employee will be theirs for a lifetime. "We'd rather have our students at twenty-three and spend two or three years educating them in our company's needs, technologies, and policies, than take them at twenty-eight with a Ph.D.," one manager says. He goes on to explain that a postgraduate degree is sometimes seen as a liability. Its possessor

From Edward A. Feigenbaum and Pamela McCorduck, *The Fifth Generation: Japan's Computer Challenge to the World* (Reading, Mass.: Addison-Wesley, 1983) pp. 144–47. © 1983 Addison-Wesley Publishing Company, Inc. By permission of the publisher.

has a status that prevents him from being moved around as flexibly within the firm as an employee with a mere bachelor's degree.

In short, industry uses the university as a filtering device, acting on the assumption that the strict entrance exams will identify the brightest and most tenacious. The quality of education offered is almost irrelevant, because the firms reserve to themselves the actual training of talent.

As a consequence, computer science training in the universities is not of high quality. Two years is not enough to train a computer scientist, even if all other dimensions of university education are excellent, but, as it happens, they are not. A group of interrelated circumstances makes computer science in the universities neither stimulating nor up-to-date.

To begin with, everybody moves off to firms or the government after receiving a bachelor's degree. There are a few graduate students around to further new research and prevent intellectual stagnation.

University computer science laboratories are equipped at the poverty level, since the national universities, at least, must look to the Ministry of Education for funds to buy equipment. But compared to the Ministry of International Trade and Industry (MITI), which supports industrial research, the Ministry of Education is relatively poor and impotent, and moreover must support all educational efforts more or less equally, regardless of their usefulness to the future of the nation. Funds disbursed by the Ministry of Education must be waited for in line, which can mean several years of waiting, and when they come, they are paltry. What is worse, funding approvals tend to depend more than is comfortable in science on clout, not merit. Thus, the extremely high cost of computing equipment and its rapid obsolescence causes university laboratories to fall further and further behind.

Finally, the universities have a deep resistance to the interdisciplinary contact which, in the computer field, is essential to the enterprise. On sabbatical at Tokyo University, Feigenbaum gave a series of 12 lectures on artificial intelligence and knowledge engineering. The lectures were announced only in the information science department and not in the engineering or medical schools. When he asked why, his hosts were astonished by the question.

The system makes no allowance for late bloomers and practically no allowance for people who find, partway along in a career, that they have made the wrong choice. Many Western observers see all this and presume that such inherent rigidity will prevent the Japanese from innovating at the high level necessary to achieve a new generation of computers. But that remains to be seen. A mediocre university system might not matter in a culture where the firms, with their lavish support for research from MITI, take on the function of grooming young talent. On the other hand, company training might (though it need not) be less imaginative and far-ranging than university computer science training in the West. The system is certainly less likely to encourage mavericks, though mavericks exist despite the system and may be about to have their day.

Still, nobody in the West should underestimate the overall cultural impact of the schools of Japan. If the universities can be termed a four-year vacation, the situation is quite different in the primary and secondary schools. One observer has written:

The great accomplishment of Japanese primary and secondary education lies not in its creation of a brilliant elite . . . but in its generation of such a high average level of capability. The profoundly impressive fact is that it is shaping a whole population, workers as well as managers, to a standard inconceivable in the United States, where we are still trying to implement high school graduate competency tests that measure only minimal reading and computing skills.

A highly literate workforce, not necessarily college trained, is precisely what is needed for worker flexibility and adaptability in the postindustrial society, with its ever more rapidly changing circumstances. Thus, even if university training is poor, Japan can count on its primary and secondary school systems to prepare the workers who can use the Fifth Generation of computers to best advantage.

53. Innovations: A United States–Japan Perspective

Henry E. Riggs

Traditionally, the Japanese have been seen as adapters rather than innovators, yet recent technological developments have shown that they are capable of both. In this selection, Henry E. Riggs, Professor of Industrial Engineering at Stanford University, examines the processes of technological creativity in an attempt to predict the areas of innovative strength and weakness of both Japan and the United States.

I start with two conventional wisdoms that I believe are basically correct. First, most observers feel that Japan has, as a nation, been a follower rather than a leader in technology developments. That is, Japanese companies have been very able at adopting, assimilating, and incorporating technologies originated elsewhere, particularly in the United States and Western Europe. Over the last forty years, there can be no question that this observation is correct, since Japan has spent those four decades catching up with the West in many dimensions, including technology particularly. Following the lead of other nations in the use of new technology has been a wholly sensible strategy for Japan while it has been playing catchup. However, Japan has now caught up, and now the "follower" strategy may not be either appropriate or successful in the years ahead.

The second conventional wisdom with which I agree is that Japanese companies have been enormously successful in producing products of very high quality and in making product improvements that are very attractive to customers. One has only to look at the competition in video recorders, in stereo equipment, and in many other areas of consumer electronics to know that this conventional wisdom

From Henry E. Riggs, "Innovations: A United States–Japan Perspective" (unpublished paper presented to the United States–Japan Project on High Technology, 1984). By permission of the author.

Table 53.1.   *Observed Technological Strengths of Japan and the United States*

United States	Japan
Basic research	Applied development
Software	Hardware
Fundamental new products	Miniaturization
High-technology systems	Process equipment and technology
New industry creation	Product variety
Advanced development	Process engineering

must be true. The accuracy of this second conventional wisdom is confirmed by the extent to which American companies have recently acknowledged that they have much to learn from their Japanese competitors and are getting on with the task of learning useful techniques to both enhance quality and improve productivity.

So much for the past and the present. The more interesting questions have to do with the future. Now that the Japanese have caught up technologically and dominate certain markets for high-technology products, what does the future bring? Their adaptive capacity is proven, but are they creative and innovative? Are they capable of doing more than imitating others? Is there something about their culture, or their educational system, or their management practices that defines just how creative Japanese scientists and engineers are or will be? When the question is asked in a simplistic form—Are the Japanese people creative?—the answer is unquestionably yes. But both the question and the answer are too general. The more appropriate question is this: Are there segments of technology and areas within industry where the Japanese are particularly creative? And as a corollary question, Are there other areas of technology and industry where American companies may have some particular advantage?

Some of the contrasts in technological strengths of the United States and Japan can be seen in Table 53.1. There is little debate about the accuracy of these contrasts, but, at the same time, we have neither (1) a categorization or classification of these strengths, nor (2) an explanation of the factors or conditions from which these strengths are derived.

High-technology industries in the two countries have very different technological strengths, but each possesses a significant set of such strengths. The contrast in technological strengths is depicted in the matrix shown in Figures 53.1 and 53.2. This matrix recognizes along the X-axis the widely understood distinction between process (or production) and product technology. It draws the distinction on the Y-axis between developments for which the target specifications are known in advance—that is, cases in which the criteria for judging the success of the development project are well understood and delineated at the outset of the project—from those in which the target specifications are unknown at the outset, either because scientific breakthroughs are the objective or because entirely new products for new markets are the result.

We must quickly acknowledge that the technical world cannot in fact be divided

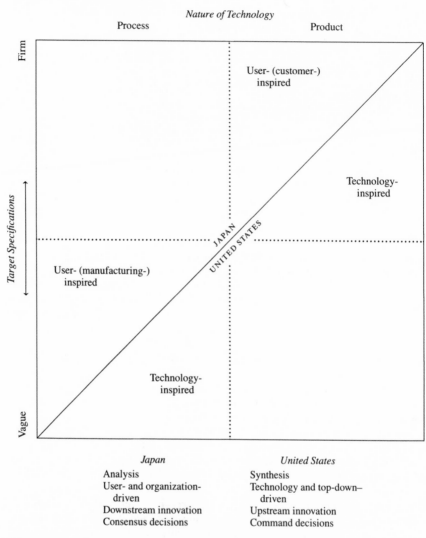

Figure 53.1.   Contrast in technological strengths.

into four tidy boxes. Many developments involve joint product-process improve-ments; the integrated circuit industry is replete with examples. Moreover, speci-fications are not all known or all unknown. Rather, they range from highly exact at one end of the spectrum, through general, to vague, to unknown (basic scien-tific inquiry) at the other. Further, the areas within each of the cells of the matrix are not at all indicative of the relative importance of each type of technical devel-opment. For example, product-engineering projects for which target specifica-tions are predetermined consume the large portion of the development budget in

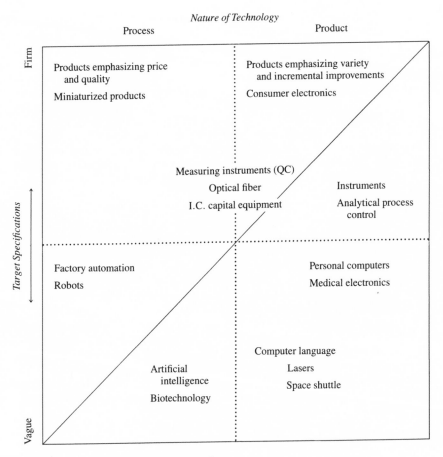

Figure 53.2. Examples of products/markets.

most high-technology companies. Nevertheless, this simple representation can assist our discussion.

Along the X-axis, Japan has demonstrated great abilities in the area of process technology, whereas the United States has been relatively more capable in product development. The upper-left quadrant of this matrix involves process development to known specifications. Price/performance improvements of manufactured products are very often the result, as are miniaturization and quality improvement. Japan's phenomenal success in consumer electronics is a result of technical capabilities that are defined by this quadrant. The lower-right quadrant involves, on the other hand, product development to unknown (or vague) specifications. Technical breakthroughs are the result of capabilities defined by this quadrant, and so are the creations of new industries—that is, new products offered to new markets. The United States has had particular success at developments defined by this quadrant. Most new industries have been created and defined in the United States, even though, in a number of cases, Japanese manufacturers have dominated them after a very few years. Note that new industry creations require market innovativeness as well as technical innovativeness and are the peculiar province of entrepreneurial high-technology companies in the United States.

But what about the other two quadrants: product development to known specifications (the upper-right quadrant) and process development to unknown specifications (the lower-left quadrant)? It appears that Japan has the advantage over the United States when advances in either of these two quadrants are inspired or driven by the user (the user being either an external customer or the firm's own manufacturing department) or by incremental suggestions emanating from one company's organization. On the other hand, the United States high-technology companies are better able to capitalize on opportunities in these two quadrants which are derived from, or inspired by, technology (the research laboratory) or imposed by a "top-down" management decision.

Put a different way, when the technological development is one that requires primarily analysis, as contrasted with synthesis, the Japanese have a significant advantage over the United States. Conversely, where synthesis is involved—that is, bringing together various technologies or matching new technologies with new market opportunities—United States industry has had and, I believe, is likely to continue to have a substantial advantage over its Japanese competitors.

Let me cite some examples. The fundamental technology for integrated circuits involves synthesis—a combination of electrical engineering, materials technology, chemistry, and so forth. The United States has led in this fundamental technology. When this technology is pushed to provide greater density of circuits and higher yields, the emphasis is on analysis—analyzing the inherent limitations in the existing process and making incremental improvements to overcome those limitations—and here the Japanese currently excel.

Original work on robots was done in Japan. It involved the bringing together of mechanical, electrical, and, in some cases, optical technology: a process of synthesis. The Japanese have taken the lead, according to some observers, in applying robots, utilizing applications engineering that is largely a process of analysis. Artificial intelligence and intelligent robots require substantial synthesis among scientific disciplines. The United States has led in these areas, and I think it will continue to do so.

The diagonal in Figure 53.1 defines the comparative technological strengths of the two countries. Japan appears to have an advantage in those technological development projects in which the target specifications can be well defined and are reasonably firm. That is, when the engineers know what they are looking for—incrementally higher speed, tighter tolerances, lower cost of manufacture, or higher yield—Japanese industry is extraordinarily capable and highly innovative. On the other hand, when target specifications are vague, as they necessarily are when basic research is involved or when entirely new products for new applications are the objective, United States industry seems to be particularly capable and creative. Note that this reasoning does not argue that the Japanese are more or less innovative than Americans, but rather asserts that engineers in the two countries have comparative advantages in quite different spheres of technological development.

Figure 53.2 contains some examples of product-market segments that fall in various parts of the matrix. Of key importance to American high technology is the fact that all products and processes have a tendency to move both up and to the left on the matrix. That is, as products, processes, and markets mature, process technology becomes more dominant as the basis for competition, and development effort geared to known or firm (improved) specifications takes over from research effort.

Now, if these are the observations, what are the reasons why Japan seems to be particularly good at analysis? Management practices within Japanese companies are major factors. These have been so thoroughly reported by others that we need only remind ourselves of the several factors listed below and relate them to technological development:

1. consensus decision making;
2. on-the-job training;
3. job rotation and training;
4. suggestion systems;
5. technology monitoring;
6. closeness to customers;
7. organization of research and engineering; and
8. intense competition.

A heavy emphasis on job rotation and on-the-job training, as well as a tradition of consensual decision making, assure intense communication, shared knowledge, and uniform and strong technological expertise. They are also the important underpinnings of a successful suggestion system that is in turn the source of many organization-inspired developments.

Japanese companies have perfected the art of monitoring technological improvements in other companies and other countries. Technology thereby transferred becomes widely disseminated within the company and serves as the basis for incremental improvements but not for radical new technological developments. Lifetime employment, a condition that is vastly overstated by Western observers, encourages user-inspired developments but sharply reduces the opportunities for synthesis of dissimilar technologies that can and do arise from the mobility of scientists and engineers.

Japanese companies get very close to their customers (a condition, by the way, that is not equated with strong marketing). Other research has verified the importance of customers as sources of ideas for product improvement and variety. At the same time, excessive dependence on customers also inhibits the development of radically new products to fulfill needs of which customers are unaware or only vaguely aware.

Japanese companies have traditionally been organized to emphasize process engineering; most large companies have for years maintained a centralized process- or production-engineering staff, but only in the last few years have they adopted the United States practice of organizing a central research and development (R&D) function focused on new technologies and fundamentally new products.

Finally, intense competition between large Japanese companies creates great pressure for both incremental product improvements and productivity improvements to permit price reductions. Fighting competitive brushfires demands much more emphasis on analysis than on synthesis.

54. The Maekawa Report

An advisory group known as the Maekawa Committee was organized at the request of Prime Minister Nakasone in October 1985 to study medium- and long-term policy measures dealing with Japan's economic and social structure in a changing international environment.

Japan's international balance of payments has tended to show increasing current accounts surpluses in the 1980's. In 1985, in particular, this surplus was unprecedentedly large, i.e., 3.6 percent of the gross national product (GNP). It is imperative that we recognize that continued large current accounts imbalances create a critical situation not only for the management of the Japanese economy, but also for the harmonious development of the world economy. The time has thus come for Japan to make a historical transformation in its traditional policies on economic management and the nation's lifestyle.

Expanding Domestic Demand

Promoting the transformation from export-led economic growth to growth driven by domestic demand requires that the government put firmly in place domestic demand expansion policies that have large multiplier effects and will lead to increased private consumption.

Promoting Housing Policies and Urban Redevelopment

Efforts should be made toward a fundamental reform in Japanese housing policy, and the strengthening and broadening of measures to promote housing is required. In large urban centers, in particular, creation of new residential areas closer to offices through redevelopment of existing areas and construction of new residential neighborhoods are to be promoted. Also, urban facilities should be expanded and improved.

A number of points should be kept in mind in carrying out these efforts.

1. The scale of such projects is to be expanded, centering on the mobilization of private-sector energies. Steps must therefore be taken to ease regulations and to provide pump-priming financial incentives.

From the Report of the Advisory Group on Structural Economic Adjustment for International Harmony, submitted to Prime Minister Nakasone Yasuhiro on April 7, 1986.

2. Tax deductions should be expanded for those buying houses.

3. Measures should be taken to keep land prices stabilized, e.g., by rezoning urban areas, relaxing local governments' residential development guidelines, and easing the restrictions on building size and land use.

4. Efforts should be made to accelerate the settlement of problems arising from land use among those concerned.

Stimulating Private Consumption

Along with the appropriate distribution of economic growth in wages, tax cuts increasing disposable income are effective in expanding private consumption. People should have more free time through reduced working hours, and the active use of paid leaves for longer periods should be encouraged. The total working hours per year should be brought into line with the industrialized countries of Europe and North America in the private sector, and early realization of the five-day work week should be pursued. At the same time, efforts should be made for speedy implementation of these policies in the public and financial sectors.

Promoting Social Infrastructure Investment

A radical increase in capital formation by local governments is essential to spreading nationwide the impact of stronger domestic demand. Accordingly, in order to promote infrastructure developments, local projects should be enlarged by making use of local government loans.

Moving to an Internationally Harmonious Industrial Structure

The shift to an internationally harmonious trade and industrial structure should basically be pursued through market mechanisms, but additional efforts should also be made through the following measures.

Promoting Positive Industrial Adjustment

Positive industrial adjustment must be promoted to encourage the international division of labor. To this end, it is necessary, while giving due consideration to the impact on small and medium-sized businesses, to actively promote the transformation of the nation's industrial structure. In this connection, the structural reforms now being promoted under current laws should be accelerated. While taking into account the serious impact on local economies, coal mining policy should be reviewed with a view to lowering the level of domestic output drastically and increasing imports.

Also, in promoting industrial restructuring, it is important to encourage technological research and development, the growing diffusion and application of information technology in the economy and society, and the development of the service sector, which will be accelerated by the greater availability of free time and diversification of consumption patterns.

Promoting Direct Investment

Direct overseas investment plays an important role in rectifying Japan's external economic imbalances and in promoting the host country's economic development. Overseas investment has been expanding rapidly in recent years, and, with due consideration to the impact on domestic employment and the economy, this should be further encouraged. Accordingly, the conclusion of bilateral agreements on the protection of investment should be encouraged, overseas investment insurance schemes should be improved, participation in the Multilateral Investment Guarantee Agency (MIGA) should be undertaken, and other governmental measures to support overseas investment should be reinforced. It is also necessary to expand economic cooperation to improve the environment for investment in the developing countries.

Foreign investment in Japan should also be encouraged, with improved conditions for financial assistance, an increased supply of information, and other measures. Furthermore, industrial cooperation should be actively promoted, including technology exchanges and cooperation in third-country markets. In particular, the establishment of a private-sector-led institution for industrial cooperation for the purpose of enhancing personnel exchanges should be encouraged.

Promoting Forward-Looking Agricultural Policies

In order to achieve maximum productivity given land conditions and other constraints, the Government should have a clear perspective for the future of Japanese agriculture. To this end, the Government should work to achieve a thorough structural improvement, thereby promoting agricultural policies befitting an "age of internationalization." In so doing, priorities should be given to policies focused on fostering core farmers for the future, and price policies should be reviewed and rationalized toward greater use of market mechanisms and active promotion of structural policies. With the exception of basic farm products, efforts should be made toward a steady increase in imports of products (including agricultural processed products) where the domestic price and the international market price differ markedly. These price disparities should be reduced, and at the same time agriculture should be rationalized and made more efficient.

With regard to products subject to quantitative import restrictions, efforts should be made to improve market access with a view to making the Japanese market more open, while taking account of developments in the relevant consultations, including the new round of GATT (General Agreement on Tariffs and Trade) negotiations.

Improving Market Access and Encouraging Imports

Improving Market Access

Full implementation of the Action Program for Improved Market Access should be promoted in the areas of tariffs, import restrictions, standards and certification, government procurement, and so on. Also the Office of Trade and Investment Ombudsman should be reinforced, and the possibility of giving it a legal basis studied, in order to further improve market access.

Encouraging Imports

Efforts should be made to encourage imports of manufactured goods. Distribution mechanisms should also be streamlined and efforts should be made to ensure the enforcement of the Antimonopoly Law for the prevention of unfair business transactions. Imports should be promoted by intensifying domestic consumption of foreign products and by making information on the Japanese market and distribution systems widely available.

Prudent Behavior of Private Companies

Considering the strong possibility of frictions caused by the behavior of private companies that pursue expanded market share at all costs, it is hoped that Japanese companies will behave with awareness of their international responsibilities.

Stabilizing and Sustaining Appropriate Exchange Rates

In achieving a proper balance between domestic and external demand, it is essential that exchange rates be stable and in line with economic fundamentals.

Under the present circumstances, arrangements for stability must be considered within the framework of floating exchange rates, and elimination of major disparities in the economic performance of the leading industrialized countries is the underlying basis of exchange rate stability. There is, therefore, a clear need for a high level of policy coordination among these countries. However, since there is no guarantee that exchange rates will always reflect the fundamentals, cooperation and intervention by the countries concerned can be effective tools for correction.

Liberalization of Financial and Capital Markets and the Yen

With the liberalization of financial and capital transactions, transactions now take place on a global scale, and Japan should ensure that its financial and capital markets are commensurate with its economic importance. This will facilitate the internationalization of the yen. Thus, efforts should be made to further liberalize financial and capital transactions and to expand transactions by nonresidents both for financing and for investment.

Internationalization with respect to the latter has been relatively slow in Japan. It is now essential to develop market facilities for funds from abroad in order to achieve a better balance between financing and investment. In strengthening investment markets, there is a need, first, to diversify investment instruments; the development of short-term financial markets is a particularly urgent task.

Second, the expansion and strengthening of secondary markets and the internationalization of trading requires international compatibility of market arrangements and trading practices; in particular, taxation policy should give due attention to the international point of view.

Promoting International Cooperation

Efforts should be made to encourage imports of manufactured goods from developing countries through such means as technology transfer and expanded investment from Japan; these steps will contribute to the development of export industries in Third World countries.

Japan should work in cooperation with other leading industrialized countries to promote efforts for lower interest rates, to increase the official financial flow to developing countries and to strengthen the financial basis of multilateral development banks.

Japan should actively contribute to the creation of new science and technology for the twenty-first century. In addition to promoting research and development in basic science and technology, Japan should promote cooperative international research in these fields.

Efforts should be made to promote Japanese language education and Japanese studies overseas, to support personnel exchanges, and to strengthen international broadcasting. Efforts must also be made to adapt to the age of internationalization, by opening doors of academic and research institutions to foreigners, for example, arranging to accept more foreign teachers and students, and accommodating Japanese students returned from overseas.

Active Promotion of GATT Negotiations

While responding positively on matters of interest to developing countries, the Government should take an active part in establishing international rules in such new fields as trade in services and intellectual property rights. The Government should also seek to improve the GATT rules and strengthen the GATT system in order to restore the credibility of the GATT.

On Fiscal and Monetary Policy Management

In the implementation of these recommendations, fiscal and monetary policy have a significant part to play.

In implementing fiscal policy, it is necessary to maintain the basic policy stance of fiscal reform to end dependency on deficit-financing bonds.

The tax system should be reviewed from the perspectives of equity, fairness, simplicity, and economic vitality. The preferential tax treatment accorded savings, in particular, should be fundamentally reviewed in light of these principles, including abolition of the tax exemption for interest on small savings accounts.

While ensuring currency stability, flexible management of monetary policy is necessary to realize an economy led by domestic demand.

Conclusion

The Government obviously has a very important role to play in transforming Japan's social and economic structure for greater harmony with the international community, but each and every Japanese should also be fully aware that Japan cannot develop unless it also contributes actively to the international community. It is imperative that every effort be made for attainment of this national goal, and the Advisory Group thus very much hopes that the Government will make every effort to implement these recommendations with the full understanding and support of the entire nation.

55. Japan's Ultimate Vulnerability

James C. Abegglen

Despite Japan's remarkable economic successes since World War II, James C. Abegglen argues, the country's narrow definition of self-interest has damaged its image in the world and may ultimately lead to its downfall. The article was first published in 1980. Abegglen was trained as a sociologist and now acts as a business economist.

When everything is taken into consideration, it may well be the case that Japan's vulnerability as an economy lies in the very nature of its economic success.

It is a commonplace observation, and an accurate one, that Japan is critically dependent on the rest of the world for the import of the entire range of raw materials and foodstuffs it needs to support its sophisticated and powerful economy. Any event that would cut off this external supply would at a single stroke reduce Japan's economy to the level of a century ago or more. Yet it must be clear by now that such external events are unlikely, and moreover, that the various predictions of shortages of materials are becoming increasingly improbable. Even the projections of a shortfall in crude oil supply are being moved steadily forward in time. And the Japanese economy has amply proved its strength and resilience in dealing with inflation, recessions, and exchange rate fluctuations.

Indeed, the Japanese economy is today, despite several years of external and internal difficulties, in robust shape. Inflation is low, the currency is strong, and domestic demand is rising. Mild concern about possible inflation and about continued increases in crude oil prices hardly even ripples the current confidence of both the Japanese business community and the political leadership. It can only be concluded that the strength of the Japanese economic system and the competence of its managers are of a very high order.

It is the burden of this essay that Japan's economic vulnerability in fact lies in Japan's successful maintenance of an internal focus—that, by defining national self-interest in the most narrow terms, and by refusing to undertake initiatives in international policy, Japan is actually risking all that its narrow definition of self-interest has so far gained the country.

Japan's International Actions

A nation interacts with other nations in only a few dimensions. First of all, it trades with outsiders, an interaction that includes the movement of technology as well as goods across boundaries and currencies. Direct foreign investment represents another interaction, one that is closely related to trade. A nation also provides economic assistance to other countries. Finally, and critically, a nation interacts with others in its defense or military policies. There are other forms of interaction, such as travel and political involvement, in addition to those congeries called "cultural interchange," but these are secondary to and derivative of the principal interactions, when they are not downright trivial.

Trade Interaction

Japan's trade interaction with the rest of the world is now a monstrous burden on the world trade system. This burden has fallen most heavily upon Japan's closest trading partner, its critical and still irreplaceable market, the United States. It would seem to be entirely within Japan's self-interest to work actively to help ensure that this market, the American economy, remains strong and vigorous. Yet the lack of clear and visible initiatives in this area conveys the strong impression that Japan will act to redress the trade balance only when the United States presses for such action and then will act only with the greatest reluctance.

Indeed, even when pressed, Japan's responses are in doubt. At the Bonn Summit, Japan's Prime Minister, Fukuda Takeo, rashly promised a 7 percent domestic growth rate, a commitment his successor retracted immediately upon taking office. Granted that no leader can in fact promise a given economic growth rate, granted that Fukuda was perhaps carried away by the splendid occasion at the expense of his better judgment, still, other commitments were offered as well, and they also went unmet. Japan promised to reduce its trade surplus from $10 billion to $6 billion within the year; in fact, the surplus passed $16 billion. Japan promised an actual deficit on the basic balance of payments; in fact, the surplus is $4 billion.

With respect to trade, the first area of interaction with other nations, Japan is an uncommonly powerful economy, achieving a large and increasing trade surplus for more than a decade with only brief interruption. This surplus was accumulated at a time of considerable difficulty for Japan's principal trading partners and is a substantial source of damage to the trade positions and currencies of those putative partners. While causing these difficulties, Japan presents itself as a nation that only grudgingly, under the greatest pressure, and with all manner of domestic excuses, makes some modest effort to deal with the problem. Furthermore, even under those external pressures, pledges of policy change seem not to be credible.

Overseas Investment

It might be argued that Japan's trade surplus and accretion of foreign reserves are, in the short run, unavoidable, pending exchange rate shifts and other adjustments, although, of course, these surpluses are not of recent origin and seem unlikely to melt away. Therefore, Japan's trade partners must look to the second area of international interaction for some relief—foreign investment.

In this area, too, Japan offers little balm either to resource suppliers or to purchasers of its merchandise. Japan's total cumulative foreign direct investment remains small. All the investments *ever* made abroad by Japan add up to a figure somewhat smaller than the 1978 trade surplus. Nor has foreign direct investment risen rapidly in recent years. Even granting the fact that investment requires lead time, one cannot help but notice that Japan's foreign direct investment has failed to rise above the modest peak it reached in 1973.

The fact that Japanese firms have not invested in the United States in increasing amounts in recent years is the more remarkable in view of the special conditions that have obtained during this period. The yen has strengthened sharply against the dollar, making United States assets relatively inexpensive. American share prices have been low, and their purchase has thus been doubly attractive. United States economic growth has been higher than normal. At the same time, the savings and investment rate in Japan, and liquidity in general, have remained high. Yet while European companies, particularly German firms, have taken advantage of these very conditions to invest heavily in the United States, Japan, under pressure to help redress the American balance-of-payments deficit, has done little or nothing in this area. Thus, in the second area of international interaction, Japan also remains internally preoccupied, offering little relief from trade surpluses in the way of direct investment, choosing instead to concentrate its investment in its domestic economy.

Aid and Assistance

What, then, of the third broad area of international interaction, economic aid to less developed countries? Here Japan's record of generosity and initiative is even less impressive than its effort in the areas of trade balances and direct investment. The World Bank reports that Japan's direct development assistance has been maintained for fifteen or more years at about .2 percent of its gross national product (GNP). This compares poorly with Germany's direct assistance level of .3–.4 percent of GNP and France's .6 percent. Whatever one might assume about the effectiveness of foreign aid programs, it must be concluded that the free world's second-largest economy, running the world's largest trade surplus, and accumulating the world's second-largest cache of foreign reserves, has been somewhat less than generous in providing development assistance.

Furthermore, a recent promise to increase aid appears to have been lost in a cloud of niggardly domestic disputes. An undertaking to increase Japanese aid has become the subject of controversy over the appropriate standard to use in measuring that increase. The discussion, rather like the trade discussions, leaves an impression of meanness and reluctance, vitiating whatever advantage Japan might have derived from an expanded aid program. Even more damaging in terms of world opinion is the Japanese policy toward refugees from Vietnam. To date, a grand total of three Vietnamese refugees have been granted permanent residence in Japan. This performance is from a wealthy country, an Asian country, and a country that aspires to the leadership of a peaceful Asia. Whether the opportunity is the munificent one of providing aid, or the humanitarian one of providing refuge, Japan must be seen as acting ungenerously.

Defense Arrangements

Nothing illustrates Japan's military participation in international affairs better than its attitude toward the recent Soviet moves in the islands immediately to the north of Japan. Only twenty kilometers from Japan, the Soviets have just established a full airstrip and are reported to be building a missile capability on an island over which Japan—futilely—claims sovereignty. To date, the only observable Japanese response to this move has been the suggestion that Japan might spend as much as 1 percent of its GNP for its military budget by 1983.

The fact is, of course, that Japan is utterly dependent on the United States for its national defense. There is now no significant opposition in Japan to that position, nor is there any substantial support for a program to build an independent capability. Yet it must be evident that the capacity and willingness of the United States to provide Japan's entire defense are becoming increasingly doubtful. Indeed, Japan's trade balance, by its effect on the dollar and its impact on United States public opinion, erodes America's ability and willingness to continue to defend Japan. Yet Japan's contribution to the United States defense expenditure on its behalf remains modest. The current total contributed by Japan to the maintenance of American forces is some $600 million. When reckoned against the total cost to the United States of its Northeast Asia military establishment and its nuclear umbrella, that offering must be deemed insignificant.

The Japanese Explanation

These are familiar facts. For the most part, Japanese explanations are equally familiar. They are many and need only be noted briefly here. For example:

1. Japan has been isolated for a long while, and internationalization has been thrust on the nation suddenly. A truly international response takes time.

2. Japan has special problems with respect to trade, both because of its trade structure with its raw-material-import dependency and because of the difficulties of rapidly changing domestic economic patterns.

3. Direct investment is often not really justified in terms of competitive costs, and, in any event, Japanese companies have no experience with acquisitions, takeovers, and other techniques of large and rapid foreign investment.

4. Aid programs, to be effective, require careful planning by both donor and recipient, and, to cite one example, the Association of Southeast Asian Nations (ASEAN) countries have not provided proper conditions for massive development assistance. With respect to refugees, Japan is a small and homogeneous country into which refugees cannot be introduced without great difficulty.

5. Japan's war experiences, and the resultant public antipathy to the military, makes substantial defense expenditure politically impossible. Furthermore, an immediate threat from the Soviets or any other quarter seems unlikely.

These and the many other explanations offered by Japanese apologists are all valid. Each of Japan's policies does indeed have a basis for justification. Indeed, much time is devoted by non-Japanese to advancing these arguments. However, the real issue is not a question of any single behavior or policy. Rather, the issue is the totality of these behaviors and the image of Japan which they present to the world.

While friendly observers can reasonably offer these justifications for Japanese policy, it is also reasonable to regard each of these arguments as simply self-serving, as a rationale advanced by a nation that defines its self-interest narrowly and takes selfish advantage whenever and wherever it can. All of Japan's interactions with the rest of the world in trade, investment, aid, and defense can be interpreted as those of a country acting purely in self-interest, with regard only to consequences for itself. Japan seems to change its international policies only in response to threats and thus appears to the rest of the world to act in a defensive and ungenerous manner. It is this perception of Japan, and the reactions and interactions that flow from this perception, that may well prove to be Japan's ultimate vulnerability.

The Definition of Self-Interest

Assume for the moment a Japanese commentator on these remarks, one of a rather cynical frame of mind. Such a commentator might well offer the view that all nations should, and in fact do, act in their own self-interest. He or she might argue that the world would be much better served if more nations defined self-interest with the precision that Japan appears to have used. Indeed, such a Japanese commentator would gain a sympathetic and supportive audience among many Americans who feel that their nation, too, might be better served by a narrower definition of self-interest. What, after all, does it matter what others think of Japan?

The fact that nations, like individuals, act according to their own self-interest, and that, indeed, they *should* do so, is clear enough. But in the case of Japan's apparent policies, two questions arise. First, is Japan really acting in its own interest, especially with respect to trade? And, second—and far more important—is Japan defining its self-interest so narrowly as in fact to jeopardize its own well-being?

Narrow Self-Interest

Japan's trade surpluses, especially since they are not deployed in investment or aid, must be viewed as a tax on the Japanese public. Materials are purchased from abroad and value is added in capital, labor, and technology in Japan to produce goods. These goods can then be consumed. However, in Japan's case, some surplus of good is needed for sale abroad in order that more materials can be purchased. The problem arises when more goods are produced and sold abroad than are necessary for Japan's purchase of materials. The fact that Japan has accumulated a trade surplus means that goods are sold abroad rather than consumed in Japan, in exchange for currencies that, given Japan's other policies, are not put to use. This imposes on the Japanese public a lower standard of living than the high level of productivity might otherwise attain. In this sense, the United States deficit serves self-interest better than the Japanese surplus does. The world provides the United States with goods of real value which are paid for with a depreciating currency and with borrowing. A still more cynical observer might conclude that the American public does better on the exchange than the Japanese public does.

The tax on the Japanese public can be illustrated very plainly. Take the example of food, surely the most basic of family needs. As it happens, the Japanese family eats about 45 percent less food than the American family—509 kilograms as compared with 758 kilograms. At the same time, the food expenditure per family is 15 percent *higher in Japan* than in the United States: the American family spends less than one-fifth of its income on food, while the Japanese family spends one-third. Japan's level of direct taxation is relatively low. Yet in the case of food, a massive hidden tax is being imposed on the Japanese family as a result of the unwillingness of the Japanese government to make foodstuffs readily available from the world market. Japanese rice prices are four times world levels, wheat prices three to four times, and for such less basic items as beef, the multiple can only be guessed.

Trade restrictions impose many such taxes on the Japanese public. International telephone charges and air fares are held at very high levels. The entry of new pharmaceuticals to the market is delayed. The fact is that, even according to a narrow definition of self-interest, it would appear that Japan's trade policies are actually hurtful: far from benefiting from these policies, the Japanese people are often penalized by them.

Japan's Real Self-Interest

The more important aspect of Japan's policies, however, is their second-order effect. It must be evident that Japan is the most interdependent of the world's major economies. That is, Japan is least able to maintain itself separately from other nations. Japan is dependent on an *increasing* supply of materials, foodstuffs, and fuels, with no prospect other than that of heightening this dependency. Therefore, it is in Japan's interest to encourage investment in resource development abroad, as well as a steady flow of supplies from those investments. More than any other developed nation, Japan needs a world monetary system and a healthy world trade system to ensure its continued access to the materials it lacks. And, above all, Japan requires either an American defense apparatus to protect it or a world order so benign as to make defense systems unnecessary.

Thus, it is in Japan's purest self-interest to actively promote the health of its major markets in North America and Europe, and especially in the United States. Those markets provide the funds that enable Japan to purchase materials. Damaging those irreplaceable markets in the short run damages Japan in the long run.

The case of investment is similar. It is entirely in Japan's own interest to invest heavily on a global scale in the development of new resources to ensure Japan's supply of raw materials. Their full availability assures Japan of reasonable prices, and the flow of funds and materials supports the trade system upon which Japan ultimately depends. Finally, the health of the American economy in the world system determines whether Japan has a defense capability or not.

The point need not be belabored. It is evident that narrow self-interest, as manifested by massive trade surpluses and niggardly investment and aid programs, in fact works against Japan's real national interest. Japan has prospered during, and in good part because of, a lengthy post–World War II period of relative peace, world economic growth, and international trade. Japan's continued prosperity depends upon the continuation of those trends. Japan can hardly withdraw at this point to a narrow band of Asia; its economy and its needs have outstripped regional solutions and require that the world be receptive to, supportive of, and interactive with Japan.

The Question of Image

The problem of Japan's image is neither remote nor abstract; it finds expression in the current behavior of other nations toward Japan. Japan is seen as narrowly self-interested, and the responses of other countries to that perception are becoming overtly hostile. Images *do* matter. They are not merely the products of advertising or public relations campaigns, and they do not yield to the mere cosmetics of media treatment. Images are formed out of facts, and they shape responses and decisions.

For example, it appears to be the case that, in general, the United States is perceived as a well-meaning, if frequently wrong-headed, country. The image of benevolence was formed out of many things, some as tangible as the Marshall Plan, some as slight as the Peace Corps. Still, the general image of the United States has allowed this nation to make the most dreadful errors in policy and to be on occasion egregiously self-serving, and still retain some stock of goodwill on which to draw in need. This image has been, after all, not inappropriate, and, while it may be changing, it still has real value.

In contrast, the rest of the world does not perceive Japan as being generous or well-meaning, and that perception matters. For example, the Japanese government recently engaged an American research organization to examine nontariff trade barriers in order to advise on those that might be lifted. Even if we leave aside the oddness of commissioning a foreign group to make such a study, the exercise seems to miss the point of present reality entirely. Japanese trade barriers of all kinds have been removed steadily and rapidly over the past fifteen years. They are no longer more substantial than those of other advanced countries. Yet the magnitude of hostility toward Japan with respect to trade matters has risen rapidly during that same period. Indeed, there seems to have been a rather neat inverse relationship. It can be argued that the issue is not a particular trade barrier or two, nor one particular government policy or another. The issue, rather, is the generally held view that Japan is an ungenerous and narrowly self-seeking participant in world affairs. If general goodwill toward Japan prevailed, it seems unlikely that hostile feelings about trade would have reached their present pitch; instead, Japan's trade behavior would have been regarded as temporarily aberrant and would have been tolerated accordingly. But given the actual existence of a strongly negative view of Japan throughout the world, hostile feeling may well find even further expression.

Image matters. And image is built in large part from substance. Japan's image in the world includes many components that are unfavorable, and no amount of friendly publicity will remove them as long as they are based on fact. In most of its interactions with the rest of the world, Japan does in fact act according to narrow self-interest. Of course, it has its reasons, but these reasons do not alter the facts. Continued pursuit of narrow self-interest, without changes in policy and practice, will in fact damage Japan. The damage is unlikely to be restricted to the area of trade discussions. Global hostility toward Japan manifests itself over trade issues because the problems with Japan are currently most acute in this area. But the more critical issues of resource allocation and defense policies will eventually become sources of friction if Japan's current preoccupation with narrow and parochial concerns continues.

The challenge to Japan is evident and enormous. Quite drastic changes are called for in trade policy, in investment policy, and in aid policy. Japan urgently needs to change its pattern of interaction with the world, since the consequences of Japan's past and present self-centered behavior are being felt. The question is whether Japan can alter its traditional role in world affairs rapidly enough and drastically enough to meet its own needs. The passive, receptive role Japan still plays in the international arena is now obsolete, and the burden of change rests with Japan.

Afterword

D I V E R S E and divergent points of view have intentionally been represented in this book. Each reading, hopefully, has contributed to an evolving set of
understandings that the reader has formulated for him- or herself along the way.
Here, we only wish to point out a few of the general themes we feel important to
underscore as fundamental to the whole.

Let us return to one question raised in the Introduction: namely, what characteristics set Japan apart from industrial systems in the West? If the answer can be
divined from the readings, Japan's distinctiveness appears to lie in the reciprocal
nature, pervasiveness, and durability of long-term ties binding groups—for example, bonds between government and industry, lead banks and businesses, parent firms, subsidiaries, and subcontractors, or companies in the same *keiretsu*
grouping. Although stable ties exist in market economies everywhere, the scope
of the Japanese organizational nexus goes beyond anything observable in the
United States or Europe.

Organizational principles are deeply embedded in the structure of Japanese labor and capital markets. Characteristics of Japanese labor markets include permanent employment for regular employees of large corporations, seniority-based
promotion and compensations, and almost no lateral entry from the outside. From
the company's standpoint, the impact of permanent employment is far-reaching.
It structures the company's organizational hierarchy, conditions the calculus of
risk, dictates the development of manpower resources, and helps determine which
activities the company is willing and able to undertake.

From the standpoint of Japan's industrial structure, the practice of career-long
employment is a key reason for the pattern of company specialization (that is, not
diversifying into unrelated fields), and the preference for relying on subcontractors and creating new subsidiaries as alternatives to vertical integration. The persistence of Japan's "dual industrial structure," consisting of a handful of big,
blue-chip corporations at one level and myriad small to medium-sized companies
at another, can be understood, in part, against the background of career-long employment. Hence, many of the most renowned features of Japan's management
system, such as the development of highly sophisticated internal labor markets,
can be traced back directly to distinctive conditions of employment that have no
exact parallel in the United States or Europe.

Postwar peculiarities in Japanese capital markets have also given rise to distinctive organizational characteristics, such as the pervasiveness and strength of intercorporate linkages in Japan. The closeness of ties between lead banks and businesses and the structure of keiretsu affiliations, for example, can be understood within the context of still-maturing equity markets and corporate dependence on indirect external financing. The nature of capital markets has also contributed to the structure of government-business relations in Japan, especially the power of the Ministry of International Trade and Industry (MITI) to administer industrial policy.

Nowhere is the strength of organizational ties more evident or important than in the extensive cross-company pattern of stock ownership, to which Okumura Hiroshi calls attention in this reader. This pattern of intercorporate stockholding carries far-reaching implications for the behavior of Japanese firms. It may be the main reason why Japanese firms are typically under less pressure to yield high, short-term returns on equity than their American counterparts, an unusual feature of Japanese corporate behavior that has struck many foreign observers as one of the underlying sources of its competitiveness. Unlike most American shareholders, corporate shareholders in Japan tend to place more emphasis on long-term stock appreciation than on big dividends based on quarterly profits. This gives Japanese companies more leeway to forsake short-term profit maximization in favor of a strategy of pursuing long-term market share.

The pattern of intercorporate stockholding is also an explanation for, and reflection of, the premium placed on long-term business relationships based on mutual reciprocity and trust. By holding an equity position in companies with which they do business, Japanese firms can reinforce the ties of interdependence and reciprocal trust. Although such links run the risk of creating rigidities and inefficiencies, as Ronald Dore points out, they can significantly reduce the transaction costs that often accompany arm's-length market relationships. Low transaction costs are evident in the comparatively low costs of legal litigation, high reliability of intermediate goods supplied by subcontractors, close coordination of delivery schedules, meticulous attention to servicing, and other well-known features of Japanese intercorporate behavior.

The emphasis on organizational networks and human relationships, based on structural interdependence, is so strong that Japanese capitalism might perhaps be called (at the risk of simplification) "relational capitalism," in contrast to the American model of "transactional capitalism," which gives greater weight to the "invisible hand" of the market. An illustration of transactional capitalism in America can be seen in the disposition of many corporations to award contracts to vendors who tender the lowest bids. Although price signals are certainly important to Japan, they are not always decisive. As pointed out earlier, market transactions in Japan take place within an institutional framework that modulates the singleminded pursuit of individual and corporate profit. There is, in consequence, a much greater spirit of accommodation and cooperation among sectors of the political economy that in the West are prone to conflict and confrontation—labor and management, large and small industries, city and countryside, public and private sectors, sunset and sunrise industries, the legislature and bureaucracies, and central and local governments. As the readings in this book convey, the Japanese system of relational capitalism has both strengths and weaknesses. With its stress on long-run production, manufacturing and process technology, market share expansion, and incremental improvements, the system has functioned admirably to meet the needs of rapid industrial catchup.

One of Japan's most striking features is the mutually reinforcing nature of politico-economic institutions. Compare the remarkable fit of such institutions in Japan to that in most industrial systems, where institutions up and down the political economy either do not mesh well or are in open conflict. Imagine the difficulties highly leveraged Japanese companies would have encountered if labor unions had not been enterprise-centered. Imagine what problems the high fixed costs of permanent employment and heavy debt financing would pose if banks were to operate at arm's length on the basis of legal contracts, or if some of the adjustment costs of cyclical downturns could not be shared by small to medium subcontractors. How would Japanese companies fare if they were locked into antagonistic rather than cooperative relations with the government?

Among the many strengths of the Japanese system, the circulation of information, capacity to reach consensus, overriding focus on the common good and the national interest, mobilization of finite resources, widespread diffusion of costs and risks, and the ability to adapt to ever-changing circumstances stand out as perhaps the most unusual and significant. Such strengths emerge out of a complex of factors, including some of the distinctive, extramarket institutions that function within the framework of a market economy. The combination of stable organizational parameters and a dynamic market system has made postwar Japan one of the fastest-growing and most competitive industrial systems in the world.

At the same time, however, the strengths of the system for latecomer catchup may not be especially well suited for firstcomer development. Now that the era of catchup is behind, can the Japanese system meet the new challenge of technological innovation? Are such Japanese institutions as permanent employment conducive to state-of-the-art invention? How well positioned is the Japanese system to adapt to an information-based society? Just how decisive has culture been in forming relational capitalism, and how capable of change are its basic organizational patterns?

The international environment is clearly evolving rapidly, and so is the nature of the Japanese industrial system. The leading edge of Japan's industrial economy is shifting progressively from smokestack to the service and high-technology sectors. This shift brings a new set of functional requirements that need to be met. Furthermore, the transition is reshaping some of the basics of the Japanese system. The once heavily regulated financial system, a cornerstone in Japan's latecomer structure, is being liberalized under the dual impact of structural maturation and foreign pressure. This is but one example of a situation in which Japan's distinctiveness is under assault by the forces set in motion by economic success. How the Japanese system adapts to the quickening pace of international and domestic change remains to be seen. What appears to the outside world as a well-oiled dynamo is on closer examination a system undergoing the normal stresses associated with adaption and change.

If some selections in this book are indicative of future trends, the Japanese system may be moving toward an erosion of some of its distinctive organizational characteristics (e.g., intimate banking-business ties) and toward a greater role for market forces. As capital markets mature, for example, the reliance of Japanese corporations on bank lending may decrease. If so, this could conceivably weaken the solidarity of banking-business ties. Further, as high technology advances, will MITI's role in the economy be eroded? For that matter, will prosperity produce the individualism and consumerism familiar in the West? Will Japan's relational model give way gradually to a transactional form of capitalism based on contracts, spot-market prices, and arm's-length relationships? It is tempting to think that Japan's system will converge with America's, for then we will know the future and understand that it is benign.

Our hunch is that this will not happen. The differences between the two countries have narrowed and some of the sharpest contrasts have been modulated, but the Japanese and American systems are likely to remain distinct, even though the two now find themselves at similar stages of development. While both face the same kinds of changes, indeed compete in trying to solve them, the readings in this book suggest that the social, cultural, political, and economic contexts of the two systems will remain very different. There are few compelling reasons to predict that the prominence of Japan's extramarket institutions will recede significantly, much less that the Japanese and American systems will emerge from the crucible of the postindustrial era looking the same. The differences may well determine the outcome of the competition for economic leadership; they also describe the many opportunities for creative forms of cooperation as the Western world orients toward Japan.

Index

Index

In this index an "f" after a number indicates a separate reference on the next page, and an "ff" indicates separate references on the next two pages. A continuous discussion over two or more pages is indicated by a span of page numbers, e.g., "pp. 57–58." *Passim* is used for a cluster of references in close but not consecutive sequence.

Library of Congress Cataloging-in-Publication Data

Inside the Japanese system: readings on contemporary society and
   political economy / edited by Daniel I. Okimoto and Thomas P.
   Rohlen.
      p.   cm.
   Includes index.
   ISBN 0-8047-1425-8 (alk. paper). ISBN 0-8047-1423-1 (pbk.)
      1. Japan—Economic conditions—1945–   2. Japan—Social
   conditions—1945–   3. Japan—Politics and government—1945–
   I. Okimoto, Daniel I., 1942–   II. Rohlen, Thomas P.
   HC462.9.I587   1988
   330.952'04—dc19   87-18820
                                                   CIP